Sister Circle

Sister Circle / Black Women and Work

EDITED BY

SHARON HARLEY

AND

THE BLACK WOMEN AND WORK COLLECTIVE

WITH A FOREWORD BY NELLIE Y. McKAY

RUTGERS UNIVERSITY PRESS
New Brunswick, New Jersey, and London

LIBRARY OF CONGRESS CATALOGING-IN-PUBLICATION DATA

Sister circle : Black women and work / edited by Sharon Harley and the Black Women and Work Collective.
    p.   cm.
   Includes bibliographical references and index.
   ISBN 0-8135-3060-1 (cloth : alk. paper) — ISBN 0-8135-3061-X (pbk : alk. paper)
   1. African American women—Employment—History—Sources.   2. African American women—Interviews.   I. Harley, Sharon.   II. Black Women and Work Collective.

HD6057.5U5 S576 2002
331.4'089'96073—dc21

                                                                    2001048613

British Cataloging-in-Publication information is available from the British Library.

Manufactured in the United States of America

To Professor Rhonda M. Williams, 1957–2000
Sister Scholar/Political Economist Extraordinaire

Contents

Foreword   ix
   Nellie Y. McKay

Preface: Sisters in a Circle   xv

Acknowledgments   xxi

Introduction: Historical Overview of Black Women and Work   1
   Sharon Harley
   Francille Rusan Wilson
   Shirley Wilson Logan

PART 1 ▪ *Work It Sista!*

The Black Side of the Mirror: The Black Body in the Workplace   13
   Taunya Lovell Banks

Flying the Love Bird and Other Tourist Jobs in Jamaica:
Women Workers in Negril   29
   A. Lynn Bolles

"Working for Nothing but for a Living": Black Women
in the Underground Economy   48
   Sharon Harley

Between a Rock and a Hard Place: Mothering, Work,
and Welfare in the Rural South   67
   Bonnie Thornton Dill
   Tallese Johnson

Getting Paid: Black Women Economists Reflect on Women and Work   84
   Rhonda M. Williams

PART 2 ▪ *Foremothers: The Shoulders on Which We Stand*

*"Don't Let Nobody Bother Yo' Principle": The Sexual Economy
of American Slavery*   103
  ADRIENNE DAVIS

*"And We Claim Our Rights": The Rights Rhetoric
of Black and White Women Activists before the Civil War*   128
  CARLA L. PETERSON

*"What Are We Worth": Anna Julia Cooper Defines Black Women's
Work at the Dawn of the Twentieth Century*   146
  SHIRLEY WILSON LOGAN

*"All of the Glory . . . Faded . . . Quickly": Sadie T. M. Alexander
and Black Professional Women, 1920–1950*   164
  FRANCILLE RUSAN WILSON

*A Sister in the Brotherhood: Rosina Corrothers Tucker
and the Sleeping Car Porters, 1930–1950*   184
  MELINDA CHATEAUVERT

PART 3 ▪ *Women's Work through the Artist's Eyes*

*Declaring (Ambiguous) Liberty: Paule Marshall's
Middle-Class Women*   199
  MARY HELEN WASHINGTON

Searching for Memories: Visualizing My Art and Our Work   218
  DEBORAH WILLIS

PART 4 ▪ *Detours on the Road to Work: Blessings in Disguise*

*Labor above and beyond the Call: A Black Woman Scholar
in the Academy*   231
  MARILYN MOBLEY MCKENZIE

When the Spirit Takes Hold, What the Work Becomes!   254
  JUDI MOORE LATTA

About the Contributors   273
Index   279

FOREWORD

*S*ister Circle: Black Women and Work is the end product of almost a decade's commitment made to each other by a small group of interdisciplinary black and (one) white "Sister Scholars" at the University of Maryland in 1993. None could have known when they first met on that winter evening, over a potluck supper, to share research interests, what would come of it. But, to their delight, they discovered a common interest in exploring together the meaning of work in the lives of black women. Energized by the idea, they met regularly over a two-year period, then widened the circle to include additional women from nearby universities. With a grant from the Ford Foundation, they constituted themselves into a faculty and graduate student seminar, Meanings and Representations of Black Women and Work. In the collective spirit of the research seminar, the Sister Scholars enlarged their circle to include a public audience with the "Roots, Resistance, and Representation: Sister Scholars Study Black Women and Work" symposium held in 1997 at the Smithsonian Institution. The essays within are informed by the wise comments of both seminar participants and conference participants.

The genesis of the project reminds me of similar academic Sister Circles in the 1970s and early 1980s when African American women, as a recognizable cohort, first entered the white academy. Then there were not twelve or six or even five black women scholars in any white college or university in the country. Instead, those were years when the one or two in their departments or institutions experienced aloneness, alienation, and feelings of job insecurity. Yet, making a way where none previously existed, young black women scholars in colleges and universities within reachable distances of each other met together to try to understand what it meant to be African American women in the academy. Those were also the years when all the black writers or black history makers were men; the years when Sojourner Truth and Harriet Tubman, neither of whom could read nor write, so we could not hear their unfiltered words, represented the experiences of black women; the years before Harriet Jacobs, Frances Watkins Harper, Zora Neale Hurston, Ida B. Wells, Mary Church Terrell, and the dozens of others whom we now know, teach, and write about were still largely undiscovered. But also in those years audacious black women, in figurative hands-on-hips, defiant poses, looked at each other and asked, Where were the black women writers and thinkers? Those words were a challenge they refused to dismiss, and they went out to find the lost women. And find them they did. But that was only the first step. The next was the struggle for job security for themselves and the emergence of black women's studies as an undeniable academic area of study.

Sister Circle: Black Women and Work is a pathbreaking scholarly work that blends old traditions with new directions and launches an exciting new era in black women's studies. Sister Circles are not a late-twentieth-century phenomenon in the experiences of African American women. Beginning in the ninteenth century, African American women have met regularly with each other for purposes of communication and mutual support in spaces as diverse as beauty parlors, book clubs, and sorority and church group meeting places, among other places. In fact, the survival of black women in America, physically, emotionally, and psychologically, has largely been the product of the support these women have given to each other in these nontraditional venues over the centuries of their collective American lives. "Sister" defines their relationships with each other, always in dimensions spiritual and secular, social and religious, and idealistic, without ever losing sight of the harsh reality of what it means to be black women in white America. Romanticists they are not.

This definition of "sister" in this context makes a renaming at Spelman College in the 1990s intellectually and culturally interesting. For when students at this all-women's (historically black) institution lovingly named Johnnetta Cole, the first black woman to occupy the presidency of that college, Sister President, they altered the received power of her office by bestowing on it an image of wholeness grounded in the shared humanity of everyone within it. In so doing, they further enhanced the safety already inherent in the structure of the black women's college for young black women and created a new, empowering space for themselves. Their action incorporated the physical and emotional environment of Spelman College into thousands of past and present Sister Circles where black women offer to and are assured of receiving from each other reliable comfort and succor that make it possible to know, however difficult individual conditions are, that somewhere there exists a safe space for them. Some years earlier, Maya Angelou, in the brilliant and popular first volume of her autobiography, *I Know Why the Caged Bird Sings* (1970), clearly articulated the meaning of "sister" when black women use it outside of their blood kin. When the adult Angelou records her childhood consternation on hearing her poor, uneducated, but strong, proud, and self-sufficient grandmother, Mrs. Henderson, address the sophisticated Mrs. Flowers, "the aristocrat of Black Stamps," Arkansas, as Sister Flowers, she remembers that she had thought, "Why on earth did she [her grandmother] insist on calling her Sister Flowers . . . [when] Mrs. Flowers deserved better than to be called Sister" by one of such low social standing. As an adult woman, Angelou responds to the question out of her own experiences: "It didn't occur to me for many years that they were as alike as sisters, separated only by formal education." By then Angelou had long recognized that Mrs. Flowers and her grandmother, who from her child's eyes saw their lives as worlds apart, were joined to each other in a circle created by mutual concerns and the trials they faced as black women, including the self-inflicted muteness of Maya, the confused young victim of rape. Black sisterhood has been a powerful force in the lives and achievements of all black women, even for those who do not recognize it. As a collective work, *Sister Circle: Black Women and Work* proves that point.

Working together, the Black Women and Work Collective has produced a publication that takes a gigantic step toward strengthening black women's studies by foreshadowing future developments in this area. This is a collective effort even beyond the inclusion of ideas from others who participated in the research seminar and who attended the symposium but are not in the book. The achievement is much more than that of a single group of dedicated Sister Scholars in the 1990s with a brilliant idea. The germ of that idea was theirs for a longer time than they were aware of. Many of these women were Sister Circle group members in the 1970s and early 1980s, even if they never recognized themselves operating out of that framework (the informal often accidental meetings at professional conferences with other scholars they did not know or know well, over coffee or wine or food, meetings that develop into valuable networks; the papers generously read by already-overworked sisters before their authors submit them for publication; etc.). They were the ones who also responded to the early challenge to search for and illuminate the lives and experiences of the missing women whose names they did not know. They, with many others, participated in that early excavation project, and when they found their subjects, they insisted that their names also receive recognition from the academy as agents of history. They were also among those who taught and wrote about individual or discreet groups of women and participated not only in creating studies of individual women's lives, as important as those are, but also in helping to compile the dictionaries and encyclopedias that make the women truly visible in the academic community. What would it be like today for the study of black women's lives and work without such volumes as Jessie

Carney Smith's *Notable Black American Women* (1991), Darlene Clark Hine's *Black Women in America* (1993), Beverly Guy-Sheftall's *Words of Fire: An Anthology of African American Feminist Thought,* and Henry Louis Gates Jr.'s *Schomburg Library of Nineteenth-Century Black Women Writers* (1988), to name the most obvious? Today younger scholars in African American studies openly admit they cannot imagine the world of black scholarly research before the 1980s.

In its expansive interrogation of one of the most significant defining aspects of black women's lives, *Sister Circle: Black Women and Work* takes important steps beyond previous achievements in this area of participatory scholarly endeavor in black women's studies. The centrality of work to the lives of black women has always been of interest to black intellectuals. Written at the end of the nineteenth century, Mrs. N. F. Mossell's *The Work of the Afro-American Woman* (1894), was the first volume to bring together the accomplishments of black women from every field of endeavor, from writers, educators, artists, journalists, and medical practitioners to small farmers and inventors. It is a celebratory work, one intended to offer not critique but an accounting of the achievements of a group less than fifty years removed from chattel slavery and even then experiencing the horrors of Jim Crowism. But if, as many of us believe, progress in eliminating racial discrimination and implementing full and free access to equal opportunity in all aspects of American life, the credo the country espouses, still eludes the nation's poor and nonwhite population, we are aware that there have been changes over the century since Mossel published her book. Mrs. Mossell could not have imagined *Sister Circle: Black Women and Work.*

Divided into four groups, the fourteen chapters in *Sister Circle* offer an interdisciplinary perspective on black women and work from slavery to the present. Each essay opens with a brief autobiographical statement by its author, who situates herself in relationship to her work before launching into the body of her essay. The groups include an identification of the places where black women perform paid and unpaid work; black women's work in the nineteenth and early twentieth centuries; black women as seen through literature, drama, and the visual arts; and the connections between black women's personal lives and professional lives. The members of the Sister Circle felt that it was important that their book represent black women across generations and that each author read and critique the work of the other authors. Thus, each story is influenced by all the authors and those who otherwise commented on the work.

Even readers who consider themselves familiar with the subject of this book may be surprised at some of the findings of these authors. For example,

I did not expect to discover that there were black women who made lucrative livings in the worlds of bootlegging, gambling, and the numbers. Some will be surprised to discover that there were black women who ran high-priced houses of prostitution. Other discussions include intra-racial discrimination based on skin tones and hair textures and demonstrate that lighter-skinned African Americans can feel discriminated against by those of darker skin tones and are especially aggrieved when the treatment comes from those with authority over them. One essay points to the depreciation of the value of services performed by menial workers in the tourist industry, especially in countries where the living standards are lower than those in the United States and where no wage protection for workers exists. Single mothers as sole economic providers for their children also come in for scrutiny, especially in light of the difficulties they have receiving training to improve their economic status while supporting their families simultaneously.

Each essay and story in this volume, many based on interviews conducted by the authors with their subjects, offers an abundance of new insights into the nature of black women and work. Together they are powerful and constitute a model of serious black women's interdisciplinary studies. This is black women's studies at its best. These essays and stories put human faces on the social science statistical research that has for a long time marginalized and stigmatized poor black women. The authors in this text explore the nature of the work in which black women engage through their personal identity, locating them in their historical and cultural spaces to give readers an opportunity to evaluate their circumstances as individuals within a special group. In this way, this work becomes another weapon in the struggle against racism and sexism, breaking silences and demolishing lingering stereotypes of the nature of African American women's work in America.

Nellie Y. McKay, Evjue-Bascom Professor
University of Wisconsin, Madison
4 September 2001

PREFACE / *Sisters in a Circle*

I can say that for three hours, I'm going
to be around people who feel the same
way I feel about black culture. I won't feel
the isolation.   —Deborah Willis-Kennedy

We get intellectual nourishment in many places,
but in the group we get personal and intellectual
nourishment, which is a very, very rare combination.
                                            —Sharon Harley

This is the space we come into where we feel intellectually
valued, where we feel a sense of community, where we feel a
sense that people *know* your work . . . we have each other's
histories in the palms of our hands.   —Anonymous

*S*itting in a circle at a potluck dinner, we were a small group of black women academics at the University of Maryland sharing our research interests, joys, and frustrations. As the evening progressed, we discovered a mutual interest in exploring black women's work. Ideas flew. We hatched an action plan in the kitchen over coffee and cleanup. By then it was so late that our hostess, Sharon Harley, suddenly appeared in her pajamas and told us to go home. We paused long enough to dub ourselves the "Sister Scholars," and we vowed to keep meeting. That Thursday night in the winter of 1993, we began an eight-year exploration of how we could work together, what our individual and collective work could become, and what the meanings of work could be in the lives of black women. This collection of essays is the result of our efforts.

Over the next two years we met informally at each others' homes, over lunch, coffee, or dinner. We became an energized, interdisciplinary group of scholars discussing black women's work from multiple perspectives. Our conversations were liberating and invigorating, but our efforts to meet were often compromised by the many demands on black women. How could we maintain a process of discovery and develop new ways of understanding black women

workers? Three professors at the University of Maryland, College Park—
Sharon Harley, Mary Helen Washington, and Bonnie Thornton Dill—proposed a project to the Ford Foundation, one which would make it possible for
the Sister Scholars to widen the circle and support our mutual interests. This
became a faculty and graduate student seminar called "The Meanings and
Representations of Black Women and Work." Twenty women historians, literary critics, artists, social scientists, and legal scholars from the University of
Maryland and other universities in the region began meeting monthly in 1995
to discuss and critique our work. During these meetings we discovered new
and unanticipated ways to collaborate. We challenged each other's thinking, we
laughed a lot, and we nudged each other out of our disciplinary boxes. We
became better scholars.

   Our project meetings evolved through panel discussions at scholarly
meetings across the country and at our own 1997 symposium, entitled "Roots,
Resistance, and Representation: Sister Scholars Study Black Women and
Work," at the Smithsonian Institution. We modeled each of our public presen-
tations after the interactive, interdisciplinary meetings of the Black Women
and Work Project, and, through exchanges with project members, our audiences also became part of the circle. As you read the essays and stories in this
volume, reflect on your own personal and professional work and the power
that comes when groups of women assemble. The Sister Scholars invite you to
join the Sister Circle.

Through a New Lens: Black Women Tell Their Own Stories

   Too often, stereotypes and misinformation—images, stories, and historical records presented to others—obscure existing representations of black
women. The storyteller's identity and history often interfere with his or her
willingness and ability to tell the story of black working women. Work brings
pain as well as joy, personal satisfaction as well as anguish, economic success as
well as continued poverty, and sometimes all at the same time. Stories of black
women's labor must recognize the connections between their work in the marketplace, in their communities and organizations, and in their homes. There
are also connections between work and personal identity, relations with others,
and historical and social conditions such as racism and sexism.

   In the past, the study of black women's work has been marked by the twin
sins of silence and omission. To break the silence about black women's work,
we must give voice to past generations of black working women. As black journalist and women's rights activist Gertrude Bustill Mossell wrote in *The Work
of the Afro-American Woman* in 1894, "The intellectual history of a people or

nation constitutes to a great degree the very heart of its life. To find this history we search the fountainhead of its language, its customs, its religion, and its politics expressed by tongue or pen, its folklore, and its songs" ([reprint, Freeport, N.Y.: Books for Libraries Press, 1971], 48).

Although black women's labor was essential to the very development of the United States and the Caribbean, studies of black women as workers lagged far behind the study of black men's or white women's labor for most of the twentieth century. Scholars and governmental agencies paid little attention to black women workers, except as domestics and during the labor shortages of World War I and II. Among the few solid studies existent between 1900 and 1970 were those conducted by a tiny group of black women social scientists and clubwomen who were as underemployed, unappreciated, and marginalized as their sister workers.

More recently the study of black women's work has been marked by disciplinary blind spots and dead ends. The new labor history, Afro-American studies, and women's studies of the 1960s and 1970s focused on black men and white women as workers, thereby continuing to slight black women's work. Since the 1970s important work has been isolated by disciplinary traditions, and, therefore, they fail to speak to and connect to each other. Despite whatever scholarly work has been done, there is a ongoing stream of images that negatively portray black women's work in film, television, magazines, and music. Images in popular culture are a continuation in both type and tone of existing stereotypes.

What the Ford Foundation–funded Black Women and Work Project offers is an interactive, interdisciplinary approach. Throughout the six years of the project, we have listened to, read, and offered critical comments on each other's representations of work in the lives of black women. This book is our collective representation of black women's work. It is a testimony to the multiple ways in which black women are linked, thereby widening the Sister Circle. All of the authors of this anthology were part of the Black Women and Work Project, with the exception of Tallese Johnson. Other scholars who were also a valuable part of the Black Women and Work Project at various times include Caleen Jennings, Nicole King, Saundra Murray Nettles, Cynthia Neverdon-Morton, Ronica Rooks, Janet Sims Wood, Susan Strasser, and Rosalyn Terborg-Penn.

/ / /

The fourteen chapters in this book include explorations of women in the tourism industry, nineteenth-century women activists, low-income single mothers, women as visual artists, church workers, and women facing workplace challenges, and depictions of women's work in fiction and in the mass media. Each author includes an autobiographical statement that makes a connection between her life and her work. All of the sisters in the circle influenced each of the essays by way of discussions, suggestions, criticism, and, in some cases, hands-on editing. Just as a circle has no beginning and no end, the chapters in this book are linked to each other and to larger themes in black women's lives. Each chapter has a story, but the whole volume tells a story as well.

The first groups of essays, "Work It Sista!" identifies the many places where black women perform paid and unpaid work. In "The Black Side of the Mirror: The Black Body in the Workplace," Taunya Lovell Banks argues that black women whose skin tone and hair texture do not fit society's standards of physical attractiveness are often victims of biased employment practices. A. Lynn Bolles takes us to the Caribbean in her essay, "Flying the Love Bird and Other Tourist Jobs in Jamaica: Women Workers in Negril." She shows us the work of thousands of invisible women responsible for the tourists' good time in the Islands. "'Working for Nothing but for a Living': Black Women in the Underground Economy" reveals the experiences of a worker who earned her income in the male-dominated world of bootlegging, gambling, numbers, and prostitution. Sharon Harley tells the story of Odessa Marie Madre, who led this bold, nontraditional life. "Between a Rock and a Hard Place: Mothering, Work, and Welfare in the Rural South" shows the difficult choices that low-income mothers make; Bonnie Thornton Dill and Tallese Johnson capture two compelling narratives of coping and survival in rural Mississippi. Rhonda M. Williams, in her essay, "Getting Paid: Black Women Economists Reflect on Women and Work," writes about Phyllis Wallace, Margaret Simms, Barbara A. P. Jones, and Julianne Malveaux. These four outstanding economists argued for the importance of bringing race and gender into the studies of work in black communities.

In "Foremothers: The Shoulders on Which We Stand," the authors turn to the past to examine the different kinds of work that nineteenth- and early-twentieth-century black women did. Adrienne Davis, in "'Don't Let Nobody Bother Yo' Principle': The Sexual Economy of American Slavery," shows how American slavery used black women for sex and reproduction and blurred the distinctions between sexual, family, and economic relationships. "'And We Claim Our Rights': The Rights Rhetoric of Black and White Women Activists before the Civil War" compares the speeches of black and white women activists. Carla L. Peterson demonstrates how black women argued for the rights of black men and women, particularly the right to work with dignity, free from racial oppression. "'What Are We Worth': Anna Julia Cooper Defines Black Women's Work at the Dawn of the Twentieth Century" is an essay in which Shirley Wilson Logan examines Cooper's views on work, as well as those of her contemporaries, by discussing Cooper's 1899 essay, "Colored Women as Wage Earners." Sadie T. M. Alexander's push to have a career of her own choosing is the subject of Francille Rusan Wilson's essay, "'All of the Glory. . . Faded . . . Quickly': Sadie T.M. Alexander and Black Professional Women, 1920–1950." Melinda Chateauvert's essay, "A Sister in the Brotherhood: Rosina Corrothers Tucker and the Sleeping-Car Porters, 1930–1950," gives an account of Tucker's life and work, exploring the tensions between the brotherhood and wives and between women workers and women union members.

"Women's Work through the Artist's Eyes" is a collection of essays that highlight black women's work through literature, drama, and the visual arts. Mary Helen Washington uses the fiction of Paule Marshall to counter negative stereotypes of black middle-class career women in her essay, "Declaring (Ambiguous) Liberty: Paule Marshall's Middle-Class Women." In her essay, "Searching for Memories: Visualizing My Art and Our Work," Deborah Willis weaves a history of women's work and a history of her own family as she explores her photography and quilts and her work as a museum curator.

The two essays in the fourth section, "Detours on the Road to Work: Blessings in Disguise," explore the connections between black women's personal and professional lives. In "Labor above and beyond the Call: A Black Woman Scholar in the Academy," Marilyn Mobley McKenzie looks at the toll taken when black women juggle various roles in higher education and proposes positive changes. The final essay in this section looks at the long-overlooked labor of black church women. In "When the Spirit Takes Hold, What the Work Becomes!" Judi Moore Latta recounts the activities of two contemporary black church women, concluding that this spiritual work differs sharply from their work in paid jobs. The central goal of this volume is to counter the many misrepresentations of black women's work with more accurate representations. Our essays reveal how we find meaning in these multiple representations.

Acknowledgments

$\mathcal{T}$he Sister Scholars' hard work, selfless commitment of time, generous spirit, and sisterly critiques made this book possible. A special debt of gratitude is owed to the original coprincipal investigators, Sharon Harley and Mary Helen Washington, and to program coordinator Bonnie Thornton Dill. A special thanks to Nellie McKay, Evjue-Bascom Professor at the University of Wisconsin-Madison, for taking time from her extremely busy schedule to write a foreword that both reflects the collaborative spirit of the project and places our work in a feminist tradition. The final completion of the book greatly benefited from the generous assistance of Caitlin Phelps.

Thanks to all of the people at the University of Maryland who helped to make this book and the Ford research seminar a reality, especially Valencia Skeeter, Behavioral and Social Sciences dean Irv Goldstein, Caitlin Phelps, and the many graduate and undergraduate assistants, including Kumari McKie, Ivy Forsythe-Brown, Jasmine Palmer, and Maria Clark. Anne Carswell and Ronald Zeigler of the Campusís Nyumburu Cultural Center generously provided a meeting place for the three-year research seminar. Over the course of the initial three-year seminar, we were also generously hosted by our Sister Scholars, Adrienne Davis, Marilyn Mobley McKenzie, and Rosalyn Terborg-Penn, at their respective campuses, American University, George Mason University, and Morgan State University.

In addition, the Smithsonian's Center for African American History and Culture, under the direction of Steve Newsome and Deborah Willis Kennedy (former collections coordinator), hosted several seminar meetings and the public symposium. Attorney Rachelle Brown graciously offered pro bono legal advice about intellectual property issues related to publishing a multi-authored text.

Thanks to the program committees that selected panels submitted by members of the Black Women and Work group, particularly the American

Studies Association, the Association for the Study of African American Life and History, the Berkshire Conference of Women Historians, the Eastern Sociological Association, and the Organization of American Historians.

We appreciate the generous support of the program officers and directors at the Ford Foundation who made our vision of a collaborative research project and this book a reality—Sheila Biddle, Margaret B. Wilkerson, Janice Petrovich, and Gertrude Fraser. Thanks especially to Margaret Wilkerson and Alison Bernstein of the Ford Foundation for their presence and support of our Black Women and Work sessions at the Black Women in the Academy II conference. We also wish to thank Columbia University and Zora Neale Hurston Professor and Ford Foundation consultant Robert O'Meally for his early support of our Sister Scholar project.

The cover of the book reflects the brilliant spirit, the joy, and the multifaceted dimensions of work that have been the foundation of the book and the Ford-funded Black Women and Work/Sister Scholar project. Thanks to Jonathan Green and his agent, Richard D. Weedman, for permission to have *Field Hands* appear on the front cover.

Finally, we extend our thanks to our Rutgers University Press editor Leslie Mitchner, who supported the book project and shared our vision of a collaborative text, and to her tireless staff, Theresa Liu, Melanie Halkias, Adi Hovav, Marilyn Campbell, Brigitte Goldstein, and Karen Johnson.

Sister Circle

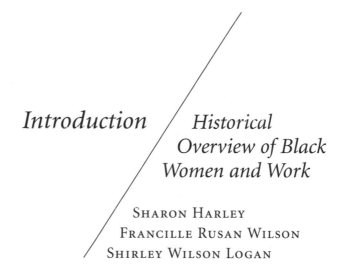

Introduction / Historical Overview of Black Women and Work

Sharon Harley

Francille Rusan Wilson

Shirley Wilson Logan

The Antebellum Period

Black women's antebellum work history unfolded within a range of oppressive contexts for those both enslaved and marginally free. While there are some distinctions to be made, depending upon geographical location, conditions of servitude, societal conventions, and time period, most of those differences ultimately seemed to have made little difference in employment opportunities for black women. But while free women performed the same kinds of labor as their enslaved sisters, all of their work was for themselves. The dichotomy between enslaved and free black women's labor will frame this discussion of antebellum black women's labor history.[1]

Women in Slavery

Almost every act enslaved black women performed could be considered labor, in that, denied ownership of their own personhood, their daily existence ultimately produced marketable goods for the slaveholder with little control over the amount and type of work performed. Their work benefited their owners and included such activities as plowing, hoeing, picking cotton, working in rice fields, serving as field hands, harvesting sugarcane, performing roadwork, feeding the farm animals, caring for livestock, childbearing, midwifery, splitting rails, sewing, managing the slaveholder's household, cooking, cleaning, spinning, candle and soap making, canning, laundering, and serving as personal attendant. Contrary to common belief, household labor was not necessarily more pleasant, because the worker was under the constant eye of the slaveholder and his wife, and she was more likely to be chastised, punished, and sexually exploited. Rural slave women in the North took on more domestic service in the wake of a growing trend toward replacing servants with slaves in the mid-eighteenth century. Along with domestic duties, slave women in the agricultural North continued to perform fieldwork as well.

Aside from the work black women performed under the supervision of slaveholders and overseers, slave women found ways to work for themselves and the survival of their families. For example, Harriet Jacobs writes, in *Incidents in the Life of a Slave Girl*, of her grandmother, who acquired permission to bake pastries at night after her household chores were done and to sell them, hoping to use the profits to purchase her children. Many gained permission to hire their own time, which allowed them to maintain some independence from masters, who generally received a stipulated amount of their slaves' wages. Both enslaved and free black women could generally find work as laundresses, a position even immigrant white women often shunned, sometimes doing washing for two or three families a week.[2] Black women also worked as hairdressers for white women. One black hairdresser, Eliza Potter, had customers up and down the eastern seaboard and also trained other black women, enslaved and free, to dress hair.[3]

Urban slavery presented labor opportunities that were different from those in plantation slavery. Urban slaveholders usually kept only a small number of slaves. They either lived in the same house with the slaveholder or on their own, often "working out" as porters, draymen, or stevedores. Urban slave women worked not only as cooks, seamstresses, and weavers, but also, in many port cities, as marketers, often selling merchandise, such as fish and prepared foods, from street carts or selling sex to supplement their incomes. Urban slave women and men also ran food and drink establishments supported by black patrons.[4]

Free Antebellum Black Women

Records for the colony of pre-Revolution Maryland indicate that about 4 percent of the black population was considered free. After the Revolution, the number increased considerably when blacks exchanged bondage for military service in negotiations with British, French, and Colonial troops. Further, after the war many states liberalized their manumission laws, making slaves' emancipation a slaveholder's prerogative; thus, more slaves were freed.

In an 1832 Boston speech, Maria W. Stewart described the labor conditions faced by northern black women: "Let our girls possess whatever amiable qualities of soul they may; let their characters be fair and spotless as innocence itself; let their natural taste and ingenuity be what they may; it is impossible for scarce an individual of them to rise above the condition of servants. . . . O, horrible idea, indeed! to possess noble souls aspiring after high and honorable acquirements, yet confined by the chains of ignorance and poverty to lives of continual drudgery and toil. Neither do I know of any who have enriched themselves by spending their lives as house domestics, washing windows, shaking carpets, brushing boots, or tending upon gentlemen's tables."[5]

As Stewart's words testify, free antebellum black women in the North as well as the South were only marginally free. Whites began to put into place restrictive racial codes governing their existence, codes that would carry over into the postbellum period. But an important distinction between free and enslaved blacks was that free blacks worked for themselves and were able to bring home the profits of their labor, although limited. There were more free black women than men in the antebellum South. One possible reason for this was that women were more likely to be manumitted, as the males were considered more valuable and more of a threat as free persons.

In the Upper South (North Carolina, Kentucky, Missouri, Tennessee, Delaware, Maryland, and Virginia) free antebellum black women provided temporary domestic work for families that could not afford slaves or permanent servants. Free women of color in the Lower South (Alabama, Arkansas, Florida, Georgia, Louisiana, Mississippi, South Carolina, and Texas) fared better. One example was the city of Savannah, said to have in the early 1800s the highest number of free blacks in Georgia. Working women outnumbered men in the city. In 1823, the Savannah Register of Free Colored Persons listed the following occupations for women: laundress, seamstress, cook, seller of small wares, housekeeper, and nurse. As did their enslaved counterparts, free black women hawked fruits, cakes, and other goods in the streets, to such an extent that officials restricted the issuing of licenses. Dressmaking in Savannah grew more popular as free blacks developed a preference for fine clothes; a number of seamstresses made a respectable living sewing for black and white customers, as did some laundresses, many accumulating enough money to purchase real estate. A number of Savannah black women were teachers in small secret schools; since it was illegal to teach blacks to read the occupation of teacher was not among those listed.[6]

In addition to the better-known women educators Frances Watkins Harper, Charlotte Forten Grimké, and Ann Plato, there was a committed cadre of black women who taught in the African schools established shortly after the Revolutionary War. For example, these women educated children at the Sharp Street Church School in Baltimore and the Richmond African School. These schools developed in response to the denial of admission of blacks to the existing schools in many cities with substantial free black populations.

Unlike their enslaved counterparts in southern coastal regions, generally most free women of color in the North were limited to unskilled labor, for example, working as cooks and seamstresses, and did not have the same opportunities for independent entrepreneurial ventures. However, an 1826 Boston city directory lists some black women as proprietors of boarding houses.[7] A few black women sold such products as oysters and cakes, but white farm women controlled the selling of farm goods. The most common occupation of the post-Revolution northern black woman, free or enslaved, was laundry work, with many doing their work within the employer's home. One census indicated that by 1847 nearly half the black women in Philadelphia were laundresses and domestic servants; 10 percent were needlewomen, and 5 percent were in jobs they could perform at home, such as hairdressing.[8] In spite of the fact that northern industrial escalation led to more factory work for single white women, black women, free and enslaved, were excluded from these jobs.

Black women performed a variety of jobs, many of them still undocumented, especially those due to conventions that define employment as men's work. But they say little about the women who no doubt occupied them.

From Emancipation through the 1930s

Although black women were now legally free, their postbellum work differed little from that of their enslaved and free ancestors. The vast majority of black women were employed as farm laborers and domestic workers during the latter decades of the nineteenth century, and that situation did not change much well into the twentieth century. Migration to towns and cities, in the North and South, often did not mean a change in the type of work available to black women, as black women were still overwhelmingly concentrated in service jobs as domestic workers, servants, laundresses, cooks, and nurses. Industrial work did not open up for black women until World War I, and then only a tiny proportion of black women worked in war-related industries. Despite the opening up of factory work to black women in the North, these gains only lasted through the war, as black women lost their jobs in the postwar economic downturn. Black women workers thus constituted the most disposable segment of the American labor force. As last-hired, first-fired workers, black women would experience the same fate during and after World War II. For black women, the decades between the Emancipation and the 1930s represented nominal gains in employment status and in the types of work available to them. While employment varied somewhat by geographic region and time period, black women after slavery and in the first few decades of the twentieth century were still concentrated at the bottom of the economic ladder, largely employed in various types of service work and agriculture, in the least desirable and dirtiest jobs.

Upon emancipation, freed women were able to labor for the benefit of their own families for the first time. The nature of their work, however, resembled that of work performed during slavery, as black women continued to engage in physical labor without the benefit of labor-saving devices. As was also the case during slavery, black women were responsible for household work and child care in addition to their outside labors. For some black women, freedom meant that they could withdraw completely from the labor force and concentrate their energies on their children and homemaking while their husbands worked outside of the home in order to support the family. However, this was not an option available to most black women throughout their entire lifetime, as economic necessity drove many black women into outside employment. Black women found many ways to supplement the family income; even if a woman did not work outside of the home, she might raise vegetables and collect eggs to sell for cash in a nearby town or take in laundry to provide extra income. These types of self-sufficient economic activities allowed black women a measure of autonomy and control over their work; in addition, taking in laundry allowed a woman to work at home, where she could be around her children and not have to be under the watchful eye of an employer.

While economic self-sufficiency, and usually land ownership, was the goal of freed women and men, this goal eluded most black farmers after Emancipation. With the rise of sharecropping, black families were mired in debt, not being able to break even at the end of each year when accounts were settled. Agricultural work, regardless of whether a family owned their own land, rented land, or were sharecroppers, was difficult work, with long hours and uncertain gains. Black women's work was therefore essential for the sheer survival of their families, especially those families who worked the land. Women worked in the fields in addition to their daily household chores and child-care duties. Farming involved the entire family; children, depending on their age, helped out with various tasks, thus contributing to the family economy. Farming was a collective enterprise, as a farm family could not survive without the labor of all of its members.

The importance of family members' contributions to family survival represented a collectivist ethos regarding work and family, an ethos that extended beyond blood relations to include an entire community. Black families, and, by extension, their communities, worked toward mutual goals that drew upon communal strengths in order to advance the entire community. This emphasis on community welfare, one which helped to ensure survival during slavery, was often sharply at odds with notions of rugged American individualism. Black women, especially those who had moved to towns and cities, took an active

part in performing unpaid work in organizations that were designed to benefit the whole community, such as churches, mutual aid societies, and various
charitable organizations. In urban areas of the South in the last decades of the
nineteenth century, black women outnumbered men because it was more difficult for single women (unmarried or widowed) to support themselves as agricultural workers.[9] Black women in southern cities found jobs as domestic
workers, servants, laundresses, cooks, nurses, and seamstresses. These women
also supplemented their incomes by keeping boarders, selling produce, or finding employment in seasonal work, which varied by region. Part of the year,
these women might work in agriculture, tobacco factories, or oyster-shucking
plants.

In the 1890s, middle-class black women in urban areas sought to help by
establishing working women's clubs in order to help find better employment
opportunities for the migrant black female workers and all black women.
These clubs dealt with a myriad of issues, including community welfare, individual self-improvement, education, lynching, suffrage, and employment, and
were geared toward bettering conditions for black women socially, economically, and politically. A tiny percentage of black women were able to combine
income-earning with social activism by working as teachers.[10] Middle-class
women employed in the teaching profession worked toward improving the
conditions of the race as a whole. It was yet another example of how black
women worked toward both the individual and the collective betterment of
African Americans. In early twentieth-century Richmond, Virginia, one such
woman, Maggie Lena Walker, helped found a bank designed with black working women in mind, small depositors who could only spare pennies per
week.[11] In addition, Walker provided white-collar work for black women in a
black-owned department store affiliated with her work in a mutual aid society, the Independent Order of Saint Luke. By employing black women as store
clerks and as office workers in the mutual aid society, Walker hoped to
improve black women's employment status and work conditions. For Walker,
the department store benefited individual families as well as the whole black
community, as women employed by the store contributed to their families'
welfare and the patrons of the department store kept money within the black
community.[12]

However, despite the efforts of women such as Maggie Lena Walker and
Nannie Helen Burroughs, who sought to professionalize domestic service in
order to make black women domestics more competitive with white immigrant women, most black women continued to labor in some sort of service
work well into the twentieth century.[13] Domestic work and laundry work
involved long hours and low pay; efforts to unionize such workers usually met
with failure as such service work revolved around oral, individual agreements

between employer and employee; and national and state legislation rarely improved their working conditions, wages, or hours.[14] Nevertheless, despite the difficulty of organizing domestic and laundry workers, there were several attempts to unionize these workers during this period, including an 1881 washerwomen's strike in Atlanta. By the 1930s, organizations of domestic workers, such as the Domestic Workers Union, founded in 1934 in New York, could be found in many cities, in the North and South. But they generally were short lived. Domestic workers found other ways to exert some control over their labor: dishonest employers were blacklisted through word of mouth; workers failed to report to work in protest of conditions, hours, or pay; and the time-honored tradition of pan-toting (taking home food leftovers) helped to supplement the diet of domestic workers' families.

Regardless of occupation, black women from Emancipation through the 1930s experienced discrimination based on both race and gender; this kept the majority of black women relegated to the lowest-paying, least desirable jobs. Until the beginnings of the Civil Rights movement helped to open up other employment opportunities for black women during World War II, despite the promises of freedom, black women continued to do work similar to that performed during slavery.

From World War II to 2000

Black women workers courageously faced immense challenges and new opportunities as the Great Depression deepened and soaring urban unemployment and mechanization severely eroded their already meager earnings. In 1940, Nannie Helen Burroughs lamented that black women's traditional jobs in agriculture and domestic service had "gone to machines, gone to white people or gone out of style."[15] Burroughs's comment captures the economic shifts in industries such as tobacco, cotton, and laundry. Racism barred black women from the clerical jobs that employed one in three white women, so they had no choice but to continue to work as domestics. But now black domestics were much less likely than before the depression to live in, and more worked as janitors and charwomen in offices, factories, and schools. They were specifically excluded from social security coverage, the protection of wage and hour laws, and worker's compensation. The Fair Labor Standards Act and the Committee on Fair Employment Practices did little to address pervasive racial and gender segregation and economic discrimination.

The intensive wartime labor shortages and the accompanying black activism of World War II brought a brief but exhilarating period when six hundred thousand black women got industrial jobs with good salaries, making army vehicles, riveting aircraft and tank parts, working in ship and rail yards, in munition plants, and in arsenals. "I was working not for patriotic reasons, I was working for the money," remembered Lillian Hatcher, United Auto Workers official and one of the first black women to obtain an operative's job at an auto plant.[16] Large-scale improvements for black women workers came almost solely from union and collective action by community groups and civil rights organizations despite the high-profile employment and the sincere efforts of black clubwomen in New Deal agencies, women such as Mary McLeod Bethune at the National Youth Administration in Washington and Crystal Bird Fauset at the Works Progress Administration in Philadelphia. Many states and cities tried to reserve relief monies and jobs for whites. White women workers led hate strikes in Detroit and other cities, refusing to share lunch-, bath-, or changing rooms to prevent black women from getting higher-paying factory jobs during the war. It took the concerted efforts of black male United Auto Workers officials, the National Association for the Advancement of Colored People (NAACP), the National Urban League, and a coalition of community organizations to get ten thousand black women hired in Detroit's war industries, but twenty-five thousand black women who wanted to work remained unemployed. In Winston-Salem, North Carolina, the "militant and determined" black trade unionist Miranda Smith led ten thousand black and white female tobacco workers in successful strikes in 1943 and 1947. Smith and trade unionists also registered eight thousand new voters, who elected the first black alderman in the post-Reconstruction South.[17] The greatest income gains for professional women came as NAACP lawyer Charles Hamilton Houston won equal pay suits for black teachers.

Women's wartime income gains had vanished by 1948, and black male and female unemployment remained double the rate for white workers from 1948 to 1995, making immediate postwar prosperity a chimera for black families. Throughout the 1950s black women were overrepresented in the labor force in general and concentrated at its lowest end, but the large difference between black and white women's wages began to narrow. At war's end employed black men and women earned half of what their white counterparts took home, making two-income households both an important bulwark against deprivation and more financially fragile. From the 1950s through the 1980s black married women had the highest labor-force participation rate, while white married women had the lowest, making black families more dependent on women's income than white families were. Civil rights and economic activism were closely related for black women workers, such as the seamstress Rosa Parks and the sharecropper Fannie Lou Hamer, and for the thousands of workers who boycotted and demonstrated. Black women's wages grew to 90 percent of white females' earnings by the late 1970s. Black women were able to hang on to their share of better paying operatives' jobs in manufacturing in the 1970s because of trade unions, but they would be hard hit by deindustrialization in the 1980s.[18]

In the post–civil rights era, on the one hand, professional black women, entertainers, and athletes were widely thought to have advanced and even surpassed white women and black men due to affirmative action. Black women appeared on television in more glamorous non-maid roles, such as Diahann Carroll's portrayal of a widowed nurse, Julia. Alexis Herman became the director of the Women's Bureau of the U.S. Department of Labor under President Jimmy Carter, who also appointed the first black female cabinet secretary, attorney Patricia Roberts Harris. Harris served as secretary of both Housing and Urban Development and Health and Human Services. By contrast, poor black women were often thought of as nonworking welfare queens. In fact, most black women were neither executives nor stay-at-home moms but still worked in the lowest-paying sectors of the economy. The most significant change for black women workers from 1950 to 1980 was their shift from being farmworkers and servants to being service and clerical workers. In the 1970s and 1980s one in four black women workers was in the service sector, compared to one out of every six white women. The number of professionals and managers, overwhelmingly schoolteachers, did rise in the 1970s.[19] But the 1980s saw no progress in eliminating wage discrimination for black workers in general as earnings ratios between blacks and whites did not change at all between 1979 and 1991.

The 1990s continued the mainstream public perception of a dichotomy of black working women. Oprah Winfrey became one of the highest paid and most popular entertainers in the country, writer Toni Morrison won the Nobel Prize, and Carol Moseley-Braun was elected to the U.S. Senate. Under the Clinton administration, Joycelyn Elders became surgeon general and Alexis Herman served as the secretary of labor, but national debates seemed to remain focused on eliminating welfare queens. Even law professor Lani Guinier was falsely characterized as a "quota queen." The economic upturn of 1993–2000 did cause black unemployment to drop to slightly less than double that for whites for the first time in fifty years and made a small dent in the situation of the poorest and most vulnerable, as the poverty rate dropped from a third to a quarter of all black people, but a racial wage gap persists today at all educational levels. Black women workers have maintained their high labor-force participation rate but, contrary to popular belief, continue to earn significantly less than black men or white women. The challenge for the twenty-first century will be for black women workers to eliminate the gender and racial barriers which have kept their wages low and restricted their occupational choices.[20]

Notes

1. The history of women's labor and employment follows a different path in Jamaica. This is due to the social and economic structure of Jamaican society and to British rule, which did not end until 1962. V. Shepherd, *Women in Caribbean History: The British-Colonised Territories* (Princeton, N.J.: Markus Wiener, 1999).

2. Jacqueline Jones, *Labor of Love, Labor of Sorrow: Black Women, Work, and the Family from Slavery to the Present* (New York: Random House, 1985).

3. Lelia Bundles, *On Her Own Ground: The Life and Times of Madam C. J. Walker* (New York: Scribner's, 2001).

4. Ira Berlin, *Many Thousands Gone: The First Two Centuries of Slavery in North America* (Cambridge, Mass.: Harvard University Press, 1998), 156–159.

5. "Lecture Delivered at the Franklin Hall," in *Maria W. Stewart, America's First Black Woman Political Writer: Essays and Speeches*, ed. Marilyn Richardson (Bloomington: Indiana University Press, 1987), 46.

6. Whittington B. Johnson, "Free African-American Women in Savannah, 1800–1860: Affluence and Autonomy Amid Diversity," in *"We Specialize in the Wholly Impossible": A Reader in Black Women's History*, ed. Darlene Clark Hine, Wilma King, and Linda Reed (New York: Carlson, 1995).

7. Marilyn Richardson, ed., *Maria W. Stewart, America's First Black Woman Political Writer: Essays and Speeches* (Bloomington: Indiana University Press, 1987), 4.

8. Paula Giddings, *When and Where I Enter: The Impact of Black Women on Race and Sex in America* (New York: Bantam, 1984), 48.

9. Jones, *Labor of Love*, 74.

10. In 1910, 1 percent of southern black women were employed as teachers. Jones, *Labor of Love*, 144.

11. Elsa Barkley Brown, "Womanist Consciousness: Maggie Lena Walker and the Independent Order of Saint Luke," in *Black Women in America: Social Science Perspectives*, ed. M. Malson, E. Mudimbe-Boyi, J. F. O'Barr, and M. Wyer (Chicago: University of Chicago Press, 1990), 183.

12. Ibid., 187–190.

13. Sharon Harley, "Nannie Helen Burroughs: 'The Black Goddess of Liberty,'" *Journal of Negro History* 81, no. 3 (December 1996).

14. Jones, *Labor of Love*, 207.

15. Ibid., 296.

16. Ibid., 236, 251, 257–258; William Harris, *The Harder They Run: Black Workers since the Civil War* (New York: Oxford, 1982), 121–122.

17. Jones, *Labor of Love*, 264.

18. Ibid., 262–269, 278–288; Harris, *The Harder They Run*, 131–136, 171; Reynolds Farley and Walter R. Allen, *The Color Line and the Quality of Life in America* (New York: Russell Sage, 1987), 266, 305.

19. Farley and Allen, *The Color Line*, 233, 256–266; Bureau of the Census, *Blacks in America, 1992 Statistical Brief* (Washington, D.C., May 1994).

20. Bureau of the Census, *U.S. Department of Commerce News*, February 24, 1999, and September 26, 2000.

PART 1 / *Work It Sista!*

The Black Side of the Mirror / The Black Body in the Workplace

TAUNYA LOVELL BANKS

> Black women bear the brunt of racist
> intimidation resulting from western standards
> of physical beauty. . . . Such intimidation also is a
> crucial instrument to limit the economic and social
> position of black women.
>
> —Paulette Caldwell, 1991

PERSONAL STATEMENT I grew up in black bourgeois Washington, D.C., a middle-class, conventionally respectable, materialistic, capitalistic, somewhat reactionary, racially isolated society. I grew up in the 1950s and the early 1960s, during the waning days of the blue vein societies, those social institutions that discouraged participation by dark-skinned blacks. I grew up thinking I was dark, but not *black*. Many of the more popular members of my social set had very light, almost "white" skin. The Washington I remember was a very color-conscious community with nuanced notions of skin color. Where one fit in this color hierarchy—very light, light, medium brown, dark brown, and black—was very subjective and affected women's lives, perhaps more than men's.

I do not remember exactly when I became aware of color difference, but I remember being keenly aware of its social impact within the colored, Negro, black, Afro-American, African American community, especially for black women. Initially, I thought that my childhood memories of coloristic practices had only social implications, but these memories came to mind whenever I walked to Lexington Market for lunch. The market is located on the edge of downtown Baltimore in an overwhelmingly poor black working-class neighborhood. Usually standing in front of the market are a number of unemployed, periodically employed, or unemployable people. As I pass them each day, one thing always stands out in my mind—their skin color.

Given the neighborhood, I would expect most of the men (and most are men) to be black. What is most noticeable about the black men standing in front of Lexington Market is that almost invariably they have dark skin. This uniformity in skin tone is surprising since black people have a vast variety of skin tones. It seemed statistically unlikely that the overwhelming majority of black men standing around Lexington Market on any given day would be more dark-skinned. One possible explanation is that dark-skinned women *and* men suffer more economic discrimination than light-skinned blacks based on a combination of "race" (a problematic term) and skin color, i.e., *colorism*.

Over the years I learned that having this conversation about skin tone among black women is dangerous territory. There is a lot of anger among black women about skin tone and hair texture. Much of this anger focuses on the social implications of skin tone and hair texture. I have been a target of this anger from women with both light and dark skin tones because of my café-au-lait hue. Some light-skinned women think my life is easier because I am more identifiably "black," whereas some dark-skinned women think my life is easier because my skin tone is lighter than theirs. My experiences left me wondering whether attitudes about skin tone and hair texture spill over into our jobs and are reinforced by the conditions under which we work.

My personal experiences with colorism and my observations at the Lexington Market remind me of black women's writings. Literature by and about black women is replete with references to colorism and hair. I wanted to document the legal and economic implications that undergird these literary references. We know, but often cannot document, how the legal and economic status of being black and female in the United States is further complicated by our skin tone and hair texture. Moving beyond the pages of literature and documenting the more nuanced aspects of being black and female in the workplace is a step toward ensuring that black women workers are treated more justly by both employers and courts.

Three generations: Taunya Banks with her mother, Nancy Boykin, and daughter, Rachel, December 1992.

PHOTO BY TONI WARD.

$\mathcal{I}$n 1986 Tracy Walker, a black clerk typist in the Atlanta office of the Internal Revenue Service (IRS), was terminated. Her supervisor, Ruby Lewis, wrote that Walker had an "attitude problem" and was late for work, lazy, and incompetent.[1] Tracy Walker filed an employment discrimination suit against the IRS, saying these reasons were fabricated and attributing her termination to the hostility of Ruby Lewis, her dark-skinned black female supervisor. In other words, Tracy Walker alleged that Ruby Lewis disliked her because of her light skin tone.

Black women face tremendous pressure to conform to dominant American cultural notions of attractiveness and style. As literary critic Mary Helen Washington wrote, this subject "occurs with such frequency in the writing of black women that it indicates they have been deeply affected by the discrimination against the shade of their skin and the texture of their hair."[2] She continues: "If the stories of these writers are to be believed, then the color/hair problem has cut deep into the psyche of the black woman. It is that particular aspect of oppression that has affected, for the most part, only women. . . . The color theme almost always plays at least a peripheral role—more often a significant one—in the lives of the women characters created by women writers. . . . The idea of beauty as defined by white America has been an assault on the personhood of the black woman."[3]

Washington calls attention to the psychological damage caused by dominant appearance standards. In this essay I focus on the economic impact of these cultural standards. Specifically, I argue that skin tone and hair texture often pose insurmountable economic barriers for black women when employers use them as racial markers while making employment decisions. Despite federal and state laws prohibiting race and gender workplace discrimination, too often the law and legal institutions permit employment decisions based on racial markers largely because they remain hidden behind nonracial explanations for imposing appearance or grooming standards.

The Rockettes: Skin Tone as a Surrogate for Race

The long-term exclusion of black women from the Rockettes, a Radio City Music Hall dance troupe, represents an extreme example of this phenomenon. For sixty-two years, all of the five thousand dancers on the Radio City Music Hall stage were white. In 1987 the *New York Times* ran a news item that read "Rockettes and Race: Barrier Slips." Before then, candidates for the Rockettes had to be between five foot five-and-a-half inches and five foot eight inches tall, slender, long-legged, able to dance, and white. Russell Merkert, who founded the group in 1925, insisted on rigid skin tone uniformity, even forbidding suntans for a white dancer because "it would make her look like a colored girl."[4]

Violet Holmes, director of the Rockettes in the 1980s, defended this all-white practice, saying that "the dancers were supposed to be 'mirror images' of each other. . . . One or two black girls in the Line would definitely distract."[5] Patricia Williams, a law professor, writing about the breaking of the Rockettes color bar, notes that "there are infinite ways to get a racially mixed lineup to look like a mirror image of itself." "Mere symmetry," she argues, could be achieved by hiring all black dancers, hiring an equal number of black dancers, or even placing black dancers at each end of the line "like little black anchors."[6]

Although color uniformity was the stated justification for excluding black women (women with any African ancestry), behind this transparent explanation was the conscious decision to maintain race uniformity or the appearance of race uniformity. Here skin tone was an obvious marker for race. Over the years, millions of tourists saw the Rockettes and absorbed the message transmitted by this visual image—attractive women are slender, tall, and white. The discrimination against black women in the Rockettes case is clearly illegal because the uniform skin tone requirement excluded women who were phenotypically black. The mirror image requirement therefore acted as a surrogate for race.

Conceivably, however, at least one or two of those five thousand dancers may have considered themselves black. Some light-skinned black women also can capitalize economically on skin tone by passing for white. Cheryl Harris, another law professor, writes about her grandmother, a light-skinned black woman, who used her white skin to secure a better-paying department store job which she needed to support her family.[7] By hiding her ancestry and capitalizing on her white European physical features, Harris's grandmother got a better-paying job.

Harris uses this story to illustrate how her grandmother's skin tone served as a proxy for race. She concludes that whites continue to have a property interest in their white skin because it confers certain economic privileges denied those whose skin is not white. But as the Tracy Walker case illustrates, in the workplace even light brown-skinned women, although clearly identified as black, may gain some economic advantage over dark-skinned black women by virtue of their skin tone.

Tracy Walker: Color Discrimination?

Since both Tracy Walker and her supervisor were black, the IRS asserted there could be no race claim. This argument suggests that blacks can engage in race-based workplace discrimination against other blacks with legal impunity. Such an interpretation of antidiscrimination law undercuts its very purpose.

Next the IRS argued that Walker's claim should be dismissed because *color*, as used in Title VII of the Civil Rights Act of 1964, is synonymous with *race*. Title VII of the Civil Rights Act of 1964 makes it unlawful "to fail or refuse to hire or to discharge any individual, or otherwise to discriminate against any individual with respect to his compensation, terms, conditions, or privileges of employment, because of such individual's race, color, religion, sex, or national origin."[8] The federal trial judge rejected the IRS's arguments and refused to dismiss the lawsuit. Instead, the judge wrote, "There is evidence that Ms. Lewis might have harbored resentful feelings towards *white people*, and therefore by inference, possibly towards light-skinned black people."[9] So, Tracy Walker, unable to prove directly that Ruby Lewis disliked light-skinned blacks, becomes a surrogate white woman in the eyes of the law because of her light skin tone.

In *Reena and Other Stories*, Paule Marshall's character Reena expresses the dilemma faced by black women in the United States: We "live surrounded by white images, and white in this world is synonymous with the good, light, beauty, success, so that, despite ourselves sometimes, we run after that whiteness and deny our darkness, which has been made into the symbol of all that is evil and inferior."[10] In 1904 the essayist Nannie Helen Burroughs wrote a series of articles criticizing color consciousness among black men "who would rather marry a woman for her color than her character."[11] Thus, "skin color may . . . constitute a special trauma for black women, since a woman's worth traditionally rests on her physical appearance much more than a man's for whom money and position count more than looks, at least on the marriage market."[12]

Black marriage patterns reflect this economic valuation of black women's physical appearance, especially their skin tone. In the 1930s a study by social scientists St. Clair Drake and Horace R. Clayton concluded that skin tone has more significant consequences for black women than black men.[13] A more recent social science study reached a similar conclusion. Researchers Verna M. Keith and Cedric Herring, using data from 1979 and 1980, found that skin tone is a more significant stratifying factor for women than men when "determining education, occupation, and family," but not personal income.[14] Both pairs of researchers attribute the differential effects of black women's family, as opposed to personal income, to a preference by successful black men for light-skinned wives. Thus, black women are more likely than black men to suffer adverse economic consequences because of their skin tone.

Given these findings, it seems ironic that Tracy Walker, a light-skinned black woman, claimed that she was economically disadvantaged by Ruby

Walker, her dark-skinned supervisor. The discrimination claim in the *Walker* case appears to turn the premise of a light-skinned economic advantage on its head because Tracy Walker claimed that her light skin tone caused the loss of her job at the IRS. Tracy Walker, a black woman, experienced a different type of employment bias, race discrimination based on her nonblack ancestry! Her light skin was as much a racial marker for this black woman as dark skin tone is for other black women.

Author and poet Alice Walker writes that colorism, skin color discrimination, is an especially divisive influence on black women and encourages dissension within the black community.[15] Thus, the alleged animosity between Tracy Walker and her supervisor, Ruby Lewis, is not surprising. What gets lost in most discussions of colorism is its economic impact on black women.

"Natural" Hair: Afros, but Not Braids, as Racial Markers

Hair, like skin color, also is a racial marker and a focal point in literature by and about black women. Essayist Pearl Cleage notes, "You can't be a black woman writer in America and not talk about hair."[16] A series of Title VII employment discrimination cases demonstrates the adverse economic impact on black women of employer-imposed white aesthetic norms.

In 1972 Beverly Jeanne Jenkins, a black woman, sued her employer, Blue Cross–Blue Shield (Blue Cross), alleging that she was denied a promotion and a better job assignment and ultimately was terminated from her job because of her race, sex, and black style of hair and dress.[17] Jenkins claimed she never had a problem during her three years at Blue Cross until she adopted an Afro or "natural" hairstyle. When she was denied a promotion, her supervisor allegedly said that Jenkins "could never represent Blue Cross with [her] Afro."[18] The implication was that Jenkins's appearance, and her hair in particular, did not conform with Blue Cross's desired corporate image for women employees. Ultimately, Beverly Jenkins was forced to leave her job.

In her lawsuit Jenkins alleged that by "requiring employees to stay within strictly delineated confines of dress codes and hairstyles. . . [Blue Cross] not only discriminate[s] against blacks because of their race, but more invidiously imperils the ability of blacks to rid themselves of a vestige of slavery by requiring them to accept white hairstyles and dress styles as a term and condition of employment."[19]

After losing in the trial court, Jenkins appealed. Although divided over certain aspects of the case, the higher court agreed that an employer policy prohibiting an Afro or other natural hairstyle constituted race-based discrimination. The problem left unresolved by the *Jenkins* case is what constitutes a *natural* hair style for black working women. Courts in later cases struggled with this question.

Renee Rogers, a black woman, had worked almost ten years for American Airlines when in the late 1970s she was assigned work as an airport operations agent. Her duties included "greeting passengers, issuing boarding passes, and checking luggage."[20] All these activities involved interactions with customers. On September 25, 1980, Rogers appeared at work with her hair in braids. American Airlines had a policy prohibiting employees who have extensive contact with the public from wearing "all-braided" (cornrow) hairstyles. Nevertheless, American Airlines permitted Rogers to retain her braids provided she "pull her hair into a bun and wrap a hairpiece around the bun during working hours."[21] In other words, Rogers would have to conceal or minimize her braided hair. She complied, but found that the hair piece caused her severe headaches. Finally, she filed a discrimination charge against American Airlines, alleging that its braid policy constituted race and gender discrimination.[22]

The New York federal district judge who heard Renee Rogers's case rejected her claim that American Airlines' policy, although applicable to both men and women, only had a "practical effect" on women. The judge said that even if Rogers's sex discrimination claim was true, different employer grooming standards for women and men would not violate Title VII.[23] Then the judge rejected Rogers's claim that American Airlines' braid policy impermissibly regulated employees based on an "immutable (unchangeable racial) characteristic," hair. Distinguishing an all-braided hairstyle from an Afro or natural one, the judge said that a braided hairstyle is an "easily changed characteristic," unlike an Afro, and thus not an immutable or unchangeable characteristic.[24]

Anticipating this conclusion, Rogers argued that all-braided hairstyles have a long cultural and historical significance for black women, as opposed to black men or white women. She said, therefore, that employment decisions based on a hairstyle's sociocultural association with a particular race or nationality constitutes race-based discrimination in violation of Title VII.[25] Once more, the trial judge disagreed. Questioning Rogers's cultural claim, he noted that she adopted her braided hairstyle shortly after a white actress, Bo Derek, wore an all-braided hairstyle in the movie *10*. The judge suggested that Rogers's problem of complying with American Airlines' hair grooming code could be cured by getting a larger hairpiece!

Further trivializing Rogers's discrimination claim, the judge said that the hair-grooming code restrictions involved no legally protected fundamental right like "the right to have children or marry." Courts traditionally give employers greater latitude in setting appearance and grooming standards for employees who interact with the public. Renee Rogers's freedom to adopt an "all-braided hairstyle" was a matter of relatively low importance in terms of those constitutional interests protected by the Fourteenth Amendment (equal and fair treatment) and Title VII.[26]

According to the court, Rogers's claim did not involve race at all. She could have worn an Afro without employer sanctions because Afros, but not braids, are natural hairstyles—racial markers. Instead, Rogers, a vain, stubborn black woman, wanted to wear her hair in a style unacceptable to her corporate employer.

Her case, *Rogers v. American Airlines, Incorporated*, is a widely cited decision. Some legal scholars have criticized the court's reasoning. Paulette Caldwell, in a powerful legal essay, entitled "A Hair Piece," on the *Rogers* case, argues that braids are just as natural as an Afro. She writes: "[W]herever they exist in the world, black women braided their hair. They have done so in the United States for more than four centuries."[27] Pointing out the illogic of the court's conclusion in the *Rogers* case, Caldwell argues that many black women wear Afros, like braids, as a symbol of black pride. Thus, Afros, like braids, also constitute cultural aspects of race.[28]

The hairstyle options available to most black women because of their hair texture are not economically feasible because of white distaste for the styles. Some hairstyles, worn easily by white women, can only be worn by most black women if their hair is chemically altered. Thus, black women's preoccupation with their hair often reflects the limited options imposed on them by a society which measures attractiveness using white aesthetic norms.

The court's constricted interpretation of racial discrimination in the hair cases supports legal scholar Alan Freeman's claim that antidiscrimination laws are ineffective because they adopt the perspective of the perpetrator or discriminator.[29] Courts, therefore, can rationalize that Afros or natural hairstyles "are permitted because [black] hair texture is immutable [whereas] braids . . . are the products of artifice—a cultural practice—and are therefore mutable[,] the result of choice."[30] Afros or natural hairstyles are *phenotypical* aspects of race, while braided hairstyles are *cultural* aspects of race, unprotected by federal antidiscrimination law.

In essence Renee Rogers claimed that braided hair is directly related to hair texture and thus constitutes an immutable or unchangeable racial characteristic. The judge, dismissing the possibility that black women's complaints about employer hair-grooming standards may be substantially different from grooming claims raised by white women, remarked that American Airlines only required Rogers to camouflage as opposed to completely restyle her hair. Therefore, the judge considered American Airlines' policy a reasonable effort to "project a conservative and business-like image, a consideration, recognized as a bona fide business purpose."[31] Thus, the *Rogers* court viewed employer grooming codes as more closely related to an "employer's choice of how to run his business than to equality of employment opportunity."[32] The court, by rejecting Renee Rogers's claim, treats all cultural practices as voluntary actions devoid of racial significance.

Another court almost a decade earlier in *Smith v. Delta Air Lines, Incorporated* was more truthful, acknowledging that employer hair-grooming requirements "may impose some additional burden on persons of the [N]egro race, because . . . hair . . . tends to be a general attribute of the race. . . . Where there is no great difficulty in complying with the [employer's] rule, . . . the rule does not have to go out on that account."[33] In essence, the courts in the *Rogers* and *Smith* cases believed that employer-imposed grooming rules reflect a biological distinction but reasoned that this distinction was just not significant enough to invalidate the rules.[34] Law professor Karen Engel adds that courts facilitate their denial of hair-grooming code discrimination claims by insisting "that Title VII is violated only by rules that affect 'natural' racial characteristics." While courts concede that there are differences between the races, they maintain that "those differences are not embodied in volitional grooming practices."[35]

The focus in the *Jenkins* and *Rogers* cases on what constitutes a natural versus an artificial hairstyle developed because the court in each case ignored the essence of the discrimination claim. Black women such as Beverly Jeanne Jenkins and Renee Rogers must adopt white hairstyles in order to acquire and retain jobs requiring interaction with the general public. This is not a nonracial explanation because the general public as invoked by employers is a euphemism for white customers. Implicitly, the employer demands that black working women conform to facially neutral hair-grooming codes that reflect both white aesthetic norms and white customer preference. In theory, antidiscrimination laws generally prohibit race and gender discriminatory employment policies based on customer preferences of a racial group. Thus, the court's approval of allegedly neutral corporate hair-grooming codes constitutes willful blindness to employers' racially subjective decision making.

Barbara Flagg, another legal scholar, calls the unconscious use by employers of criteria more strongly associated with whites than nonwhites in business decisions transparently white subjective decision making. Employers apply these criteria when assessing the speech, dress, hairstyle, attitudes, and beliefs of an applicant or employee.[36] When assessing the appearance of applicants or employees, employers can legally apply corporate or business norms based on unacknowledged white aesthetic values and preferences.

As a result of this racial transparency, employer resistance to braided hairstyles continues and black women continue to be unsuccessful in the courts. In

1996, a federal district judge in Georgia upheld the dismissal of Corrine McBride, an administrative assistant with Lawstaf, a temporary legal staffing service, who claimed that she was fired because she protested her employer's policy prohibiting the referral of "qualified applicants with 'braided' hair styles for employment positions." Lawstaf responded that its refusal to place applicants for employment with "braided" hair did not constitute an "unlawful employment practice" under Title VII, and the district court agreed, citing *Rogers v. American Airlines*.[37] Despite the continuing popularity of braids among black women, employers, with the courts' consent, continue to treat braided hair as unnatural, deviant, unprofessional, or unbusinesslike, reflecting both white aesthetic norms and white customer preferences.[38]

Nevertheless, black women continue to resist the imposition of white personal-grooming styles in the workplace. In 1995, by taking their grievances to the press rather than the courts, three black female college students successfully prevailed upon a Richmond, Virginia, Wendy's fast-food restaurant franchisee to allow them to keep their shoulder-length braided hair. The franchisee became embarrassed after the local press published a story saying that his manager called the braided hair unsanitary and prone to bugs and lice.[39]

In January 1997 "LaToya Rivers, a twenty-two year-old student at Umass Boston, . . . quit her job at the Boston Harbor Hotel after a manager told her to change her conservatively braided coif or leave."[40] Like Renee Rogers's hairstyle, Rivers's hairstyle did not comport with white aesthetic norms. She challenged her forced resignation by filing suit with the Massachusetts Commission against Discrimination. In June 1998, *20/20*, a television news magazine, highlighted the plight of Rivers and other black women.

An important point, often overlooked in the analysis of these cases, is that the black women most adversely affected economically by employer decisions that focus on hair and skin tone interact with or are seen by the white general public. At least one expert claims that "people whose livelihood does not depend on the *image* they present are not having a problem, but women at hotel counters, at airline companies, in restaurants, and some department stores are encountering a backlash."[41] Yet courts assume that employee grooming-code restrictions have a "de minimis effect" on employment opportunities.[42] Renee Rogers, Corrine McBride, LaToya Rivers, and other black working women who wear braids challenge this conclusion.

Attractive Public Image: Not Simply a Racial Issue?

Despite laws prohibiting discrimination based on race or gender, courts continue to give employers tremendous leeway to protect their business image by dictating employee grooming standards. In essence, courts consistently allow "de facto attractiveness standards for women to sneak in under the guise of 'gender-neutral' grooming codes."[43] Corporate policy literature suggests that dress and appearance matter a great deal in the workplace.[44]

Disneyland is perhaps the most extreme example of corporations that use appearance and dress requirements to promote a certain business image. Homogeneity, the same justification advanced by the Rockettes' director, is also an important component of the Disneyland image. The Disney Corporation maintains its desired image by hiring only what it considers young, attractive, and enthusiastic employees.[45] Thus, the business image justification simply masks employment policies and practices that pander to white customer preference and demand adoption of white aesthetic personal styles, unrelated to competency. These policies and practices result in the exclusion of qualified people who cannot or will not adopt appearance styles that satisfy the corporate customer. Thus, black women would be compelled to comply with these grooming codes even if the codes imposed greater burdens (like chemically treating one's hair) on black as opposed to other women.

Although black women disproportionately bear the brunt of white American cultural notions of beauty, white women also suffer to a lesser degree from so-called gender-neutral grooming codes that impose appearance standards for women generally. In the early 1980s Christine Craft, a white television news anchor in Kansas City, Missouri, was at the center of a widely publicized case that raised these issues.

Craft resigned after she was demoted because her superiors repeatedly criticized her makeup and clothing. She alleged that the television station's "appearance standards were based on stereotyped characterizations of the sexes and were applied to women more constantly and vigorously than they were applied to men."[46] The station denied Craft's claims and offered the findings of a communications consultant, hired by the station, who testified that all viewers, and women in particular, are more critical of other women's on-camera appearance. The consultant blamed society for the viewing audience's more critical examination of women's on-camera appearance.[47] Thus, the employer argued, the criticism and subsequent demotion of Christine Craft simply reflected Kansas City, Missouri, community standards and not some impermissible employer discrimination based on Craft's gender.

The federal court, while conceding that Craft's employer overemphasized physical appearance, concluded that the station's action did not violate Title VII because "the appearance of a company's employee may contribute greatly to the company's image and success with the public and thus . . . a reasonable dress or grooming code is a proper management prerogative."[48] The court also

rejected Craft's argument that Title VII prohibits employers from using different appearance standard for women and men based on customer preferences.
According to the court, the antidiscrimination law only prohibits dress
requirements that involve "demeaning stereotypes [about] female characteristics and abilities or stereotypical notions of female attractiveness or use of
female sexuality to attract business."[49] It was Craft's "'below-average aptitude'
in matters of clothing and makeup," the court said, and not any unlawful gender-based discrimination, that caused the television station to pay greater
attention to Craft's appearance.[50]

Feminist legal scholars argue unsuccessfully that employment decisions
based on women's physical appearance constitute unlawful sex discrimination
because physical appearance standards tend to perpetuate sex-specific stereotypes about how women should look and dress.[51] Employers successfully
counter that business decisions based on a woman's physical appearance
simply reflect societal or community norms. Courts, the legal entities assigned
to mediate these claims, consistently uphold employers' prerogatives to make
employment decisions based on the dress and physical appearance of women
applicants or employees.

Nevertheless, using feminist arguments to attack employer appearance
standards as sex discrimination is a dangerous strategy. The braid cases illustrate how race complicates any discussion of employer grooming requirements
directed at women. Sometimes the claims of black working women are distinct
from the claims of white women and black men, and in those situations, black
women should be treated as distinct legal subjects.

The Intersection of Race and Gender

Although Renee Rogers sued, claiming both race and gender discrimination, the court disposed of her gender discrimination claim with little discussion, saying only that American's no-braid policy implicated no characteristics
that were immutably tied to one gender.[52] Paulette Caldwell calls the *Rogers*
decision a prime example of the distinctive difficulties black women face when
trying to secure protection under Title VII.[53] Other critical race feminists argue
that race and gender often work together or "intersect" when laws affect black
women in ways that are distinct from their effect on either white women or
black men.[54]

Initially, federal courts treated each of the protected categories under Title
VII as mutually exclusive.[55] These courts reasoned that gender and race could
not combine to form a distinct type of unlawful discrimination. In *Degraffenreid v. General Motors Assembly Division*, for example, it was shown that Gen-

eral Motors had a history of hiring black men and a more recent history of hiring white women, but not black women.[56] When the company laid off employees based on their seniority, black women, the most recently hired group, were disproportionately represented among those employees most likely to be laid off. Several black women sued General Motors, alleging discrimination based on gender and race because of the employer's last hired, first fired seniority policy. The women asked that they be considered a "special class (separate and distinct from either black men or white women) to be protected from discrimination."[57] The court, however, refused to recognize that black women experience a distinctive type of discrimination, saying that such a "super-remedy . . . would give them relief beyond what the drafters of the relevant statutes intended . . . . [and would] create a new classification of 'black women' who would have greater standing than, for example, a black male."[58]

Four years later another court accepted the argument that some employment discrimination claims by black women are distinctive, presenting an intersection of race and gender discrimination. In *Jeffries v. Ham's County Community Action Association*, a federal district court ruled that unlawful employment discrimination can exist against black women when it does not exist against black men or white women based on black women's dual identities as black and female.[59] Otherwise, the court said, black women would not have a viable remedy to challenge the type of discrimination they experience in the workplace. Most later court cases that have decided this question agree. While recognizing "sex plus" claims (sex discrimination *plus* race discrimination), courts still do not recognize more subtle forms of race-gender discrimination represented by the braid cases.

Conclusion

Black women experience a distinctive and subtle form of employment discrimination embodied in so-called neutral employer-imposed appearance or grooming requirements. Courts, when applying federal antidiscrimination law, fail to acknowledge that these grooming standards rely heavily on notions of physical appearance predicated on white aesthetic norms. Employers justify grooming requirements by saying they contribute to the company's image, a transparent cover for their pandering to the preferences of white customers. Courts uncritically allow employers to use the so-called neutral (nonracial) grooming requirements when making hiring, retention, and promotion decisions.

Although employer-imposed grooming standards disproportionately affect black women, some white women suffer economic harm as well. Rather than assume, as courts do, that grooming and appearance requirements do not discriminate based on race and gender, black and white women need to work together to persuade courts and policy makers that employer-imposed appearance or attractiveness standards, masquerading as neutral grooming requirements, are unlawful mechanisms that foster gender and race discrimination. Otherwise, black and white women litigants who challenge negative employment decisions based on physical appearance face little chance of success.

Notes

1. *Walker v Internal Revenue Service*, 713, *Federal Supplement* 403, 404 (N.D. Ga. 1989).

2. Mary Helen Washington, ed., *Black-Eyed Susans: Classic Stories by and about Black Women* (Garden City, N.Y.: Anchor Books, 1975), xiv–xv.

3. Ibid., xvii.

4. Bruce Lambert, "Rockettes and Race: Barrier Slips," *New York Times*, 26 December 1987, 25, col. 6.

5. Ibid.

6. Patricia Williams, "The Obliging Shell: An Informal Essay on Formal Equal Opportunity," *Michigan Law Review* 87 (1989): 2128, 2138.

7. Cheryl Harris, "Whiteness as Property," *Harvard Law Review* 106 (1993): 1709.

8. *United States Code* 42, § 2000e–2(a)(1), 1994.

9. Ibid., 404–405 (emphasis added). Tracy Walker ultimately lost her case after a trial on the merits. *Walker v Secretary of the Treasury*, 742 *Federal Supplement* 670 (N.D. Ga. 1990), *affirmed*, 953 *Federal Reporter* 2d 650 (11th Cir. 1992).

10. Paule Marshall, *Reena and Other Stories* (Old Westbury, N.Y.: Feminist Press, 1983), 79.

11. Paula Giddings, *When and Where I Enter: The Impact of Black Women on Race and Sex in America* (New York: W. Morrow, 1984), 115.

12. Brita Lindberg-Seyersted, "The Color Black: Skin Color as Social, Ethical, and Esthetic Sign in Writings by Black American Women," *English Studies* 73 (1992): 51, 64.

13. St. Clair Drake and Horace R. Clayton, *Black Metropolis* (New York: Harcourt, Brace and Co., 1945).

14. Verna M. Keith and Cedric Herring, "Skin Tone and Stratification in the Black Community," *American Journal of Sociology* 97 (1991): 760, 773.

15. Alice Walker, *In Search of Our Mothers' Gardens: Womanist Prose* (San Diego, Calif.: Harcourt Brace Jovanovich, 1983). 290–291, 311.

16. Pearl Cleage, "Hairpiece," *African American Review* 27 (1993): 37.

17. *Jenkins v Blue Cross Mutual Hospital Association*, 522 *Federal Reporter* 2d 1235 (7th Cir. 1975), *affirmed*, 538 *Federal Reporter* 2d 164 (1976) (*en banc*).

18. *Jenkins*, 522 *Federal Reporter* 2d at 1240.

19. Ibid.

20. *Rogers v American Airlines, Inc.*, 527 *Federal Supplement* 229, 231 (S.D. N.Y. 1981).

21. Ibid., 233.

22. Ibid., 231.

23. Ibid. The court gave no reasons, simply citing the following cases: *Longo v Carlisle DeCoppet and Co.*, 537 *Federal Reporter* 2d 685 (2d Cir. 1976); *Fountain v Safeway Stores, Inc.*, 555 *Federal Reporter* 2d 753,, 755 (9th Cir, 1977); *Willingham v Macon Telegraph Publishing Co.*, 507 *Federal Reporter* 2d 1084, 1092 (5th Cir. 1975) (*en banc*).

24. *Rogers*, 527 *Federal Supplement*, 232.

25. Ibid.

26. Ibid.

27. Paulette Caldwell, "A Hair Piece: Perspectives on the Intersection of Race and Gender," *Duke Law Journal* 1991 (1991): 365, 379.

28. Ibid., 384–385.

29. Alan Freeman, "Legitimatizing Racial Discrimination through Antidiscrimination Law: A Critical Review of Supreme Court Doctrine," *Minnesota Law Review* 62 (1978): 1049.

30. Caldwell, "A Hair Piece," 378.

31. *Rogers*, 527 *Federal Supplement*, 233. Ultimately, the court dismissed all of Rogers's complaints except her allegation that the hair grooming policy had been applied to her in a discriminatory manner. Ibid., 234.

32. *Rogers*, 527 *Federal Supplement*, 232–233.

33. *Smith v Delta Air Lines, Inc.*, 486 *Federal Reporter* 2d 512, 514 (5th Cir. 1973) (quoting the trial judge in *Smith v Delta Air Lines, Inc.*, 6 *Fair Employment Practice Cases* (BNA) 1097, 1098 (N.D. Ala. 1971).

34. Barbara J. Flagg, "Fashioning a Title VII Remedy for Transparently White Subjective Decisionmaking," *Yale Law Journal* 104 (1997): 2009, 2028–2029.

35. Karen Engel, "The Persistence of Neutrality: The Failure of the Religious Accommodation Provision to Redeem Title VII," *Texas Law Review* 76 (1997): 317, 330.

36. Flagg, "Fashioning a Title VII Remedy," 2029.

37. *McBride v Lawstaf, Inc.*, 1996 *West Law* 755779 (N.D. Ga. 1996).

38. John W. Fountain, "The Afro Enjoys a Growing Popularity: A Big Political Statement in the '60s and '70s, It's Back in Vogue as a Symbol of Black Pride," *Chicago Tribune*, May 9, 1994, 5, 1; Tasneem Grace, "The '90s Afro: Hairstyle Is Now a Fashion Choice, Not a Political Statement," *Post-Standard* (Syracuse, N.Y.), Aug. 31, 1994, D1. These articles note not only the use of Afro hairstyles as a political symbol in the1960s, but also a resurgence of the Afro in the 1990s.

39. "Fast-Food Workers Allowed to Wear Braids," *New York Times*, September 3, 1995, 16, col. 4.

40. Diane E. Lewis, "No 'Braiding' Policies Have Some Firms in a Twist: On the Job," *Boston Globe*, May 6, 1997, C6.

41. Ibid.

42. See, for example, *Earwood v Continental Southeastern Lines*, 539 *Federal Reporter* 2d 1349, 1351 (4th Cir. 1976) ("Discrimination based on factors of personal preference does not necessarily restrict employment opportunities and thus is not forbidden."); *Barker v Taft Broadcasting Co.*, 549 *Federal Reporter* 2d 400, 401 (6th Cir. 1977) ("Employer grooming codes requiring different hair lengths for men and women bear such a negligible relation to the purpose of Title VII that we cannot conclude they were a target of the Act."); *Lanigan v Bartlett and Co. Grain*, 466 *Federal Supplement* 1388, 1392 (W.D. Mo. 1979) ("Employment decisions . . . based on either dress codes or policies regarding hair length are more closely related to the company's choice of how to run its business rather than to its obligation to provide equal employment opportunities.").

43. Karl E. Klare, "Power/Dressing: Regulation of Employee Appearance," *New England Law Review* 26 (1992): 1395, 1424.

44. Gordon L. Patzer, *The Physical Attractiveness Phenomena* (New York: Plenum Press, 1985).

45. John Van Maanen and Gideon Kunda, "Real Feelings: Emotional Expression and Organization Culture," *Research in Organizational Behavior* 11 (1989): 43, 58–70.

46. *Craft v Metromedia, Inc.*, 766 *Federal Reporter* 2d 1205 (8th Cir. 1985).

47. Ibid., 1214.

48. Ibid., 1215.

49. Ibid., 1215.

50. Ibid., 1209–1210.

51. Katherine T. Bartlett, "Only Girls Wear Barrettes: Dress and Appearance Standards, Community Norms, and Workplace Equality," *Michigan Law Review* 92 (1994): 2541; Meg Gehrke, "Is Beauty the Beast?" *Southern California Review of Law and Women's Studies* 4 (1994): 221.

52. *Rogers*, 527 *Federal Supplement*, 231.

53. Caldwell, "A Hair Piece," 376–381.

54. Kimberle Crenshaw, "Demarginalizing the Intersection of Race and Sex," *University of Chicago Legal Forum* 1989 (1989): 139; Angela Harris, "Race and Essentialism," *Stanford Law Review* 42 (1990): 581.

55. Elaine W. Shoben, "Compound Discrimination: The Interaction of Race and Sex in Employment Discrimination," *New York University Law Review* 55 (1980): 793; Judy Scales-Trent, "Black Women and the Constitution: Finding Our Place, Asserting Our Rights," *Harvard Civil Rights–Civil Liberties Law Review* 24 (1989): 9.

56. *Degraffenreid v General Motors Assembly Division*, 413 *Federal Supplement* 142 (E. D. Missouri 1976).

57. Ibid., 143.

58. Ibid., 143, 145.

59. *Jeffries v Ham's County Community Action Association*, 615 *Federal Reporter* 2d 1025, 1032 (5th Cir. 1980).

Flying the Love Bird and Other Tourist Jobs in Jamaica / Women Workers in Negril

A. Lynn Bolles

PERSONAL STATEMENT Like most women of African descent, I come from a long line of female workers. Some of that work was wage labor, and some was unpaid domestic work. Regardless of the remunerative nature of that labor, it was necessary and valued by my foremothers and forefathers. Their labor was skilled blue- and pink-collar and professional work. Work made you honest, provided goods and services that improved the material conditions of the family. Work was something you took pride in, even if it was backbreaking labor.

In 1948, my mother, an established, educated hairdresser, met a former GI from West Virginia at a party in Harlem. He was finishing graduate school at New York University, and within five months they married and moved to Passaic, New Jersey. They put up a double-tiered sign in front of the house. One read, "Beebe's Beauty Shoppe," while the other (on top) said, "Dr. George W. Bolles, Psychologist." This, my natal home, was where I lived until my parents' divorce.

In the eighth grade, I found out that there was a profession that involved traveling all across the world, learning and studying different ways of living, and listening to people tell their own stories of motherhood, gender relations, and work. They wrote down what they saw and heard in ethnographic accounts. At once I knew I had found my calling, to be an anthropologist.

My parents—the psychologist and the hairdresser—were required, as professionals, to listen. Patients and clients alike bared their souls in my house. While one group talked upstairs quietly in the office, the others spoke in loud and soft voices over the spraying of water or the din of the dryer in the shop in the basement. I was not privy to those stories told upstairs, but I was a participant-observer downstairs in the shop. It was clear to me then, as it is now, that black women's stories have value and meaning for those who listen well. This work I do as an anthropologist is work I have been doing all of my life: I listen, observe, and tell tales.

*Managers' cocktail: woman in print skirt
is the assistant manager.*

PHOTO BY A. LYNN BOLLES.

Hair braiders certified by the Chamber of Commerce.

PHOTO BY A. LYNN BOLLES.

Hotel bungalows, in foreground, overlooking the Caribbean Sea in Negril.
PHOTO BY
A. LYNN BOLLES.

*F*rom the moment you land at Sangster International Airport in Montego Bay, you meet the smiling faces of Jamaican women tourist workers. If you flew Air Jamaica, the encounter began when you boarded the plane. Here, and elsewhere in the world, women are the predominate tourist workers.

It takes about two hours to travel from Sangster International Airport to Negril. Although it's a mere fifty miles between points, Route A-1 is a narrow winding road built in the seventeenth century when the travelers rode on horseback, in carriages, on sugarcane carts, or walked. Along the way, on one side of the road is the incredible aquamarine Caribbean Sea that shimmers in the sunlight. On the other side of the road are the green fields or villages that proclaim that this is rural Jamaica. It is obvious that if you are going to Negril you are not looking for bargain-packaged attractions. You've come to Negril for its free and easy style, seven miles of white sandy beaches, good food, and breathtaking views. With the passing of each of the miles, you take in the unfolding vista and begin to unwind, putting the responsibilities and worries of jobs and decisions and the like in the far, deep recesses of the mind—no problem.

As the bus or car nears its designation, Route A-1 becomes Norman Manley Boulevard (named after one of Jamaica's national heroes), the road that follows the beach and defines the village of Negril. Waiting for you to pile out of the vehicle are tourist workers, the people whose purpose it is to cater to your personal needs so well that you will be a return visitor. Just like the ad says, you will "come back again and again." Most likely one of the first persons you will meet (after the bellman) will be an official hotel greeter or a clerk at the registration desk. On the way to the room, you will pass household staff, a member of the chef's staff, a table server, and perhaps a member of the recreation staff, who welcome you on their way to their assigned duties.

Overwhelmed by the unfamiliarity of the place—new surroundings, different flora and fauna and new voices—you begin to make the transition. It is an easy one, since there were smiling faces and warm words of welcome that came from each employee whom you passed on the way to your room. By the time you open your bags and don appropriate activity attire, you are a part of the Negril scene, at home and feeling good. Who helped to make this quick transition possible? The dozen or so women who welcomed you, made you comfortable, and organized the creature comforts for you, the guest. This is what tourism is all about.

In contrast, let's envision tourism from the point of view of the tourist worker. In this way you can see the invisible or hidden underside of this most important sector of the Jamaican economy.[1] Not only is tourism the predominate industry of the country, it is also one of the major employers, particularly for women—and not just chambermaids and flight attendants. Included in the tourist trade, for example, are transportation (travel and car rental agents); commerce (basket sellers, duty-free shop clerks); industry (managers); agriculture (farmers); and personal service (housekeepers, personal trainers). Tourist work crosses class and other social divisions of society, replicating the Jamaican social structure and representing all walks of Jamaican life. Needless to say, there is a history of which set of women possesses the necessary requirements for different kinds of jobs. Differential access to education and training is rooted in Jamaica's legacy of slavery and colonialism.

Historically, Jamaican society can be characterized in terms of a class and color hierarchy. The majority of people are black-skinned, poor, or working class.[2] For the most part, they have not gone past elementary school and more than likely do not own land or other property. Then, there are those who took advantage of secondary education and advanced training. Depending on their family's social mobility, they may or may not own land, but they may have acquired other kinds of property. Ranging in skin color from the darkest to lightest brown hues, this group occupies the middle strata of Jamaican society. Finally, there are those who are the beneficiaries of education, family connections, wealth, and privilege.[3] Often members of this elite strata are phenotypically of lighter shades of brown skin color, deep cinnamon to café au lait, than the others and include people known as "white Jamaicans," descendants of Europeans, the inheritors of the old plantocracy and colonial expatriates. Since independence in 1962, the opening up of opportunities have modified this historical class and color characterization. Jamaicans of African ancestry as well as members of various ethnic groups, such as Arab Christians (known as Lebanese or Syrians), Chinese, and those descended from subcontinental Indians, are included in the elite group. Color or ethnicity no longer stymies success on the basis of racial discrimination. Further, because of great strides in education and the breaking down of gender barriers, more women than ever before are moving up the social ladder. However, certain criteria, such as home or land ownership, education, training, and the ability to save, still mark social differences. These are the basics for the social inequality very evident in Jamaica, as the following discussion of women tourist workers in Negril illustrates.

Going to Work with Women Tourist Workers

Going-to-work stories help to identify the social markers of class and, by association, color among the cadre of women who make their living in tourism. These stories are composites of women's lived experiences.

It is about 6 A.M.: a dark-skinned black woman draws her sweater close to her body and picks up the bag that holds her lunch. She double-checks on her children as they ready themselves for school. Closing the door behind her, the woman walks down to the coastal road, Route A-1, to wait for the bus. She joins a group of similarly hued women who are also waiting for their transportation to work. Three of the women look down the road for their bus, owned by their employer, a resort complex on the beach in Negril. They see it, a U.S.-style school bus, barreling around the bend. It stops and the women climb on board. In unison they say "Good morning" to the driver and the other passengers/coworkers. They are greeted by a similar response. Taking their seats, the coworkers chat among themselves as the bus makes several more stops along the way as it travels from Lucea to Negril. Another resort-owned bus travels from the opposite direction, picking up hotel workers who live in the Sheffield area, a community southeast of Negril. The hotel provides this transportation for the majority of its workers—the housekeeping staff—so they can get to work safely, in relative comfort, but more importantly on time. When the bus arrives at the hotel property, the women change into their uniforms, which invariably include an apron and cap. They report to the head of housekeeping, get an update of the daily routine, and head off to clean guest rooms.

A little after the first set of women board the hotel bus, another group of dark-skinned women workers stand by a designated stop on the same highway. After making sure that their children are ready for school, they are off. They await their transportation to work, one of the many minibuses that follow route A-1 from Montego Bay to Negril. This passenger van is rarely early and sometimes late, but it is the most reliable transportation available for these women. Since they are regular passengers, the minibus driver looks out for them and stops right in front of them. They pile onto the bus, pay their fare, make room for their bundles and their bodies in the tight squeeze of the over-crowded vehicle. Some of these women work in hotels that do not provide worker transportation.

At about 7 A.M., a set of women of varying shades of blackness leave their homes also headed for work. They make sure their work clothes hang properly so as to make a smart and professional image. Some don the uniform that marks their status as bank tellers, administrative staff, or agents. They double check to see that their children are readying themselves for school. If they are driving a car, they retrieve their car keys from their handbags. If a husband or partner or friend is giving them a lift to work, they wait for the honk of the car horn before going out of the door. Cars start down the street and turn onto Route A-1. They drive to hotels, banks, and assorted offices to prepare for the start of the day. Entering their places of work, this group of trained, professional women place their handbags in their desk drawers. After they arrange their work area, they turn on the computer or other pieces of office equipment and are ready for the day.

Another, smaller group of women are also getting ready for the workday. Dressed for success, these light-brown-skinned women wear the latest fashions, both casual and business attire acquired during their trips abroad to New York, Miami, London, Toronto, or wherever. They arrange their briefcases, check their recharged cellular phones, and head out the door. The helper (housekeeper) has already arrived and is attending to the last requests from the children. As they drive down the road, they pass the minibuses and other buses full of predominately women workers, some of whom are their employees. Stepping on the accelerator of their Volvos, BMWs, or Grand Cherokees, a few of the briefcase set must arrive before their secretaries, cooks, and clerks do. These women own tourist businesses, and their success in these establishments depends on their own ingenuity, managerial skills, and punctuality.

The last group of black women, morning workers, stand by a designated stop on Route A-1. Their children are already off to school. They await the arrival of their regular minibus. The driver looks out for them and stops right in front of them. They pile onto the bus, pay their fare, make room for their bundles and their bodies in the vehicle. They are vendors in the two craft markets in Negril. Extracting themselves from the van at their stops, the craft vendors cross the road and enter the grounds of the craft market. They open the doors to their locked booths and check to see if anything is amiss. Once everything looks proper, they begin to unpack their bundles and rearrange their displays for the beginning of the daily sales.

By 9 A.M. the majority of Negril's daytime female labor force is in place and already hard at work.

There are a few clear markers that distinguish one group of women tourist workers from another identified in these going-to-work scenarios. Differentiation quickly surfaces in the examples of child care, clothing, and modes of transportation. Although all of the women make sure that their children are ready for the school day, only the briefcase set gives the job over to the helper, their private housekeeper. School starts early, and most children must travel on the same minibuses that travel Route A-1, but probably going in the opposite direction, toward Montego Bay. Children's time of departure for school depends on how far they have to go.

Only the housekeeping staff changes clothes on the job. The other women tourist workers dress for work at home, donning professional uniforms assigned to clerical staffs in hotels, businesses, and banks. Company-designed ensembles consist of a suit (jacket, skirt, blouse, maybe a vest) with a pair of matching pants for variety. Market women make sure that their very casual dress is clean and tidy so as to be presentable to customers. Often they will wear a T-shirt they are promoting for their shop. Those of the briefcase set, needless to say, dress according to their business, their clientele, and fashion trends. Of particular importance are the accessories with designer labels and those made of precious metals and stones. Bracelets, earrings, rings, as well as handbags, shoes, and manicured hands and toes, all make their appearance quite distinctively elite.

The transportation used by the women to get to work is a clear mark of class and occupational difference. For example, the difference between riding a school bus or a minibus has to do with cost, safety, and efficiency on the part of both the women and their employers. A number of hotels provide free school bus transport for their employees. This benefit is critical for the house-keeping staff, whose labor is necessary for a smoothly run resort. Each worker has a seat and does not arrive on the job exhausted from the hassle of the trip. There are few road mishaps with the large buses. More importantly, workers get to their jobs on time. All of these points are cost effective for workers and employers alike.

In comparison, the minibuses charge each passenger a fare. The vans are packed way beyond their recommended passenger load to maximize the prof-its of the minibus owner. Consequently, because of the overcrowded condi-tions, there are often road mishaps. Commuting by minibus often means a high probability that workers may arrive at work worn out and crushed up from an uncomfortable ride, especially during the morning rush hour. For the self-employed, such as the craft market women, minibus travel can be man-aged because of the flexibility of their own work schedule. They travel after and before the peak rush hours. Nonetheless, unless the worker establishes a rela-tionship with a reliable driver, minibus travel can create havoc with a work schedule.

A passenger car allows for the greatest individual freedom, but most women who work as housekeepers or in the craft market cannot afford one. Those workers who do own cars follow their own schedules, are assured com-fort, but must pay to maintain the vehicle and buy gas. Of course, cars are dependable until repairs become unavoidable. However, coworkers and friends will come to the aid of a stranded commuter.

As evident in the vignettes above, tourist work is characterized by a range of jobs requiring a broad spectrum of abilities. Women tourist workers fill these jobs based on their educational attainment and according to their class position in Jamaican society. Taken together as a group, these women provide the wide range of services necessary to make Jamaica a place to which you'll always want to return.

A Day in the Life: Craft Market Vendor

Penny Lewis sells T-shirts, straw crafts, and beads at one of the two craft markets in Negril. She has been doing this work for ten years, enjoys it immensely, and takes her turn being the president of the craft market associa-tion. Penny finished eight years of school but recently took advantage of man-agement courses offered by the Chamber of Commerce. The classes were run by a Peace Corps volunteer interested in small businesses. Tall, slim, dark-brown-skinned, with a flashing smile, Penny, at age thirty-four, is a single mother of three children aged sixteen, twelve, and five.

I started the day off early as usual, about 5 A.M. In the old days, my mother, she didn't have no clock, just the sun come up and she start about her business—she work the land. This morning, after I got my daughters up and the boy, to go to school, we had a little breakfast, made sure there was lunch money for them, and then they went off. Tidy up the place, and then I look at my list again and go over my money. I decided last night that I need to get a new style T-shirt and more colors for the straw [raffia]. What I've a do is go to MoBay to the factory for the T-shirt, . . . go look for the goods at the shop.

So, here it is morning time and I nyah go to the shop to make money, I go to town and spend money! That takes all morning and way after noon, till what is it, almost time to close up shop? But I need those new things to keep up, so the trip was OK. Tourists like new styles, especially them that repeaters. See this shirt? It costs me more than this one here, but it feels nice—nice and soft. Now, I could not make this trip in high season, unless somebody I trust run the shop, they don know how the price go. We keep the same price here [referring to the craft market association members], but sometime we do our own thing for a special customer. You know what I mean? But now, what is it, November? I can take the time.

When I leave here, it's late now, I take the van home to Orange Bay. My daughter starts the dinner when she gets in from school. It's a help. The boy does [washes] his own uniform now, too. I finish the dinner. We eat. The kids do their homework. After tidying up the house, I set on the verandah and work on the straw. You know, put things on the basket like "Jamaica," "Negril," "One Love," tings like that and flowers. More details cost more to make and make a high price, too. I work a bit, listen to a program on the radio, then lock up for the night. Sometimes somebody comes to call, but tonight, I too tired.[4]

A Day in the Life: An Accountant

Mrs. Gwendolyn Hicks Brown is an accountant for a large resort in Negril. She began her work at the hotel as a bookkeeper and worked herself up the ladder. Gwendolyn "took accounts" (bookkeeping and accounting) in high school in MoBay, (Montego Bay), as there is no secondary school in Negril. She went on to attend a commercial school and received a certificate in accounting. Married for three years, she has a four-month-old baby girl. A small, dark brown woman, Gwendolyn is twenty-three years old. Just coming back to the job after maternity leave, she begins her workday at 8 P.M.

I like working nights because you really don't have all the problems of the phone ringing, people asking you different things all of the time. Yes, with the baby, I guess I am used to being up [in] the night. It's quiet; you can do the work and that's that. I come on work at eight, so I leave my house at about quarter past seven, twenty [minutes] after. By that time I have given my daughter her feed [cornmeal porridge in a bottle], bathe her, dress her, and give her over to her father. We eat when my husband comes home at five. It seems a bit of a hurry, but he usually is hungry and I have time to cook. He loves the baby, so when I hand her over to him, they have a grand time together. He puts her to bed, then watches TV. The dishes? No, but he does put them in the sink. I do them when I get home in the morning. Sometimes I take the car and drive here myself. Sometimes I get a lift. Sometimes my husband drives me to work.

When I arrive here, I retrieve the guest chits [register charges] that must be lodged, prepare the next day's bill for departing guests, etc. Sometimes, like tonight, I am in charge of reception, too. There is a bookkeeper who does the actual figures—I used to do that job before I got my promotion.

Tourist industry is very good for Jamaica, and, well, I should say good for me. I always thought I would work for a hotel because in high school that was seen as *the* employer. I was lucky that I grew up in the Negril area and saw Negril develop, so I got a job in the business. It was good timing.

Next job for me here? Well, I don't know. If I go back and take more courses maybe I could try to go higher. It is hard after a point. Not here, at another hotel, maybe. Maybe here, who can say? Fees and books my family cannot afford now, and we have plans. I want to travel to Brooklyn. My sisters and brothers want to see the baby. Buy some things up there for the baby and for the house. So, I am saving for that trip.

A Day in the Life: A Chambermaid

Miss Mary Palmer has been a chambermaid for a "very long time" at the same hotel. She has seen Negril grow from a handful of hotels to the two dozen or more now. Working at the same property has given her benefits, including seniority among the household staff. Her daughter has a new baby. Miss Mary helps her extended family financially, too. A cinnamon-colored woman, Miss Mary is very plump. Miss Mary's father was a sugarcane cutter on an nearby estate, and her mother worked her garden plot. Like many working-class women of her generation, Miss Mary never went past the fifth grade.

> I am one of the old-timers all right! We just watch the place grow from a few villas to now hundreds of rooms. C block—that is all new. We staff see changes—managers come and go. Some of them are standoffish, some friendly. You know a good one when you see one though. I guess you can say that I train new girls on the job. I show them how to do things right, do it quick, quick, and make the guest dem feel comfortable. You 'ave a certain number of rooms, and you wanna to be done before it is time to go. If the guests from a foreign country, then they check out early, and you can finish the work.

My day? It start at daybreak. That is the old way—start at sunup. I do my chores, tidy up, get my lunch in the pail for me to carry, dress, and walk down the hill to the road. The hotel has a bus for the workers. Before the bus, we had to flag a van. Sometimes it come late, or packed up with people. You get to work all crush up. When the kids were young, me, them, all had to be out at the same time. That was a time all right. Now, with just the baby girl and my grandson, I can take my time. We have to be ready to work, uniform on, at 7 a.m.

On the third Friday [of the month] is staff meeting and we go over what is going right and what we must improve on. Last month, I was employee of the month. Thanks. Sure, I have gotten that award before, but this time the money was bit more, and I got a day off. I gave a little to my daughter for the baby, bought something for the house, and put some up.

What do I do? Let's say a guest is coming in. First I check to see if everything is proper—towels, bed linen—freshen up the room, make it nice. I like nice flowers in the little vases, not some dead-looking thing. In the villas I make sure that the kitchen things are in order, TV work. You know, the little things. When a villa guest wants dinner, I do that too. It costs extra. I ask them what they want, and the guest buys the provision, meat, fish. A truck comes every day and delivers to the chef and then comes around here. Guests can buy all their vegetables, ground provisions, fruits from the truck. I buy (for myself for home) what I see I cannot get at the market. Guests can go the supermarket too, or the little store [on the hotel property], but the price too dear.

Most of the guests here are quite nice. Most give good tips and leave good comments. Some places I hear them nasty. Nobody wants to clean up behind that kinda business. We lucky here.

When it is slow, like it now, the staff is let go, starting with the new one, then go up. Long time ago, I used to be let go, but now I am one that stays on permanent. Tourism is good for Negril. It's getting bigger, but not as friendly like it used to be. Just as long as it don't get too big. [I asked her if a trade union ever tried to come here.] No, not that I remember. [I asked her if a trade union would help workers keep their jobs.] Not in this business, no; it too up and down. That is the bad side of the job, not knowing if management change, staff let go, hotel shut down, all that happen all of the time.

A Day in the Life: A Hotel Manager

Ms. Regina Hakkem is a twenty-eight-year-old hotel manager. She has a bachelor of science degree in hotel management from the University of Miami. She was raised in the business; her parents also own a farm that produces most of the fruits, vegetables, eggs, and chickens for the hotel. Her brother became a physician, so, in order to keep the hotel in the family, Regina went abroad to study. She then came back home to take up managing her legacy. Single and not looking for a husband, Regina is a dutiful daughter of Lebanese-Jamaican origins.

My day begins whenever a crisis interrupts my sleep. A broken water pipe at midnight means the day starts at midnight. One time last year, it was not a hurricane, but a storm, I worked two days straight. We had guests! It was a mess! The hotel is very open—it's a natural Caribbean style—so when the wind blows and the rain comes, it can cause problems, especially for Americans. Europeans seem to handle things a bit better. So, take yesterday: my day started not bad, around 8:30 A.M. I live on property, but my apartment is not exactly on top of the guests. One of the perks, you might call it, is that my breakfast is prepared by the kitchen. I take it here, right on this balcony [off the office]. One of the things I missed about home (when I was in Miami) was Blue Mountain coffee, but sometimes I do not get to finish my coffee before things happen (here). Yesterday my day was regular for summer season. I go over arrivals and departures of guests, meet with housekeeping and grounds staff. I do the food and beverage management, so that has to be dealt with, too. By then it's way past midday. Usually I walk the grounds and look at things. I speak with guests, and if there are repeat visitors, I take extra time. Before tea, I work with accounts, make sure our bills are paid and that sort of thing. Of course, if a problem comes up, which usually happens, everything stops and I have to look to it. Like the other day—you noticed that we are building on— well, one of the pieces of machinery broke down stopping all work. The contractor called a meeting and we had to reschedule the next week and look at the time line for completion date, which was behind time already. Then I had to recalculate the financial situation and so forth. This is low season, so at least there aren't a lot of guests to get in the way.

My day ends about 9 or 10 P.M. If it's a Monday, we host a welcome reception for guests, and that is a great social event—rum punch, cocktail patties, cod fritters, you know, a real Jamaican thing. I am on duty until it's over and then some.

Do I have a social life, being single and all? The answer to that question is no. One day, but not now. Maybe I will go on holiday for a week or so in September, do some shopping, visit family, but nothing else. Yes it is hard to meet someone in Negril because I am always working. Where would I meet someone? Everyone is in town [Kingston], not here. The construction must finish.

I am fortunate that my father bought this business years ago and built it up. I like doing this work. When I went to the States, I thought that I might like it and stay. And I thought that the studies would be easy because I learned the hotel business as a child. What a shock! I missed Jamaica, even in Miami, and I realized, too, that unlike my classmates, I did not have to look for work after graduation—one was waiting for me.

Tourism has really gotten stronger here in Jamaica and in Negril; things are growing fast. Soon there will be no idle beach land; you know the problems of the reefs. What worries me the most is the sanitation problem needs to be dealt with. We passed the code for the new construction, but I was in conflict the whole time. My father spent extra money and time to make sure that we were way above the standards, for our sake and because we take care of the community, too. I spent my summers here and know the people.

Tourist development should not be done without thought. Those days are finished. I am in business to make money for sure, but not to spoil everything, too. The government of Jamaica must work on that on a community level. But you know Jamaica—a lot of talk no action.

/ / /

These four women are doing well in the tourist business, but they recognize that tourism is a precarious industry. Its success depends on the weather, the government, and the healthy economies of North America and Europe. The history of tourism on the island clearly demonstrates how the lifestyles of individual women shift and change in relationship to modifications of the industry.

The Banana Boat before Harry Belafonte's Song

At the turn of the twentieth century, an American sea captain, Lorenzo Dow Baber, of the United Fruit Company (now known as Chiquita Banana), brought visitors with him when he traveled to Jamaica to buy bananas. Baber is crediting with first having brought visitors to Jamaica solely for recreation.[5] At that time, Jamaica was still very much a part of the British Colonial Empire. For the British upper class (those who could afford leisurely adventure), the island was not seen as a destination for rest and relaxation. But those sentiments changed after the Second World War. A 1947 Cunard Steamship Line advertisement featured Jamaica as a premier travel destination for the wealthy. Twenty years later, following Jamaica's independence in 1962, tourism had become a way of life for Jamaicans and a major sector of the economy.

By the 1970s, tourism took on new aspect, expanding its clientele beyond the affluent, mobile traveler who continued to visit. The majority of guests were now middle-class Americans looking for bargains as well as unaccustomed luxury. The result was the birth of mass market tourism. This kind of tourism provided a Modified American Plan, or MAP (three meals a day, based on middle-class American food preferences), discount coupons, and most activities based on the U.S.-style hotels. At the same time, Jamaica experienced a national debt crisis, due in part to the price increase of crude oil and the oil embargo. In addition, there was the 1970s political ideology promoting self-reliance in all aspects of citizenry and questioning the motives of the United States in Jamaican economic relations. International attention, however, focused on Jamaica's position as a leader in the nonaligned movement and its friendship with Cuba. Sensing a "red scare," tourist agents and their middle-class clients looked elsewhere for vacation spots.

In keeping with the spirit of self-reliance, and to make Jamaica more than just a beach and more like a country, alternatives to mass market tourism were created, including a meet-the-people program. This was also the moment when Negril's tourist development took off. Unlike mass market hotels in the well-established tourist areas, Negril attracted travelers looking for less luxury, less structure, and more adventure. The cottages and small hotels brought hippies and young professionals to this relatively secluded western part of the island, long a favorite retreat of the Jamaican middle class. What many middle-class Jamaicans had known about for years was now open to all who wanted something different for their vacation plans.[6]

When the conservative Jamaican government was elected in 1980, the Jamaican Tourist Board slogan said it all—"Return to how things used to be." The emphasis again rested with the heightened degree of service and seemingly greater degrees of servitude on the part of tourist workers. The numbers of visitors as well as spending increased dramatically. So did another type of tourism, the "all inclusive." This new arrangement was modeled on the profitable club. All-inclusive vacationing means that all expenses for travel, food, drink, lodging, entertainment, gratuities, and the like are paid in advance. Moreover, all activities are located within the confines of the hotel property. A tourist can visit a country without touring the place. One can land at the airport, go directly to a waiting bus, arrive at the hotel, and never leave it until it is time to retrace the steps to the aircraft bound for home. Not all hotels became all inclusive, but it is a growing trend. Though Negril has all-inclusive compounds, including some catering to special interests such as sports, most lodgings are still firmly in the community-based cottages, guest houses, and small hotels.

In 1989, when the national election brought the People's National Party back into power again, the tourist sector was flourishing despite setbacks caused by Hurricane Gilbert. In an joint effort, government and the private businesses poured capital, incentives, and expertise into the sector. Jamaica's natural beauty and strategic, aggressive marketing by the Tourist Board placed Jamaica as one of the top two destinations in the Caribbean—a position it still holds. Since 1995, almost two million U.S. citizens have traveled to

Jamaica per annum. Further, tourism has become the largest source of foreign exchange for the country.[7]

Jamaican Economy and Women Tourist Workers

Between the street vendors and the cottage and hotel owners, there are numerous categories of jobs considered women's work. However, domestic work stands out because of the numbers employed in the occupation and the ideological underpinnings of women's necessary, but unpaid, domestic work. By understanding the primacy of the chambermaid, it will be easier to see why, when we hear the phrase "woman tourist worker," it triggers images of members of the housekeeping staff rather than women in any other jobs found in the industry.

Cynthia Enloe, in her book *Beaches, Bananas, and Bases,* mentions that certain Caribbean nationalists have criticized their government's promotion of tourism as turning their society into a "nation of busboys."[8] Putting aside the sexism of the statement for a moment, the image of the declaration is powerful. Independence, national autonomy, and the end of colonial rule should not equate with the reconstitution of subservience for anyone. In reality, however, tourism *is* turning Caribbean societies into "nations of chambermaids" as the industry has become the top earner in the majority of countries of the region. Not only does the categorization of domestic service underscore the division of labor within the industry, but it indicates the pay scales within the industry. Not so subtly, there is an evaluation of various kinds of labor that constitutes tourism and who performs it.

The range of opportunities available to women in the tourist industry exemplifies the paradox of Jamaican social mobility. In an earlier study of Negril, Deborah D'Amico-Samuels found that women vendors were engaged in creating economic opportunity in the narrow space between the "rock" of doing poorly paid, scarcely available wage labor and the "hard place" of living in abject poverty.[9] D'Amico-Samuels also observed that middle-class and upwardly mobile working-class women made significant contributions to Negril's successful tourist business. As proprietors of cottages and guest houses, crucial to Negril's person-to-person ambiance, middle-class women, and those who aspired to that status, reaped the rewards of doing good business.

Tourism is a labor-intensive industry. It requires a high ratio of employees to paying customers. People who come to Jamaica as tourists need and expect a lot of service. Furthermore, the kinds of jobs typed as labor-intensive are also unskilled, low skilled, and low cost in terms of wages and benefits. Unskilled or low-skilled work is generally assumed to be work that needs little training, work that the worker already knows how to perform. Most of the jobs in the tourist sector are viewed, in most societies and definitely in Jamaica, as the ones that women not only know how to do, but do naturally. Therefore, housekeeping, laundry, cooking, serving, and so forth are female-dominated jobs. Located in a labor market already rife with gender inequality, low-skilled and unskilled female workers receive low pay in the tourist sector.[10]

In addition to the low-skill jobs, however, women tourist workers are also employed in a variety of occupations that require a secondary education or higher education, technical skills, and advanced training. These primary sector female tourist jobs include accounting, bookkeeping, hotel management, recreation, medical services, commerce, and business services. Even in areas of nontraditional female work, such as accounting, women tend to receive lower pay than their male counterparts. However, this is changing as new hires demand higher salaries than were commonly given in the past.

Tourism provides decent and in some instances fairly substantial livelihoods for Jamaican women. One cannot assume that the impact of a developing tourist sector will always result in negative consequences for the people or for their communities. What accounts for the success of some women and the rock of impoverishment for others as well as points in between? Some of the differences can be accounted for by individual hard work, ambition, family support, training, and education. Those individual attributes cut across class and color lines. However, other differences stem from social inequality. A working-class woman's chance of upward mobility to the middle-class strata is decidedly less if she comes from parents who are landless laborers or domestic servants.

Across the occupational categories in tourism, class and color intersect, illustrating the divisions of Jamaican society. However, the overall status of women's labor contributes to their invisibility in the success of the sector because their labor seems to come naturally. Furthermore, even in the highly technical areas of tourism, women's efforts are done in such a efficient or creative manner that they still warrant the "natural" nomenclature. Of course, this view disregards or makes invisible the training, education, and expertise that guaranteed that these women would receive high performance ratings.

Seven Days, Six Nights

The week has gone so fast; it seems that you just got here. Most U.S. visitors to Jamaica spend just a week in the country, unlike their European counterparts, who stay for a fortnight (two weeks). During the seven days, you tried to experience as much of the Negril scene as possible. You relaxed on the beach, swam in that aquamarine water that you now refer to as "the sea" and not "the ocean" as you did when you first arrived. The pool was lovely, especially the whirlpool. You tried your hand at sailing or played nonstop tennis. Perhaps you did a "Robinson Caruso" trip. A schooner picked you up at the hotel's dock and you joined a group that sailed to one of the nearby small islands. There you snorkeled around a reef, ate barbecue, and partied up a storm before being dropped off back at your hotel. You saw the sights that are highlights of Negril, the Lighthouse, and the Negril cliffs on the West End. Negril's location at the most western part of Jamaica provides a spectacular view of sunsets. You had drinks at any one of the bars and restaurants on the West End, which made for a extraordinary ending of a lovely day. For the last two days you decided to do some shopping. Negril's two craft markets and malls with boutiques provided many handicraft items as mementos for those back at home. The upscale boutique was very special—the batik and the ceramics were out of this world. Some inclusive hotels arrange for craft vendors to sell in designated areas near the beach, so their visitors never have to leave the property and go exploring on their own. And, of course, the duty-free shops with jewelry, liquor, fine china, crystal, and electronics were a shopper's delight. Checking off your list, you see that everyone is covered.

Your flight leaves before noon, so you checked out last night to save time. Your bill was itemized down to the last moment before departure. It was as if someone had read your mind. The clerk asked about your stay, and you replied with a broad smile of satisfaction. This morning, while you pack your bag, you decide to leave half-full bottles of this or that right there on the shelf in the room. As you stuff in that last item, the chambermaid helps you with the last tug on the zipper. She wishes you "God speed" as your bag is carried down to the car or the bus that will take you back. As you leave Negril, you sigh a bit. Is it really over? You retrace your trip back to Sangster International Airport, now nodding to the familiar view of the aquamarine sea, the small villages, and the city of Montego Bay as it appears down the road. You unload the car or the bus and get in line for airline departure. Soon, you are in the friendly skies, perhaps flying the Love Bird—Air Jamaica—bringing you back to the States. A lovely time was had by all, and you *will* come home to Jamaica, again and again.

The labor of women tourist workers made you feel comfortable, welcomed, and taken care of during these seven days and six nights. All of the creature comforts of being on vacation were prepared by the invisible hands of women working on your behalf. True, this is their job, but do visitors recognize it as such when there are no problems, or only when the job is not done to their satisfaction? Think of the small touches—the flowers in the room, the bed turned down with the extra fluff of the pillow, and the general advice as to what to do and where to go, given by the chambermaid. When you left half-full bottles of this or that right there on the shelf in the room, did you say to her, "This is nothing, but if you can use it, please do so." Even though gratuities were included in the bill, did you leave a little extra beside that flower vase? How about the comment card? Did you fill it out? Did you include the name of that most attentive woman server, or housekeeping staff, or the woman clerk with that infectious smile who helped you send that fax back to your office, or the young woman from recreation who got you out on the dance floor? They knew your name, and in a friendly fashion did you learn theirs? When you signed up for the snorkeling trip, how many times did you ask the woman representative, "What time will I be picked up?" She smiled one more time, repeated the information, and then went out of her way to personally escort you to the dock. A special thanks was in order. Did you do it? The shopping was good and you did your best in haggling for the best prices. Did you assume that the straw basket that you bought cost the market vendor next to nothing? That saying written in rattan—you asked for a special monogram—did you pay extra for that custom work with the time, energy, and skill required when you started to negotiate for that price?

Women's work in the tourist industry is depreciated by its invisibility. A smoothly run office is attributed to the man in charge, not to the woman secretary or file clerk who does the bulk of the work. In this inequitable world, the market does not reward women as it does men in wages, benefits, or prestige. Further, in the construct of class and color, working-class or poor black or dark brown women become more invisible because of the compound effect of their social status. Therefore, in tourism, a sector that is both predominately female and characterized as a service industry, merit is quite invisible. The visitors expect the best and respond by coming to Jamaica again and again. But do they attribute their repeat business to the women who make it all happen, or are those actions so invisible that they blend in with the lush fauna, aquamarine sea, and spectacular sunsets?

NOTES

1. Baker noted that tourism accounts for almost 50 percent of foreign income and employs 72,000 Jamaicans, plus 217,000 indirectly—a quarter of all jobs. Christopher Baker, *2000 Jamaica* (Victoria, Australia: Lonely Planet Publishers, 2000), 50. A survey stated that 62 percent of all women were in the labor force. Government of Jamaica, *Economic and Social Survey* (Kingston, Jamaica: Planning Institute of Jamaica, 1994), chap. 18, 4.

2. During the years of research, 50 percent of the workforce was unemployed. Government of Jamaica, *Economic and Social Survey*, chap. 18, 7.

3. Gordon argued that researchers must confront the paradox of large-scale social mobility generated by the opening up of new positions coexisting side by side with gross, and per-

haps even widening, inequalities of opportunity between the minority at the top and the majority at the bottom of the social order. Derek Gordon, *Class, Status, and Social Mobility in Jamaica* (Kingston, Jamaica: Institute of Social and Economic Research, University of the West Indies, Mona, 1987). Beckford and Witter schematized Jamaica in a five-part triangle: whites and foreign and Jamaican capitalists at the apex, one-fifth; black and brown capitalists, professionals, bureaucrats, big peasants, small businesspeople, intelligentsia, and worker aristocracy occupying two-fifths, and the remaining two-fifths composed of the black masses of workers, peasants, the unemployed, and hustlers. George Beckford and Michael Witter, *Small Garden . . . Bitter Weed* (Morant Bay, Jamaica: Maroon Publishing House, 1980), 71.

4. The interviews with the women represented here were conducted during anthropological fieldwork carried out over a three-year period (1992–1994) in Negril, Jamaica. I thank all of the women who spent time talking to me and sharing their lives. The names used in the narratives are pseudonyms. Sections of this chapter appeared elsewhere.

5. These both provide good histories of the tourist industry: Frank F. Taylor, *The Hell with Paradise: The History of the Jamaican Tourist Industry* (Pittsburgh: University of Pittsburgh Press, 1991); and Polly Pattullo, *Last Resorts* (Kingston, Jamaica: Ian Randle Publishers, 1996). See Bolles for a study of tourism promotional literature: A. Lynn Bolles, "Sand, Sea, and the Forbidden: Media Images of Race and Gender in Jamaican Tourism," *Transforming Anthropology* 3, no. 1 (1992): 30–35.

6. Pattullo, *Last Resorts,* 20; A. Lynn Bolles, "Women as a Category of Analysis in Scholarship on Tourism: Jamaican Women and Tourism Employment," in *Tourism and Culture: An Applied Perspective,* ed. Erve Chambers (Albany: State University of New York Press, 1997), 77–92.

7. Baker, *2000 Jamaica,* 50.

8. Cynthia Enloe, *Bananas, Beaches, and Bases* (Berkeley: University of California Press, 1989), 34.

9. Deborah D'Amico-Samuels, "You Can't Get Me out of the Race: Women and Economic Development in Negril, Jamaica, West Indies" (Ph.D. diss., Graduate Center of City University of New York, 1986).

10. Bolles, "Women as a Category of Analysis," 84.

"Working for Nothing but for a Living"
Black Women in the Underground Economy

SHARON HARLEY

PERSONAL STATEMENT I am not sure of the exact reason or the exact moment I chose to write about a member of Washington's underworld, but there are several possibilities. It may be my recollection that the first person among my high school friends to have her own car was the daughter of a "numbers" backer. Or it may be my knowledge of the ease in which the Washington criminal element moved throughout the black middle class, sometimes on the periphery, other times as members of the group. Or is it the echo of Dr. Mary Frances Berry's words on the eve of my doctoral defense—"You have not included any in the formal and informal underground economy in your study of black women's economic and social lives?" Or it may be my personal and intellectual fascination with women (and men) who go against the racist and capitalist patriarchy. I suspect focusing my essay on black women and work on Odessa Madre, the black female "Al Capone," is a combination of these and other yet unknown and unacknowledged factors.

Writing about two women's profitable work in the male-dominated underground economy—taking bets on numbers (prior to legalized gambling in the form of state-run lotteries), operating prostitution hours, and eventually peddling illegal drugs—without glamorizing what sociologists and many middle-class and poor blacks would classify as deviant behavior is a difficult task. Although Odessa Marie Madre, unlike most black women and men, was born into a family of some means, including successful businesspeople and educators, she chose a life of crime. The mixture of the criminal element with middle-class professionals and working-class blacks in many of Washington's segregated neighborhoods earlier on exposed her, as it did me and other Washington residents, to criminal activities. While impressed as a young girl with the financial resources of the neighborhood numbers backers, the likes of educated, churchgoing, law-abiding blacks held greater fascination for me, as they did for most black people.

In Madre's case, the excitement of criminal life was combined with her deep feelings of rejection by the Washington color-conscious, black middle class. She was dark and self-described as unattractive and was the subject of many taunts by her classmates at Washington's exclusive Dunbar High School. To pursue a college education would have required Madre to join the Washington elite who had rejected her repeatedly. Moreover, she would have found the underground world far more accepting of her homosexuality.

While it was not a life most blacks or whites would choose, we have felt the rejection that Odessa felt. We recognize that during her lifetime and ours the life of the criminal—the wheeling and dealing, the illegal and extralegal maneuvering—in many ways resembles the wheeling and dealing and, yes, occasional criminal activities of America's corporate executives. She wanted a much bigger piece of the American pie, a piece she felt she would not get following the traditional route of the educated black. Too proud to operate in the world of the middle-class, frequently light-skinned black professional, Madre chose the more exciting life, and, as she said, the one that paid well.

Odessa Madre and her lawyer after she testified before a grand jury in Washington, D.C., on February 12, 1952.

PHOTO COURTESY OF THE WASHINGTON, D.C., PUBLIC LIBRARY.

*T*wenty years ago, on the eve of my scheduled doctoral defense, I was informed of a glaring omission in my historical study of black women's social, economic, and organizational lives—the absence of black women who worked in the criminal underground economy.[1] The expectation was that I would immediately correct this situation. Not a comforting thought, but nonetheless, I eagerly gathered a few newspaper entries on the criminal activities of black women and strategically inserted the information in my manuscript. During the early years of my graduate studies, my excitement about the abundance of largely unknown and untapped manuscript sources about the work and organizational lives of black female educators in Washington, D.C., and the large number of elderly black women available to interview about their work lives as domestic servants occupied my attention. Besides, workers in the complex and largely secret world of the illegal underground economy remained invisible to most outsiders because the nature of their work required even more anonymity than was usual for the black working class.

Nearly two decades later I return to the subject of women in illegal and extralegal jobs in the underground economy in an effort to understand the complex, intermingling relationships between work, gender transformation, sexuality, class, and the oppositional strategies of black women. This essay focuses on black women largely in the pre-1950 United States, women who earned part (or all) of their income in the male-dominated world of gambling and bootleg liquor and in the female-dominated world of prostitution, where women were sex workers or controlled the services of other women who sold their bodies.

My interest in black women who earned a living through various criminal activities focuses primarily on the process by which black women who worked in legal and illegal jobs in nightclubs, dance halls, "jook joints" (a term commonly used to refer to makeshift dance places such as barns, backrooms, and basements frequented by the poorer working class), and private homes that featured unlawful activities helped transcend gender roles. It is a story of how certain resourceful, ambitious, and courageous black women with limited legal economic opportunities resorted to criminal activities to earn a living for themselves and support kin and black institutions—goals which they shared with their law-abiding neighbors and family members. These women's work and family lives provide a window through which we can view the complex web of gender formation resulting from a frequently uneasy amalgamation of black core strategies and goals within black communities and the middle-class norms of the larger white patriarchal culture.

Before examining the work and lives of black women in the subterranean economy in the early twentieth century, it is important to explore why I and other scholars routinely marginalized these women and their work. Certainly, the dearth of traditional manuscript sources and the middle-class biases of many scholars (often regardless of their own familial background) have collectively resulted in few historical studies of the black working class until recently. Rarely do these works address the labor of women in the illegal underground economy.

For me, writing about women bootleggers, numbers backers, and bawdy house operators required an honest reassessment of my personal view of "mojo" women—a common term for certain women operators in the criminal world. My own political consciousness prompted me to study explicitly race-conscious feminist women, which, in my thinking at the time, excluded black women who engaged in criminal enterprises. Erroneously and naively, in my earlier academic life I operated from an intellectual stance that political activism and criminal behavior were mutually exclusive. This posture differed quite remarkably from my affiliation in the late 1960s and early 1970s with the Black Panther Party, in which political action, such as supporting a free breakfast program, might involve the appropriation of the master's goods. Moreover, I recall my interest in such gun-toting, race-conscious black women as Harriet Tubman and Ida Wells-Barnett. But, of course, there is a difference between women and men who break unjust laws in the name of racial justice and those who do so for personal and community survival—or is there? Aren't they both about racial justice? Denied an opportunity to make a decent living solely because they were black, certain law-abiding black women, men, and children turned to criminal enterprises in order to buy food, pay the rent, and, in the case of parents, educate their children. Certainly, my own self-conscious concern about the moral imagery that such female prostitutes, bootleggers, and numbers backers might project figured into my decision to exclude them from my earlier labor studies.[2]

As I recalled my personal and intimate knowledge of some of these women in my own community, I thought about Toni Cade Bambara's grandmother's response to her when she pretended (much as I had) not to know something (or, as in my case, someone). Bambara said that her fictive grandmother would look at her and ask, "'What are we *pretending* not to know today?'"[3] As I discussed my project with the other Sister Scholars, some in the group acknowledged knowing at least one black woman or man (including an occasional relative) who either earned a living or supplemented her or his income from the numbers business, card games, or bootleg liquor.

Any apprehension that I or others might feel that a study of female numbers backers (writers), numbers runners, and bootleggers would contribute further to the dehumanizing stereotyping of blacks in the media must take into consideration the fact that racial and other forms of stereotyping exists in the face of factual evidence to the contrary. We must accept that telling this story is neither to glorify nor to suggest a universal acceptance of criminal behavior in black communities. Indeed, recent scholarship on the black working class—specifically, *Race Rebels: Culture, Politics, and the Black Working Class,* by Robin D. G. Kelley; *To 'Joy My Freedom: Southern Black Women's Lives and Labors after the Civil War,* by Tera W. Hunter; and "The Black Community: Its Lawbreakers and the Politics of Identification," by legal scholar Regina Austin—has contributed significantly to our understanding of the black subterranean world as a possible site of autonomy and power for African Americans.[4] Literary accounts of the lives and thoughts of ordinary black folk and their culture have greatly transformed contemporary scholars' understandings of the complexity of black core values and actions. Recent critical and literary studies of black working-class communities present insights into the resistant impulses and multidimensional nature of black folk without forgoing a critique of working-class men and women's values and lives.

Moreover, I experienced scholarly affirmation and personal joy from reading about and listening to black folk tell the story of their lives. My reading of the scholarly works mentioned above and the detective fiction of Valerie Welsey Mitchell, Barbara Neely, and Walter Moseley further encouraged me to think anew about the jook joint women absent from my earlier scholarly studies of black working women. As I am drawn more and more to the women who openly challenged gender, race, and sexuality in their work and leisure lives, as a lens through which to understand the complicated sex-gender systems in black communities, I recognize that my decades-earlier attempt to insert a few tidbits about women in the criminal world was a missed opportunity to understand more fully the nexus of women's work, gender, and class in black communities in the United States.

"Jook Joint" Women

The world of the mid-twentieth-century underground economy was exciting or morally despicable (or both), depending upon one's individual perspective. Yet it was the site of employment for thousands of black women, men, and children throughout the United States. The majority of the women workers in the underground economy (1) were bootleggers who sold illegal whiskey or numbers runners who took bets on a three-digit number; (2) were from working-class backgrounds; (3) tended, like women in the legal market economy, to earn less and occupy less prestigious positions than their male counterparts in the hierarchical structure; (4) were often introduced to or were in the business with a male partner, either a relative or friend; (5) often moved back and forth from the legal to the illegal economy even at the same job site; and

(6) for some, had as their only income monies collected from numbers running and bootleg liquor sales.

Faced with the difficulty, indeed the near impossibility, of making a living wage in the legal labor market, they turned to the illicit underground economy. Despite occasional arrests and feelings of regret more fully articulated upon retirement from "the business" or during periods of incarceration, most women and men in the underground economy (illegal and extralegal) needed their jobs as attractive alternatives to the vast majority of low-paid menial jobs reserved for blacks or as the only alternative to homelessness or starvation. For some, avoiding intra-race colorism was a hidden motivation. Black and white folk with legal job options who chose to work in the numbers or bootleg business did so because the income was usually higher, the work conditions were typically better, and they encountered fewer racial insults or attacks. In addition to being an alternative to unemployment and the demeaning, low-paying jobs available to most blacks, the excitement and glamour of the underground work world, centered largely around black nighttime leisure and pleasure, was unmatched in the mid-twentieth-century black job market in the United States.[5]

Odessa Marie Madre was a prominent figure in the mid-twentieth-century black Washington, D.C., underground economy. As a graduate of Washington's elite Dunbar Senior High School, she likely could have found employment in the legal labor economy or lived comfortably due to her parents' financial successes. Neither poverty nor the absence of intellectual ability forced Madre to accept any one of the usual menial jobs available to black women. For good reason, she recognized that the few professional and clerical jobs open to educated black women were more likely either to be filled by light-skinned, so-called attractive women or to have a predominance of such women. Believing that she was both too unattractive and too dark-skinned to be employed in elite professional settings, in addition to not desiring to work in such settings, Madre chose an alternative path to earning money—lots of it. With her "disarmingly charming and biting quick wit," from the 1930s to the 1950s Madre became "one of the most prosperous and flamboyant hustlers who ever operated in the shadows of the nation's Capitol."[6] People who knew her remarked that she was smart and tough and that "no one messed with Odessa."[7]

As the "Queen of Washington's Underworld" and the "Al Capone" of Washington, Odessa Marie Madre was unusual, particularly for a woman, in that she was a member of Washington's criminal upper echelon. At one point, Madre's financial operations reportedly included an "empire of joints" that sold everything from bootleg liquor to sex.[8] Madre also owned a legitimate nightclub, Club Madre, frequented by famous black entertainers such as Moms Mabley, Count Basie, and boxing legend Joe Louis. Whenever Moms Mabley performed at Club Madre, she was usually Madre's houseguest. In addition to their friendship, there was speculation at the time that they may have been lovers.

Newspaper accounts of Madre's life and career provide a rare glimpse into the personal perspective and complicated life of a key female figure in the complex world of the black underground economy. Madre was born in 1907 into an entrepreneurial family; her mother was a seamstress, her father, Lindsay Madre, and her uncle, Moses Madre, operated Madre Brothers barbershop, and later her father owned a pool hall. Her aunt, a teacher at M Street High School (a predecessor to Dunbar High School), made it possible for Madre to live with her family and to attend the academically elite Dunbar High School. The prestigious neighborhood of LeDroit Park, home to a number of black academics at Howard University, was not nearly as attractive to the young Madre as the sights and sounds of Barry Place, the neighborhood off Georgia Avenue in northwest Washington where her parents lived. This multiethnic neighborhood of Irish and blacks on one side of the street and Germans and Italians on the other had a mixture of modest homes, tin-roof shanties, and bootleg ("jill") joints. The latter was one of the reasons Madre's uncle, a reverend and her math and oratory tutor, forbade her to return to the neighborhood where her parents still lived. However, Madre regularly visited the community where she had grown up, to play and occasionally fight with other black and Irish children. Based upon Madre's recollections of her old neighborhood, known as "Cowtown," *Washington Post* reporter Courtland Milloy wrote: "On weekends, the air there was laced with the smell of cooking collard greens and of lye bubbling in pitch-black kettles. Boys shot marbles on grassless backyards. Her grandmother, with her head wrapped in rags, rocked on the front porch, corncob pipe locked in her jaws. Jill joints did a brisk business selling bootleg. Dice and dancing feet clicked through the night."[9] The Irish boys who were Madre's playmates and became members of the Metropolitan Police Department, like their fathers and uncles, proved invaluable to Madre's eventual rise to the top of the underground hierarchy.

As a 1925 honors graduate of Dunbar High School, Madre, it was thought, would become a teacher, like her aunt and a number of her classmates, or maybe a legitimate businesswoman. Her graduation present from her parents, a sleek Whippet automobile, was one indication of how Madre, an only child, benefited from her family's financial successes. With the proceeds from the sale of some family property, she purchased two houses in Cowtown; one she used as her residence, the other as a "jill joint—selling that bootleg."[10]

So why didn't this young honors graduate of one of the nation's most elite black high schools, with money, property inheritances, and significant familial connections, pursue a career as a teacher or legitimate businesswoman rather than become an owner and operator of a jill (jook) joint at the youthful age of seventeen? In an extensive interview conducted by Courtland Milloy and published in a 1980 issue of *Washington Post Magazine,* the seventy-three-year-old Odessa Madre revealed part of her painful past that led her to despise the "E-lites" (the term she used to describe prominent black families) and the "yella gals" and thus vow never to follow in their professional or their social paths. Madre offered this explanation:

> "You wonder what made me choose the life I did? I wonder, too, sometimes," she said. "I just figure that I didn't want to be like them—them 'yella gals.'" The bitterness is gone, but the vivid memory reveals a deep wound. "They called me 'the big, black mutha with the television eyes.' . . . There was only three blacks at Dunbar back then—I mean black like me," she said. "I had good diction, I knew the gestures, but they always made fun of me. . . . Like on days when we were having drill competition and we were supposed to wear the school colors—red and black. The 'yella gals' would say, 'oh, big, black Dessa—you don't have to wear the school colors, just stick out your big fat red tongue.' I would try to kick 'em where they said it from, but could never get my foot no higher than their butts."[11]

A former Washington nightclub dancer who knew Madre repeatedly stated, "Odessa was very, very dark and not attractive, but she was smart, very smart." She confirmed that Madre's classmates teased her about her skin color, offering a slightly different version of the high school's colors story. She remembered Madre being told that she only needed to wear red clothing because she already had on black, her skin.[12] While far more privileged than most blacks of her youth, Madre was not part of Washington's educated social elite and firmly believed that her physical appearance, including her skin color, made it impossible to join the black elite even if she so desired.

Indeed, her experiences at Dunbar remind me of those of another graduate, Nannie Helen Burroughs, who graduated near the top of her class but never received the teaching assistant position she claimed had been promised her. Burroughs felt that being dark-skinned and being the daughter of a washerwoman were significant factors in her failure to secure an appointment in the colored public schools of Washington, D.C. Burroughs left Washington, D.C., and worked at a variety of teaching and clerical positions before returning in 1909 as the founder and president of the National Training School for Women and Girls. Madre's family's entrepreneurial spirit, her lack of interest in teaching (and all that it represented), and her early exposure to the life of the jill joints contributed to her early decision to engage in various criminal enterprises, in contrast to Burroughs's endeavors. It appears that Madre had too much pride and independence and, in her case, also lacked the financial pressure to work as a domestic servant or to face the possibility of continued social rejections if she pursued the teaching profession. Consequently, as former undercover Washington vice squad detective Robert Lee concluded: "'Odessa was basically forced into a life of crime. . . . There weren't hardly any jobs for black people like her when she was coming along . . . and once you got an arrest record, you could hang it up.'" Ironically, as a possible cover for her illegal activities, Madre reported her occupation as a "domestic" in the 1929 Washington, D.C., city directory.[13]

Mrs. Joyce Jean, an owner of two local nightclubs from the 1940s to the 1970s, recalled Madre walking into her establishment with several "beautiful ladies-in-waiting" trailing behind. According to Jean, in addition to houses of prostitution, Madre reportedly owned "two illegal saloons and an elaborate bookmaking operation at 16th and U Street, N.W."[14]

As the Queen of Washington's Underworld for nearly forty years, Madre achieved both of her expressed goals—financial success and fame. At one time, she was said to have controlled six houses of prostitution, employing approximately twenty women (more than most black legitimate businesses at the time) and to have a net annual income of $100,000. One of a very few black women brothel owners, Madre indicated, "'I didn't set out to get into the "trick" trade. But I had come to know so many white fellows, and you know how they are, they love some colored gals. So I'd pay a girl $25 and tell her to be at such and such a place at a certain time and, hell, we'd both make out like fat rats.'"[15]

Like other bigwigs in the illegal business community, Madre operated at least one legitimate business, Washington's fashionable Club Madre, that deflected attention from her substantial illegal earnings. According to her obituary in Washington's *Capital Spotlight* newspaper (1 March 1990) on nights when famous black entertainers frequented her club she became well known for her grand entrances. Dressed in furs and diamonds from head to toe, Madre would be followed by an entourage of beautiful, light-skinned black as well as white and Asian women—all for sale.

The Thin Line between the Legitimate and the Criminal Economy

Many of the women and men who worked in the underground economy, whether as numbers operators, bootleggers, or prostitutes, had other full- or part-time jobs either as fronts or because they needed both incomes, while others worked in legitimate businesses that included one or more illegal spin-off activities. On the criminal fringes were women and men who operated restaurants, bars, and nightclubs frequented by the criminal element and those who worked as domestics, cooks, or barmaids in the brothels, jook or jill joints, and nightclubs.

In the early twentieth century, Ruby Owens worked as both a cook and maid, alternating these jobs with another black woman at Atlanta's Sans Souci Hotel, which doubled as a brothel and gambling den. It was common for brothels to employ black women as domestics and black women and men as entertainers. Blues singers were required to have heavily sexualized lyrics in their songs.

In a published interview, Owens recalled that on the days she cooked, the other black female employee would "be tending to white folks business and when I be tending to they business she be cooking." During her tenure, Owens occasionally managed the brothel in her employer's absence and discovered that her benefit to her employer extended beyond her work as a cook, maid, confidante, and occasional manager of the brothel. Owens learned that the liquor that was being illegally sold at the brothel had been obtained in her name and in the names of other black employees without their consent or any financial remuneration. Earning, with wages and tips, from five to ten times as much as the typical black domestic, however, far outweighed Owens's fear of being arrested for working at a brothel or any ethical concerns she might have had about working in the criminal underground economy.[16]

Also operating on the fringes of the criminal world were black business-women and -men whose clientele included bootleggers, hustlers, and number backers. Cecelia Scott, a successful black businesswoman, operated a bar on the U Street corridor, in the black entertainment district of Washington, D.C., and later owned the popular Cecelia's restaurant and nightclub adjacent to the legendary Howard Theater. Her clientele included a pre-integration mix of black professionals and hustlers. Scott boasted that her barmaids and wait-resses were some of "the best-looking women in Washington, D.C." Attractive, light-skinned young women, Scott alleged, were good for business because her patrons, who spent freely on liquor and tipped handsomely, preferred such women. Indeed, some of her friends approached her about hiring their daughters because, as she stated, "I paid a decent wage and because of the type of clientele we attracted—doctors, and big-time hustlers who paid large tips. Besides they knew I would take care of their daughters."[17]

The presence of "big-time hustlers" (including an occasional visit by Odessa Madre) in Scott's establishments reflects the blurred lines between legitimate and illegal business activities and the class mixing common in pre-1960s black communities, especially in entertainment and leisure time activities. One legitimate businesswoman in the nation's capital blurred the legitimate and illegitimate lines more than most. Seeking to directly benefit from the criminal underground economy beyond the liquor sales and the generous tips her barmaids collected from hustlers, this businesswoman entered into a business arrangement with the numbers backers. In exchange for allowing them to occupy window seats in full view of the customers and permitting them to collect illegal bets on the daily numbers there, they paid a fee for the use of her property.[18]

Except for the most God-fearing folk and the social elite, widespread poverty, homelessness, and hunger forced even wider acceptance and participation in the numbers game, dice games, and bootlegging among entrepreneurs and the poor, and also some churchgoing folk. Still, there were public denunciations of these activities, especially among the most devoutly religious working- and middle-class blacks, and they were the most pronounced when directed toward women, rather than men, in the criminal underground economy. Yet even with women the views expressed often varied depending upon the type of work (the numbers business was less vehemently criticized than the prostitution business), the amount of money earned (the largesse of the middle-class numbers backers often blunted criticisms of them), and the familial and class background (prominent middle-class number-backing families were more widely accepted than the so-called common criminal). Odessa Marie Madre, for instance, was well known and respected in some quarters for her generous gifts to poor people, including donating clothes for destitute children in the Shaw community, where she lived and did business. On occasion, she special-ordered clothes from "boosters" (shoplifters) and had them gift wrapped and delivered to neighborhood children. Madre recounted, "'Some of the kids' mothers would be outdone but nobody ever sent a present back.'"[19]

The women and men at the very top of the numbers game and bootlegging business, like Odessa Marie Madre, often flaunted the fact that they made good money by the clothes they wore, the cars they drove, and the money they doled out, which had a certain cache in working-class black communities, especially among the regular patrons and workers in the nightclubs, bars, and jook joints. Their influence could spread beyond nightclubs and bars to churches and other black institutions, where ministers and community leaders pretended not to see.

A Little Tomboy in Me

Women who visited public dance halls, bootleg joints, and gambling dens, whether as patrons or workers, were way beyond the private and public spaces;

a distinction most respectable black women at the time allegedly recognized. Single black working women gained more and more independence from familial and domestic control with each move further away from the community in which they grew up and with each paycheck they cashed. As they did so, they determined more and more how they spent their money and their leisure time. The all-black dance halls and jook bars patronized largely by working-class men provided their black female patrons with a world that at once affirmed traditional black cultural values and lifestyles and, at the same, enabled women to exercise greater autonomy and independence. Angela Davis asserts that "women like Gertrude Rainey and Bessie Smith helped to carve out new spaces in which black working people could gather and experience themselves as a community. The tent shows in the South and the clubs and buffet flats in the North, where the Devil's music was performed by irrepressible and sexually fearless women, helped to produce a new feeling of community, one in which black culture was affirmed and the male dominance of the black church powerfully contested."[20]

Women's presence in the traditional male world of bars and nightclubs, coupled with their public drinking and freestyle dancing, contributed to the loosening of constraints on female sexual behavior and gender roles. "Street life is public life," as Regina Austin maintains; therefore, "it entails being 'Out There,' aggressive and brazen, in a realm normally foreclosed to women."[21] Conscious of how much their presence in these male-dominated public sites challenged their gender-defined roles and expectations, or having already transgressed them in their private sexual lives, some female patrons and workers in jook joints, bars, and gambling dens dressed, acted, or referred to themselves as men or tomboys. Quite possibly these women were merely reflecting how others defined them based upon the strength, courage, and aggression they exhibited alone or with their male co-conspirators. Or perhaps they were adopting characterizations designed to prevent other women from emulating them. Among the Memphis Beale Street regulars, Lillie May Glover, also known as "Big Mama Blues" and "Ma Rainey Two," earned a reputation as a "pretty tough boy" chiefly because she was a "pistol-toting blues singer and hoodoo woman." While women occasionally passed as men to secure jobs classified as men's, they were more likely to accept or adopt male characterizations to work and play in male-defined jobs and public spaces. According to economist Julie A. Matthaei, "only if they acted as men was their presence in such jobs [and public spaces] acceptable."[22]

The masculinization of black women predated the twentieth-century black woman who both worked and played in male-defined public spaces. As black women were forced into arduous, backbreaking work in the antebellum United States, it was not uncommon for a black woman to "work like a man." Some women even proudly boasted of their ability to do so.

Female blues singers were among the first groups of women whose working lives and work spaces defied traditional sexual and gender roles and assumptions in black communities. As traveling entertainers, turn-of-the-twentieth-century blues singers joined other women in the illegal underground economy in refusing to conform to dominant gender norms and expectations. Kate McTell sold bootleg whiskey alongside her husband, fellow blues singer Willie McTell, and occasionally worked as a numbers runner. Prior to becoming a recorded blues singer, Minnie Douglass sang and played on the streets of Memphis, Tennessee, and in local barbershops along Beale Street for dimes in the early 1900s. As a recorded artist, "Memphis Minnie" was said to have had a voice that was as "loud and as strong as a man's" and to have "played a guitar like a man."[23]

Based upon her assessment of Ma Rainey's career and her musical lyrics, Angela Davis reveals how Ma Rainey's work helped redefine post-emancipation gender expectations. She maintains that "like vast numbers of men, she [Ma Rainey] was exercising the freedom to travel—her music also invited her female audience to glimpse for themselves the possibility of equaling their men in this new freedom of movement. The female characters in her songs also left home, and they often left their male partners behind. They were female subjects who were free of the new, post-slavery fetters of domestic responsibilities and domestic service outside the home."[24]

Rather than appreciating women whose courageous entry into one of the last bastions of male territory expanded the limits of women's public roles and actions, most middle-class reformers condemned them for what they perceived as the immoral character of their work and their presence in nightclubs, dance halls, and jook joints. Hidden behind questions of morality were the efforts of male members of black communities to control and limit women's public lives and behavior. Certainly jook joint women experienced a world of sexual freedom and equality unprecedented in post-emancipation black community life, and for that they were often labeled "mannish."

In her youth and the years before her successful career in the criminal underworld, Madre said, "I always was a bit tomboyish and curious, so I hung around the jill joints and the gaming houses and I wanted to get in on some of the fun, too. Shoot. Why should just boys have all the fun?" Besides, she remarked, "I just couldn't keep no whatchamacallit—a man? I guess I was just born to give orders, not take 'em. What kind of man wants a woman like that?"[25]

If, by passing through the portals marked "male," black women in the underground economy rejected their subordinate status, claimed equality and freedom for themselves, and were required to adopt or self-consciously accept the moniker of "mannish," then they welcomed it as a characterization. The pistol-packing jook joint women and the elite of the underground economy, like Odessa Marie Madre, refused to accept the hierarchical patterns of a dominant male heterosexual and class-conscious culture that would have confined them to a separate sphere of work and play for women. To the extent that it occurred in the criminal underground economy, the radicalization of the gender and sexual norms was a secondary aspect of the life of black women who just wanted to make a living and possibly have a little fun in the process. Rejecting a work life characterized by low wages, poor work conditions, and frequent abusive treatment, a group of courageous, independent-minded women sought first and foremost the economic benefits of working in the largely black underworld.

Conclusion

Whether stepping out dressed in one's finest attire for a nighttime of dance and frolic, collecting number bets, selling bootleg liquor from the confines of their home or business establishment, or working as a domestic or prostitute in a brothel, these black women, with their activities and presence in the underground economy, helped to redefine gender norms and relations in black working-class urban communities and foresaw women's expanded economic and community roles. Notions of respectability and morality, notions that undergirded black middle-class women's quest for equality in the job market and in the home, had limited influence on female workers and patrons of nightclubs, jook joints, and brothels. The ability to earn a living, enjoy themselves just as the men in their communities did, and occasionally become financially successful far outweighed questions about moral and feminine character and the fear of arrest. Indeed, for many jook joint women, having fun or making a living in an illegal venture did not automatically purge them from the Lord's redemption and forgiveness or from playing an active role in the church and civic groups. As the Reverend Adam Clayton Powell Sr. in New York City and others have reported, many a pew in Sunday services were filled by folk who had partied all Saturday night, including some who sold bootleg liquor, engaged in illegal numbers operations, and ran or worked in houses of prostitution.[26]

In her later years, Owens, for one, expressed regret for having worked in the sordid environment of a brothel but reconciled her delayed feelings of guilt with the fact that she was able to earn enough money to make a living and even to purchase a home for her family. As she succinctly stated, "I wasn't working for nothing but for a living."[27]

In addition to making a living for themselves and providing for their family members, successful black women number backers and bootleggers used some of their earnings to launch successful businesses and to support civic and church activities in their communities. Indeed, in Madre's lifetime, Madame C. J. Walker and Maggie Lena Walker may have been two of a few black woman entrepreneurs to match Madre's financial success. In the end, Madre's extensive economic undertakings produced significant financial gains that provided her with a life of luxury and a wellspring of power and fame, largely unattainable to most blacks both within and outside the mid-twentieth-century underground economy. This is remarkable, especially, as she asserted, for an "unattractive" brown-skinned woman like herself. The works of legal scholar Taunya L. Banks and others reveal the extent to which skin color and physical appearance influenced black women's work lives no less than gender, class, and racial identities in the legal employment sector.[28]

Still, the work in this employment sector was not without its obvious downside, which Madre and others, especially black women, knew—the likelihood of being arrested and incarcerated. The frequent response of police to women walking down the public streets and frequenting bars, dance halls, and jook joints was to arrest them. Arrest figures in large urban communities often give the impression that black women are the only ones or are disproportionately engaged in these types of economic enterprises. Instead, they represent the greater likelihood of black women being arrested rather than their white counterparts. In some southern communities, both black male and female criminal arrests and convictions were economically motivated as much as driven by an attempt to punish women who were operating outside acceptable race and gender boundaries. For instance, for minor criminal offenses black women and men, especially in the South, were likely to be sentenced to work on chain gangs or leased to work for private firms.

Women who not only ignored laws prohibiting them from patronizing salons, but also drank alcohol in alleys and streets or sold beer, whiskey, or sex encountered the anger and ire of various segments of the black community. As Evelyn Higginbotham, Tera Hunter, and others reveal, the outrage expressed was part of a larger discourse on the virtue of the subordinate women in an urban setting.[29] For respectable middle- and working-class blacks, the behavior of these "public" women, some feared, would be the basis for how the entire race would be judged. Hunter maintains that many women from immigrant, working-class, and African American backgrounds helped to reconfigure gender conventions by their mere presence in show business as performers and patrons. This defiance of the Victorian standards of "true womanhood" resulted in women becoming major targets of middle-class criticisms of public amusements. Others, particularly devoutly religious working-class blacks, seemed not the least bit concerned about how persons outside the black community viewed jook joint women. Their focus was on saving the souls of women who frequented nightclubs as patrons or workers.

Historian Robin D. G. Kelley reveals the sense of collectivity and comradery among the working women (and men), whether enjoying the sights and sounds of the underground as a patron or as a worker. For most black workers, nightclubs, jook joints, and house parties represented "an escape from the world of assembly lines, relief lines, and color lines." Furthermore, a night on the town provided black women with an opportunity to be with "people with whom they felt kinship, people to whom they told stories about the day or the latest joke, people who shared a common vernacular filled with grammar and vocabulary that struggled to articulate the beauty and burden of their racial, class, and gender experiences in the South."[30]

Indeed, under closer examination we discover that despite middle-class denunciations of dancing and gambling, cross-class intermingling occurred. Many black women who were middle-class frequently grew up in working-class families or socially mixed neighborhoods where they were aware of, if not directly exposed to, the leisure activities and legal or illegal income-producing activities of the black men and women anxious for Saturday night diversions.

Besides, as Higginbotham argues, the condemnation of the reformers was not nearly as effective in influencing the moral character of the working poor as the sermons and religious race recordings of the 1920s and 1930s were. One of the most popular of these records was Reverend A. W. Nix's "Black Diamond Express to Hell." An advertisement for the record offered the following details: "Here she comes! The 'Black Diamond Express to Hell' with sing, the Engineer, Holding the throttle wide open; Pleasure is the Headlight, and the devil is the conductor. You can feel the roaring of the express and the moanin' of the drunkards, liars, gamblers and other folk who have got aboard. They are hell-bound and they don't want to go. The train makes eleven stops but nobody can get off." The names of the stops—"Liar's Ave," "Dance Hall Depot," "Stealing Town"—offer a glimpse into the passengers' characters.[31]

While Madre and the women workers were more akin to the zoot-suiters in Kelley's *Race Rebels* than the law-abiding, hardworking black folk in John Langston Gwaltney's *Drylongso: A Self-Portrait of Black America* (1980), they were no less respected for their wit, race consciousness, and financial acumen. As Gwaltney observed, "[T]he primary status of a black person is that accorded by the people he or she lives among. It is based upon assessments of that person's fidelity to core black standards."[32]

In keeping with her desire to maintain a certain lifestyle and to remain at the top of the illegal financial world following a series of criminal arrests, Madre expanded her economic enterprises to include drug sales—a highly unusual endeavor for women during the mid-twentieth century and one that few, if any, members of the black community supported.[33] In 1980, seventy-three-year-old Odessa Madre, newly released from prison, lived in a spacious five-bedroom house that she owned in Northwest Washington. Although she died penniless in 1983, several people who remembered how she had so generously abided by one of the core values of the black community—communal sharing with the needy—collected money to bury her. Despite her financial situation when she died, when asked whether crime pays, Madre's response, with her typical bravado, was, "Yes, it pays. It pays a helluva lot."[34] Her work life was, in fact, a double-edged sword—it paid well, but she also paid dearly with the years she spent in jail and the dire financial straits in which each jailing left her.

NOTES

1. Mary Frances Berry, currently the Geraldine R. Segal Professor of American Social Thought at the University of Pennsylvania and author of *The Pig Farmer's Daughter: Women, Crime, and the Law* (New York: Vintage Press, 1999), requested that I present information about women in the underground economy. The term "underground" represents, in part, the extent to which members of the black working class attempted to keep their illegal as well as their legitimate nighttime lives and actions hidden from public view, although their actions were no secret in most black circles. Labor scholars often use the term "underground economy" to refer to undocumented (usually illegal) work not performed or considered part of the traditional labor market.

2. My personal reflections in this essay represent, in part, a continuation of an earlier essay, "Reclaiming Public Voice and the Study of Black Women's Work," where I examine the twists and turns of my personal journey as an black feminist research scholar. That essay appears in *Gender, Families, and Close Relationships: Feminist Research Journeys,* ed. Donna L. Sollie and Leigh A. Leslie (Thousand Oaks, Calif.: Sage Publications, 1994), a collection of essays in which feminist researchers seek to recapture the intersection of their personal lives and their feminist scholarship.

3. Quote taken from "Voices beyond the Veil: An Interview of Toni Cade Bambara and Sonia Sanchez," by Zala Chandler, in *Wild Women in the Whirlwind: Afra-American Culture and the Contemporary Literary Renaissance,* ed. Joanne M. Braxton and Andree Nicola McLaughlin (New Brunswick: Rutgers University Press, 1990), 347.

4. Robin D. G. Kelley, *Race Rebels: Culture, Politics, and the Black Working Class* (New York: Free Press, 1994); Tera W. Hunter, *To 'Joy My Freedom: Southern Black Women's Lives and Labors after the Civil War* (Cambridge, Mass.: Harvard University Press, 1997); Regina Austin, "The Black Community: Its Lawbreakers and the Politics of Identification," *Southern California Law Review* 65, no. 4 (May 1992): 1769–1817.

5. See the "Madre" listings in *Boyd's Directory of the District of Columbia*, vol. 58–67 (Washington, D.C.: R. L. Polk & Co., 1921–1925), Mfilm 31–35, 39, Washingtoniana Division, D.C. Public Library, M. L. King Branch.

6. Courtland Milloy, "The Odessa File," *Washington Post Magazine*, 28 September 1980, 2.

7. Mrs. Lilly Butler, interview by author, Washington, D.C., 14 February 2001.

8. Thomas Bell, "Once the 'Queen' of Washington's Underworld, Odessa Madre Dies Penniless," *Washington Post*, 8 March 1990, J-11.

9. Milloy, "The Odessa File," 16.

10. Ibid., 17.

11. Ibid., 15.

12. Butler interview.

13. Milloy, "The Odessa File," 20; see the "Madre" listings in the *City Directory of Washington, 1921–1925*.

14. Mrs. Joyce Jean, interview by author, Washington, D.C., October 1998. This is a pseudonym to protect the identity of the sixty-year-old woman whom I interviewed who knew Madre and operated legitimate businesses frequented by Madre and other women and men like her.

15. Milloy, "The Odessa File," 20. In the criminal underground economy, some women who chose to become sex workers were drawn by the higher salaries and glamour; others were "occasional prostitutes." Moreover, as historian Joanne Meyerowitz writes, occasional prostitutes "did not necessarily see themselves as prostitutes, they simply played the 'sex game' for somewhat higher stakes." The latter group of women combined their day jobs with offering "sexual services on occasional nights for extra money." Joanne Meyerowitz, "Sexual Geography and Gender Economy: The Furnished-Room Districts of Chicago, 1890–1930," *Gender and History* 2 (autumn 1990), cited in *Unequal Sisters: A Multicultural Reader in U.S. Women's History*, ed. Vicki Ruiz and Ellen Carol DuBois (New York: Routledge, 1994), 192.

16. Hunter, *To 'Joy My Freedom*, 113.

17. Scott interview, September 1998.

18. Jean interview.

19. Milloy, "The Odessa File," 20.

20. Angela Y. Davis, *Blues Legacies and Black Feminism: Gertrude "Ma" Rainey, Bessie Smith, and Billie Holiday* (New York: Pantheon Books, 1998), 137.

21. Austin, "The Black Community," 1798.

22. Julie A. Matthaei, *An Economic History of Women in America* (New York: Schocken Books, 1982), 192

23. Paul Oliver, *The Story of the Blues* (Boston: Northeastern University Press, 1997), 122.

24. Davis, *Blues Legacies and Black Feminism*, 72. For a fuller discussion of gender politics in the lives and lyrics of black blues singers, see Davis, *Blues Legacies and Black Feminism*.

25. Milloy, "The Odessa File," 17.

26. Most ministers, such as Adam Clayton Powell Sr., who acknowledged that among their congregants were numbers (policy) backers, pimps, and those "who were operating houses of ill repute" openly condemned their work. Powell Jr. recounted how his father ranted and raved in the church and in the streets against such people through a practice called "gospel bombardment." Other ministers accepted the financial support and presence of "prominent" policy kings. See, for instance, Wil Haygood, *King of the Cats: The Life and Times of Adam Clayton Powell, Jr.* (Boston: Houghton Mifflin Co., 1993), 68; and St. Claire Drake and Horace R. Clayton, *Black Metropolis: A Study of Negro Life in a Northern City* (1945; reprint, University of Chicago Press, 1970), 490–494.

27. Hunter, *To 'Joy My Freedom*, 114.

28. See Taunya Lovell Banks, "The Black Side of the Mirror: The Black Body in the Workplace," in this volume.

29. Evelyn Brooks Higginbotham, *Righteous Discontent: The Women's Movement in the Black Baptist Church, 1880–1920* (Cambridge, Mass.: Harvard University Press, 1993); Hunter, *To 'Joy My Freedom*.

30. Kelley, *Race Rebels*, 47.

31. Evelyn Brooks Higginbotham, "Rethinking Vernacular Culture: Black Religion and Race Records in the 1920s and 1930s," in *The House That Race Built: Black Americans, U.S. Terrain*, ed. Wahneema Lubiano (New York: Pantheon Books, 1997), 157–177.

32. John Langston Gwaltney, *Drylongso: A Self-Portrait of Black America* (New York: Random House, 1980), xxii. This book is among the most insightful recent texts of this genre.

33. Anthropologist Tony Whitehead reports that the young men and women engaged in street-level drug sales in the Baltimore, Maryland, communities studied maintained that they are no different from the nation's corporate executives, except that they had a few blocks to peddle their goods whereas corporate giants have the whole world. Tony Larry Whitehead, James Peterson, and Linda Kaljee, "The 'Hustle': Socioeconomic Deprivation, Urban Drug Trafficking, and Low-Income, African-American Male Gender Identity," *Pediatrics* 93, no. 6 (June 1994): 1050, part 2.

34. Milloy, "The Odessa File," 21.

Between a Rock and a Hard Place

Mothering, Work, and Welfare in the Rural South

BONNIE THORNTON DILL

TALLESE JOHNSON

PERSONAL STATEMENT **BONNIE THORNTON DILL** ▪ At a dinner party given shortly after I moved to Memphis, Tennessee, in 1979 an older, genteel white woman asked if I liked southern cooking. I replied that I had always eaten southern cooking as the granddaughter of a black cook who had migrated to Chicago before 1920. So, while I had never lived in the South or even visited it much before I moved to Memphis, I was well aware of my southern heritage. Much of my upbringing, at home, in the neighborhood, and in church, had been influenced by manners and traditions that were characteristic of black southerners. My parents, in fact, were two of the most northern people among their friends. My mother had come to Chicago in 1921 at the age of eight and my father had grown up in a number of cities in the Midwest, including Battle Creek, Michigan, and St. Paul, Minnesota. In fact, he was the only black person I knew who had lived in those seemingly remote places, and I remember thinking it rather odd that he was not from the South. But black Chicagoans often referred to the city as "up South," which captured both the southern roots of many of the city's black residents and the new forms of racism and discrimination they experienced there. So, while I read and heard about "down South"—a place where Jim Crow determined where people could sit on the train, drink water, use a restroom, or eat and where racial exclusion limited opportunities for blacks so much that my grandfather reputedly turned a deaf ear to the pleadings of his former boss, who promised to pay for the college education of his children if he would only return to Louisiana and continue to be his cook—I experienced "up South"—the food, sense of community, religious practices, and cultural traditions that southern blacks held onto in the cold and impersonal North.

Moving to Memphis after living in Chicago and then New York was both a shock and a pilgrimage. It provided me with an opportunity to get to know and understand the South better and, in doing so, to understand myself better as well. It helped me to see both my southern heritage and my northern experience in bold relief. Memphis, in addition to being the home of such music legends as Stax records and Elvis Presley, was also referred to as the capital of northern Mississippi. Many of its black and white residents had moved there and were still moving there from Mississippi. Until I moved to Memphis, I had forgotten that I had been there once before. It was on my way to join James Meredith's March against Fear in 1966. The airplane I had taken from New York had landed in Memphis, where I had been met and driven to join the march somewhere in the Mississippi Delta. Memphis was both entry and exit point for Mississippi, and participation in the Meredith march provided me with a brief glimpse into a state that was legendary for its mistreatment of poor black folk.

My long-term research interests were in work and family for black women. My mother had always worked, as a teacher, and so had most of her friends. They worked in professional jobs and did well, but many women of their generation faced much harsher working conditions, and I had long had an interest in how this group of women had managed not merely to survive but to build lives for themselves and their children. I took those interests with me when I moved to Memphis, and when I had the opportunity to transfer some of those concerns to the lives and experiences of poor women in rural Mississippi, I jumped at the opportunity. Though I had never lived in a rural community, I relished the opportunity to get out, meet and talk with people, and hear their own stories about their lives.

PERSONAL STATEMENT / **TALLESE JOHNSON** ▪ I grew up in an extended family composed of my mother, my two sisters, and my maternal grandparents in the Deep South during the 1970s and 1980s. My parents divorced when I was three years old. I was reared in the segregated city of Birmingham, Alabama, where remnants of the Civil Rights movement were and still are salient to the residents of the city. One of the strong tenets from the movement for equal rights was the importance of access to education as a key to success in America. Education was strongly emphasized within my working-class family, particularly from my maternal and paternal grandmothers, who were employed as domestic workers: one as a maid in private homes and the other within a business office. A familiar phrase I heard from these two women while growing up was, "You're not going to have to wait on white people when you grow up; you're going to get an education." My mother also stressed the importance of education by example, through attending college part time to become a nurse while working as a nurse's aide and home health-care sitter for the elderly.

Most members of my family (aunts, uncles, cousins) were employed in blue- and pink-collar occupations. A few members, like my father, who was a postal worker, and an aunt who was employed by the telephone company, were employed in the "good jobs," jobs that provided a good salary and medical benefits.

Of particular interest to me was how the women in my family were able to raise children on limited resources and balance work and family. Although these women worked full time, their jobs did not pay enough to make ends meet. So for brief periods of time they received public assistance in the form of medical care, food subsidies, or public housing assistance. Medicare and Medicaid were common forms of health insurance for working family members who did not receive health benefits from their jobs. Memories of complaints of poor treatment in county hospitals and long waits in lines before work for food subsidies are part of my childhood.

My family background nurtured my interest in conducting research on issues of gender, work, and family. I feel strongly about contributing to our knowledge of how poor women balance work and family. These concerns are similar to those of Bonnie Thornton Dill in her work on rural families in Mississippi. Thus, when the opportunity to work with her developed, it seemed a perfect fit. My current research on the relationship between job quality and returns to welfare (recidivism) is quantitative. In it I analyze data from national surveys to learn about the types of jobs that help women get off and potentially stay off welfare. Dill's work complements mine because it focuses on women's own stories about how they manage to cope, survive, and make ends meet. Working with her on this project allowed me to stay in touch with the lived experiences of women who, like my mother and grandmother, spent their child-rearing years balancing work and family.

---

*W*ork and welfare: most people have thought that the two were mutually exclusive, that women who received welfare prior to welfare reform in 1996 didn't work and didn't want to work, and that women who worked didn't need welfare. Contrary to popular opinion, however, most women who received welfare (a term which was often used to refer to the specific federal program entitled Aid to Families with Dependent Children [AFDC]) worked for pay.[1] In fact, most often they combined welfare with work because their low-wage jobs did not pay enough for them to become self-sufficient in providing for their families and because welfare did not provide enough money for them to be dependent on it alone.[2] Poor women on welfare worked or sought paid work, not only to support their families, but also to have a sense of self-reliance and independence. They worked because they knew they needed to establish a record for themselves in the workplace. They also knew that marriage alone would not support them. Racism has caused both black men and women to suffer in the labor force, to experience higher rates of unemployment, underemployment, layoffs, and low wages. As a result, even middle-class black families are far more likely than comparable white families to depend on two wage earners to maintain their standard of living. Poor black women are likely to marry men whose economic prospects are limited and thus to continue to struggle financially, even when married.[3] Therefore, a woman's independent ability to support her family becomes an important part of her role as a mother.[4]

Between 1989 and 1992, Bonnie Thorton Dill interviewed a number of low-income single mothers living in rural southern communities to explore how they managed their multiple roles of homemaker, provider, and mother. In the process, the women described themselves, their children, and families and discussed their goals and aspirations as well as their survival strategies. They talked a lot about work, especially the kind and amount of work available in their rural communities. What they said belies traditional stereotypes and images of poor single mothers as lazy and unwilling to work.

This chapter presents the story of one of those women, Loretta Samms, and explores the issues of work and welfare through her life.[5] Loretta's story highlights some of the dilemmas faced by women who must find ways to support their families when paid work opportunities are limited. In contrast to the idea that work and welfare are opposites, it illustrates how they are related, two sides of the same coin, with welfare filling the void created by limited work opportunities. Loretta also challenges contemporary notions that marriage, more than a job, will solve problems of poverty among low-income single mothers. Loretta had this to say about it: "That don't mean 'cause you got a good man, you got a good job. *You* ain't got that. That's that man's. If that man don't want to give you nothing, that man ain't got to give you nothing. . . . That's still not you. I like to have my own money. It's good for [him] to help you out, but, you know, your money is best. You do what you want. You can get whatever you want. You ain't got to worry 'bout 'What you go on 'n buy this for?' 'You don't need this.' I [want to] have my own money so I ain't got nothing to worry 'bout . . . 'cause, see, it's mine. I worked for it. I made it. I do whatever I want."

Loretta Samms, a twenty-six-year-old single mother of two young children, is looking for a job, not a husband. It's not that she has anything against having a husband. She is engaged to the father of her two children, and they plan on getting married as soon as he has regular work. However, from her per-spective, having a husband does not relieve her of the responsibility of provid-ing for herself and her children. In fact, in her view, being dependent upon a man's wages to support her and her family would limit her freedom because she fears she would have to account to someone else for every penny she spends.

Dill met Loretta in 1991. She lived in a small town in the Mississippi Delta with her two children, her brother, three sisters, and six nieces and nephews. Her house was located in a subdivision of about twenty Federal Housing Administration–financed single-family homes. Of average height and slim build, she was energetic, friendly, and outgoing. She talked about her life in a straightforward and open manner, describing her two daughters, ages four and two, with pride and pleasure. The oldest child attended Head Start, and Loretta was an enthusiastic observer of her daughter's progress and participation, visit-ing the program every couple of weeks to observe and assist.

During the two and one-half hours in which they talked about how she managed as a single mother in a rural community, Loretta repeatedly returned to the issue of finding work. She had begun receiving welfare when her first child was born in 1986. Five years later, in 1990, at the time of this interview, she said that the children's father, his family, and her own helped out in pro-viding for the children. As she put it, "They [the children] not needy. Only thing needy is that I just needy for a job. They ain't in need, but I'm the one in need. You see I need a job for to help them out too."

For Loretta, work was an important aspect of her goals for herself and of her definition of being a mother. "I can be a Mama and a working woman at the same time," she proclaimed early in the interview. When asked if she would ever move away from this community for a job, she enthusiastically responded: "Uh-huh! Yeah! Yeah! I'm not choosy 'bout no job. Long as I'm working, it don't make me no difference what I'm doing, long as it's work. Yeah, I'll move for a job. Yeah, it would be hard to leave my family, but, I can't worry about them. If I can't see 'em, I'll keep up to date; call and write. . . . 'Cause, see, all my life I wanted to work, have my own place, raise my kids up the way I want them to be raised up, and get them what they want. That's my dream. Because I want to work. I look for work 'bout every month—look for something to do. I say I'm gone keep on till I find me a job soon."

In the early 1990s, Dill, along with several colleagues, conducted a study of black and white low-income single mothers living in four predominantly rural counties in the South. The research focused on the women's coping and sur-vival strategies and on how the opportunity structures of the communities in which they lived—structures developed through a legacy of racially exclusive and gender discriminatory social, economic, and political practices—shaped the women's choices and options. Loretta Samms was one of the women who participated in the study.

The region, referred to as the Lower Mississippi Delta, includes portions of Missouri, Tennessee, Arkansas, Mississippi, and Louisiana. For most African Americans born before 1965, the Delta area of the state of Mississippi is associated with the names of people such as Medgar Evers, James Meredith, Fannie Lou Hamer, and Bob Moses; with such organizations as the Mississippi Freedom Democratic Party, SNCC (Student Non-violent Coordinating Committee), and the 1964 Freedom Summer Project; and with the murders of Emmit Till, Mickey Schwerner, James Chaney, Andrew Goodman, and Viola Liuzzo, along with countless others, named and unnamed.

The counties in this region are still among the poorest in the nation.[6] Overall, more than 20 percent of the population is poor, and many of those are workers who earn low wages. Rates of infant mortality and substandard housing are high. Educational levels are generally lower than the national average and health and health care are poorer. In the Delta, these indicators of poverty are shaped by race: the large African American population is overwhelmingly and severely disadvantaged when compared to the white population. Rural African Americans experience poverty rates which exceed those of both urban blacks and rural whites. And while half of all southern poor children are white, southern black children are two and a half times more likely to live in poverty than southern white children.[7] Increasingly, the overwhelming majority of these children live in single-parent households with their mothers.

The county in which Loretta Samms lives is typical of the region. Cotton, soybeans, and now catfish are the primary agricultural products in the area, and there are also a number of small factories. In the early 1990s, when Dill drove on Highway 61 from Memphis into the Mississippi Delta, she was struck by the vast rolling fields stretching as far as the eye could see. If the sun was shining, and it usually was, it was bright and penetrating, unremitting in its heat and glare. Every mile or so a small grove of trees providing a break in the broad landscape would appear. Wooden shacks, abandoned to the elements, appeared at intervals along the roadside, and occasionally small groups of people with hats or scarves covering their heads could be seen bending over, working in a field. Though the county seat is the commercial and residential hub of each county, there are a number of small towns dotted across the countryside. Every ten or fifteen miles along the highway, parts of these towns would appear; a water tower, silos, or perhaps a grain elevator signaled their agricultural roots. On the highway, you might find a gas station, quick food mart or general store, and perhaps a group of small frame houses, which were part of a housing development. Driving into this part of the Mississippi Delta, even as recently as ten years ago, felt like a journey back in time.

In the year that Loretta Samms was interviewed, 64 percent of the population of her county was black and over one-half of all residents were poor. Slightly more than one-fourth of the families in the county were considered female-headed households. Poverty, especially among black single mothers, was due in large part to the legacy of racial exclusion, the dearth of jobs, and the fact that the few jobs that exist pay low wages. Almost 22 percent of black people living in Loretta's home county were poor in 1990, compared to just under 5 percent of whites. Women's poverty followed a similar pattern: 23 percent of black women and only 4 percent of white women were unemployed. Young black women close to Loretta's age fared considerably worse with a full 55 percent counted as "not in the labor force" and only 22 percent counted as employed. Those women who did work found jobs in restaurants as cooks and servers, in hotels as maids, in nursing homes as aides, and in factories as operatives. In light of these data, it is not surprising that Loretta has struggled to find work. Her choice, to spend roughly two years in a training program to become a cashier clerk, provides an interesting commentary on the interface between individual skills and experience and the structure of the local labor market.

At twenty-six, Loretta had held only one paid job in her life and it was a job as a student worker at the local community college. She dropped out of high school after ninth grade after a fire destroyed her family's home and all of their possessions. She recalled: "We lost everything and I had [to] start back from scratch all over, had to start buying clothes, shoes, 'n stuff all over for everybody. That's when I dropped out. And then, you know, by the time I got back on my feet, able to go back to school, you know, I went and took me a trade out to the college."

Loretta says she spent about two years training to become a cashier clerk because she wanted to get a job at the new Wal-Mart that was opening in a nearby town: "At the time I wanted to work at Wal-Mart. 'Cause, see, at the time they were hiring at Wal-Mart and I wanted to work, you know, with the Wal-Mart. I thought, if I take up a trade out there as a cashier—cause that's what I wanted to be, a cashier—I probably would have had a opportunity to get me a job there. But, you know, it didn't work out in my plan. I graduated from there, of course, but I didn't get no job from them. . . . They had got the people they needed and . . . At the time when I graduated . . . they weren't hiring no more. And so I looked for another job."

The qualifications for a job as a cashier at Wal-Mart do not generally require specialized training. Most cashiers are people with high school diplomas who are trained by the company with or without prior related work experience. Loretta's employment strategy was to substitute trade school training, certifying her as a cashier clerk, for her lack of a high school diploma in order to obtain the job she sought at Wal-Mart. The problem, however, was that the market for cashier clerks was small in her community, and once Wal-Mart had filled its jobs, there was virtually no place to sell a skill for which people were easily trained. Loretta was caught between the rock of her own lack of a high school diploma and the hard place of a local job market that offered a limited range of employment options. Like her older sister, she had chosen job training as a means to overcome this dilemma. But it had not yet paid off for either her or her sister. "It's a lot of folk out there at Wal-Mart . . . they don't have no . . . job experience, that was they first job experience, and they don't have no high school diploma and stuff like that. Some tell you that you have to have your high school diploma; then some of them say you don't. So you'll never catch the truth about that."

In the face of the failure of that plan, her employment-related work became looking for work, but few opportunities were related to her newly acquired skills. "We [Loretta and her sister] put us a application at the personnel office in town, you know, trying to get a housekeeping job or work in the kitchen. And so, you know, didn't nothing come through there. And, I have put me an application at the Quality Hotel and the Johnson Motel. And I got one at Wal-Mart, and I got an application out there at McDonald's and at the gas station. You know, I be putting in application all over, but they never come through, 'cause the first thing they looking at, you know, I didn't finish high school. I ain't got no high school diploma. That's what really messing me up I believe. But, like you say, it's just who you know."

Issues of education, training, and the limitations of the local job market are confounded in small towns and rural communities by the benefits and liabilities of who you know. Loretta described her community with the following words: "We have a small town. Most folk like to run your business."

In most small rural communities, individuals are known as members of families. Family membership marks people. It labels them hardworking or "no-count," from the right or wrong side of town. It is often the lens through which others view them. Opportunities for employment are often shaped by personal history and family relationships.

For many of the years while she was growing up (and until the fire), Loretta and her brothers, sisters, mother, and grandmother lived in the home that her grandfather had owned, built, and left for his family when he died. Even though Loretta's mother was receiving aid from Aid to Families with Dependent Children (AFDC) for herself and her children, they all lived in this family home, an ample brick house. In their community, a brick house is as a symbol of financial security. According to Loretta, this aspect of her family life affected her search for employment: "Okay, like Mr. C, when he was the mayor, his folk got everything they needed. That's all he was really concerned about— his folk. He ain't really concerned about what the other folk needed. You go to ask him about a job [and he'd say,] 'Naw, Ms. Samms. Y'all got everything. Look at that big old fancy house. Look how y'all dress. Y'all don't need nothing.' But, like I say, he don't know what's behind closed doors." And, Loretta's mother added, upon entering the room, that he would say, "You ought to find y'all some good men, and things like that."

Objective factors, such as education, training, and the job market, tell only part of the story of finding work in this rural community. Loretta's story makes it clear that personal factors such as family and friendship are critical. And beyond that, she contended that men in a position to hire workers often expect personal favors from young single women like herself: "Get ahead in life? Get in the racket. They tell me if you don't get in that racket you gon' be left by a long time for jobs, place to stay, anything. I'll always be left out 'cause I'm not going to bed with nobody for no house or for no job. . . . 'I'll get you the job. What you gon' get me?' That's what they really say. I'll say, 'Nothing. Well, you keep the job then. I don't need that.' But I need it bad, but not bad enough to go to bed for no job."

Although she did not talk about this issue at length, several times during the interview Loretta made it quite clear that the request for sexual favors in exchange for a job or other service was not at all unusual. As a poor young single woman who had children and few marketable skills, she, and other women like her, were particularly vulnerable to those kinds of requests and expectations. Though most of the women interviewed were, like Loretta, quite critical of this racket and refused to get into it, several other women confirmed that the request to exchange sex for money and services was not unusual.

Loretta's fate in the job market was limited by a number of factors. On the personal side, her age and lack of education and experience as well as the lack of family or personal connections that could help her with employment choices and preparation were major limiting factors. On the structural side, the lack of jobs in the community, the legacy of racial discrimination, and sexism in the treatment of women and the jobs open to them further narrowed her opportunities.

Since she was unable to find employment that would permit her to provide for her family, Loretta's primary source of steady support, beginning with the birth of her first child, was welfare. For her, that meant AFDC and food stamps with free medical care through Medicaid. In 1990, Mississippi ranked lowest of all the states and the District of Columbia in monthly benefits. AFDC awards were based on family size, with a family of two (mother and child) receiving $96 per month and a maximum benefit of $144 for a family of four or more. Food stamps provided additional cash assistance "and often became the major source of income for families receiving AFDC." (For example, a family of three that receives $120 a month is likely to receive, in addition, about $315 a month in food stamp benefits.)[8] AFDC families received free health care through the Medicaid program. All other expenses, including rent, utilities, clothing, household items, toiletries and furniture and school supplies and other educational expenses had to be purchased using the monthly benefit or some other unreported income.

Loretta was not the first person in her family to receive welfare. Her mother had received welfare and food stamps for all eight of her children as far back as Loretta could remember. And at least two of her sisters, at the time of the interview, were also receiving AFDC. Since her welfare case had been opened, Loretta had struggled to make ends meet. She was adamant in her feelings that the money was insufficient to support her family: "Naw, they ain't doin' you fair, and we ain't getting enough money. 'Cause, you see, two children, and, you know, cost of living is done gone up. A hundred and twenty dollars cannot do nothing for no two children especially when you got to clothe 'em, feed 'em, and got to help take care of bills and stuff. Naw, we ain't getting nothing but a lot of heartaches and pain. We just suffering."

Though she had proudly stated earlier in the interview that her children were "not needy," as the conversation progressed, it became apparent that there were times when they had been without food as well as without gas and electricity because they could not afford to pay the bill. The heartaches and pain that she describes are a result of those circumstances and of her inability to provide the kind of financial resources she feels her family needs to survive. Though welfare was her major source of income, its inadequacy meant that her family's survival depended on supplements from a variety of sources including the children's father, his family, and, primarily, her own kin.

Loretta's family's strategy for making ends meet was interesting and distinctive among the people interviewed. They took advantage of the fact that they were a close-knit group that had grown up learning to rely on one another. According to Loretta, "My mama growed us up to help one another and love one another. Help 'em when they need help. . . . We been together all our lives. We ain't never been separated and we all still together. I don't care what it is. If we got it, they got it."

Using their ability to live and work together, they pooled their resources to enhance their family's ability to survive. Yet despite their ingenuity, they often fell short of meeting their basic needs. At the time of the interview, Loretta shared a house with three sisters, her brother, and their eight children. The family was purchasing the house through the Federal Housing Administration (FHA), but they were having a difficult time keeping up with the payments and the taxes. The only person in the household who had a job that paid above minimum wage was Loretta's brother. However, his job was seasonal and he was employed only three to four months a year at the local manufacturing plant where he had returned to work each year for nine years. Nevertheless, he paid the mortgage. Two of her sisters had three children each and received welfare benefits of $144 per month. One of them had recently begun working in a local restaurant chain, making between $70 and $200 weekly, depending on the number of hours she was given. She anticipated that these earnings would be deducted, dollar for dollar, from her welfare check after the first month. The third sister had no income and no children. Together, the sisters paid the household expenses, including utilities, telephone, and other home care items. The entire family of five adults and eight children were eligible for food stamps and received coupons worth $991 monthly. Loretta reported that they ran out of food almost every month, usually about a week before it was time to pick up food stamps. Dill's rough estimate of expenses and income for the family (excluding food stamps) found that in the best of times, they would have only about $150 left for all other expenditures after rent and utilities were paid. Managing these meager resources was made even harder by the fact that family income varied widely from week to week, with the only consistent money being Loretta's and her nonworking sister's welfare checks. When her brother was working, he was paid fairly well at his job. When that job was over, he had no other employment and was not eligible to receive unemployment insurance. Additionally, his earnings as well as those of the sister who worked in the restaurant were expected to reduce the family's food stamp allowance.

For Loretta, then, welfare offered a source of income when she had none, along with the additional benefits of Medicaid coverage. But life on welfare was hard and unsatisfying in many ways. She could not rely on it to meet all of her and her children's needs, it offered no source of self-esteem, and, while pooling resources facilitated her ability to cope and survive, it was not the life she hoped and planned for herself and her children. When asked how long she thought she would continue on welfare, she responded: "By the help and grace of the Lord, I hope I be done found me a job, my boyfriend be done got him a good job, you know, be done got married. I was hoping this year could be my las' year on 'cause you do better by working. 'Cause you don't get enough. . . . If I can get me a job right now, they can have that ADC [AFDC] 'cause I wanta work for my money. I don't wanta be on no ADC all my life. . . . I'd rather work than to get that 'cause I know I be working more than $120 just once a month. . . . I want me a job getting paid off every week 'cause I won't have to worry about no ADC."

Loretta's dream for her family is a modest version of the American dream, to be married, to have a family, and for both her and her husband to have jobs that provide wages that can support that family. Her family was clearly her most important resource, providing child care, money, companionship, and a team approach to survival and provisioning.

Even for women who are able to find employment, family becomes a key means of survival, supplementing wages that are too low to create self-sufficiency. Alfrenell Thomas, a divorced mother of two sons, who also participated in the study, has a job like the one Loretta wants. She works at a local retail store in town.[9] She works six days a week: from 8:30 A.M. until 4:00 P.M. on Mondays and Tuesdays, until 6:00 P.M. on Wednesdays and Fridays, until noon on Thursdays, and from 7:30 A.M. until 6:00 P.M. on Saturdays. She earns $4 an hour and brings home $165 per week. Though divorced, she receives no child support or other money from her ex-husband, whom she describes as "continuously unemployed." Her wages make her ineligible for welfare; however she does receive about $80 to $100 monthly in food stamps. After work on Mondays, Tuesdays, and Thursdays (her early days), she drives to a trade school about forty miles from her home, for cosmetology classes that begin at 5:00 P.M. She does this because she is confident that her trade-school training will provide her with a marketable skill that will raise her earnings and her standard of living. She has been encouraged in pursuing this line of work by her aunt, who owns a business in a midwestern city and wants her to move there to work with her when she is fully trained. Alfrenell, however, is doubtful that she will leave this community, even for the prospect of a better standard of living. And, when one looks closely at how she manages to juggle all of these aspects of her life, children, work, and school, it is apparent that she is deeply indebted to family members who live nearby and without whom all of this would not be possible.

Alfrenell and her two boys live in a small housing complex containing approximately twenty garden-style rental units arranged around a cul-de-sac. Her brother and sister-in-law also live in the complex. Her older son and his first cousin (her brother's son) attend the local parochial school together; it is only a block away. Her younger son is in the local Head Start program and he is picked up daily by a school bus. Because their uncle lives nearby, her sons view his house as a second home. Each day after work, Alfrenell's sister or mother comes to her home to take care of the boys until Alfrenell gets home. On the days that she has trade-school classes, her sister helps the children with their homework, prepares their dinner, and stays until Alfrenell returns from school, usually about 10:00 or 11:00 P.M.

In addition to child care, the other thing that makes it possible for Alfrenell to take advantage of a training program forty miles from where she lives is her car. Although a car is essential for traveling to work, shopping, and obtaining services in rural communities, most of the low-income women whom we interviewed did not have one. Transportation is a major barrier to opportunities outside their households, and many told of paying money to people who had cars in order to go grocery shopping, make clinic visits, or get to work. The few women who, like Alfrenell, have a car usually have an old one that requires considerable maintenance. Alfrenell's car is maintained by her father and brother, both of whom are mechanics.

Alfrenell's family provides the grease that keeps the multiple gears of her life turning together, and income from long hours of work at low pay is supplemented by assistance from her siblings and parents and by government aid in the form of food stamps. The combination of these factors facilitates her ability to make choices that she hopes will improve her children's futures and her own.

Though Loretta and Alfrenell are in very different points on the work-welfare continuum, their stories show that their similarities are greater than their differences. Both cases illustrate a finding we reported earlier: in the rural southern communities we studied, low wages and limited employment opportunities for African American women, along with low welfare payments and a meager social support system, result in a strong reliance on kin and friendship networks for survival.[10] As is the case in many developing countries, the costs of low wages and underemployment in the rural South are borne by small groups of kin and friends. The literature on development in the Third World also helps us see Loretta's unemployment and Alfrenell's low-wage employment as a direct result of the structure of available occupational opportunities in local labor markets. In these small southern towns, the job market is primarily characterized by low-wage agricultural and service jobs, limited industrial opportunities, and a predominance of seasonal work, underemployment, unemployment, and discrimination. In this framework, Loretta's own lack of education and experience is seen more as a direct reflection of these conditions than as a personal failure or a lack of motivation.

What we have tried to show through both of these stories is that neither work nor welfare *alone* is able to support and sustain these families. Both women found themselves in a kind of double-bind situation, facing either low-wage work or welfare, neither of which provided adequate support for their families. Each made a number of strategic choices designed to improve her economic circumstances and her family's future. Their motivation and desire for improvement and upward mobility is clear. Loretta's failure to fully achieve her goals (at least at the point at which the conversations ended), when contrasted with Alfrenell's ability to take steps in the direction of achieving hers, illustrates the importance of work, even at low wages, at the same time that it points up its limitations. In both of these cases, kin are key to buffering and/or overcoming the barriers created by an interlocking system of economic exclusion, racial oppression, and gender discrimination deeply rooted in the region, the state, and the nation.

We also hope this chapter has demonstrated the close link between work and welfare in the lives of all of these women. Though Loretta has not been a wageworker, her desire for work and her efforts to find work shape much of her life. Welfare, for her, is a means of support because she cannot find a job. For Alfrenell, work provides her the means to seek alternative educational opportunities for her children and herself. Yet, in a small town with limited work opportunities, Alfrenell's future as a worker is precarious, dependent upon the sustained health of the business in which she is employed. A layoff or store closing would quickly erase the differences between her life and Loretta's.

The lives of these two women and others whom Dill interviewed demonstrate that even before the recent changes in welfare programs, changes tying benefits directly to wage work, poor rural women experienced work and welfare not as mutually exclusive but as directly related to one another. In fact, more often than not, women receiving welfare are displaced workers, people who seek paid work but, for many reasons, both structural and personal, cannot find steady employment that provides sufficient funds for them to support their family. Thus, when jobs are scarce, when they are laid off from work, when family demands are great, or when their wages are insufficient to provide for their children, welfare along with help from kin provides a safety net that helps these families survive.

Epilogue

Shortly after the interviews with the women in this article, the 1996 welfare reform act was implemented. The act, the Personal Responsibility and Work Opportunity Reconciliation Act (PRWORA), eliminated the federal entitlement program of Aid to Families with Dependent Children (AFDC). Control was shifted to the states through a new program called Temporary Assistance for Needy Families (TANF), which offers time-limited cash assistance in order to move women off welfare and into work.

The new policy emphasizes work as the key to economic self-sufficiency for poor women with children. The policy's emphasis on work seems to imply that poor women were not working before TANF was instituted. However, the stories of Loretta Samms and Alfrenell Thomas and subsequent research show that most AFDC recipients combined welfare and work in the past in order to make ends meet.[11] The stark reality of life, as was shown through these earlier case histories, involves a delicate balancing act in order to maintain low-wage work, receive welfare benefits, especially health coverage, and provide for one's family. Factors such as low wages, lack of child care, and lack of transportation, factors especially problematic in Mississippi, make it very difficult for women to stay employed.

Jason DeParle, a columnist who has reported extensively on the new welfare act for the *New York Times*, described the impact of welfare reform in Mississippi.[12] By some standards, the 1996 welfare reform legislation appears to be a success in Mississippi: welfare caseloads have dropped in record numbers.[13] Some of that success has been attributed to Work First, a trial program, implemented prior to the passage of TANF, that focused on employment. Work First was initially implemented in six counties and required recipients to spend thirty-five hours a week in a job-search class or work program or lose all their benefits, including cash awards and food stamps.

The true success of welfare reform in Mississippi is yet to be determined. DeParle reported, "During one recent period, the families dropped for violating the new work rules outnumbered those placed in jobs by a margin of nearly two to one."[14] Families were dropped for violating work rules, which included such things as missed appointments and failure to take jobs. It appears that many women may have turned down job offers or missed appointments because they did not have adequate transportation to travel to work, which in rural areas is a common problem. Nevertheless, these women lost all of their benefits. Thus it appears that the reduction of welfare caseloads is not entirely a result of getting women into the workforce.

One quarter of Mississippi's welfare caseload lives in the eleven counties of the Delta, all of which have inadequate employment opportunities to meet the needs of their residents. In many cases residents must travel long distances away from home in order to work. The particular county where Loretta resided is representative of those counties. We saw also that Alfrenell, an employed woman with a car who lived in a county outside the Delta (one with scarcely better opportunities and resources), had to travel forty miles from home to attend cosmetology school. The employment situation in Mississippi's Delta counties is so dire that even the executive director of the state's Department of Human Services, Donald Taylor, compared the situation of contemporary welfare recipients to the plight of the characters in the novel *The Grapes of Wrath*. "He [Mr. Taylor] warns that the only alternative for some of the 8,000 welfare families there may be to move to places that have jobs. . . . He added, 'But you've got some people in rural Mississippi who are tied to the land, and I understand their reluctance to leave.'"[15] Alfrenell's reasons for staying, as is the case with many single mothers, were not so much because of ties to the land but because of a strong kinship network that she depended upon for assistance with child care, transportation, and other help which supplemented her low-wage job. Loretta, however, boldly stated that she would relocate to get employment. In fact, during the summer of 2000, when researchers returned to the small town where she and her family lived, they were informed that the entire Samms household had left the town some years earlier and moved to Nebraska.

In addition to the difficulties surrounding getting and securing transportation to jobs and training programs, critics of welfare reform have also sought more information about outcomes for those who leave welfare. Groups such as the Mississippi Legislative Black Caucus have criticized the state for failing to provide information on people who left the rolls and disappeared.[16] "'The rolls have been reduced. We know these people are out there, but we must see where they really are,' said Sen. Hillman Frazier, D-Jackson (MS). . . . 'We might be creating a class of homeless people, of children with no future.'"[17]

Although the new welfare reform legislation in Mississippi can be viewed as a success from the standpoint of a reduced welfare caseload, economic factors that predate that legislation continue to plague the state. In 1999, "the state [Mississippi] offer[ed] child care, transportation, tax credits and up to six months benefit extension to new workers to help them adjust. . . . Richard Berry, director of resource development for DHS' economic assistance division, . . . stated that the reality is what's available often depends on where a client lives—jobs, transportation, child care, other necessities."[18]

Hence, even when given resources to aid in the transition from welfare to work, recipients who are located in rural areas are operating at a serious deficit that begins with the lack of jobs. Thus, welfare recipients living in rural Mississippi continue to face the prospect of no job or a low-wage job and must rely heavily on family and friends to meet the challenges of everyday living. As we saw in the case studies of Loretta and Alfrenell, their families were key in helping them resolve issues of child care, housing, food, and transportation.

The high unemployment and underemployment rates that characterize Mississippi continue to forecast a bleak economic future for many of the state's low-income rural single mothers for whom, despite their own desires and the stated intent of the new welfare reform legislation, achieving even a modest version of the American dream appears a long way off.

NOTES

1. See Kathryn Edin and Laura Lein, *Making Ends Meet* (New York: Russell Sage, 1997); Kathleen Harris, "Life after Welfare: Women, Work, and Repeat Dependency," *American Sociological Review* 61 (1996): 407–426; and Roberta Spalter-Roth et al., "Welfare That Works: The Working Lives of AFDC Recipients" (Washington, D.C.: Institute for Women's Policy Research, 1995).

2. Bonnie Thornton Dill, "A Better Life for Me and My Children: Low-Income Single Mothers' Struggle for Self-Sufficiency in the Rural South," *Journal of Comparative Family Studies* 29, no. 2 (summer 1998): 419–428.

3. Maxine Baca Zinn uses the term "reshuffled poverty" to describe this pattern in "Family, Race, and Poverty in the Eighties," in *Rethinking the Family: Some Feminist Questions,* ed. Barrie Thorne and Marilyn Yalom (New York: Longman, 1993).

4. See Patricia Hill Collins's discussion of "motherwork" in Collins, *Black Feminist Thought: Knowledge, Consciousness, and the Politics of Empowerment* (Boston: Unwin Hyman, 1990).

5. In order to protect the confidentiality of the participants in the study, names used herein are pseudonyms and the exact location of the interview site is disguised.

6. The descriptions that follow are based on 1990 census data that provides county-level data on percentages of the population: how many live in poverty, educational levels, health outcomes, and other indicators of economic and social well-being. Michael Timberlake, Bonnie Thornton Dill, and Bruce Williams, "Race, Gender, and Peripheralization: Rural Poverty and Development in the Mississippi Delta," paper presented at the 23rd World Congress of Sociology, Germany, 1994.

7. Children's Defense Fund, "The High Price of Poverty for Children of the South," Washington, D.C., May 1998.

8. Gretchen G. Kirby et al., "Income Support and Social Services for Low- Income People in Mississippi," Washington, D.C., The Urban Institute, 1998, 3.

9. This description is taken from an earlier paper. See Bonnie Thornton Dill and Bruce Williams, "Race, Gender, and Poverty in the Rural South: African American Single Mothers," in *Rural Poverty In America,* ed. Cynthia M. Duncan (New York: Auburn House, 1992), 106–107.

10. Dill and Williams, "Race, Gender, and Poverty," 105–106.

11. Edin and Lein, *Making Ends Meet;* Harris, "Life after Welfare"; Spalter-Roth et al., "Welfare That Works."

12. Jason DeParle, "What about Mississippi? A Special Report: Welfare Law Weighs Heavy in the Delta, Where Jobs Are Few," *New York Times,* 16 October 1997, late ed., A-1.

13. Butch John, "Mississippi Welfare Reform Reports Produce Successes and Failures," *Times-Picayune,* 4 July 1999, 1st ed., B-5; DeParle, "What about Mississippi?"

14. Deparle, "What about Mississippi?"

15. Ibid.

16. John, "Mississippi Welfare Reform Reports Produce Successes and Failures."

17. Ibid.

18. Ibid.

Getting Paid / Black Women Economists Reflect on Women and Work

Rhonda M. Williams

PERSONAL STATEMENT As best I can remember, my interest in matters of work, wages, and wealth has deep roots in southeastern Ohio, circa 1964. My family had moved twice since I was five years old. The first move took us from Cleveland, birthplace of both my parents and migration destiny for all four of my grandparents. With my grandmother's support and against my grandfather's wishes, my mother attended Western Reserve University in the early 1950s. My father did not last long in Cleveland's steel mills after returning from World War II. He eventually used the GI Bill's benefits to enroll at Western Reserve University, where he met my mother.

Arlene and Ronald Williams shared a side-by-side midwestern duplex with my paternal aunt Fay and her family, the Gandys. My brother Bob and I were both born in Cleveland and stayed there until the first move to a small college town, thirty miles away. Liberal whites, trying to integrate Oberlin College in the early 1960s, recruited my father, master's degree fresh in hand. My mother withdrew from the university after marrying and starting her family. She would complete her college degree many years later, when Bob and I were much older.

The whites I met in Oberlin seemed friendly enough, not that much different from my parents' Italian and Greek-American friends in Cleveland. Many of these adults shared my parents' commitment to the Civil Rights movement. Many of my classmates in first and second grade were the middle-class daughters and sons of Oberlin College professors. My memories of first and second grade in Oberlin are pleasant. My report cards document that I talked too much in class and was sometimes disruptive.

Ohio University in southeastern Ohio was a different story. My family made its second move to Athens, Ohio, the summer before I entered third grade. Athens was close to the West Virginia border, and Athens County was home to many formerly rural and quite poor white families. For the first time in my life, I saw dirt-poor white people. I already knew about job discrimination—that whites excluded capable blacks from high-paying jobs. Thus I had the rudiments of an understanding of black-white economic inequality. I had no idea, however, that white people accepted a world in which other white people lived in shacks without bathrooms and in which poor white children got on the school bus dirty, funky, and with teeth rotting in their mouths.

This early recognition of class differences among whites troubled me—I wondered what chance black folk had for civil rights and well-paying work if white folk accepted such material want among their own. My childhood resolution of this troubling quandary was simple: it had to be a lot of misinformation and ignorance. It simply couldn't be that all these intelligent adults would stand by and let these parents toil under such harsh conditions and with such meager results.

My preteen and teen years whisked away some of my youthful confusion, but by no means all. White violence against black, Latino, and Native American activists at home and the Vietnamese abroad was a sobering and often frightening lesson. Yet still, I figured that economic problems had to be much easier to solve. I just could not figure out how so many U.S. citizens could consent to hunger, oppression, and want among their sister citizens and their children. Somewhere in my teens, I learned that economists were the professional experts on this business of who gets what and for how much, so I resolved to take at least one economics course in college, right away.

My choice of Radcliffe College at Harvard University came after my brother attended Yale University. He advised me that Harvard was a good school with an excellent reputation and had ample opportunities for a good social life. That was good enough for me. Each of us had modest scholarships that paid for less than a third of our university expenses. My parents paid the rest on monthly payment plans. I remember watching them sweat over our college bills during holidays and in the summer. Looking back, I marvel at their ability to make the payments from their very modest salaries and without any reserves from which to draw.

I enjoyed my economics classes. They were challenging and engaged historical and political issues. I began to consider pursuing graduate work in economics. One of my professors told me about a summer economics program at Northwestern University designed to fast-track students of color into the economics profession. I applied and was accepted. That summer institute was a turning point—I met older and younger black economists and developed the sense that I could do well at this work. I believed that economists could help reduce racial economic injustice. Meanwhile, my mentors at Northwestern were professors like my father. I had already decided that I must have my own work and income. The professor's life looked increasingly appealing. Professors seemed to have some control over what they did and how they did it, and I certainly enjoyed reading, writing, analyzing, and problem solving. Graduate school in economics seemed like a real possibility. I eventually decided to do it.

My professors at the Massachusetts Institute of Technology (MIT) provided a rather more grim and hostile perspective on persistent racial economic inequalities. They were less inclined to focus on the past and present effects of white economic supremacy; rather, they focused more on the things that black folk didn't have or didn't do. When writing about work and wages, they imagined a world in which equally able persons eventually and generally got rewarded for their efforts. Worst of all, their analyses of racism and its economic impact on African American communities often were stories outside of history and ignored and denied the power relations between whites and blacks.

Thus did I confront the powerful connections between theory and ideology and the important role that mainstream economists play in explaining to us all why inequalities of wealth, work, and income are often efficient and socially beneficial. Because my interest was in these matters of distribution, and because these stories of pervasive black deficiencies ran counter to all I had learned from my family, historical studies, and critical observation, I began to look around for other possible analyses. Did all economists share this same view, that this was basically the best of all possible worlds?

In the library and with the help of my brother and friends, I soon discovered what we call other "schools of thought" among economists and among noneconomists who engaged economic issues. I began to read the works of Karl Marx and black male labor historians such as Abram Harris and Charles Wesley. In my early years as a professor, I began to read the works of white feminist economists, an up-and-coming group of scholars who wrote about gender, but much less often and much less deeply about race. I began to see the pattern noted by black feminists worldwide—that the "sisters" were often missing in these stories; all the blacks were men, and all the women white or European. I began to think about the importance of who gets to tell the economic stories, of how a researcher's views of and experiences in the world inform the questions and policy recommendations she or he makes (albeit not in some simple mechanistic way, such that all black men think alike).

MIT's graduate program in economics was a white, male-dominated world with a strong Jewish presence. The professors were self-confident and sometimes arrogant. I was shocked by the cultural dynamics of the graduate program—the professors and older graduate students were intense and competitive. After my studies at Harvard-Radcliffe and my summer at Northwestern University, I felt prepared for the academic work; I quickly learned, however, that even with my three semesters of calculus and one semester of statistics, I was one or two math courses behind many of my peers. A low point in my first year came during an oral examination in one of our theory classes. I had not completely solved the take-home problem—only a few of us had done so. My professor told me that "not everyone has what it takes" to be a professional economist and that I might want to consider other work possibilities. I was shocked and hurt by his dismissiveness.

My chapter in this volume presents the writings of four black women economists who were writing and publishing about race, gender, and work in the 1980s. Phyllis Wallace was teaching at MIT when I was a student there. She was in a different department, and I didn't have the good sense or vision to seek her advise and counsel. Julianne Malveaux fortunately had that good sense, and Wallace became her mentor and coauthor. Barbara A. P. Jones was already out of school and working at Clark University, and Margaret Simms was working at a research organization in downtown Washington, D.C. Phyllis Wallace passed away several years ago; Simms, Jones, and Malveaux are alive, well, and writing, and they remain professionally active.

When I look back at my years in graduate school, I know the deep significance of the absences in my reading lists and my mentoring; amidst the recurrent messages, from some of my professors, that I didn't have the right stuff to become an economist, my classmates were a source of support and joy. I know my journey through MIT would have been less alienating if I had spent more time with Phyllis Wallace. I know that my research journey would have taken a different course had I read these black women economists more thoroughly in the mid-1980s. Yet I also rejoice in the opportunity to reclaim their works now, to publicly reflect on and share their gifts with an audience that otherwise might not have the chance to benefit from their insights. They write about gender, class, race, and work from different perspectives than most of my MIT professors circa 1980, and for this I am truly grateful.

---

*A*lthough their writings remain unknown to many African Americans, black women economists were important advocates for race and gender justice in the workplace during the 1980s. While President Reagan and his corporate allies orchestrated a decade-long assault on affirmative action and the living standards of many U.S. workers, these scholars insisted that race- and gender-conscious policies were necessary to smash the barriers of occupational segregation. Some white economists celebrated the momentary reduction of income gaps between black and white women in the late 1960s and 1970s, proclaiming a declining significance of race and racism in the lives of black workers. However, most black economists—both men and women—did not embrace the "declining significance" perspective. Like many African American feminist writers in the 1980s, black women economists challenged social science writings that either assumed or concluded the insignificance of race and racism in the lives of working black women.[1]

Few black women had Ph.D.'s in economics in the mid-1980s.[2] Although African American women worked as social scientists before World War II, very few enjoyed the privilege of full-time employment as scholars and researchers.[3] By the time I arrived in graduate school to study economics in 1978, Dr. Phyllis Wallace of the Massachusetts Institute of Technology was a respected senior professor with a distinguished record of research published in the 1960s and 1970s. Wallace wrote extensively on black workers and economic discrimination. In 1980, she was the senior author of *Black Women in the Labor Force*, the first academic press publication solely devoted to the economic status of black women. Six years later, one of her students coedited a second such volume. Wallace's protégé and former student Julianne Malveaux joined forces with sister economist and Stanford graduate Margaret Simms to edit *Slipping through the Cracks: The Status of Black Women.*[4]

I am interested in four specific chapters in the Simms-Malveaux volume; they address the ongoing significance of race and gender in the economic lives of African American working women. When writing about black women and work, Julianne Malveaux, Barbara A. P. Jones, Phyllis Wallace, and Margaret Simms address a common set of themes. Each asserts the importance of racial community, i.e., each economist studies black women's work in the context of connections to and responsibilities for neighbors, family, and kin. They also address the gender dimensions of racial oppression—they examine challenges and constraints that black women do and do not share with black men workers.

Because they simultaneously consider racial differences between women *and* the significance of gender in studies of African American workers, these economists also advance an analysis unlike those developed by most of their white feminist peers and liberal brother economists. In comparison to the small post–Civil Rights era brotherhood of black men economists, these sister economists led the way in making the case, to scholars and activists alike, that a consideration of gender is a must for those seeking a fuller understanding of the economic conditions confronting African American communities. And, like so many of their predecessors in the tradition of black women writing about work, these economists speak with eloquence about how black women's working lives are unlike those of similarly educated white women workers. Their writings display a remarkable dedication to the practice of taking seriously how institutionalized racism and race privilege have shaped and continue to shape the working lives of women in the United States.

A Brief Economic Overview of the 1980s

The late 1970s through mid-1990s were years of heightened economic strife for millions of African American workers and their families. Real wages—wages adjusted to correct for the fact that rising prices reduce the purchasing power of a fixed salary—fell for most U.S. workers, including millions of high-school-educated white men. Young black workers experienced dramatic declines in income and employment; among those who were working, young workers were increasingly employed in jobs and industries that did not reward them for increased levels of education. Moreover, job and wage losses in working-class black communities affected both sexes—both black women and men lost economic ground relative to their white peers. White women, however, continued to slowly close the employment, earning, and education gaps in relation to white men, despite a decade of reduced federal enforcement of affirmative action and other antidiscrimination polices. More so than their black counterparts, white women continued to close the earnings gap with white men by increasing their representation in higher-paying, male-dominated jobs and in many white-collar and service industries.[5]

As the evidence and stories of economic distress among African Americans accumulated, journalists, academics, and policy makers in the 1980s reignited an old and ongoing debate as to the causes and appropriate responses to black-white economic inequality. Much of the popular and academic debate focused on the relative importance of race-based economic discrimination. Scholars and commentators alike again posed the question: To what extent is racial discrimination still a major determinant of employment and wage outcomes for African Americans? Had economic racism largely vanished, leaving behind a racial inequality largely caused by deficiencies in African Americans' family backgrounds, skills, and the quality of the schools they attend?[6]

Recurrent Themes: Class, Race, Community, and Black Women's Work

The Simms and Malveaux volume provided a publishing vehicle to a group of black economists—almost all women—who specialized in the study of race, racism, gender, and economics in the 1980s. I begin with Barbara A. P. Jones's essay, "Black Women and Labor Force Participation: Analysis of Sluggish Growth Rates." Jones's focus is black-white gaps in labor-force participation

rates ("labor force participants" are individuals who are either working or seriously looking for work). Economists study labor-force participation rates
because they are an important indicator of who has a job or wants one within
a given community. For example, the government only counts as unemployed
those who have looked for a job but not found one. If you are retired, a full-
time student, or a full-time homemaker, economists do not count you as
unemployed.

In her discussion of black women's patterns of labor force participation,
Jones repeatedly describes and emphasizes black women's ties to black men
and children. Consider her discussion of the percentages of women working
and looking for work in the 1970s. During that decade, young black women's
labor-force participation rates did not increase, but young white women's participation rates increased by 40 percent. As part of her discussion of these racial
differences, Jones observes, "Any attempt to explain the economic plight of
black women and the implications of their labor market experiences must consider economic conditions in the total black community and assess the economic well being of black women in different social classes. The economic
problems of black women in general and their problems as workers cannot be
separated from the economic plight of the black community. The same forces
which affect the employment opportunities of black women tend to affect
those of black men."[7]

What were the forces that affected black workers of both sexes in the late
1970s and 1980s? Jones accords great weight to what economists sometimes
define as "capital flight," which means that businesses change the location of
their operations in pursuit of lower costs and higher profits. Specifically, Jones
documents that many U.S. manufacturers closed their plants in the United
States. In so doing, they eliminated hundreds of thousands of good-paying
blue-collar jobs in metropolitan centers of the West and Midwest and sent
them to the southern United States (where unions were less powerful) and over-
seas (where unions were fewer in number and weaker). Jones argues that this
decline in working-class jobs injured both black men and women. Jones was
right on target—my research shows that black employment in manufacturing
declined 16.7 percent in the 1980s, much less than the overall manufacturing employment decline of 7.1 percent.

Jones also argues that massive job losses in the black community increased
the ranks of "discouraged workers" among young black women in the 1970s
and early 1980s. Discouraged workers are those who leave the labor force without a job. Recalling the earlier definition of "labor force participation," discouraged workers are not counted as members of the labor force. Even though
they are jobless, they are not counted as members of the unemployed! Jones

notes that black women's earnings and levels of educational attainment increased in the 1970s, and that these are changes economists often associate with increased propensity to seek work for wages. Nonetheless, black women's labor-force participation rates increased only modestly and less so than similarly educated white women.

Jones also argues that a family's socioeconomic status or class shapes the economic opportunities and decisions made by the family members. In this context, a class consists of individuals with similar family incomes, educational attainments, and occupational achievements. For example, women from poor families generally complete fewer years of schooling than women from higher-income homes. They likewise have higher rates of unemployment, are more likely to be working in the lowest-paid service jobs, and are less likely to be sharing a man's income. Because they also are more likely than their male counterparts to be financially responsible for children, these women are among the most economically vulnerable members of the African American working classes. Jones's evaluation of class leads her to conclude that economic justice for black communities requires more than one set of policy solutions.

Julianne Malveaux analyzes comparable worth in her chapter "Comparable Worth and Its Impact on Black Women." The principle of "comparable worth" mandates that workers whose jobs are of similar value should receive similar pay. Comparable-worth advocates argue that women and people of color often receive less pay than their white male counterparts who perform work that is similar in the skills required and working conditions. Moreover, they have documented that many employers use hiring practices that foster race- and gender-based job segregation and use job evaluation systems that systematically undervalue women's work.

Because black women are overrepresented in traditionally female occupations and also are segregated racially within women's work, Malveaux argues that a policy of "equal pay for work of equal value" definitely would benefit African American women workers. However, like Jones's analysis, Malveaux's analysis locates individual black women workers in their ethnic community and prioritizes how their experiences vary by class. Consider the following passage, where she argues that the entire black community benefits from successfully implemented comparable worth: "The black community, as well as black women will accrue gains when comparable worth is implemented. The first gain is an obvious one—the gain from higher black family wages when black women earn equitable pay. Given the large number of black women heading households, the need for black women to earn equitable pay cannot be overstated. But even where there is another household earner, black women's contributions to black family income frequently make the difference between black family poverty and black family survival."[8] Thus Malveaux sees black women's earnings as central to the economic well-being of black households, whatever their composition. Black women's wage work is neither incidental to nor peripheral to family and community well-being. For Malveaux, it is a given that black families and communities need black women's wages.

Malveaux also notes that black men will benefit from comparable worth because they, more so than white men, worked in typically "female jobs," for example, clerical and secretarial jobs. Indeed, Malveaux was among the first African American economists to advance the argument that comparable worth would help black men who confront their own forms of race- and gender-based job segregation. Because white men have often used their economic power (sometimes as employers and sometimes as workers) to exclude black men from high-paying "men's jobs"—professional, managerial, and craft jobs—African American men are more likely to work in traditionally lower-paying women-dominated occupations. Malveaux was optimistic that re-searchers assessing the gender bias of job evaluation systems would also find race bias in jobs that hire large percentages of African American men—that is, researchers would find that employers "undervalue" and therefore underpay jobs with high percentages of black male workers. Thus the comparable-worth strategy would yield pay benefits for African American men and women and multiply gains for black families and communities.

Her support for comparable worth notwithstanding, Malveaux carefully identifies the class-based limitations of this activist strategy. Neither unem-ployed workers nor Aid to Families with Dependent Children (AFDC) clients would benefit from fairer job evaluation systems. Most blue-collar black work-ers similarly could not look to comparable worth to improve the terms of their compensation. In light of these class realities, she recommends multiple policy strategies, ranging from affirmative action and expanded unionization to full-employment legislation and job creation. Like Barbara A. P. Jones, Malveaux argues that employment equity for black women requires more than any one social policy can provide.

The Simms and Malveaux volume also includes the editors' coauthored, ten-point policy program, "A Legislative/Policy Agenda to Improve the Status of Black Women." Here again, they vigorously assert black women's deep ties to their ethnic community and a conviction that any serious improvements in the economic lot of black women would be a rising tide that lifted all black boats:

> It is important for us to note that our focus on the status of black women
> is not at all meant to divert attention from the very drastic problems that
> face the total black community. Instead, our effort is meant to talk about
> ways we can *strengthen* the status of the black community, both now and

in the future. The majority of black children, at this time, live in families headed by black women. These children share their mothers' jeopardy as their future options are limited by the present constraints their mothers face. The status of black women is connected with the status of black communities—of black men and black children. But a specific look at black women's status is warranted at this time, especially since researchers have, all too frequently, studied men who are black and women who are white, with the status of black women an invisible one.[9]

In this passage, Malveaux and Simms are responding to African Americans who question the woman-focused thrust of their research. One can hear their critics in the background—the men *and* women who dispute the legitimacy of any scholarship that foregrounds the experiences of black women. Yet Simms and Malveaux remain undaunted by their critics: they reject both definitions of community that make black women invisible (via the equating of black community well-being with that of black men) *and* analyses of women and work that assume away the significance of race. They opt for a third way, an examination of African American women's economic status in black communities, where class and gender relations shape socioeconomic opportunities and outcomes.

Malveaux and Simms are strident in their call for continued affirmative action. They chastise President Reagan and his Justice Department for seeking to dismantle affirmative action programs and name the racist ideologies that inform the policy shift: "Preserve affirmative action. Justice Department efforts to dismantle affirmative action systems are misguided, ill-informed attempt to erode limited gains made by black workers in the past 15 years. . . . It should be noted that detractors of affirmative action have indicated that affirmative action 'assumes' inferiority. Yet black competence was not invented in the post-1965 period."[10] Like their coauthors, Malveaux and Simms accord scholarly importance to policies that seek to overturn racism's economic legacy. In their analyses of women and work, Jones, Malveaux, Wallace, and Simms do not theorize or recommend policy on behalf of "race-less" women (or men).

Phyllis Wallace's opening line to her proposed research agenda on black women's economic status affirms her commitment to race-specific labor studies: "In the economic sphere, black and white women share many common concerns, but there are significant differences in their employment, occupation, and income status." Like Malveaux and Simms, Wallace argues that community context is an important source of difference between white and black women. Wallace warns her readers that the emergence of "the greatly impoverished black female head of family household" will have significant social and

economic consequences. Yet for Wallace, the significant policy issue is the inci-
dence of poverty among these families, not the fact that they are female-headed
households.[11]

Returning briefly to Jones's chapter, I note that she similarly documents
racial economic inequalities among women: "White women are able to move
into more desirable jobs with fewer years of schooling than black women. . . .
A higher proportion of white women with limited education held the better
paying operative and craft positions, and one-third of employed white female
high school dropouts held technical, sales and administrative support positions compared to one-fifth of comparably educated black women."[12] From
Jones's perspective, racial barriers to black women's economic advancement
are still very much present, and not a relic from the past. She finds that African
American and white women do not receive the same rewards for their education and skills, and she affirms that although the quality of some black
women's work has changed, it is *not* the case that they collectively have moved
out of traditionally defined women's work. Rather, Jones suggests that black
women moved from one set of sex-segregated jobs to another between the
1960s and 1980s. As was the case at earlier moments in U.S. women's economic
histories, racial-ethnic occupational boundaries between women were quite
evident.[13]

From a historical perspective, it is important to note that the so-called
mainstream white liberal policy leaders and journalists in the mid-1980s did
not foreground the works of Malveaux, Wallace, Simms, and Jones. Indeed, the
liberal corporate media's black expert of choice on race and work then and
now is sociologist William Julius Wilson. Unlike the authors cited here (and the
preponderance of African American social scientists), Wilson's 1987 book, *The
Truly Disadvantaged*, argued that present-day discrimination did not significantly affect the lives of urban working-class African Americans in the 1980s.
Wilson's thesis argued the potential importance of what he termed "historic
discrimination" and gave short shrift to the evidence of ongoing white economic privilege.[14] From his perspective, poor black workers' major problems
lay in their membership in a jobless and culturally adrift underclass.

Although Wallace and company did not share Wilson's perspective on the
declining significance of race, Wilson did have allies within the ranks of liberal
white feminist economists. As has often been the case in the course of U.S. history, black and white women crafted disparate accounts of race, gender, and
work. In contrast to their black peers, at least two prominent liberal white feminist economists argued that racial discrimination was in decline. One reached
this conclusion based on analyses of earnings data from the 1970s, the other on
the basis of evidence that remains unclear.

Francine Blau argued for the declining significance of race based on her examination of a closing earnings gap between black and white women. In her 1984 review of the literature, "Discrimination against Women: Theory and Evidence," Blau suggested two causes for the earnings convergence.[15] First, she argued that black women had closed the earnings gap by working more hours than white women. Second, she suggested that racial job barriers between women were eroding faster than racial job barriers between men. According to Blau, black women were able to enter white women's jobs faster than black men were able to enter white men's jobs. Why? Her explanation is that there were no substantive skill gaps between black and white women—black women acquired the skills they needed to compete for women's work prior to actually getting the job. Only the pernicious practices of racist exclusion kept African American women out of white women's jobs (for example, secretarial work or retail sales). Thus federal antidiscrimination policies were more effective in racially desegregating women's work. Many older black women had plenty of the qualifications necessary to do better-paying (white) women's work, but lacked the opportunity.

By contrast—or so Blau asserted—black men did not have the high level of training, education, and experience needed to secure high-wage white men's jobs. According to Blau and many other economists (then and now), the death of job discrimination would help some African American men seeking to enter white men's jobs, but many more would have to upgrade their education and skills. In other words, black men's job plight reflected the combined negative consequences of job discrimination and a lack of qualifications. Yet why don't some black men have the required experience and training? For the working-class majority seeking entry-level jobs, an important component of the answer is job discrimination. Like black female workers, many black male workers have faced employment discrimination—i.e., white men denied them access to white men's jobs—and therefore were not able to acquire valued on-the-job training and skills needed to secure and maintain blue-collar jobs that paid a decent wage.

Liberal white feminist economist Barbara Bergmann shared Blau's conclusion—that ours is an economy where sex discrimination creates two separate labor markets, a men's market and a women's market, and where racial differentiation among women is of secondary importance.[16] Employment discrimination forces most women into a small set of women's jobs, thereby increasing the number of workers competing for a limited set of slots. This process forces wages down and leads to the earnings gap between men and women. In this story, women have the skills, but not opportunity.

However, Bergmann adds her own twist: she sees gender exclusions as fundamentally more debilitating than class exploitation and racial subordination. After explaining women's confinement to the domestic sphere, and its negative consequences for many women, she observes: "Of course many men have been denied opportunities, for reason of class or race or religion or origin. But the denial of opportunities to women has always been more severe, more pervasive, and harder to evade." Indeed, Bergmann predicted that a woman's gender, but not her race, would continue to affect labor market outcomes for years to come: "But we appear to be moving toward a system where males compete for jobs on the basis of merit. Traditions subordinating and segregating women, which go back thousands of years, are dying more slowly."[17]

Yet her analysis falters before the previously discussed statistical reality: white women, more so than black men, collectively continued to move up the earnings and occupational ladder during the 1980s, a decade of limited government enforcement of antidiscrimination laws and orders. What made possible their continued upward mobility? Was it due to a sudden spurt in skills and more women working year round, full time? Some economists did and do argue that the key to white women's improving economic status is that many are now working more hours per year. However, we must recall that prior to the 1980s, many white women did work full time but could not get men's jobs and earn a man's wage. Perhaps a greater commitment to wage work may have been necessary for some white women's upward movement, but in the past, such commitment had not been sufficient for many white women.[18]

What then does account for white women's slow but steady climb up the wage ladder? We do not yet have a final and all-encompassing answer. However, I suggest that recent scholarship on race and economics points us in some helpful directions.[19] First and foremost, economic analyses of gender must move beyond the mere assertion of the declining significance of race. Blau's and Bergmann's analyses of discrimination fall short in part because they view race only through the lens of work and wages. Bergmann thinks of gender as a universal relation that unifies women across all racial-ethnic boundaries; moreover, she explicitly identifies all types of gender oppression as more tyrannical than any form of race-class exploitation. Yet she remains silent in the face of an abundance of scholarly evidence that disputes this position. Absent a richer framework for thinking about the political, economic, and cultural significance of race, Blau and Bergmann fall prey to wishful thinking. Their analyses prematurely presume the death of race as a determinant of self-understanding, as a shaper of collective identities, and as a factor in the organization and distribution of economic resources, power, and authority. In light of the previously discussed growing gaps between white women's economic fortunes and the economic standing of blacks of both sexes, their predictions of the coming cheery world of male meritocracy simply miss the mark.

Additionally, I suggest that Jones's, Wallace's, and Malveaux's observations on gender, race, and community also are necessary for the development of a fuller account of the workings of labor markets in a capitalist economy where race continues to matter. White women, like their African American counterparts, are members of racially identified communities. They are the mothers, daughters, partners, wives, sisters, cousins, neighbors, and/or friends of white men. We do not have to believe that white male sexism against white women is dead in order to believe that at least some of these white men—and more of them today than thirty years ago—are interested in following the law and breaking down the economic barriers of gender for their women kin.

We also must note the growing presence of white women in the labor force. Married white women with children have dramatically increased their presence in the wage labor market in the past thirty years. Employers need workers and find white women very numerous in their applicant pools. Meanwhile, white men are a shrinking percentage of the labor force and are simply too few in number to fill all the traditionally defined men's jobs. Furthermore, in the 1980s and 1990s, more white families than ever before became dependent on an adult woman's income in order to sustain a working- or middle-class living standard. When viewed in this light, white women's economic advances are less surprising. Black women and men, in contrast, are infrequent members of white men's race-class communities and a much smaller share (less than 10 percent) of the employed workforce.

For those who reject or simply ignore the connections between racially defined communities and the distribution of work, the idea that white women have improved their positions simply because they are now more willing to work like men is a tale of hope. If white women make the right choices about schooling and work (albeit what is right is by no means obvious), they can compete on level ground with their white male kin. To the extent that whites increasingly view white women's access to education as a given, the work-like-a-man story also hides the extent to which white women have benefited from affirmative action and race privilege in colleges, universities, and professional schools. And because it is a story of the "cream rising to the top," this vision also suggests that sexism at school and work are largely nonissues.

Indeed, conservative opponents of affirmative action paint a world in which poorly qualified African American and Latino students, and not institutionalized white male sexism, are the more serious threat to the economic ambitions of young white women of the late 1980s and 1990s. Consider contemporary public debates about academic merit and race-conscious admissions policies for the nation's colleges and universities. The public debate on merit generally focuses on the capabilities of African Americans and Latinos. Opponents of affirmative action conclude that low scores on standardized tests are proof that blacks and Hispanics are intellectually weak. Although some white men still resist white women's entry into specific occupations and professions, they generally do not do so on the grounds that white women are cognitively deficient. After all, white women's test scores are closer to white men's than are those of blacks and Latinos.

The case of *Hopwood v. Texas* is illustrative.[20] In this instance, the named plaintiff is a white woman denied admission to the University of Texas law school, despite the fact that her test scores were higher than those of most of the black and Latino law school applicants who were accepted. Cheryl Hopwood is the voice of white expectations denied. Hopwood and her co-plaintiffs proclaimed themselves victims of reverse discrimination who were denied the proper reward for their achievements; the courts affirmed her expectation that she, as a white woman, was entitled to admission to the University of Texas based on her test scores.

She, in turn, vigorously asserted her difference from, and greater merit than that of African Americans and Latinos in Texas. The importance of whiteness as status looms large here. Recall that Hopwood did not contest the admission of *white men* with test scores lower than hers. Gender fairness among whites is not the issue here—she did not protest her competitive loss to white men with low test scores. Rather, it is her race, her status as a white person, that defines her claim of reverse discrimination. It is one thing to lose in the competition for access to law school to white men with lower test scores; it is apparently unacceptable to lose to similarly situated blacks and Latinos.

For many middle-class and working-class whites of the late twentieth century, higher education continues to be an important key for unlocking the economic fruits of citizenship. In this ongoing era of white racial backlash, neither African Americans' access to higher education nor the benefits thereof are guaranteed. The insights of black women economists and other scholars who demonstrate the importance of race, classes, communities, and gender remain relevant: a young women's racial community of origin still shapes her path toward economic inclusion.

NOTES

The author thanks the Black Women and Work editorial collective for their numerous suggestions for reworking and revising this paper. I particularly benefited from the comments made by Professors Mary Helen Washington, Sharon Harley, and Tauyna Banks.

1. Professor Lynn Burbridge recently wrote a very useful review of the economics literature on black women. See her chapter, "Black Women in the History of African American Economic Thought," in *A Different Vision: African American Economic Thought,* vol. 1, ed. Thomas D. Boston (New York: Routledge, 1997).

2. In 1980, approximately 150 African Americans held Ph.D.'s in economics. Black women held fewer than half of these degrees.

3. See historian Francille Rusan Wilson's chapter in this volume. According to Wilson, black women social scientists before World War II generally lacked the institutional support, full-time research opportunities, and teaching positions held by their white female and black male peers.

4. Phyllis Wallace, *The Black Woman in the Labor Force* (Cambridge, Mass.: MIT Press, 1980); Margaret Simms and Julianne Malveaux, *Slipping through the Cracks: The Status of Black Women* (New Brunswick, N.J.: Transactions Books, 1986). The Simms and Malveaux volume is based on a special issue of the *Review of Black Political Economy,* the only U.S. economics journal focusing on the economic issues facing the black people of the world.

5. For discussions of race, gender, work, and economic inequality in the 1980s, see M. V. Lee Badgett and Rhonda M. Williams, "The Changing Contours of Discrimination: Race, Gender, and Structural Economic Change," in *Understanding American Economic Decline,* ed. Michael Bernstein and David Adler (New York: Cambridge University Press, 1994); and Teresa Amott, *Women in the U.S. Economy Today* (New York: Monthly Review Press, 1993).

6. The 1999 *The State of Black America,* ed. William Springs (New York: National Urban League, 1999) includes several reader-friendly articles, by African American economists, that deal with this debate. For a discussion of the impact of class, race, and family background on work and educational outcomes, see Dr. Patrick Mason's chapter, "Family Environment and Intergenerational Well-Being: Some Preliminary Results." For a discussion of the relative importance of discrimination and skills in shaping black-white wage gaps, see the chapter by Dr. William M. Rodgers III, "A Critical Assessment of Skill Explanations of Black-White Employment and Wage Gaps."

7. Barbara A. P. Jones, "Black Women and Labor Force Participation: Analysis of Sluggish Growth Rates," in Simms and Malveaux, *Slipping through the Cracks,* 27.

8. Julianne Malveaux, "Comparable Worth and Its Impact on Black Women," in Simms and Malveaux, *Slipping through the Cracks,* 54.

9. Margaret Simms and Julianne Malveaux, "A Legislative/Policy Agenda to Improve the Status of Black Women," in Simms and Malveaux, *Slipping through the Cracks,* 297.

10. Simms and Malveaux, *Slipping through the Cracks,* 298

11. Phyllis Wallace, "A Research Agenda on Black Women's Economic Status," in Simms and Malveaux, *Slipping through the Cracks,* 293, 294.

12. Jones, "Black Women and Labor Force Participation," 23.

13. See Julie Matthaei and Teresa Amott's book *Race, Gender, and Work* (Boston: South End Press, 1995) for historical perspectives on the racial-ethnic segregation of women's work.

14. See William J. Wilson, *The Truly Disadvantaged* (Chicago: University of Chicago Press, 1987). Although he diminishes the importance of racial discrimination, Wilson also argues that whites will not support race-based social policies designed to economically empower African Americans.

15. Francine Blau, "Discrimination against Women: Theory and Evidence," in *Labor Economics: Modern Views,* ed. William Darity Jr. (Boston: Kluwer-Nijhoff, 1984).

16. Barbara Bergmann, *The Economic Emergence of Women* (New York: Basic Books, 1986).

17. Bergmann, *The Economic Emergence of Women,* 7, 93.

18. Both Blau ("Discrimination against Women") and Bergmann *(The Economic Emergence of Women)* provide critiques of the notion that a limited commitment to the workforce historically has caused the wage gap between white men and white women.

19. See Patrick Mason and Rhonda M. Williams, "The Janus-Face of Race: Reflections on Economic Theory," in *Race, Markets, and Social Outcomes,* ed. Mason and Williams (Boston: Kluwer Academic Publishers, 1997).

20. *Hopwood v Texas,* 518 US 1033 (1996).

PART 2 / *Foremothers: The Shoulders on Which We Stand*

"Don't Let Nobody Bother Yo' Principle"

The Sexual Economy of American Slavery

ADRIENNE DAVIS

> Many . . . young women are afraid to speak,
> let alone write. When I witness their fear, their
> silences, I know no woman has written enough.
> —bell hooks, *Remembered Rapture*

PERSONAL STATEMENT I was an Afro-American studies major in college. Yes, *Afro-American* studies, so you can imagine this was the 1980s. Not the hard-edged black studies of the 1970s or the gentle chicness of African American or Africana studies in the 1990s. Afro-American. Language situates us in time and politics.

The two events that remain most impressed upon my mind from college occurred in the course of pursuing my major. I was a student of black feminist theorist bell hooks, Gloria Watkins, who taught courses in literature, specializing in fiction by black women. For Gloria, as we called the woman, and her classes into which we crowded, the rigorous study of literature yielded the greatest gift of all: mastery of language, the fundamental Western tool of self-articulation and representation. The students of all races who "took Gloria" learned how, through language, one acquires a voice, thus demanding recognition by others. Through these linguistic eruptions into existence, people achieve subjectivity, agency, humanity. Her courses, unable to contain the student excitement over the possibilities that language suggested for our agency, spilled over into her office. There, she encouraged black undergraduate women to use the study of literature to reclaim our sexuality, our lives, to realize that in a world structured to deny our humanity, we had choices, options. Through language, we could represent, and thus reclaim, our intimate selves.

This conversation, which continued over the course of two years, was punctuated by a moment when Toni Morrison came to campus to speak. Post-*Sula* and *The Bluest Eye*, pre-*Beloved* and *Paradise*, she talked about the paucity of

103

language to describe the horror of American slavery. What language can we use to represent human bondage, to describe the conversion of humans into property, to capture the experience of being possessed or, even more grimly perhaps, of *possessing* another? The emptiness of language to describe the process of enslavement mirrors the void of slavery in the nation's memory.

Yet slavery, like our sexuality, lies continually at the periphery of our consciousness; eluding representation, it hovers over us. It disrupts our lives with unpredictable eruptions. Mimicking the American conspiracy of silence around slavery, black women often avoid speaking of sex and intimacy. But in its repression, black women continually create images, representations, which we then either embody in flat unidimensional cartoons of "respectable good girls" or reject, thereby risking sanction by our sisters. Without language, slavery and black women's sexuality each remains unspeakable—repressed, yet ever present.

Comprehending and filling the linguistic vacuums around slavery and black women's sexuality are directly linked to the project of this book: representing black women's work. What I now realize, as a scholar and a woman with her own sexual battlegrounds to conquer, is how the unspeakability of slavery contains the seeds of the unspeakability, for black women, of our own sexuality. As I say in my essay, the economy of American slavery systematically expropriated black women's sexuality and reproductive capacity for white pleasure and profit. As their descendants, we continue to suffer from the silence. The failure of language to document and archive the sexual abuse of reproductive exploitation of enslaved women is the origin of the absence of language to articulate for contemporary black women sexual identities that are empowering, fulfilling, and joyous.

In much of my professional adult life, through my research and my writing, I have tried to restore and engage that voice, to offer myself and other black women a voice sketched through history and law. My essay in this volume tries to combine and, to an extent, reconcile those two defining moments from a decade ago in my life when Toni Morrison and bell hooks urged me and other black women students to see that understanding both history and ourselves lay in mastering language and its mysteries. Without a vocabulary to describe slavery, contemporary black women have been without a voice to describe and confront the history of sexual and reproductive expropriation and exploitation that slavery entailed. In my essay, I propose to label slavery as a "sexual economy," hoping that this may give us the tools we need to excavate black women's history, document our exploitation, and archive our resistance. We can use this vocabulary to understand our collective sexual histories and then confront our choices, realizing that each of us makes different ones.

Toni Morrison and bell hooks were right, without language we can't represent; without representation, we can't imagine; without imagination, we can't
comprehend; without comprehension, we can't move forward.

*B*eyond the backbreaking, soul-savaging labor that all enslaved people
performed, American slavery extracted from black women another form of
"work" that remains almost inarticulable in its horror: reproducing the slave
workforce through giving birth and serving as forced sexual labor to countless
men of all races. The political economy of slavery systematically expropriated
black women's sexuality and reproductive capacity for white pleasure and
profit. Yet what discourse has confronted and accused this national horror?
What documents record its effects on enslaved women? In the face of this
unspeakable work, chroniclers of American history have all but erased its existence. This essay attempts to initiate the beginnings of just such a conversation
by naming the world of these legal conflicts a "sexual economy."

Voice and vocabulary are vitally important in antiracist and antisexist
politics. Vocabulary is much more than grammatical choice, as represented
in debates as diverse as the validity of Ebonics and whether "sex worker" or
"prostitute" is the better word. Word choices represent political views of
the world, especially when describing the topic of this book: work. We may
need new terms, such as "sexual economy," to capture that history and reality
and begin a discourse of national confrontation and, ultimately, of personal
reconciliation.

This essay examines two cases in which enslaved black women's sexuality
was at the heart of the dispute. It starts with an 1806 Virginia case in which two
enslaved women used slavery's rules of reproduction and race to argue that
they were not legally black and hence should be set free. The second case, an
1859 Mississippi case, involved the rape of an enslaved girl. I use these cases to
investigate some of the primary legal doctrines that enabled elite white men to
extract forced sexual and reproductive labor from enslaved women. Taken
together, these cases and rules reveal how law and markets of the antebellum
South seized enslaved women's intimate lives, converting private relations of
sex and reproduction into political and economic relations. This interplay of
sex and markets leads me to name this world a sexual political economy.

The idea of a "sexual economy of slavery" may seem odd on first impression. We divide our economic relationships in the workplace from our intimate,
family interactions. We view these relations as taking place in two segregated
spheres: the market and our intimate lives. It is in this latter space that we feel
enabled to make our decisions, conduct our lives, love our own families. We

may experience dissonances when sex and economics are juxtaposed. In addition, many of us imagine slavery as an institution of racial hierarchies, not gender hierarchies. But the cases and rules I will examine expose a different relationship between sex and markets for enslaved black women. In the process, they expose the brutal gender subordination that slavery entailed.

One quick caveat: slavery varied from region to region and slaveholder to slaveholder. It also evolved and mutated during its 250-odd years. I use two cases from two significantly different regions and periods (Virginia in 1806 and Mississippi in 1859). I do not mean to suggest that these cases are representative of slavery. However, I use them because individually and taken together they raise intriguing questions about the central and distinctive role that black women's sexuality and reproductive capacity played in the southern political economy.[1]

A Life of Labor: Production and Reproduction

When we think of enslavement, we think of labor. Recent studies of enslaved women have shown that they labored no less than enslaved men. As activist-scholar Angela Davis put it, "As slaves, compulsory labor overshadowed every other aspect of women's existence. It would seem, therefore, that the starting point for any exploration of Black women's lives under slavery would be an appraisal of their role as workers."[2] Historian Jacqueline Jones discovered that "in the 1850s at least 90 percent of all female slaves over sixteen years of age labored more than 261 days per year, eleven to thirteen hours each day."[3]

But the labor that slavery compelled of enslaved women was distinct from the way others worked in two ways. First, unlike white women, they performed the same work as men, while also doing the domestic work typically reserved for women, free and enslaved. In the middle of the nineteenth century, seven-eighths of enslaved people, regardless of sex, were field workers.[4] In 1800, when the Santee Canal was built in North Carolina, enslaved women constituted 50 percent of the construction crew.[5] Deborah Gray White notes: "[I]t appears that [enslaved women] did a variety of heavy and dirty labor, work which was also done by men. In 1853, Frederick Olmsted saw South Carolina slaves of both sexes carting manure on their heads to the cotton fields where they spread it with their hands between the ridges in which cotton was planted. In Fayetteville, North Carolina, he noticed that women not only hoed and shoveled but they also cut down trees and drew wood."[6] Thus, enslaved women performed much of the same productive labor done by men who shared their race and status as slaves.[7] Jones notes that while the form of *extracting* their labor differed from that of a free labor system, the content of what enslaved men did could be analogized at some level to the work that all men did on farms, including in New England and on smaller southern farms.[8] This was not so for enslaved women, whose labor differed markedly from that performed by white women.

In colonial American society, privileged white women rarely worked in the fields. Occasionally, white female indentured servants were forced to work in the fields as punishment for misdeeds, but this was not a common practice. In the eyes of colonial white Americans, only debased and degraded members of the female sex labored in the fields. And any white woman forced by circumstances to work in the fields was regarded as unworthy of the title "woman."[9] Historians caution us not to overstate the point: there was gender differentiation in enslaved men's and women's labor.[10] Still, enslaved women did not perform gender-segregated labor nearly to the same extent that white women did.[11]

Performance by enslaved women of conventionally male work distinguished their labor from that of black men, white women, and white men. Enslaved men, and free whites of both sexes, worked in accord with gender roles. In fact, when enslaved men were assigned "women's work," it was often for the specific purpose of humiliation or discipline.[12] And historians Nell Painter and Chris Tomlins reinforce the intriguing point that, for those white women who did work in the fields, the reality of their daily lives departed from the rhetoric of white femininity.[13] The existence of this disjuncture in the lives of many working white women stemmed from the cultural and racialized importance of rigid gender roles. "[W]hile white women's field labor challenged gender roles, African women's field labor *confirmed* racial roles. Enslaved African women's substitution for white women field workers (occurring far earlier than the late 17th/early 18th century 'transition to slavery' would suggest) then increased opportunities for white women's participation in household formation, stabilizing white culture with an approximation of 'good wife' domesticity."[14] Within a society that enforced strict adherence to sex roles, only enslaved women were compelled to labor consistently across gender boundaries. This aspect of their physical work is one of the distinguishing features of their experience.

But slavery's political economy forced enslaved women to labor in a second way that was not required of any other group. As the remainder of this essay shows, enslaved women, and only enslaved women, were forced to perform sexual and reproductive labor to satisfy the economic, political, and personal interests of white men of the elite class. Even more so than crossing gender boundaries in physical labor, this second distinguishing feature of their experience under slavery foregrounds their gender and demonstrates how embedded their sexuality was in slavery's economic markets.

In an 1806 case, *Hudgins v. Wrights,* two enslaved women, Hannah and her unnamed daughter, sued for their freedom.[15] They alleged the wrongful enslavement of the woman who was, respectively, their mother and grandmother, Butterwood Nan. Let me consider in some detail the arguments of both Hannah and her daughter (the plaintiffs) and the man claiming to be their master (the defendant). Ultimately, Hannah and her daughter's freedom turned on how the law decided to characterize Butterwood Nan's reproduction.

The defendant, who claimed ownership of Hannah and her daughter, did so based on a fundamental rule of slavery: *partus sequitur ventrem,* Latin for "the child follows the mother." Under this law, adopted in every enslaving state, children inherited their status as enslaved or free from their mothers. This rule dictated that enslaved women gave birth to enslaved children and free women gave birth to free children. Accordingly, the slaveholder argued that because the ancestral matriarch, Butterwood Nan, had been enslaved, her daughter Hannah had inherited her enslaved status and subsequently passed it on to her own daughter, akin almost to tainted blood.

As early as 1662, Virginia adopted the rule that enslaved black women gave birth to enslaved children.[16] By the time of the founding of our democratic nation, all of the enslaving states dictated that enslaved black women gave birth to enslaved children, regardless of the father's status or race. As one judge said, "The father of a slave is unknown to our law."[17] This is a striking conclusion, given the general patriarchal and patrilineal nature of antebellum Anglo-American law. But, it is not a surprising one, given the direction of the political economy and wealth holding. Historians agree that "land and slaves became the two great vehicles through which slaveholders realized their ambitions of fortune. . . . The usefulness of land increased in proportion to the availability of black slaves."[18] Peter Kolchin documents the need for growing numbers of forced laborers as early as the colonial period: "Cultivating [tobacco and rice], however, required labor; in an environment where land was plentiful and people few, the amount of tobacco or rice one could grow depended on the number of laborers one could command."[19] Of course, the United States was not alone in basing its economy on black slave labor. It did distinguish itself, however, in how it met the ongoing need to replenish its workforce.

Other New World slave systems continued to kidnap Africans through the international slave trade to meet their labor needs. Varying combinations of higher ratios of men to women, low fertility rates, and extreme mortality rates meant that natural reproduction did not sustain the enslaved populations of Latin America and the Caribbean. The demography of these slave societies stood in stark contrast to the United States slave system. One "unquestionable—indeed unique—mark of slavery in the Southern states was the natural increase of the slave population. In all other slave societies of the New World, the slave population failed to reproduce itself and was sustained or increased only by constant injections of new slaves from Africa."[20] This had striking demographic effects. "Jamaica, Cuba, and Haiti each imported many more slaves than the whole of the North American mainland. Yet, in stark contrast, by 1825 the Southern states of the United States had the largest slave population of any country in the New World, amounting to well over one-third of the total."[21] Thus, the rule that children's status followed their mothers' was a foundational one for our economy. It converted enslaved women's reproductive capacity into market capital to serve economic interests. In the United States, it was enslaved women who reproduced the workforce.

Thus, childbearing by enslaved women created economic value independent of the physical, productive labor they performed. Southern legal rules harnessed black reproductive capacity for market purposes, extracting from it the profits one might expect from a factory or livestock. According to historian James Oakes, "The distinguishing function of slaves in the South's market economy was to serve not only as a labor supply but also as capital assets."[22] Law and markets operated synthetically in converting black reproductive capacity into capital creation. Slaveholders used the same logic of reproductive profits to get courts to void sales of enslaved women who couldn't bear children.[23] Functionally, reproductive relations were market relations of incredible economic significance. In its centrality to the political economy, enslaved women's reproduction was arguably the most valuable labor performed in the entire economy.

Thus, when the slaveholder in *Hudgins* invoked the rule that a child inherits its status from its mother, he was drawing on a foundational cultural assumption. Slaveholders owned all of the offspring of women they enslaved. The legal rule had immense economic and political significance for antebellum culture. Not only did slaves constitute the overwhelming proportion of the southern labor force, but this rule meant that it was a workforce that reproduced itself. Enslaved women gave birth to enslaved children and did so in a system that set considerable economic importance on this fact.

One of the nation's earliest and most prominent leaders, President Thomas Jefferson, personally proclaimed the unique, dual value of an enslaved workforce. Jefferson, who enslaved more than 144 people, said, "'I consider a woman who brings a child every two years as more profitable than the best man on the farm; what she produces is an addition to capital.'"[24] The value of short-term productive labor, such as that provided by the male slaves, or by the female slaves when viewed as mere field hands, "disappeared in mere consumption."[25] In keeping with this, Jefferson instructed his plantation manager to monitor the overseers and ensure that they were encouraging female slave reproduction, the source of his wealth. Repeated references to enslaved females' fertility in advertisements and negotiations for sales indicate that Jefferson was not alone in his sentiments.[26]

The secretary of the treasury and president of Georgia Cotton Planters Association estimated that a slaveholder's workforce would double every fifteen years through the process of normal reproduction.[27] Slavery scholar Deborah Gray White estimates that 5 to 6 percent of profit came from the increase of slaves due to reproduction.[28] Indeed, many members of the planting aristocracy owed their success to initial large gifts or inheritances of enslaved persons from their families.[29] Gray White notes, "Many farmers made their first investment not in a male slave, but in a young childbearing woman."[30] As one judge stated: "With us, nothing is so usual as to advance children by gifts of slaves. They stand with us, instead of money."[31] Historian Cheryl Ann Cody found that one of the men she studied "acquired slaves, once his estate was well established in the 1790s, primarily to give his sons their economic start rather than to expand his own labor force."[32]

Finally, southern judges drew analogies to rules governing livestock. Owners of female animals also got legal possession of their offspring. Should there be any doubt that southern whites grasped this analogy, one South Carolina judge declared that "the young of slaves . . . stand on the same footing as other animals."[33] Meanwhile a famous observer of the American South, Frederick Olmsted, concluded from his travels that "a slave woman is commonly esteemed least for her working qualities, most for those qualities which give value to a brood mare."[34]

The date of the case, 1806, is significant. The United States Constitution provided that no enslaved people could be imported (legally) from abroad after 1808.[35] Yet the expanding economies of the Deep South required larger and larger workforces. In 1806, Old South slave states, such as Virginia, were poised to take over the (legal) international slave trade with a domestic trade in slaves.[36] With enormous profits from reproduction anticipated, rules determining status became more crucial than ever.[37]

Therefore, the slaveholder in *Hudgins* drew upon the strong cultural expectation that personal economic profit would and should stem from an enslaved woman's childbearing. His lawyers cast his case as a question of "rights of *property*, those rules which have been established, are not to be departed from, because *freedom* is in question."[38] In other words, white economic rights trumped black liberty rights.[39]

Against this American backdrop of property rights in people, how could Hannah and her daughter have possibly responded? One would assume that the force of this law and custom would have dictated the outcome of the case: the law would side with the slaveholder, declaring him to be the legal owner of Hannah and her daughter. But, as central as these property rights were in the slaveholding South, they were countered by another, equally fundamental tenet of slavery, the rules of race. Hannah and her daughter argued that they could not be enslaved because, by law, they were *legally not black*.

Under Virginia law, only people of African descent could be enslaved.[40] Proving membership in the Native American or white races constituted a legal defense to slavery. Southern law dictated that blacks were presumptively slaves, while whites and Native Americans were presumptively free.[41] Judge Roane stated the law in *Hudgins*: "In the case of a person visibly appearing to be a negro, the presumption is, in this country, that he is a slave, and it is incumbent on him to make out his right to freedom: but in the case of a person visibly appearing to be a white man, or an Indian, the presumption is that he is free, and it is necessary for his adversary to shew that he is a slave."[42] Accordingly, Hannah and her daughter claimed that Butterwood Nan was Native American and therefore illegally enslaved. If Butterwood Nan had been wrongfully enslaved, then as a free woman she could not have transmitted any enslaved status to her daughter, Hannah, who, in turn, could not transmit it to her own daughter. In a fascinating instance of valuing white racial privilege over white wealth, the laws of race trumped the law that enslaved the children of female slaves. From within this legal box of race and status, Hannah and her daughter asserted the only legal argument that could win their freedom, their own nonblackness.

The plaintiffs' argument rested on gender as well as racial rules of slavery. Mother and daughter claimed their freedom through Butterwood Nan. To counter this, the slaveholder argued that Nan was, in fact, black and that it was her sexual partner who was Native American. Therefore, the nonblack (and legally free) ancestor was male. The establishment of nonblack ancestry had to be done through the maternal line to a female ancestor to be grounds for a claim of wrongful enslavement. Strikingly, within this deeply patriarchal culture, neither the father's race nor his status was relevant to the legal inquiry.[43] Free black men who took up with enslaved women fathered children who were enslaved by law. Moreover, showing white ancestry through one's father's side, indeed, showing that one's father was white, was no defense to enslavement. As noted before, by American law, the child of an enslaved black mother had no father. An enslaved woman who was black could not alter the status of her children through selecting either a free black or a white sexual partner.

Even more brutally, because the race of the father did not alter the status of an enslaved black woman's child, tens of thousands of white men were able to sexually abuse and coerce individual enslaved women without the risk that the women would bear children whose legal status would be affected in any way by their own. Such a child would not be construed by law as white or free, but as black and the father's slave.

Within what we now understand to be an absurd system, the assertions of both the slaveholder and the women he claimed as his property raise fascinating questions. Was Butterwood Nan exempted from the rule by virtue of being Native American? Had she lived her entire life held illegally as a slave? Were Hannah and her daughter free or enslaved? The arguments of both sides illustrate the centrality of enslaved women's reproduction to the political economy and culture of American slavery.

Let me finally reveal the outcome of the case. Judge Roane decided: "No testimony can be more complete and conclusive than that which exists in this cause to shew that *Hannah* had every appearance of an Indian. That *appearance* . . . will suffice for the claim of her posterity, unless it is opposed by counter-evidence shewing that some *female* ancestor [*sic*] of her's [*sic*] was a *negro* slave, or that *she* or some female ancestor, was *lawfully* an Indian slave."[44] The court never described Butterwood Nan's appearance. Most likely she was deceased or had been sold out of the area and away from her family. But because Hannah and her daughter did not look black, they were presumptively free. The burden was on the slaveholder to prove that Butterwood Nan had been legally enslaved. He failed to do so. Hannah and her daughter went free.

Hannah's successful efforts to seek a racial exemption from slavery's status classifications left intact legal assumptions that relegated the overwhelming majority of blacks to enslavement. So, is this a case to be celebrated? Condemned? How do we evaluate the efforts of Hannah and her daughter to escape from the grip of *partus sequitur ventrem*? Their lawyer started his argument before the court, "This is not a common case of mere *blacks* suing for their freedom."[45] Looking backwards from the twenty-first century, should we blame Hannah for seeking her family's freedom with such arguments? What other argument could she make within a racial logic that drew a legal equivalent between blackness and enslavement? What else could Hannah argue, except that she was not black?

Earlier, this essay identified black women's deployment across the conventional sexual division of labor as one of the things that distinguished their lives from those of other groups. The physical labor of enslaved women differed from white women's work both absolutely and relative to the work done by enslaved men. The case of Hannah and her daughter exposes a second, more brutal way that the economic roles that slavery assigned enslaved women distinguished their labor from other groups. White men and black men (free and enslaved) could father children either free or enslaved, and white women could give birth only to free children.[46] Laws of race and gender merged with *partus sequitur ventrem*'s status classifications to condemn the wombs of enslaved black women. This is a point about race and gender: only black women could give birth to enslaved children, and every black woman who was enslaved and gave birth did so to an enslaved child. In other words, the class that reproduced the workforce was limited to black women.[47] It is this terrorizing aspect of enslaved women's lives that also distinguished their role in the political economy from that of black men, white women, and white men. At labor in the fields and in labor in the birthing bed—the enslaved woman was both a mode of production and a mode of reproduction.

I turn now from reproductive relations to sexual relations. Like reproduction, from a contemporary perspective, many of us tend to think of sexual relationships as intimate, noneconomic relationships. But, again like reproduction, enslaved women's sexuality played an essential role in the antebellum political economy. If the rule of *partus sequitur ventrem* reflected the southern investment in enslaved women's reproductive capacity, then the law of rape reveals the interests, economic and political, in their sexuality.

Pleasure, Profit, and Punishment: Sexual Exploitation of Enslaved Women

In Mississippi in 1859, an enslaved man was accused of raping an unnamed enslaved girl, under ten years old.[48] Convicted at trial, the defendant, named only as George, appealed to the Mississippi Supreme Court. The lawyer representing him argued: "The crime of rape does not exist in this State between African slaves. Our laws recognize no marital rights as between slaves; their sexual intercourse is left to be regulated by their owners. The regulations of law, as to the white race, on the subject of sexual intercourse, do not and cannot, for obvious reasons, apply to slaves; their intercourse is promiscuous, and the violation of a female slave by a male slave would be a mere assault and battery."[49] Influential legal commentator Thomas Cobb agreed: "The violation of the person of a female slave, carries with it no other punishment than the damages which the master may recover for the trespass upon his property."[50] This meant that an enslaved woman's master could prosecute her rape as a crime against his property, but the state would not prosecute her rape as a crime against her person. The court agreed and overturned George's conviction.

Nearly every southern court that ruled on rape and enslaved women followed this ruling.[51] As Carolyn Pitt Jones, a student, succinctly summarized it, within slavery's sexual subtext, the female slave was an extralegal creature who could not use the law to protect herself.[52]

It would be folly to overgeneralize about a society's sexual norms based solely on its laws of rape. But criminal laws of rape define the boundaries of sexual access to bodies, especially women's and children's.[53] And the doctrine in *George v. State* shows how white institutions, including law, created and legitimized black women's sexual vulnerability. The refusal of law to protect enslaved women from rape institutionalized access to their bodies. Their exclusion from rape doctrine enabled their sexuality to be seized for multiple purposes.

First, slaveholders could force the relations they had with enslaved women as their laborers beyond the economic arena and into the sexual one without significant social disruption. Not only productive labor and reproduction could be demanded of enslaved women, but sexual gratification as well. The refusal of law to recognize sexual crimes against enslaved women enabled masters to compel sex.

"Since the white male could rape the black female who did not willingly respond to his demands, passive submission on the part of the enslaved black women cannot be seen as complicity. Those women who did not willingly respond to the sexual overture of masters and overseers were brutalized and punished. Any show of resistance on the part of enslaved females increased the determination of white owners eager to demonstrate their power."[54] Sexual relations were part and parcel of what women were expected to do as members of an enslaved workforce.

Under this theory of law, and on a brutal daily basis, enslaved women's sexuality was under the direct control of men in the slaveholding class. But it is important to note that sexual abuse of enslaved women was not limited to white men in slaveholding families. This group comprised only a small percentage of whites in the South. Other men, poorer, nonslaveholding whites and black men, took advantage of enslaved women's sexual vulnerability. Overseers frequently sexually assaulted or coerced enslaved women. In addition, a slaveholder could compel an enslaved woman to have sexual relations with his friends or to "initiate" a son or younger nephew, much as he might hire her out for her productive labor. In the alternative, he might by his silence authorize sexual access for men related to him by blood or economics. In short, law granted masters not only economic and political authority, but sexual authority as well.

Sadly, there is a need for intraracial as well as interracial critiques of sexual abuse. Recall that the case of *George v. State* involved the rape of a ten-year-old enslaved girl by an enslaved man. This may be one of the reasons the case was ever prosecuted. While certainly many black men of this era respected black women's sexual integrity and rights over their own bodies even in the absence of legal dictates to do so, others did not. Black women's sexual vulnerability was created and legitimized by white institutions of law and social power, but black men as well as white took advantage of it. Intraracial sexual abuse of black women surely has a different social meaning and significance than their abuse by white men. But that should not preclude our investigating what that different meaning is, and why some black men and not others took advantage of their sisters.[55]

Second, some white slaveholders embraced the sexual exploitation of enslaved women to defend slavery against abolitionists who charged sexual abuse as one of the evils of slavery. According to Chancellor Harper, a judge: "And can it be doubted that this purity [of the white woman] is caused by, and is a compensation for, the evils resulting from the existence of an enslaved class of more relaxed morals? . . . I do not hesitate to say that the intercourse which takes place with enslaved females is less depraving in its effects than when it is carried on with females of their own caste . . . [The white man] feels that he is connecting him with one of an inferior and servile caste, and there is something of degradation in the act. The intercourse is generally casual; he does not make her habitually an associate, and is less likely to receive any taint from her habits and manners."[56] Southern white men openly justified their exploitation of enslaved women as resulting in the better treatment of white women. The same sexual norms that protected (white) female chastity with vigilance and brutality (sometimes directed at the women themselves) construed enslaved women as perpetual "outlets."[57] Elite white women, represented as delicate and often asexual, found their own sexual relations closely guarded and monitored by these same men. "Whereas the lady was deprived of her sexuality, the black woman was defined by hers."[58] Sexual access to enslaved women was central in the creation and maintenance of this repressive ideology of white femininity. Black enslaved women were therefore excluded from, yet essential to, the gender ideology of white masculinity and femininity.

Third, sexual abuse of enslaved women must be understood as an exercise of political power as well as sexual license. Contemporary feminists have demonstrated that rape entails power relations as much as sexual relations. Men rape women not only for personal pleasure, but to discipline women into conforming to certain behaviors: to achieve women's submissiveness in personal relationships or adherence to conservative dress codes or to dictate physical activity, i.e., where and when women feel safe. Slavery offers a primary and stark example of the power relations embedded in forced sexual relations.

An enslaved woman might be sexually punished for any number of perceived or actual offenses. Forced sex reminded an enslaved woman of her pow-
erlessness in the hands of her master or his agent, the overseer. It functioned to
humiliate her and demonstrate that the legal system had given control over her
body to the man who enslaved her. Angela Y. Davis offers the following characterization: "Rape was a weapon of domination, a weapon of repression, whose
covert goal was to extinguish slave women's will to resist, and in the process, to
demoralize their men."[59] Rape under slavery was an extremely powerful tool of
disciplining women workers.[60]

In addition, rape helped to maintain racial hierarchy by reminding black
women and men of black men's subordinate status to white men. As noted, a
hallmark of southern antebellum culture was the protection of female chastity
by male family members. An enslaved man who sought to do the same risked
his life and that of the woman. "Clearly the master hoped that once the black
man was struck by his manifest inability to rescue his women from sexual
assaults of the master, he would begin to experience deep-seated doubts about
his ability to resist at all."[61] Rape of enslaved women demoralized the entire
black community. Law thus endorsed the use of sexual power as a mechanism
of labor, racial, and gender control.

Finally, in addition to serving antebellum interests of pleasure and politics,
enslaved women's sexuality was a source of economic profits for those inclined
to reap them. Historians have identified an active market in enslaved women
for prostitution, called the "Fancy Trade." "Slaves selected for their grace,
beauty and light skins were shipped to the 'fancy-girl markets' of New Orleans
and other cities. At a time when prime field hands sold for $1,600, a 'fancy girl'
brought $5,000. Some ended up in bordellos, but the majority became the
mistresses of wealthy planters, gamblers, or businessmen."[62] Sex might be
extracted from any enslaved woman or girl. However, an enslaved woman sold
primarily for sex commanded a higher price than other enslaved women.[63]
The market assigned economic value directly related to sexual attractiveness. The seller reaped as extra profit the market's valuation of their sexuality,
whether in skin color, hair, or whatever the buyer happened to personally value
as erotic. As Brenda Stevenson incisively puts it, "What, after all, could be more
valuable than a woman of 'white' complexion who could be bought as one's
private 'sex slave.'?"[64] To accommodate these buyers and ensure that they were
getting what they expected, fancy-girl traders might allow the buyer to
"inspect" his proposed purchase alone. At this juncture, sexual abuse and economic profits brutally collided.

The appearance of enslaved women as explicit sexual commodities in
markets illuminates yet another way in which the South profited from enslaved

women's sexuality. The fancy-girl trade offers perhaps the most vivid image of how enslaved women's sexual relations were integrally tied to market relations in the antebellum political economy. Many historians now acknowledge that white men used enslaved women for sexual gratification. But with the above analysis I have tried to point out the nuances of their sexual labor. At the southern antebellum juncture of sex and markets, enslaved women were sexually exploited for a variety of purposes: pleasure, politics, punishment, as well as profit. In addition, as I have described earlier, slavery replenished its workforce through black women. This convergence of sexual and reproductive relations with market and political relations is what leads me to name slavery a sexual political economy.

A Sexual Economy

A political economy is characterized in some part by how wealth is defined, who owns it, and who creates it. In their descriptions of expected profits, ways to maximize yield, and transmissions of wealth between generations, elite members of antebellum society characterized enslaved women's reproductive capacity in the language of capital assets. Judges, cabinet members, and at least one president declared the economic value of enslaved women's childbearing capacity. This reproduction was integral to the plantation economy, which required a steady flow of cheap, largely unskilled labor. Hence black reproduction yielded economic profits, creating value for the slaveholding class. Enslaved black women gave birth to white wealth.

A political economy is also characterized by the interests it prioritizes and how those are served. White men established enslaved women as sexual outlets, forcing them to perform sexual labor. In the process, their sexuality could be exploited to reinforce gender conventions among elite whites and to defend slavery against northern charges. In addition, enslaved women could be sexually terrorized in order to coerce economic work or quell political resistance. Their exploitation could also be used to discipline enslaved men. Finally, as the fancy-girl trade illustrates, economic profits were to be made in slavery's sexual markets. Pleasure, punishment, politics, and profit: once laws of rape authorized elite white male legal and economic control over enslaved women's sexuality, their sexuality could be manipulated to serve any number of interests.

Taken together, *Hudgins v. Wrights* and *George v. State* show how law extracted and markets expected dual labor from enslaved women. Like enslaved men, they were coerced into performing grueling physical productive labor. But they were also compelled to do sexual and reproductive labor required of no other group. This suggests the need for attention to gender to fully understand the economics and effects of U.S. enslavement. Economists of slavery have characterized the political economy of slavery as a system in which blacks transferred millions of dollars of uncompensated labor to white slave-holders. "[Slavery] directly enriched those who bought, sold, transported, financed, bred, leased, and managed slaves in agriculture. But it was also important in other sectors, including mining, transportation, manufacturing, and public works—roads, dams, canals, levees, railroads, clearing land—and so on."[65] Wealth not only was transferred from blacks to whites, as scholars have noted, but, in addition, was transferred from black women to white men. Hence, the economics of slavery were gendered as well as racialized.

In addition, the economic impact of its sexual exploitation distinguishes the antebellum South from other enslaving systems. Other slave societies entailed sexual and reproductive exploitation.[66] Indeed, some cultures enslaved primarily women (and children). In this sense, they were more gendered than U.S. slavery with its relatively equal sex ratios. But, what I have tried to show in this essay is the extent to which enslaved women's sexual and reproductive labor was an integral and critical part of the economic and political viability of the South. One measure of slavery is how central or peripheral it is to the immediate economic functioning of the society. People might be enslaved to serve primarily as servants, political officials, soldiers, wives, or concubines.[67] Enslavement in the United States stands in stark contrast to all of these. David Brion Davis elaborates the relationship of slavery to the U.S. market economy: "No slave system in history was quite like that of the West Indies and the Southern states of America. Marked off from the free population by racial and cultural differences, for the most part deprived of the hope of manumission, the Negro slave also found his life regimented in a highly organized system that was geared to maximize production for a market economy."[68] Enslaved women both labored in and reproduced this workforce. I have also shown how their sexual exploitation was inextricably tied not only to economic viability, but also to maintaining and defending the social order, ranging from pleasure to punishment to politics. In sum, slavery's legal and cultural institutions system-atically made enslaved women's reproductive and sexual capacity available to serve any number of political and economic interests of elite white men. For all these reasons, I name the antebellum South a sexual political economy. Rules of race, rape, gender, and *partus sequitur ventrem* formed the legal core of slav-ery's sexual economy.

What, then, do we gain from viewing slavery as a sexual economy? I would suggest three things. One purpose in labeling the antebellum South a sexual economy is to draw attention to the extent to which slavery drew distinctions on the basis of sex as well as race. It was a gendered and sexualized as well as a racial institution. Or, in the language of subordination, a language that may more aptly characterize slavery's brutal hierarchies, American slavery, while obviously racially supremacist, was also fundamentally a system of gender supremacy. Designating it as a sexual economy draws attention to its axes of male power as well as racial power, thereby shedding light on the lives and exploitation of both enslaved women and enslaved men.

Viewing slavery through the sexual economy lens also suggests insights about the very nature of gender itself. "Masculine" and "feminine" mean different things in different races, classes, and ethnicities. Sexual roles and norms evolve over time and across cultural boundaries. Enslaved women offer an early, dramatic example of the political, cultural, economic, and violent forces that can shape gender. Angela Davis offers an excellent description of the manipulation of enslaved women's gender: "Expediency governed the slaveholders' posture toward female slaves: when it was profitable to exploit them as if they were men, they were regarded, in effect, as genderless, but when they could be exploited, punished and repressed in ways suited only for women, they were locked into their exclusively female roles."[69] Jacqueline Jones concurs: "The master took a more crudely opportunistic approach toward the labor of slave women, revealing the interaction (and at times conflict) between notions of women qua 'equal' black workers and women qua unequal reproducers."[70] Against the feminine delicacy and chastity ascribed to most white women in this society, enslaved women were clearly gendered differently. They were gendered as masculine when performing conventionally male work or suffering the same brutal physical discipline as enslaved men. But an enslaved woman might have her sexuality or childbearing capacity seized for pleasure, profit, or punishment at any moment, suffering rape or giving birth to white wealth. She was male when convenient and horrifically female when needed. In this sense, she was "gendered to the ground," as legal feminist theorist Catharine MacKinnon would say.[71] Comprehending gender as brutally malleable may uncover deeply buried historical facts.

Finally, seeing slavery in this way challenges the way we divide the intimate from the economic. For enslaved women, sexual and reproductive relations were economic and market relations.[72] While their family lives and personal relationships offered some solace from the daily brutality of slavery, white men could invade this sphere at will, abusing women sexually or reproductively. Excellent work by historians Darlene Clark Hine and Nell Painter invites our attention to the ongoing sociological and psychological effects of slavery's sexual economy. Clark Hine makes the powerful argument that all of these manipulations and abuses of sexuality were primary factors in shaping cultures of resistance in southern black women. Dissemblance, flight northward, and, most tragically, violence targeted at their own bodies were tactics black women employed.[73] And Painter argues that because sexual abuse of enslaved women was woven into the fabric of southern households and families, its cultural, sociological, and psychological effects reached far beyond enslaved females or even the larger enslaved and black communities.[74]

In the black community too often we still view sexuality as something to be kept private and not spoken about. Black women's magazines are filled with stories of the trauma and loss of self-esteem this repression causes. Perhaps understanding black women's sexual history as something under public control for so long can help us to see the inherently political nature of our sexuality.[75] For black women to reclaim our sexuality, our intimate selves, from all of the people and forces who would seek to expropriate it, regulate it, define it, and confine it, we must first become comfortable speaking about it. The language of the sexual economy may help in this process.

To summarize, enslaved black women shared the world of productive labor with white men, black men, and white women but also inhabited a separate world of compelled sexual and reproductive labor. By understanding American slavery as a sexual economy in which black women's reproduction and sexuality were appropriated for any number of white economic and political interests, we can see more clearly how slavery was a deeply gendered and sexualized institution in which there was a constant interplay between black sexuality and white economic profits. Such an understanding collapses the distinctions we draw between sex and work, families and markets, also showing how this distinction was itself largely under male control. It also enables us to see more clearly the institutions, including law, that slavery erected, institutions that systematically made enslaved women's reproductive and sexual capacity available for sale and consumption.

Afterword: Reclaiming Ourselves

Grandma Baby said people look down on her because she had eight children with different men. Colored people and white people both look down on her for that. Slaves not supposed to have pleasurable feelings on their own; their bodies not supposed to be like that, but they have to have as many children as they can to please whoever owned them. Still, they were not supposed to have pleasure deep down. She said for me not to listen to that. That I should always listen to my body and love it.

—Toni Morrison, *Beloved*

Beyond the brutal exploitation and abuse of the slave economy, black women have reclaimed productive work as something that can be fulfilling and affirming. But much of the labor that slavery extracted from women in the enslaved workforce was sexual and reproductive. Toni Morrison's Pulitzer Prize–winning novel, *Beloved,* is a story about a black woman who is thoroughly brutalized and haunted by the sexual economy of slavery described above. Morrison poetically renders her character's exhausting struggle to reclaim herself, and her family, from the terror of her past.

Have we, today, fully reclaimed our own intimate lives from that horror? What are the ongoing effects of slavery's systemic expropriation of black women's reproduction and sexuality for market and political purposes? How does the sexual economy of slavery continue to affect the policing of black women's sexuality? From current national debates about welfare reform to local debates within the black community about sexual aggression by black men against black women, our intimate lives cannot be tidily defined as and confined to a private space. This essay has used cases and legal doctrine that document and record the real lives and experiences of black women who were enslaved, not only for academic insight, but to enable us to combat the effects of sexual economies, past and present.

NOTES

The title of this essay comes from Minnie Folkes, a former Virginia slave. Her full statement was, "Don't let nobody bother yo' principle, 'cause dat wuz all yo' had." John Blassingame, *The Slave Community: Plantation Life in the Antebellum South* (New York and Oxford: Oxford University Press, 1972), 163

1. On the specificity of slavery, see Peter J. Parish, *Slavery: History and Historians* (New York: Harper and Row, 1989), 3–6, 97–112.

2. Angela Y. Davis, *Women, Race, and Class* (New York: Random House, 1983), 5. Leslie Schwalm's study of enslaved women on South Carolina rice plantations also reinforces this point. Leslie A. Schwalm, *A Hard Fight for We: Women's Transition from Slavery to Freedom in South Carolina* (Urbana: University of Illinois Press, 1997), 19–46.

3. Jacqueline Jones, *Labor of Love, Labor of Sorrow: Black Women, Work, and the Family from Slavery to the Present* (New York: Basic Books, 1985), 18.

4. Davis, *Women, Race, and Class,* 5.

5. Ibid., 10.

6. Deborah Gray White, "Female Slaves: Sex Roles and Status in the Antebellum Plantation South," in *Half Sisters of History: Southern Women and the American Past,* ed. Catherine Clinton (Durham, N.C.: Duke University Press, 1994), 56, 59.

7. See also Brenda E. Stevenson, *Life in Black and White: Family and Community in the Slave South* (New York: Oxford University Press, 1996), 159, 187–192; Schwalm, *A Hard Fight for We,* 19–23; Carole Shammas, "Black Women's Work and the Evolution of Plantation Society in Virginia," *Labor History* 5 (1985): 5–6.

8. Jones, *Labor of Love, Labor of Sorrow,* 12. Brenda Stevenson notes that this was not the case in many African tribes. Stevenson, *Life in Black and White,* 171 (under sexual division of labor in many African tribes, men did not perform agricultural labor, which was considered women's work).

9. bell hooks, *Ain't I a Woman: Black Women and Feminism* (Boston: South End Press, 1981), 22.

10. For instance, Deborah Gray White warns: "[I]t would be a mistake to say that there was no differentiation of field labor on southern farms and plantations. . . . Yet the exceptions to the rule were so numerous as to make a mockery of it." Gray White, "Female Slaves," 59–60 (emphasis added). In addition, "Pregnant women, and sometimes women breastfeeding infants, were usually given less physically demanding work." Ibid., 60 (footnote omitted). See also, Ira Berlin, *Many Thousands Gone: The First Two Centuries of Slavery in North America* (Cambridge, Mass.: Belknap Press of Harvard University Press, 1998), 56, 135, 168 (describing the evolution of sexual division of labor); Stevenson, *Life in Black and White*, 192–193.

11. See hooks, *Ain't I a Woman*, 22–23. Ira Berlin notes, "Only rarely—for the very young and the very old—did household labor occupy slave women on a full-time basis." See also Berlin, *Many Thousands Gone*, 168, 270–271, 311–312; Eugene D. Genovese, *Roll, Jordan, Roll: The World the Slaves Made* (New York: Pantheon Books, 1972), 495; Schwalm, *A Hard Fight for We*, 19–28.

12. See, e.g., Peter Kolchin, *American Slavery: 1619–1877* (New York: Hill and Wang, 1993), 121–122 (describing one slaveholder who used this tactic).

13. Nell Irvin Painter, "Soul Murder and Slavery: Toward a Fully Loaded Cost Accounting," in *U.S. History as Women's History: Feminist Essays,* ed. Linda Kerber et al. (Chapel Hill: University of North Carolina Press, 1995), 125, 142; Chris Tomlins, "Why Wait for Industrialism? Work, Legal Culture, and the Example of Early America," *Labor History* 40 (February 1999): 5.

14. See Tomlins, "Why Wait for Industrialism?" 32.

15. *Hudgins v Wrights*, 11 Va. (1 Hen. and M.) 134 (1806).

16. Act XII, 2 Laws of Virginia 170 (Hening 1823) (enacted 1662). For further discussion of this rule in Virginia, see Karen A. Getman, "Note, Sexual Control in the Slaveholding South: The Implementation and Maintenance of a Racial Caste System," *Harvard Women's Law Journal* 7 (1984): 115, 130–132; A. Leon Higginbotham Jr. and Barbara K. Kopytoff, "Racial Purity and Interracial Sex in the Law of Colonial and Antebellum Virginia," *Georgetown Law Journal* 77 (1989): 1967, 1970–1975; hooks, *Ain't I a Woman*, 39–44; Wilbert E. Moore, "Slave Law and the Social Structure," *Journal of Negro History* 26 (1941): 171, 184–191 (intriguing early discussion about definitions of enslavement).

17. *Frazier v Spear*, 5 Ky. (2 Bibb) 385, 386 (1811).

18. James Oakes, *The Ruling Race: A History of American Slaveholders* (New York: Knopf, 1982), 73.

19. Kolchin, *American Slavery*, 6–7.

20. Parish, *Slavery*, 23. "[T]he North American mainland was one of the smallest importers of slaves from Africa, and yet became the home of the largest slave population in the Western hemisphere." Ibid., 112, see also 16. See also Albert J. Raboteau, *Slave Religion: The "Invisible Institution" in the Antebellum South* (New York: Oxford University Press, 1978), 91. Slavery in the United States was not static, however, and at times failed to reproduce by natural increase. See, e.g., Berlin, *Many Thousands Gone*, 149 (through most of the eighteenth century, the slave population in the low country did not naturally reproduce); Parish, *Slavery*, 16 ("the first generation of slaves did not even reproduce their own population, let alone produce a natural increase").

21. Parish, *Slavery*, 12 (footnote omitted).

22. Oakes, *The Ruling Race*, 26.

23. Margaret Burnham discusses such cases in her excellent article on the legal treatment of enslaved families. Margaret A. Burnham, "An Impossible Marriage: Slave Law and Family Law," *Law and Inequality* (1987): 187, 198–199.

24. Letter from Thomas Jefferson to Joel Yancy (17 January 1819), reprinted in *Thomas Jefferson's Farm Book: With Commentary and Relevant Extracts from Other Writings,* ed. Edwin Morris Betts (Princeton: American Philosophical Society, Princeton University Press, 1953). 42, 43.

25. Ibid.

26. Stevenson, *Life in Black and White,* 245.

27. Herbert G. Gutman, *The Black Family in Slavery and Freedom, 1750–1925* (New York: Pantheon Books, 1976), 76.

28. Deborah Gray White, *Ar'n't I a Woman? Female Slaves in the Plantation South* (New York: Norton, 1985), 177 n. 22. She describes the economics in excellent detail. Ibid., 67–70.

29. In 1818, one southerner wrote: "For a young man, just commencing life the best stock, in which he can invest Capital, is, I think, negro Stock . . . ; negroes will yield a much larger income than any Bank dividend." Oakes, *The Ruling Race,* 73. Quoted in Leslie Howard Owens, *This Species of Property: Slave Life and Culture in the Old South* (New York: Oxford University Press, 1976), 16. Similarly, an uncle advised his young nephew: "Get as many young negro women as you can. Get as many cows as you can. . . . It is the greatest country for an increase that I have ever saw in my life. I have been hear [*sic*] six years and I have had fifteen negro children born and last year three more young negro women commenced breeding which added seven born last year and five of them is living and doing well." Oakes, *The Ruling Race,* 74 (quoting Alva Fitzpatrick to Phillips Fitzpatrick, Aug. 20, 1849, Fitzpatrick Papers, University of North Carolina, Chapel Hill, N.C.).

30. Gray White, *Ar'n't I a Woman?,* 67–70.

31. *Jones v Mason,* 22 Va. (1 Rand.) 577, n. 1 (Aug. 1827) (Carr, J., concurring).

32. Cheryl Ann Cody, "Naming, Kinship, and Estate Dispersal: Notes on Slave Family Life on a South Carolina Plantation, 1786 to 1833," in *Black Women in United States History: From Colonial Times through the Present,* ed. Darlene Clark Hine (New York: Carlson Publishing, 1990), 242.

33. *M'Vaughters v Elder,* 4 S.C.L. (2 Brev.) 307, 314 (1809). See also Parish, *Slavery,* 80 (describing a South Carolina planter who registered the births of enslaved children and of colts, naming the horses' sires but not the slaves' fathers).

34. Gray White, *Ar'n't I a Woman?* 177 n. 22 (quoting *DeBow's Review* 30 [1857]: 74, which is quoting Frederick Olmsted, *The Cotton Kingdom,* ed. David Freeman Hawke [Indianapolis: Bobbs-Merrill, 1971], 12, 72.)

35. U.S. Constitution, art. I, § 9, cl. 1.

36. See, e.g., August Meier and Elliott Rudwick, *From Plantation to Ghetto,* 3rd ed. (New York: Hill and Wang, 1976), 40–41 (describing the role of the United States in ongoing illegal trade). On the slave trade generally, see Philip D. Curtin, *The Atlantic Slave Trade: A Census* (Madison: University of Wisconsin Press, 1969); Herbert S. Klein, *The Middle Passage: Comparative Studies in the Atlantic Slave Trade* (Princeton, N.J.: Princeton University Press, 1978); Stanley L. Engerman and Joseph E. Inikori, eds., *The Atlantic Slave Trade: Effects on Economies, Societies, and Peoples in Africa, the Americas, and Europe* (Durham, N.C.: Duke University Press, 1992). On the domestic slave trade see, e.g., Stevenson, *Life in Black and White,* 175–176; Walter Johnson, *Soul by Soul: Life Inside the Antebellum Slave Market* (Cambridge, Mass.: Harvard University Press, 1999); Michael Tadman, *Speculators and Slaves: Masters, Traders, and Slaves in the Old South* (Madison: University of Wisconsin Press, 1989); see also Parish, *Slavery,* 56–57 (summarizing the debate over extent and effects of domestic slave trade).

37. The scope, design, and profitability of breeding enslaved females remains deeply contested among historians. See Parish, *Slavery,* 63 n. 33; Richard Sutch, "The Breeding of Slaves for Sale and the Westward Expansion of Slavery, 1850–1860," in *Race and Slavery in the*

Western Hemisphere: Quantitative Studies, ed. Stanley L. Engerman and Eugene D. Genovese (Princeton, N.J.: Princeton University Press, 1975); Richard G. Lowe and Randolph B. Campbell, "The Slave Breeding Hypothesis: A Demographic Comment on the 'Buying and Selling' States," *Journal of Southern History* 42 (1976): 401–412.

38. *Hudgins v Wrights,* 11 Va. (1 Hen. and M.), 136 (italics in original).

39. The *Hudgins* ruling suggests a different outcome when the contest is between white economic versus *white* liberty interests. See *Hudgins v Wrights,* 11 Va. (1 Hen. and M.), 140–141. For further discussion of this point, see Adrienne D. Davis, "Identity Notes Part One: Playing in the Light," *American University Law Review* 45 (1996): 695, 702–707.

40. Native Americans could be enslaved in Virginia only during a certain period of time, and whites could not be enslaved at all.

41. In an earlier essay, I joined other commentators in arguing that the decision in the case exemplifies the role of law in shaping the existence and meaning of racial categories, such as black, white, and Native American, in the U.S. law that protected those who were not black from being enslaved. One of the judges, for instance, said, "The distinguishing characteristics of the different species of the human race are so visibly marked, that those species may be readily discriminated from each other by mere inspection only." *Hudgins v Wrights,* 11 Va. (1 Hen. and M.), 141. The essay calls this assignment of race based on visual appearance a "scopic" determination of race, which it contrasts with assignments based on ancestry or genealogy. While many slave laws protected white economic interests, I argue that *Hudgins's* scopic rule of racial classification identified a second legally protected interest, the white liberty interest. Not surprisingly, under such a rule, the definition of "black" itself became a matter of legal contestation. See, e.g., Davis, "Identity Notes Part One," 702–711; see also Ariela J. Gross, "Litigating Whiteness: Trials of Racial Determination in the Nineteenth-Century South," *Yale Law Journal* 108 (1998): 109; Higginbotham and Kopytoff, "Racial Purity and Interracial Sex," 1975–1988.

42. *Hudgins v Wrights,* 11 Va. (1 Hen. and M.), 141 (italics in original).

43. See *Frazier v Spear,* 5 Ky. (2 Bibb) 385, 386 (1811).

44. *Hudgins v Wrights,* 11 Va. (1 Hen. and M.), 142 (italics in original).

45. *Hudgins v Wrights,* 11 Va. (1 Hen. and M.), 135 (italics in original).

46. At various points, white women, too, suffered regulations not unlike those suffered by enslaved black women. At times, white women giving birth to children deemed to be black could be sold into indentured servitude, and their children could be indentured. If an indentured white woman had a child, it could extend the period of her own indenture (the child would be indentured until an adult, as well). In one extreme iteration, in 1664, Maryland enslaved white women marrying enslaved men for the lifetime of the husband, enslaving also any children. This law was repealed due to fear of its abuse by white masters seeking to extend white female servants' period of service. See, e.g., James Hugo Johnston, *Race Relations in Virginia and Miscegenation in the South: 1776–1860* (Amherst: University of Massachusetts Press, 1970); 172–179; Thomas D. Morris, *Southern Slavery and the Law: 1619–1860* (Chapel Hill: University of North Carolina Press, 1996), 23; Martha Hodes, *White Women, Black Men: Illicit Sex in the Nineteenth-Century South* (New Haven: Yale University Press, 1997), 24–25.

47. Darlene Clark Hine concurs: "Slave women were expected to serve a dual function in this system and therefore suffered a dual oppression. They constituted an important and necessary part of the work force and they were, through their child-bearing function, the one group most responsible for the size and indeed the maintenance of the slave labor pool." Darlene Clark Hine, "Female Slave Resistance: The Economics of Sex," in *Hine Sight: Black Women and the Re-Construction of American History,* ed. Darlene Clark Hine (New York: Carlson Publishing, 1994) 27, 34.

48. *State v George,* 37 Miss. 316 (1859).

49. Ibid., 317.

50. Thomas Cobb, *An Inquiry into the Law of Negro Slavery in the United States of America* (Philadelphia: T. & J. W. Johnson and Co.; Savannah, Ga.: W. T. Williams, 1858), § 107.

51. See, e.g., Higginbotham and Kopytoff, "Racial Purity and Interracial Sex"; Morris, *Southern Slavery and the Law,* 304–307.

52. Carolyn Pitt Jones, "Litigating Reparations for African-American Female Victims of Coerced/Uninformed Sterilization and Coerced/Uninformed Norplant Implantation," 1999, 41 (memorandum written for class, on file with author).

53. "Serious prohibitions of rape strengthen the bargaining power of the weaker sexual player by making the stronger obtain consent from the weaker rather than force the sexual transaction. The various possible incarnations of rape—stranger rape, statutory rape, marital rape, acquaintance rape, and rape by abuse of familial or professional authority—mark the boundaries of one person forcibly claiming access to another's body without their consent and accordingly are central in setting the terms of such consent. . . .The law governing forcible rape also reflects the core beliefs of a society about the role of sexual access." Linda R. Hirshman and Jane E. Larson, *Hard Bargains: The Politics of Sex* (New York: Oxford University Press, 1998), 6.

54. hooks, *Ain't I a Woman,* 25–26.

55. Brenda Stevenson, for instance, describes a variety of factors that may have led some enslaved men to sexually objectify enslaved women. Stevenson, *Life in Black and White,* 242–243.

56. Genovese, *Roll, Jordan, Roll,* 420, quoting Robert Goodloe Harper, *Cotton Is King and Pro-Slavery Arguments,* ed. E. N. Elliott (New York: Vintage Books, 1976), 44–45, 61. See also Painter, "Soul Murder and Slavery," 142 (describing the complex reasoning of apologists defending the sexual norms of slavery).

57. Darlene Clark Hine notes: "Another major aspect of black women under slavery took the form of the white master's consciously constructed view of black female sexuality. This construct, which was designed to justify his own sexual passion toward her, also blamed the female slave for the sexual exploitation she experienced at the hands of her master." Hine, "Female Slave Resistance," 28.

58. Katherine Fishburn, *Women in Popular Culture: A Reference Guide* (Westport, Conn.: Greenwood Press, 1982), 10–11.

59. Davis, *Women, Race, and Class,* 23–24.

60. Enslaved men may have been sexually victimized for similar purposes; this topic is underexplored in the literature. For discussion, see Painter, "Soul Murder and Slavery," 137–138; Stevenson, *Life in Black and White,* 181, 195–196. Judith Kelleher Schafer discusses the sexual torture of an enslaved boy in "Sexual Cruelty to Slaves: The Unreported Case of *Humphreys v. Utz*," *Chicago-Kent Law Review* 68 (1993): 1313. In *Beloved*, Toni Morrison alludes to sexual abuse of black men on the chain gang. Toni Morrison, *Beloved* (New York: Knopf, 1987), 107–108.

61. Angela Y. Davis, "Reflections on the Black Woman's Role in the Community of Slaves," in *The Angela Y. Davis Reader,* ed. Joy James (Malden, Mass.: Blackwell, 1998) 111, 124 (originally published in *The Black Scholar* 3/4 [1971]: 3, 13); see also Stevenson, *Life in Black and White,* 240.

62. Dorothy Sterling, ed., *We Are Your Sisters: Black Women in the Nineteenth Century* (New York: W. W. Norton, 1984), 27. Deborah Gray White notes that the cities of New Orleans, Charleston, St. Louis, and Lexington seem to have been the centers of the trade. Gray White, *Ar'n't I a Woman?* 37. One trader insisted on separating a mother and daughter, speculating that when the daughter was a few years older, "there were men enough in New Orleans who would give five thousand dollars for such an extra handsome, fancy piece as Emily would be." Ibid., 38 (quoting Solomon Northrup, "Twelve Years a Slave: Narrative of Solomon Northrup," in *Puttin' on Ole Massa,* ed. Gilbert Osofsky [New York: Harper and Row, 1969],

268). See also Frederic Bancroft, *Slave Trading in the Old South* (1931; reprint, Columbia: University of South Carolina Press, 1996), 57, 102, 131, 328–330, in reprint; Stevenson, *Life in Black and White,* 180–181, 239.

63. "Only 'fancy' women commanded higher prices than skilled male slaves. . . . Joe Bruin of the Alexandria firm of Bruin and Hill placed Emily Russell, a beautiful mulatto whom he planned to sell as a prostitute in New Orleans, on the market for $1800. Bruin and Hill realized the profit that could be garnered from the 'fancy girl' market and often purchased females in Virginia and Maryland for that purpose." Stevenson, *Life in Black and White,* 180. This item appeared in a southern newspaper: "A slave woman is advertised to be sold in St. Louis who is so surpassingly beautiful that $5,000 has already been offered for her, at private sale, and refused." Bancroft, *Slave Trading in the Old South,* 329, see also 329–333. See also Kenneth M. Stampp, *The Peculiar Institution: Slavery in the Antebellum South* (New York: Knopf, 1956), 259.

64. Stevenson, *Life in Black and White,* 180.

65. Richard F. America, *Paying the Social Debt: What White America Owes Black America* (Westport, Conn.: Praeger, 1993), 6.

66. Orlando Patterson, *Slavery and Social Death: A Comparative Study* (Cambridge, Mass.: Harvard University Press, 1982), 50, 229, 230, 261.

67. See, e.g., Kolchin, *American Slavery,* 4. The sexual labor of enslaved women in the United States differed from sexual exploitation in other societies. The South was practically alone among slave systems in denying and prohibiting any legal recognition of women who built sexual families with their masters. See, e.g., Patterson, *Slavery and Social Death,* 231–232, 260–261.

68. David Brion Davis, *The Problem of Slavery in Western Culture* (Ithaca, N.Y.: Cornell University Press, 1966), 60.

69. Davis, *Women, Race, and Class,* 6.

70. Jones, *Labor of Love, Labor of Sorrow,* 12.

71. Catharine A. MacKinnon, *Feminism Unmodified: Discourses on Life and Law* (Cambridge, Mass.: Harvard University Press, 1987), 173; Catharine A. MacKinnon, *Toward a Feminist Theory of the State* (Cambridge, Mass.: Harvard University Press, 1989), 183, 198.

72. "When the profitability of slaves as capital became that great, as it did very early on, the market economy came to intrude deeply into the most intimate of human relationships." Oakes, *The Ruling Race,* 26.

73. "Rape and the threat of rape influenced the development of a culture of dissemblance among southern black women" in the late nineteenth and early twentieth centuries. Darlene Clark Hine, "Rape and the Inner Lives of Black Women: Thoughts on the Culture of Dissemblance," in *Hine Sight,* ed. Hine, 37. She continues, "Black women as a rule developed a politics of silence, and adhered to a cult of secrecy, a culture of dissemblance, to protect the sanctity of the inner aspects of their lives." Ibid., 41. She also makes the case that "the most common, and certainly the most compelling, motive for running, fleeing, or migrating was a desire to retain or claim some control of their own sexual beings and the children they bore." Ibid., 40–41. In addition, Hine argues that enslaved women understood their own sexual economic value and used that to resist slavery: "When they resisted sexual exploitation through such means as sexual abstention, abortion, and infanticide, they were, at the same time, rejecting their vital economic function as breeders. . . . 'The female slave, through her sexual resistance, attacked the very assumptions upon which the slave order was constructed and maintained. Resistance to sexual exploitation therefore had major political and economic implications.'" Hine, "Female Slave Resistance," 34. See also Stevenson, *Life in Black and White,* 245–246.

74. In two path-breaking essays, Painter argues that historians have failed to approach sexual abuse in the context of interracial households as families and enslaved women as workers and hence have missed critical psychological effects that spanned all of southern society.

Nell Irvin Painter, "Of *Lily*, Linda Brent, and Freud: A Non-Exceptionalist Approach to Race, Class, and Gender in the Slave South," in *Half Sisters of History: Southern Women and the American Past,* ed. Catherine Clinton (Durham, N.C.: Duke University Press, 1994), 93; Painter, "Soul Murder and Slavery," 126–128.

75. Darlene Clark Hine puts it powerfully: "The fundamental tensions between black women and the rest of the society—especially white men, white women, and to a lesser extent, black men—involved a multifaceted struggle to determine who would control black women's productive and reproductive capacities and their sexuality. At stake for black women caught up in this ever evolving, constantly shifting, but relentless war was the acquisition of personal autonomy and economic liberation." Hine, "Rape and the Inner Lives of Black Women," 41.

"And We Claim Our Rights"

The Rights Rhetoric of Black and White Women Activists before the Civil War

CARLA L. PETERSON

PERSONAL STATEMENT My grandmother died on September 6, 1985, at the age of 101. She had survived so many health problems—operations for glaucoma, cataracts, ovarian cysts—that I had convinced myself this day would never come. But it did, and it overwhelmed me. Since I was just starting a sabbatical leave and was not distracted by day-to-day work obligations, I had time not so much to indulge my grief as to reminisce about this amazing woman who had lived with my family as I was growing up and who had indeed helped to raise me.

Much of this reminiscing was done as I wandered aimlessly around Washington, D.C., going to bookstores, museums, and art galleries. It was on one of these occasions that I walked into a bookstore and picked up a copy of Dorothy Sterling's *We Are Your Sisters*, a book about black women activists in the nineteenth century, and stood reading it utterly spellbound. On the spot, I decided to reorient my scholarship and study nineteenth-century black women's writing as a way of paying tribute to my grandmother and remaining connected to her. Out of this decision, my book *"Doers of the Word": African-American Women Speakers and Writers in the North (1830–1880)* took shape.

Born in Jamaica in the 1880s, my grandmother came to the United States with my mother through Ellis Island during World War I. She found a job as a seamstress and the two of them lived in Harlem, where my grandmother sewed dresses for a nickel and my mother attended public school. But my grandmother wanted to give her daughter something that had been denied her, a higher education. So she scraped and saved, and as a result my mother was able to attend

Barnard College and subsequently graduate from Columbia Medical School in 1936.

In the 1930s, this was no mean feat for an immigrant Jamaican woman with a sixth-grade education and her daughter to achieve. And yet what always puzzled me was that neither my grandmother nor my mother saw themselves as "feminists" in the current usage of the word. During the 1960s, when I was in college and my mother was the director of the Smith College Medical Services, feminist talk was all around us, and yet my grandmother and mother could only talk about those "bra-burning women's libbers." I gradually came to understand that for my grandmother work was an essential part of life. To work was a given, not a choice, and no form of work was devalued. What should be a choice is the kind of work one desires to pursue; and for my grandmother, this liberation transcended gender. So it was just as important to her that she had enabled one of my mother's high school friends to fulfill his dream of becoming an engineer as it was that she had helped my mother get through medical school. Studying the work of nineteenth-century black women had enabled me to understand the tradition that so informed my grandmother's life, the tradition of work and community.

---

*I*n May 1866, black activist Frances E. W. Harper delivered a speech at the eleventh National Woman's Rights Convention. Born free in Baltimore in 1825, Harper had been at the forefront of the racial uplift, abolitionist, and temperance movements and had traveled throughout the New England, mid-Atlantic, and Midwestern regions since the mid-1850s, delivering her message in public lectures, newspaper articles, and at least two published volumes of poems. Yet Harper's affiliation with the woman's rights movement—created by white middle-class women at Seneca Falls in 1848 to protest their political, social, and legal inequality and increasingly dedicated to issues of suffrage—was new. Harper confessed, "I feel I am something of a novice upon this platform," and she proceeded to give an unusually personal lecture prompted by her memory of the recent death of her husband after a brief marriage and her dawning awareness of how little protection the law offered widowed women:

> But my husband died in debt; and before he had been in his grave three months, the administrator had swept the very milk-crocks and wash tubs from my hands. I was a farmer's wife and made butter for the Columbus market; but what could I do, when they had swept all away? They had left me one thing—and that was a looking-glass! Had I died instead of my husband, how different would have been the result! By this time he would have had another wife, it is likely; and no administrator would have gone into his house, broken up his home, and sold his bed, and taken away his

means of support. . . . I say, then, that justice is not fulfilled so long as woman is unequal before the law.[1]

In this opening statement Harper defined herself as a married woman, specifically, as a farmer's wife whose widowhood limited her capacity to work. In thus invoking her marital status, Harper suggested her commonality with the white middle-class women before her whose culture she knew placed such importance on marriage. She focused in particular on the inequities of marriage laws that leave the widow of an indebted household with her paraphernalia alone—defined by Norma Basch as "special articles of clothing and ornaments suitable to her station in life"—in contrast to the widower, who cannot be held responsible for debts incurred by his wife after marriage.[2] Deemed "unequal before the law" by a patriarchal legal system, the indebted widow is left with superfluous ornaments instead of the necessary tools of labor.

As Harper continued her speech, however, she proceeded to reject the unitary category of "woman" and to distance herself from "you white women," whose racial privilege separates them from black women and supersedes any common inequality before the law: "I do not believe that white women are dewdrops just exhaled from the skies. . . . While there exists this brutal element in society which tramples upon the feeble and treads down the weak, I tell you that if there is any class of people who need to be lifted out of their airy nothings and selfishness, it is the white women of America."[3] In contrast to such "dewdrops," Harper offered the model of Harriet Tubman, whose concern for her enslaved people had earned her the name of Moses. And she proposed to replace the category of "woman" with the more complex one of "humanity," which would include emancipated slaves, northern blacks like herself still living amidst racial discrimination, and poor whites neglected by the slaveholding powers: "We are all bound up together in one great bundle of humanity."[4]

To my mind, Harper's speech is one of the most powerful in all of nineteenth-century African American oratory; it uses a vivid personal anecdote to analyze a larger social reality: the complex relationship that existed between black and white women during this period. In this essay I extend Harper's project to engage in a comparative analysis of the antebellum rhetoric of rights employed by black and white women in both oratory and narrative in order to illuminate the profound ideological differences that existed—and still exist—between them. From this perspective, writing and speaking constitute forms of social activism and hence forms of work.

Mainstream accounts of the origins of the woman's rights movement contend that these must be located in white women's antislavery activities begun in the mid-1830s. Angelina Grimké, for example, asserted that her growing awareness of slaves' lack of rights led her to a better understanding of the lim-

its placed by male abolitionists on her own public activism. These women created a feminist-abolitionist discourse grounded in a comparison of white
woman—most especially the married woman, or *feme covert,* who, in marrying, loses her legal existence to become her husband's property—to the slave:
"Then may we well be termed the 'white slaves of the North.'"[5] This class-based
account ignores, however, the rights discourse of white working women who
were employed in New England textile factories and who organized themselves
in the mid-1830s to protest their increasing economic disempowerment, and
in the process also compared their lot to that of slaves. Taking yet another
approach, Barbara Berg has argued that white women's struggle for self- and
social emancipation existed well before these two social movements; she suggests that feminism's origins must be sought in the early 1800s in white
women's formation of female voluntary associations that functioned as organizational antecedents to the later societies.[6]

Not surprisingly, African American women are largely absent from such
accounts. Black feminist scholars need then to tell a new history that fills in the
current gaps. We need to point out that it was free black women in the North
who, in the face of severe discrimination and poverty, were among the first to
organize mutual aid and benevolent societies.[7] And we need to emphasize that,
much like their white counterparts, antebellum black women also protested
their unequal status, laying claim to the full legal and civil rights of citizenship
promised by the Declaration of Independence and the Constitution. Yet black
women's circumstances and strategies also differed radically. Confronting
white men, white women complained that their legal disabilities had rendered
them like slaves and turned to the law for remedy. In contrast, black women
addressed their appeals to three groups: white men, white women, and black
men. If they invoked slavery, it was most often not as an analogy but as a historical reality that directly affected black women's lives. And, if they referred to
white women, it was not to suggest similarity but to underscore the latters'
racial privilege that often resulted in the oppression of blacks in both slavery
and the free workforce. Most importantly, however, black women asserted their
rights not only for themselves as individuals and as women but for the entire
community. Aware of the limitations of rights claims, finally, they insisted on
complementing them with a discourse of responsibility, one that spelled out
the collective needs and obligations of both black women and men.

/ / /

In addition to Harper, Sojourner Truth, Harriet Jacobs, Maria Stewart, and
Harriet Wilson also committed themselves to the work of social activism in
the decades before the Civil War. Two of these women, Sojourner Truth and

Harriet Jacobs, were born slaves. Emancipated in 1827 with the end of slavery in New York State, Truth was an active abolitionist and one of the few black women to participate in the white woman's rights movement; unable to read or write, she made her mark as an impassioned orator. In contrast, Jacobs was a slave from North Carolina who escaped to the North in 1842; she lived at different times in New York, Boston, and Rochester, where she affiliated with both white and black antislavery groups and in 1861 published her autobiographical narrative, *Incidents in the Life of a Slave Girl*. For her part, Stewart, a freeborn northerner, married a Boston merchant; after his untimely death, she underwent a conversion experience and also became active in the city's racial uplift causes in the early 1830s. As the first American woman to speak in front of a promiscuous audience (composed of women and men), Stewart's work also appeared in writing; a pamphlet, "Religion and the Pure Principles of Morality: The Sure Foundation on Which We Must Build," was published in 1831, and four of her lectures were reprinted in William Lloyd Garrison's *Liberator*. The most obscure of the women, Harriet Wilson, is known to us primarily through her 1859 novelized autobiography, *Our Nig*, in which her life serves as a protest against conditions of indentured servitude and discriminatory work practices in New England. What these women held in common was that they all conceived of writing and lecturing not only as social activism but also as paid labor that would enable them to earn a living. And in their writing and lecturing, all five of them made the issue of work central to their discussions of African American rights and responsibilities.

From the very beginnings of black activism, African American women and men alike appropriated the dominant culture's discourse of rights to insist that full freedom and equality be granted to them as well. In her pamphlet, Maria Stewart forcefully reminded her readers that "according to the Constitution of these United States, [God] hath made all men free and equal" and went on to wonder, if this were indeed so, "why should man any longer deprive his fellowman of equal rights and privileges?" Stewart concluded her protest with the exhortation "AND WE CLAIM OUR RIGHTS," based on her profound faith in the liberatory power of rights rhetoric.[8] For most of the antebellum period, black leaders remained convinced that such claims to rights could effectively challenge white supremacist thinking and bring about full inclusion into American public life.

Many contemporary critical legal scholars have criticized rights rhetoric, arguing that it fixes claimants in a socially subordinate position and makes them passively dependent on those from whom they are seeking rights. Sojourner Truth seems to have been aware of this potential danger when, in her 1853 lecture to the Mob Convention in New York City, she tacitly acknowledged the dependency of the rights claimant on those in power. In her speech, she invoked the figure of Queen Esther, who had gained rights for her people based on the king's liberality alone: "And he was so liberal that he said, 'the half of my kingdom shall be granted to thee,' and he did not wait for her to be asked he was so liberal with her."[9] In Truth's evocation of Esther, rights petitioners are at the mercy of their grantors' liberality; they remain subordinate and passive, with the impulse for effective action deferred and the means of achieving permanent rights unresolved.

In contrast to Esther, antebellum black women recast the rights rhetoric of their speeches and writings as active struggle. They needed first of all to struggle against the limits that black men sought to impose on their activities in the public sphere. In this regard, Stewart was by far the most vocal of the five women. Her grievances were, in fact, not that different from those launched by Angelina Grimké against white male abolitionists when, in her "Farewell Address," Stewart accused Boston's black male leadership of conspiring to limit her public activism. Insisting that it was God who had "raise[d] up your own females to strive, by their example both in public and private, to assist those who are endeavoring to stop the strong current of prejudice . . . against us," Stewart demanded that black men "no longer ridicule their efforts" but support them.[10] To Stewart's voice we may add those of Jarena Lee and Mary Ann Shadd Cary, who likewise complained of the inhibitions placed by black men on their public work—preaching in Lee's case, newspaper editorship in Cary's. Yet it was not until the postbellum period that black women would craft a more fully developed rights discourse directed against black men. In the 1860s, Truth, for example, would worry that the passage of the Fifteenth Amendment, granting the vote to black men alone, would create a dangerous inequality between black men and women.

In the antebellum period, however, black women turned most especially to the dominant culture to articulate their grievances and claim their rights. As they continued to demand African Americans' right to the full privileges of citizenship, they also came to insist on black women's specific right to control their own bodies—whether for work or pleasure—and to pursue forms of self-development that would benefit both themselves and their families and communities. In the process, they emphasized their difference from white women, pointing to the latters' collusion in the degradation of black women's bodies in both the economy of slavery and northern workforces.

For these black women, freedom and equality meant first of all ownership of their own bodies. In her religious pamphlet, Stewart inveighed against the sexual work forced upon black women in a racist society—"America, America, thou hast caused the daughters of Africa to commit whoredoms and fornications"—and predicted that "Africans" would soon rise up in protest.[11] In *Incidents in the Life of a Slave Girl,* Harriet Jacobs described with great explicitness her master Dr. Flint's repeated attempts to control her body. Her narrative reaches beyond condemnation of male sexual abuse, however, to underscore white women's collaboration in it and the consequent gulf that separates black women from white; in exposing her mistress's refusal to protect her, for example, Jacobs points to the larger issue of the unavailability of the protective privileges of domesticity to slave girls. Moreover, if *Incidents* begins as an appeal to the white women of the North to help slave women gain the right to control their own bodies, it increasingly betrays a lack of faith in northern will subsequent to the passage of the Fugitive Slave Act. The narrative insists that slave girls must rely on their own agency; Jacobs herself does so by choosing another white man as her lover, hiding in her grandmother's garret, escaping to the North, and finally manipulating Flint through fictitious letter-writing.[12]

Sojourner Truth's speeches further illustrate how the slave woman's lack of control over her body is due not only to the sexual economy of slavery but to the enforced labor of the slave system as well; slavery has transformed her body into something other than a "woman" as defined by the norms of the dominant culture. In the "Ain't I a Woman?" version of her 1851 speech to the Akron Woman's Rights Convention, Truth acknowledged her difference from the white woman who "needs to be helped into carriages, and lifted over ditches, and to hab de best place everywhar, [while] nobody eber helps me into carriages, or ober mud-puddles, or gib me any best place." Slave labor has turned her into a worker whose femininity is distinctly at odds with white womanhood: her productive labor has masculinized her; her reproductive labor, which forced her to bear thirteen children for the benefit of the slave system and to suckle her masters' children, has denied her a place in the female domestic sphere. Yet a much earlier and often neglected version of this same speech, printed in the 21 June 1851 *Anti-Slavery Bugle,* suggests that Truth's real goal was to redefine the concept of womanhood for black women by reconfiguring her self-identity as a productive worker: the refrain "ain't I a woman?" becomes "I can do as much work as any man."[13]

In fact, the right to engage in productive labor pervades black women's antebellum speeches and writings. Harriet Wilson's *Our Nig,* for example, provides a fictionalized account of her own futile attempts to live as an economically independent black woman worker in New Hampshire; in and of itself, it constitutes an impassioned plea for the right to self-support. Abandoned as a child in the home of a white family, the Bellmonts, the protagonist Frado is forced into an indentured servitude which is a de facto form of slavery: working without a contract and never compensated for her labor, Frado is at the mercy of the Bellmonts, particularly the women of the household, who treat her harshly. Even after the termination of her indenture, however, Frado's life does not improve. Married and then abandoned, she is obliged to reenter the labor force. Interestingly enough, this reentry is made possible only through the intervention of white women, who once again act as her patrons. Furthermore, the labor that Frado engages in—the making of straw hats as a form of New England rural outwork—fully explodes the myth of free labor in the North. This industry was fully enmeshed in colonial and slave systems as its raw material, straw, was imported from the Caribbean and the finished product, hats, were sold in the South to slaveholders for use by their slaves. Finally, Frado's participation in this industry is dead-ended and never results in the economic advantages that accrue to her white counterparts: her wages are not a supplement to a farming family's income, nor is her labor a transition to the more remunerative work of New England factories.[14]

Even more explicitly than Wilson, Stewart chastised her "fairer sisters" for their willingness to discriminate against black women in the workforce and confine them to "continual hard labor [that] deadens the energies of the soul, and benumbs the faculties of the mind." It is in this context that Stewart resorted to a metaphor of slavery, not as a legal status that links black women to white, but as an image of drudge work that constricts the mind: "Yet, after all, methinks there are no chains so galling as those that bind the soul, and exclude it from the vast field of useful and scientific knowledge."[15] Stewart's larger goal here was to assert the right for black women to pursue an education and acquire the same forms of useful knowledge available to white women.

If grievance is the tone that dominates Wilson's narrative and Stewart's Franklin Hall lecture, Jacobs's *Incidents* records a moment of triumphal assertion of rights. Despite her escape North, Jacobs's freedom is still highly conditional: she remains a slave to the Flint family and an economically dependent servant to Mrs. Bruce, a white woman for whose child she cares. In this position, she experiences a humiliating incident of racial discrimination at a northern hotel when she faces the hostility of white nurses who oppose her presence at their table; but, as she tells us, "finding I was resolved to stand up for my rights, they concluded to treat me well. Let every colored man and woman do this, and eventually we shall cease to be trampled underfoot by our oppressors."[16] Significantly, Jacobs's appeal here is to both black men and women; given the pervasiveness of racial prejudice and discrimination, she knew that claims of individual rights or rights for women alone were not sufficient. Indeed, Jacobs and other black women activists came to complement their

discourse of rights with a discourse of responsibility that insisted on obligations to family, community, and race; in the process, they specified the kind of
work required of both black women and men; and they conceived of gender
roles as complementary or even overlapping.

Black women's appreciation of family and community was shaped in part
by their particular relationship to *coverture,* which differed substantially from
that of white women. Black women yearned for what many white women
could take for granted: the intimacy of marital relations, the protection and
material advantage these often provided, and, for women of the elite, access to
men of influence and power. For slave women such as Truth and Jacobs, legal
marriage was an impossibility. In the "free" North, socioeconomic conditions
often hindered marriage among blacks, and protection on the part of the husband was not always possible. Wilson's Frado, for example, marries Samuel
only to discover that he has been masquerading as an escaped slave in order to
acquire work as an antislavery lecturer from white abolitionists; he is forced to
imposture to make a living. Finally, in many northern communities black
women outnumbered black men, limiting their chances for marriage. As a consequence of these factors, some black women came to accept intimate relationships with men outside of the marriage bond. Others deliberately chose the
status of *feme sole,* or single woman. Indeed, considerable evidence exists to
suggest that a number of black women actively resisted *coverture,* determined
to make the most of the economic advantages allowed single women: the ability to acquire property and retain legal control over it and, most significantly,
the ability to buy enslaved relatives.[17] In this respect, black women manipulated the laws of *coverture* in ways that most white women did not.

Given the particular configuration of African American marital and familial relations, black women recognized the importance of, and responsibility to,
family and community. Adapted from African models, black households were
often based on domestic kin networks organized around blood rather than
conjugal ties; they were sometimes extended to include non-kin networks of
single boarders or relatives brought together in multifamily housing. In these
households, black women's responsibilities predominated in the formation of
kin and non-kin domestic units, child rearing, and in-house economic contributions, but they also received considerable support from black men. In *Incidents,* for example, Jacobs describes her grandmother's home as a household
that thrives on the margins of plantation and capitalist economies. Her grandmother presides over a four-generation extended family organized around
blood ties. Within this household unit she establishes an in-house economy
that produces goods for sale, the profits of which are returned to the community. When called upon, she expands her domestic network to include non-kin

members in need of shelter and protection. And she is helped in all of these tasks by her son, Phillip, who, for example, makes the necessary arrangements to hide Jacobs in the garret.

In Jacobs's text, family and community become all the more important to her once they have been disrupted by her escape North. In Philadelphia, Jacobs is convinced that she looks so foreign that people "could not easily decide to what nation [she] belonged."[18] In New York, she confronts a city of strangers when she attempts to rebuild her old neighborhood peopled by refugees from home. Unable to recreate her grandmother's household, she plans how "by dint of labor and economy, [she] could make a home for [her] children."[19] In this home, Jacobs, as a feme sole, will be her children's protector.

In her pamphlet and sermons, Stewart offered an even broader agenda for the implementation of African American community work, an agenda in which discourses of rights and responsibilities for both black men and women are inextricably intertwined and firmly grounded in the truth of Scripture. To Stewart, women's and men's racial uplift efforts were not divergent but complementary. Her attitude toward black men was highly complex as she sought both to limit and to extend their authority. If, as we have seen, she protested against black men's attempts to inhibit women's public work, she also sought to extend their responsibilities within both the community and the larger public sphere in emulation of white men's activism. If black men were to establish educational institutions and temperance societies, they must also raise their voices against the Colonization Society and send antislavery petitions to Congress. Beyond that, Stewart appropriated the rhetoric of black men themselves to invoke the concept of "manhood rights." A masculine concept, manhood rights called upon black men to claim for themselves those rights for which American men had fought in 1776—physical self-defense, economic competition, patriarchal authority within the household, political participation in the nation at large—and hence to challenge racist notions of an emasculated black race.

In so doing, Stewart paradoxically sought to extend to black men those very rights that white women complained that white men used against them, and she appeared to aspire to forms of female respectability that suggested a dangerous concession to the dominant culture's ideology of true womanhood and a willingness to be entrapped in that very prison of domesticity from which white women were seeking escape: "Have you prayed the legislature for mercy's sake to grant you all the rights and privileges of free citizens, that your daughters may rise to that degree of respectability which true merit deserves?"[20] Indeed, in many instances Stewart defined the role of black women as that of "keepers at home," where their task was to spread moral influence throughout the household and thereby shape the values of husbands and children.[21] Yet, it is important to note that Stewart here was demanding the right to respectability, a right taken for granted by middle-class white women but unavailable to black women. Stewart was, in fact, striving to move beyond Truth's definition of black women as workers to envision possibilities that were radically new to black women in the 1830s—possibilities that she believed would strengthen both family and community life.

At the same time, Stewart sought ways for black women to move beyond the domestic sphere in order to improve conditions in the black community. In her pamphlet, she evoked the possibility of a space that is neither public nor private but rather takes the values of the domestic sphere and extends them into the community. She suggested, for example, that black women follow the example of "The good women of Wethersfield, Conn., [who] toiled in the blazing sun, year after year, weeding onions, then sold the seed and procured enough money to erect them a house of worship. . . . Let every female heart become united, and let us raise a fund ourselves; and at the end of one year and a half, we might be able to lay the corner stone for the building of a High School, that the higher branches of knowledge might be enjoyed by us."[22]

In passages such as these, Stewart encouraged the further development of black women's associations created at the beginning of the century. Historians have suggested that many of these societies' constitutions followed those of white organizations as formal documents. Yet, as Anne Boylan has pointed out, black women's organizations evolved quite differently from those of white women. The latter tended to be benevolent societies, dedicated to helping the less fortunate and thereby reinforcing class distinctions, rather than mutual aid societies based on notions of self-help among equal members. In contrast, black women's societies combined mutual aid, benevolence, and self-improvement, providing services to both neighbors and strangers, indeed, to the community as a whole.[23] Even more significantly, Stewart's model is also characteristic of traditional West African societies, where no clear-cut distinction is made between women's domestic roles and their public economic roles and where women participate in the wider economy through farming and trading. Although we have no way of knowing to what extent Stewart might have been aware of the economic role of African women, her consistent identification of U.S. blacks as African points to a pride in her African heritage. Moreover, as Marsha Darling has argued, beyond the official rhetoric of these societies' documents lies a cultural ethos that is rooted in African First Principles, "a tradition based on a belief in a common good, reciprocity, accountability, right action, and compassion," linking those of means to the less fortunate.[24]

Let us now return to Harper's speech and ask how white women—both feminist-abolitionists and labor activists—might have developed it. Each group would have grounded its argument in analogy—the "slavery of sex" and "wage slavery," respectively—to give voice to women's legal and economic dispossession and claim to rights. Given the goals of this essay, I focus exclusively on the use of these analogies rather than on other forms of discourse precisely because white women based their claim to rights on this comparison of white to black. The reliance on analogy—which intimates the similarity between two unlike entities—is particularly instructive: it allows the speaker to select the term with which to compare the chosen object or idea and, in the process, to emphasize one particular feature over all others. It functions, moreover, as a form of explanation by suggesting that the same cause has given rise to the similarity of features. Finally, in emphasizing similarity, analogy often seeks to suppress what does not fit; and yet, since similarity never means exact sameness, difference always remains.[25] Hence, although the slavery analogies of antebellum white women seem straightforward enough, their use over time indicates increasing tensions and ambivalences.

The feminist-abolitionists who invoked the slavery-of-sex analogy included women such as Angelina and Sarah Grimké, sisters born into a wealthy South Carolinian slaveholding family, who moved to Philadelphia, became Quakers, and converted to abolitionism; Lucretia Mott, from Philadelphia, who not only fought slavery but decried racism within the antislavery ranks; Elizabeth Cady Stanton, one of the founding members of the woman's rights movement and convener of the 1848 Seneca Falls convention; and even Margaret Fuller, author of the feminist tract *Woman in the Nineteenth Century.* Like Maria Stewart, these women initially grounded their appeals in the truth of Scripture, insisting on the equality and moral responsibility of each individual before God; as the woman's rights movement became more formalized, however, many came to substitute legal arguments for moral arguments. And although they, too, insisted on women's right to higher education and to comparable worth in the workplace, they knew that social convention dictated marriage to be their primary form of work. Most of these women were in fact married and were not motivated by economic necessity as their black counterparts were; to them, public speaking and writing were forms of social service rather than paid labor. Hence, they focused on the legal disabilities of the *feme covert* and protested her exclusion from public life and relegation to the domestic sphere.

According to Anglo-American common law, once a marriage has been contracted, it is no longer a contract. Rather, the husband becomes his wife's protector and she is transformed into a covered woman, or *feme covert,* relegated to the private domestic sphere. Under *coverture,* a wife is absorbed into her husband, becomes one with him, and no longer has a separate legal existence: she cannot own personal property but is herself property; since she is propertyless, the right to make a will is unnecessary and the laws of dower limit what she may inherit; finally, she is excluded from commercial life and denied the ability to contract.[26] Her status contrasts sharply with that of the anomalous single woman, or feme sole, whose lack of *coverture* enables her to maintain a legal existence. It is such a loss of rights that allowed Sarah Grimké to invoke the slavery-of-sex analogy: "Laws bear with peculiar rigor on married women: 'By marriage, the husband and wife are one person in law; that is, the very being, or legal existence of the woman is suspended during the marriage. . . . Here now, the very being of a woman, like that of a slave, is absorbed in her master.'"[27]

Assertions that the legal status of married women is "like that of a slave" are indeed accurate and correctly point to the law as the common cause of this similarity. Yet the analogy works only on the level of abstraction and not on that of daily lived life; as Harper was well aware, it suppresses crucial differences of race and class. On a purely legal level, it failed to address the ways in which certain laws did help married women circumvent *coverture,* in particular, the right under special conditions to maintain separate estates and the more general rights of dower and petition. On the level of social practice, it failed to acknowledge the privileges accorded to white married women— domesticity, protected family life, placement on the pedestal, educational opportunities—however confining or limited these might be. Most particularly, the analogy obscured the importance of white women's kinship ties to men of the elite—fathers, brothers, husbands. These ties allowed them access to those in power, access denied to slave and free black women alike.

In turn, white women workers, such as the factory girls at the Lowell (Massachusetts) mills, invoked the analogy of wage slavery within the larger context of its widespread use from the 1830s on by working-class white men to describe their sense of economic disempowerment in the burgeoning democratic nation. In contrast to their elite counterparts, the ambivalence of these working women toward the comparison was more explicit. If they asserted their affinity to black slaves, they also insisted on their difference from them; in the face of economic hardship, they clung to their identity as free people based on their whiteness.

Established according to the family model of the domestic household, the mills were a racialized institution that excluded black women. The mill girls were, in fact, the unmarried daughters of independent Yankee yeomen, and they engaged in paid labor in order to enjoy a period of legal and economic autonomy before marriage and subjection to the laws of coverture. As early as 1834, however, they chose to protest wage cuts by "turning-out" (striking) and writing petitions in which they invoked the wage-slavery analogy in order explicitly to reject it and proclaim their status as free people: "The oppressing hand of avarice would enslave us . . . ; [but] as we are free, we would remain in possession of what kind Providence has bestowed upon us, and remain daughters of freemen still."[28] By the 1840s, however, this female working population had changed: the majority were foreign born and constituted a permanent force engaged in unskilled labor as a result of mechanization. Faced with a severe economic depression, these women insisted that they were driven by forms of economic necessity approaching the condition of enslavement: "Voluntary! A slave too goes voluntarily to his task, but his will is in some manner quickened by the whip of the overseer. The whip which brings us to Lowell is NECESSITY."[29] Left unexamined in this analogy is the fact that there existed a free time before necessity drove these women to Lowell, that they owned their labor and that it was paid, however meagerly.

Significantly, in both of these slavery analogies the legally and economically disabled slave almost always remained ungendered, referred to by the generic pronoun "he." In so doing, feminist-abolitionists and labor activists alike erased the specific historical experiences of the black woman worker. When they did refer to the black female slave in their public discourse, however, both groups tellingly shifted rhetorical strategies to emphasize difference rather than similarity. This distancing occurred especially at those moments when blackness was sexualized and thus made white women's kinship to black women undesirable.

In such instances, working-class women invoked the analogy of wage slavery only to reject it unequivocally. Indeed, by the 1840s many Lowell factory girls openly acknowledged that their "enslavement" was no longer confined to their lack of control over their labor power but extended to their sexual vulnerability as well. In 1846 one worker referred to "the thousands of unprotected white females of Lowell [made] slaves to the overseers [who] can do with them as any passion may dictate." Yet, having admitted her similarity to slave women as both economically and sexually exploitable, the writer then explicitly distanced herself, insisting that female slaves were more fortunate since they had "a master and an owner to protect [them]." Leaving black women behind, she concluded with a question firmly grounded in her sense of white racial privilege: "It is indeed high time for men of the United States . . . to seriously inquire . . . whether there is no remedy for such a slavish condition of American white women?"[30] Asserting racial difference rather than the common ground of labor, white working women sought refuge in their status as white Americans.

In turn, when feminist-abolitionists addressed the issue of the sexual exploitation of female slaves, they abandoned the use of comparison altogether, disassociating themselves from black women and crafting narratives that shifted emphasis from gender similarity to racial difference. In striking contrast to their black contemporaries as well as to their British predecessor Mary Wollstonecraft, these feminist-abolitionists remained reluctant publicly to discuss their own sexual enslavement—their inability as covered women to own and control their bodies—before the late 1850s; they did so only in private, unpublished documents or in the safer form of fiction.[31] The one notable exception was Fanny Wright, a radical freethinker and utopian socialist, whose views impelled feminist-abolitionists and suffragists alike to disown her and acknowledge her contributions only late in the century.

The power of white women's claims to rights lay in these slavery analogies even as these very analogies silenced black women's voices and thoughts, more often than not forced the black female slave to carry the burden of female sexual vulnerability, and finally disregarded the specific needs of black women and their communities. One of the most significant forms of redress that white women sought to acquire was the right to petition as a means of improving their civil and economic status—a right that black abolitionists like Stewart had envisioned as a political act that would allow a measure of participation in public life and hopefully facilitate entry into full citizenship. Hence, in the 1840s white women in the woman's rights movement petitioned state legislatures for the passage of Married Women's Property Acts while the Lowell girls petitioned for a ten-hour workday; significantly, however, in neither of these movements were black women included as active participants or as beneficiaries of reform. It is true that in their antislavery petitions feminist-abolitionists made slave women the object of their concern; yet the nature of their petitioning differed substantially from that of black abolitionists as it served to reinforce the racial and class differences that Harper had so dramatically underscored in her speech: as they "sent petitions up to their different legislatures, entreating their husbands, fathers, brothers, and sons," these women reaffirmed their kinship ties to white men of power while distancing themselves from those oppressed slaves in whom they "endeavoured to inculcate submission."[32]

In demanding legal redress, white women ultimately aspired to achieve what political philosopher C. B. MacPherson has called "possessive individualism," according to which an individual owns himself and hence exists freely and independently of the will of others; in this condition, he can enter voluntarily into commercial transactions with similar independent beings on an equal basis. Recent legal theorists have argued, however, that, given the coercive nature of the capitalist market, the concept of equal citizens entering of their own free will into voluntary interactions with one another is mere illusion.[33] Nonetheless, aware of the degree to which possessive individualism regulated contemporary social life, feminist-abolitionists and labor activists alike sought the right to contract as a way of improving their labor conditions whether in marriage or in the workforce. At the 1854 New York Woman's Rights Convention, Elizabeth Cady Stanton insisted that "the femme covert must have the right to make contracts"; hence, marriage itself becomes a contract.[34] If one of the by-products of contractual relations is that they do not dwell on personalities but rather envision persons as strangers, then marital relations themselves no longer are purely personal and confined to the domestic sphere, but are subject to contract law and perhaps even state regulation, providing the *feme covert* with greater legal protection. At no point, however, did feminist-abolitionists minimize the social importance of marriage, which could link them to men of power. For their part, labor activists sought to force their employers into contractual arrangements that would ensure their economic independence before marriage; but they, too, never questioned the social structures that defined their lives. Finally, in embracing contract law, neither group of women fully understood the illusory nature of the concept of equal citizens entering freely and voluntarily into commercial transactions.

/ / /

In crafting a discourse of responsibility, black women recognized that in the antebellum United States possessive individualism could not in and of itself ensure the well-being of self, community, and race. Given the constraints placed upon African American lives, these women were well aware of the unequal nature of contractual transactions. Moreover, they understood that while contractual activity might bestow benefits upon individual parties, these did not necessarily extend to the wider community; they recognized as well that such benefits are necessarily qualified and insecure when individuals remain inextricably tied to their race. Beyond these legal concerns, finally, they took full measure of the enduring presence of the "soul," which, as Stewart noted, can be numbed but never contracted for.

Yet, despite these differences, social and cultural affinities between black and white women did exist. Black women availed themselves of the right to contract whenever feasible—laboring for wages, marrying, acquiring property. In turn, some white women looked beyond possessive individualism to embrace a discourse of responsibility; the "good women of Wethersfield" whom Stewart held up for emulation were, for example, white rural women. Given the impasse that black and white women seem to have reached today, perhaps a new historicized understanding of nineteenth-century discourses of rights and responsibility can provide a groundwork for future cross-racial alliances.

NOTES

1. Frances E. W. Harper, *Proceedings of the Eleventh Woman's Rights Convention* (New York: Robert J. Johnston, 1866), 45–46.

2. Norma Basch, *In the Eyes of the Law* (Ithaca: Cornell University Press, 1982), 53; Marylynn Salmon, *Women and the Law of Property in Early America* (Chapel Hill: University of North Carolina Press, 1986), 226–227.

3. Harper, *Proceedings*, 46, 48.

4. Ibid., 46, 47.

5. Quoted in *The Public Years of Sarah and Angelina Grimké*, ed. Larry Ceplair (New York: Columbia University Press, 1989), 132.

6. Barbara Berg, *The Remembered Gate* (New York: Oxford University Press, 1978), 5–6.

7. Anne Firor Scott, *Natural Allies* (Urbana: University of Illinois Press, 1992), 13–14.

8. Maria W. Stewart, "Religion and the Pure Principles of Morality: The Sure Foundation on Which We Must Build," in *America's First Black Political Writer*, ed. Marilyn Richardson (Bloomington: Indiana University Press, 1987), 29, 39, 40.

9. Quoted in *History of Woman Suffrage*, ed. Elizabeth Cady Stanton, Susan B. Anthony, and Matilda Joslyn Gage (New York: Fowler and Wells, 1881–1922), 1: 568. For a discussion of legal scholars' critique of rights rhetoric, see Kimberlé Williams Crenshaw, "Race, Reform, and Retrenchment: Transformation and Legitimation in Antidiscrimination Law," *Harvard Law Review* 101 (May 1988): 1352–1355.

10. Maria W. Stewart, "Mrs. Stewart's Farewell Address to Her Friends in the City of Boston," in Richardson, *America's First Black Political Writer*, 69.

11. Stewart, "Religion and the Pure Principles of Morality," 39.

12. Harriet Jacobs, *Incidents in the Life of a Slave Girl*, ed. Jean Fagan Yellin (1861; reprint, Harvard University Press, 1987).

13. Quoted in Stanton, Anthony, and Gage, *History of Woman Suffrage*, 1: 116; *Anti-Slavery Bugle* (Salem, Ohio), 21 June 1851.

14. Harriet E. Wilson, *Our Nig; Or, Sketches from the Life of a Free Black*, ed. Henry Louis Gates Jr. (1859; reprint, New York: Random House, 1983); for a discussion of New England rural outwork, see Thomas Dublin, *Transforming Women's Work* (Ithaca: Cornell University Press, 1994), 33–75.

15. Maria W. Stewart, "Lecture Delivered at the Franklin Hall," in Richardson, *America's First Black Political Writer*, 45, 47.

16. Jacobs, *Incidents*, 177.

17. Suzanne Lebsock, *The Free Women of Petersburg* (New York: W. W. Norton, 1984), 99–109.

18. Jacobs, *Incidents*, 160.

19. Ibid., 169.

20. Maria W. Stewart, "Lecture Delivered at the Franklin Hall," 49.

21. Stewart, "Religion and the Pure Principles of Morality," 33.

22. Ibid., 37.

23. On the constitutions of black women's societies, see Dorothy Sterling, *We Are Your Sisters* (New York: W. W. Norton, 1984), 108; on the differences between white and black women's societies, see Ann Boylan, "Benevolence and Antislavery Activity among African-American Women in New York and Boston, 1820–1840," in *The Abolitionist Sisterhood*, ed. Jean Fagan Yellin and John Van Horne (Ithaca: Cornell University Press, 1994), 130.

24. Marsha Jean Darling, "'We Have Come This Far by Our Own Hands': A Tradition of African American Self-Help and Philanthropy and the Growth of Corporate Philanthropic Giving to African Americans," in *African Americans and the New Policy Consensus: Retreat of the Liberal State?* ed. Marilyn E. Lashley and Melanie Njeri Jackson (Westport, Conn.: Greenwood Press, 1994), 132. On women's roles in West African societies, see Niara Sudarkasa, "Female Employment and Family Organization in West Africa," in *New Research on Women*, ed. Dorothy G. McGuigan (Ann Arbor: University of Michigan Press, 1976), 53.

25. For a further discussion of analogy, see Nancy Lays Stepan, "Race and Gender: The Role of Analogy in Science," in *Anatomy of Racism*, ed. David Theo Goldberg (Minneapolis: University of Minnesota Press, 1990), 48–51.

26. Basch, *In the Eyes of the Law*, 48–55.

27. Sarah Grimké, *Letters on the Equality of the Sexes and the Condition of Women* (Boston: Isaac Knapp, 1838), 75. Among the many analyses of the "slavery of sex" analogy, see Blanche Glassman Hersh, *The Slavery of Sex: Feminist-Abolitionists in America* (Urbana: University of Illinois Press, 1978).

28. Quoted in Thomas Dublin, *Women and Work* (New York: Columbia University Press, 1979), 93.

29. Quoted in Philip Foner, *The Factory Girl* (Urbana: University of Illinois Press, 1977), 160.

30. Quoted in Foner, *Factory Girl*, 83, 84.

31. Karen Sanchez-Eppler, "Bodily Bonds: The Intersecting Rhetorics of Feminism and Abolition," *Representations* 24 (fall 1988): 33.

32. Angelina Grimké, *Letters to Catharine Beecher* (Boston: Isaac Knapp, 1838), 25, 18.

33. C. B. MacPherson, *The Political Theory of Possessive Individualism* (Oxford, U.K.: Clarendon Press, 1962), 272–275. For a critique of contract law, see Peter Gabel and Jay M. Feinman, "Contract Law as Ideology," in *The Politics of Law: A Progressive Critique*, ed. David Kairys (New York: Pantheon Books, 1982), 172–184.

34. Quoted in Stanton, Anthony, and Gage, *History of Woman Suffrage*, 1: 600.

"What Are We Worth" / Anna Julia Cooper Defines Black Women's Work at the Dawn of the Twentieth Century

SHIRLEY WILSON LOGAN

I am always glad to hear of the establishment of reading rooms and social entertainments to brighten the lot of any women who are toiling for bread—whether they are white women or black women. But how many have ever given a thought to the pinched and down-trodden colored women bending over wash-tubs and ironing boards—with children to feed and house rent to pay, wood to buy, soap and starch to furnish—lugging home weekly great baskets of clothes for families who pay them for a month's laundering barely enough to purchase a substantial pair of shoes!

—Anna Julia Cooper, "What Are We Worth?"

PERSONAL STATEMENT I've spent most of my life teaching English—first in junior high school, then high school, then college. But it is only within the last few years that I have found myself wondering, "What does it mean to say that I am an English teacher?" At social gatherings, this self-description usually produces the response, "Well, I better watch my grammar around you." For others it means that I teach literature—you know, the canon, Shakespeare, Frost, Milton, Twain, Faulkner, and the others. In the last decade, my being an English teacher for many has meant that I taught African American literature, the reasoning being that since I am at a predominantly white university, I must have been hired to teach African American literature, right?

So when I correct these assumptions by saying that I teach rhetoric, or how people use language to persuade, the reply is usually "Oh," and then the silence as we search for something else to talk about. Alas, even an established lawyer asked, "Rhetoric? What's that?" But the most disturbing response came from a potential student who entered my office at the beginning of a semester to ask about a course I had developed called "The Rhetoric of Nineteenth-Century African-American Women." I launched enthusiastically into my standard spiel, naming the women whose writing and speaking we would study, talking about the speech occasions and some of the issues we would address—lynching, slavery, woman's rights, civil rights. I was sure that I would soon be adding his name to the roll. But the student, after listening with respectful dismay, said, on his way out of my office, that it was probably a good course and that he especially liked the fact that I was "giving the sisters their props," but he couldn't understand my choice of title. "What's rhetoric got to do with it? Isn't that just hot air, the kind of empty talk that politicians produce?" I never saw him again.

Had the student stayed around, I might have told him that rhetoric has a lot to do with the way African peoples have made sense of their American encounters and the way in which white America has constructed its perceptions of African people. I might have told him about how Ida Wells developed into a powerful public speaker, though as a young person she never read a book by or about a black person. Or I could have told him about my own education at George Washington Carver High School in Spartanburg, South Carolina, in the late 1950s and early 1960s. I remember being handed my valedictory address—several typed pages prepared by my senior English teacher—and told to memorize it, and I did. I don't remember what it said, but I do remember staring out into a sea of white faces sitting in the front row, including Mr. McCraken, the superintendent, who had all come out to the colored high school commencement. Many years later I read Richard Wright's *Black Boy* and Ralph Ellison's *Invisible Man* and Sutton Griggs's *Imperium in Imperio*, all containing similar commencement narratives, and I finally understood how important such speeches must have been to the project of maintaining the status quo. I grew interested in just how they performed this cultural work.

Understanding how language creates knowledge and influences thinking fascinates me because, as Toni Morrison observes, doing language may be the true meaning of life. By studying how black women, in particular, have "done language" since their arrival in the Americas, I have made my research both personal and professional. I study black women's use of language to persuade because language provides a glimpse into their souls.

Growing up in South Carolina in the 1950s, I was read the poetry of Paul Laurence Dunbar ("Jump back, honey, jump back") and discovered the short stories of Charles Chesnutt and Langston Hughes, the speeches of Booker T. Washington and Frederick Douglass. But no one ever told me—and it never occurred to me to ask—whether black women had written poems and stories and delivered speeches as well. Much later—later than I care to admit—I learned that Lucy

Terry was writing poetry in 1746 and that Ann Plato was writing essays in 1831 and that Harriet Wilson wrote a novel in 1859 and that Frances Harper was writing short stories in 1859 and that Maria W. Stewart delivered her first public address in 1832. I was excited. These women, women who looked like me, were brave. They dared to write and to speak out against the social ills suffered by Americans of African descent during a time when such public performances were considered improper for white women and impossible for black women. I was excited, and I wanted to help tell their stories.

I write about the persuasive discourse of nineteenth-century black women, to paraphrase a character from Frances Harper's novel *Iola Leroy*, to express the fullness of my heart and to inspire a deeper sense of justice and humanity, for no one can feel the iron which enters another's soul. When I came across this essay by Anna Julia Cooper saying that women should be compensated for the work they do in the home, I thought, "Okay, a sister scholar who would earn a Ph.D. from the Sorbonne speaking up for housework! This is an essay I want to tell folks about."

---

*B*lack women have always understood the role that work plays in defining their lives and have not been reluctant to speak and write about it. One of the earliest such statements about black women and work comes from Maria Stewart, who in 1832 spoke about the trouble black women in Boston were having finding and keeping decent jobs. Frances Harper, in her 1859 short story "The Two Offers," has one character remind her friend, who is worried about becoming an old maid, of the "intense wretchedness in an ill-assorted marriage" and the value of finding one's own "earthly mission."[1] Many other black women surely expressed their unrecorded views on the matter as well. But Anna Julia Cooper was among the first to argue simultaneously for the social and economic value of the work black women performed in their own homes as well as the work they did away from it. Cooper advocated relentlessly for the right of women to participate fully in public workplaces and to be compensated for their work within the home and did so in an intellectual climate constrained to some extent by the principles of the Victorian cult of True Womanhood. According to these principles, women were to serve as guardians of morality, and their proper place was in the home. Yet aspects of this ideology encouraged women's reform activities. In order to protect and purify the home, women might attack immoral conditions in public spaces. Developed primarily with white women in mind, these concepts influenced the lives and thinking of black women such as Cooper in various ways, an influence her writings reflect. She supported in particular the notion that women had a right to honest work for self- and family improvement and expressed this support on numerous occasions. She admonished the gathering of black Protestant Episcopal clergy in 1886 that the church needed to become more active in the work of helping post-Emancipation black women develop marketable skills, pointing out that "the race cannot be effectually lifted up till its women are truly elevated."[2] In her 1890 address, "The Higher Education of Women," she argued for the coexistence of feminism and intellect, speaking of educated women "who can think as well as feel, and who feel nonetheless because they can think—women who are nonetheless tender and true for the parchment scroll they bear in their hands."[3] She here slipped unself-consciously into cult discourse, projecting women who are "tender," "true," and feeling. She herself, influenced by these principles, claimed, in *A Voice from the South,* that black women, in particular, should inhabit homes and public work spaces with "quiet, undisputed dignity," and with special feminine influence whispering "just the needed suggestion," and (in the essay "Colored Women as Wage-Earners") with "calm insight and tact."[4]

Identifying points of intersection between Cooper's own expansive working life and her views on the working lives of other black women, I consider the extent to which her essay "Colored Women as Wage-Earners" argues for a broader definition of work, a definition that recognized and dignified the labor black women performed in the home and in official work environments. Her defense of in-home work performed by black women highlighted the economic benefits of this labor, but more significantly it highlighted the role it played in the work of racial uplift. I discuss Cooper's discourse on work in the context of century-long labor debates carried on by other black women intellectuals, including Maria Stewart, Frances Harper, Fannie Barrier Williams, and Victoria Matthews, and by white women associated with the early feminist movement. Curiously, her essay can be said to represent microcosmically the range of positions black women assumed across the nineteenth century as they voiced their opinions on employment options for black women workers. Her essay "Colored Women as Wage-Earners" opens with the radical claim that women should be paid for home work, but ends by elevating that work to the morally superior realm of racial uplift, with no further mention of compensation.

The Woman

Her views on black women and work were shaped by the challenges she met over the course of her own working life. Born in 1858, Anna Julia Haywood Cooper, a working woman, supported herself and various family members for most of her 105 years of life. She began rehearsing for her career as an educator before she was nine years old by tutoring classmates at St. Augustine's Normal and Collegiate Institute in Raleigh, North Carolina, receiving an annual scholarship stipend of one hundred dollars and often standing on a chair to reach the blackboard. She attended the school, established to train teachers and ministers, for fourteen years. During her brief marriage to the institute's professor of Greek, the Reverend George Cooper, she continued to teach at St. Augustine's. Widowed after only two years of marriage, Cooper, at twenty-one, concentrated entirely on professional development. Following the denial of her request for a salary increase, she left St. Augustine's to work and matriculate at Oberlin College. Graduating from Oberlin in 1884, she taught at Wilberforce College, where she chaired the modern language department. A year later she returned to St. Augustine's to teach. Although her first year there was apparently successful, just before the spring commencement of her second year, she was fired due to alleged incompatibility. In the fall of 1887, Cooper moved to Washington, D.C., to teach mathematics and science at the M Street High School, having been awarded a master's degree in mathematics from Oberlin, based on the three intervening years' teaching experience. Hired during a period when over 80 percent of the District of Columbia's black teachers were unmarried or widowed women, Cooper, herself a widow, was appointed principal in 1902, at the age of forty-three. In the context of a curriculum controversy, she was not reappointed in 1906. From 1906 to 1910, she chaired the modern language department at Lincoln Institute in Missouri, returning to M Street High School in 1910, where she remained until she retired in 1930. During a tour of Europe in the summer of 1900, she became interested in a pursuing a degree in modern language and literature, subsequently spending the summers of 1911 through 1913 at the Guilde Internationale in Paris studying French literature and history. Building on this work, she began doctoral studies at Columbia University in 1914. After four summers there, during which she translated *Le Pélérinage de Charlemagne,* Cooper, faced with the requirement of a year in residence, changed her plans and decided to matriculate for her doctorate at the University of Paris some years later. This change of plans was no doubt influenced by the fact that in 1915, in her fifties, she became more fully a worker in the home when she assumed responsibility for rearing five great nieces and nephews, the youngest being only six months old. In 1924, when the youngest child was nearly eleven, she left for France to pursue her degree. These intellectual labors as a scholar-educator earned her a doctorate in French literature from the University of Paris in 1925, close to five months before her sixty-seventh birthday. More a scholar than a public figure, Cooper performed her unpaid work for racial uplift by lecturing and writing provocative essays. This work continued throughout her life and is best represented in *A Voice from the South*, compiled when she was thirty-four. At the age of seventy-two, she became the second president of the Frelinghuysen University, a night school described as a beacon of hope for "colored working people." She worked actively as an educator into her mid-eighties. Cooper died in 1964, one year after the labor-led March on Washington for Jobs and Freedom.

The Rhetorical Challenge

Given such a prominent and expansive work history, how did an independent, highly educated woman like Cooper see herself in relation to contemporary black women laborers? Although it would be inaccurate to say that Cooper lived a privileged life, her work experiences were materially different from those of most black women at the turn of the century, women like the ones she describes in the opening epigraph, who were struggling for fair compensation, even in the lowest-paying jobs. An article in the 1 August 1877 *Galveston Daily News* about black urban women working in commercial laundries gives evidence of this struggle. The women went on strike, demanding at least $1.50 a day for their labors, and marched through the town insisting upon the cooperation of all the women.[5]

The Response: "Colored Women as Wage-Earners" and other Essays

Cooper wrote and spoke about the entitlements and obligations of black women at every opportunity, but the essay under consideration here, "Colored Women as Wage-Earners," is not widely known. It directly addresses the labor rights and responsibilities of black women workers in and outside the home. The essay appeared in the "Contributed Articles" section of the August 1899 *Southern Workman and Hampton School Record*, at that time the official publication of the Hampton Institute in Hampton, Virginia. Hampton Institute, established in 1868, subscribed to a program of racial uplift that centered on industrial education, offered courses in domestic science for women, and minimized political and social inequality for the race. Of the two articles besides Cooper's included in this section of the *Workman*, one critiqued the participation of "colored American soldiers" in the Spanish-American War and the other described a growing resentment among the "Indian of the Plains" living on reservations, in line with the paper's stated purpose of working for the progress of "the Black and Red races of our country."[6] The specific circumstances surrounding the writing of "Colored Women as Wage-Earners" are not known, but by the time it was published, Cooper was a well-established member of the black intellectual community. She had addressed the American Negro Academy, an exclusive think tank founded by Alexander Crummell, as well as the American Conference of Educators, the World's Congress of Representative Women, the First National Conference of Colored Women, and the second Hampton Negro Conference. A frequent contributor to black turn-of-the-century periodicals, Cooper was women's editor of the *Southland*, a monthly magazine founded by Joseph Price of Livingstone College in Salisbury, North Carolina.

In "Colored Women as Wage-Earners," Cooper's opening claim is that homes were economic institutions, though not officially so designated, and that women who labored in them should be paid a fair wage for their work. She also called for pay equity with respect to women's official wage-earning activities. But along with these demands she asserted that black women have an obligation to make a contribution to the larger work of racial uplift.

Cooper first reports on Atlanta University research revealing that of 1,137 black families, 650, or 57.17 percent, were supported wholly or in part by women.[7] She continues that, since many black women were already principal wage earners, they were entitled to the rights of all other workers. Cooper characterizes such "conditions which force women into the struggle for bread" negatively.[8] It is that they must work, rather than that they do, which makes the situation undesirable. Cooper's is not an argument about black women's right to work; it identifies instead their working reality and argues for equality within it.

The second section of the piece argues for a broader definition of the term "wage-earner," one that includes women working in the home. Cooper's entire essay can be viewed in one sense as an extended definition. Scholars of rhetoric point out that all definitions are argumentative, since the audience may accept or reject them. In defining a term, a writer may select from a general definition the essential elements that support application of the term to a particular set of circumstances. Arguing in favor of a certain definition of a word slants it to influence the use which would probably not have been made of it had the preferred meaning not been put forward. Constructing a preferred definition also adjusts the term's meaning as it relates to the whole system of thought with which it is associated.[9] This characterization of definition helps to account for Cooper's tactics in "Colored Women as Wage-Earners."

She defines several paired economic principles—land and rent, labor and wages, capital and interest—all leading to the creation of wealth. Cooper then applies these definitions to the "system of thought" surrounding the work performed primarily by women in the home, arguing that women have a right to share in the wealth produced as a result of "relieving the man of certain indoor cares and enabling him to give thereby larger effort to his special trade or calling."[10] This broadened definition of wage-earner allows Cooper to claim that since the "indoor partner of the firm" facilitates the work of the "outdoor manager," she should be considered just as truly a contributor to the product gained and entitled to a share of the wages. Anticipating the charge that mothering and homemaking were being commodified, Cooper countered that as noble as this work is, the woman should not have to ask for doles; her partner should remember that she "earns a definite part of the wage that he draws; and that, though she has never figured it out and presented the bill, his account is greatly in arrears for simple wages."[11]

Although Cooper argues for wage equality, this equal partner performs her duties in the tradition of Victorian True Womanhood. Cooper writes: "The silent partner toils in the home, whether to cook the dinners or direct little feet and hands. Her heart is in her work. Faithfulness and devotion are hers. At the end of her monotonous round of days' doings she prepares to welcome in the eventide the battle-scarred veteran of the outer life. She opens the door with a smile. That smile is an important part of her program. She leads him to dinner that she has prepared; he eats with a right good relish, for he likes to be fed."[12]

In keeping with one of the cult's chief tenets, domesticity, Cooper's homemaker-as-wage-earner prepares for her husband a comforting escape from the harsh realities of the marketplace, where he can expect to be greeted with a smile and a hearty meal. We should remember that at this point in the essay, Cooper is still arguing in general terms for women's wage-earning entitlements. When she quotes Social Darwinist Herbert Spencer's claim that women should not be "artificially disadvantaged" and when she describes the economic aspects of homemaking, it is clear that she means to include all women; thus, it may be less surprising that she slips into cult discourse.[13]

Early white feminists had made the claim that wives were entitled to property rights in their household labor in the decade before the Civil War. They insisted as early as the 1850s that the work women performed for the family in the home should be valued equally with men's. Antebellum earnings statutes gave married women rights only to their work outside the home; with this claim, supporters attempted to emancipate wives' labor in the home as well as in the market through joint property laws. The claim was based on arguments from difference—not that women were the same as men or that they should be treated like men, but that they performed distinct but no less valuable work. Unfolding within the gender discourse of the time, such arguments failed to question the division of labor in marriage, but contrary to separate-sphere conventions, they did claim that both work settings should be valued if not compensated with wages.

During the years after the war, advocates began to push for independent sources of income for women and to argue less for recognition of work done in the home. Legal scholar Reva Siegel points out that Charlotte Perkins Gilman's very popular 1899 book, *Women and Economics,* marked this shift definitively. Gilman refused to view a wife's household work as in any way enabling the husband's income, reasoning that only if that labor were recognized on a market basis could it be classified as "productive industry."[14] Further, women had come to realize that, in the words of Siegel, "while legislatures and courts may have been prepared to emancipate women's labor when it looked like men's, they were in no way prepared to emancipate the work that was "woman's."[15] These activists feared that valorizing such work would only strengthen separate-sphere discourse.

Cooper may have been influenced to some extent by this labor debate, originating in the women's rights movement. For example, in her 1890 address "The Higher Education of Women" can be found traces of this argument, particularly in the section where she describes the changes to occur after women are allowed to participate fully in public affairs. One change, she predicts, is correction of the "absurdity that man and wife are one, and that one, the man—that the married woman may not hold or bequeath her own property save as subject to her husband's direction."[16] But it is clear from other essays in *A Voice from the South*, particularly, for example in "Woman vs. the Indian" and "What Are We Worth," quoted from in the epigraph, that while Cooper may have been sympathetic to the notion of women's entitlement to rights in their household labor, she found it impossible to sympathize either with the women's rights or the organized labor movements, in light of the failure of both to acknowledge the pressing needs of black women and black workers. In the chapter "Woman vs. the Indian," Cooper criticizes the Reverend Anna Shaw, prominent women's rights leader, who delivered an 1891 address to the National Woman's Council with this title: "Woman vs. the Indian." In the speech, Shaw pitted women against Native Americans instead of attacking white patriarchal institutions, the true perpetrators of injury against women, blacks, and other marginalized groups. Cooper further implicates white women leaders for their silence, charging them with complicity in a system of prejudice. Likewise, the essay "What Are We Worth" accuses organized labor of failing to defend the rights of black workers, who labored under severe conditions in both the North and South.[17]

Since black women's experiences had so often been left out of women's labor discussions, it was necessary for Cooper to define these experiences in the context of race as well as gender. Cooper located the black women's wage-earning situation within the black community as a whole. Cooper was keenly aware of the rhetorical maneuvering required to argue for black women's wage-earning rights in a sphere marked white, domestic, feminine, and private as well as in a sphere marked white, official, masculine, and public. Several paragraphs later, in "Women as Wage-Earners," when she narrows her focus to black women, Cooper seems more concerned with their rights in the public sphere: "And now let us apply what has been said to the special class of women mentioned in our subject. The colored woman as wage-earner must bring to her labor all the capacities, native or acquired, which are of value in the industrial equation. She must really be worth her wage and then claim it."[18]

She had already, in the opening paragraph of the essay, dissociated black women from the debate about whether women should work and was now returning to this "special class" for further discussion. In this third section, Cooper shifts the reader's attention to the "dusty arena" of the public sphere and the attributes that women, particularly black women, should have as they enter it. She returns to her established definitions of labor ("all human exertion") and wage-earning (the "proper corollary to the human element in the creation of wealth"), this time to highlight associations with intellectual and moral training, concluding that better-educated women will earn more. In line with her earlier call for women with "undisputed dignity" and special feminine influence, Cooper registers a distinct dislike for assertive "women with elbows." But she concedes that black women, in order to survive in the workplace, needed to demand fair labor compensation aggressively. Citing the disadvantages of a 250-year lag in educational opportunities, she writes, "But every wage-earner, man or woman, owes it to the dignity of the labor he contributes, as well as to his own self-respect, to require the rights due to the quality of service he renders, and to the element of value he contributes to the world's wealth."[19]

In the final section, Cooper turns her attention to the ways in which the rush to acquire material wealth impedes racial progress. She was discouraged to see black families scramble to imitate middle-class white society by staging costly weddings, funerals, and coming-out parties and called for the adoption of more conservative spending practices. According to Cooper, the black family, instead of striving "to reach an extravagant and unattainable standard of life" needed first to accumulate social wealth.[20] Social wealth seems to be Cooper's term for cultural knowledge of the kind acquired over time and resulting from association with certain cultural artifacts, to include books, music, and art. It is in this way, according to Cooper, that family values are secured. In making this claim she refutes fellow American Negro Academy member Kelly Miller's suggestion that the excess of women in the cities encourages promiscuity and leads to general moral decline.[21] She counters that a return to simple living—not "killing off the surplus women"—would increase the number of "honorable marriages and pure homes."[22] Black women were called to maintain home and family for the welfare of the race. Ultimately, then, Cooper subsumes the issue of wage-earning within domestic discourse. Building strong homes takes precedence over fighting for equal wages, especially within a labor market where most black women had limited opportunities.

Although the essay's title implies a focus on the black laboring woman, it ends by placing highest value on her supporting role as homemaker, performing the work of racial uplift. Toward the close of the essay, Cooper writes to and of the ungendered black wage-earner, proposing uplift policies of general benefit. Cooper, in language evoking the tenets both of true womanhood and racial uplift, advises the black woman to "Study economy. Utilize the margins. Preach and practice plain living and high thinking." Further, she must "prove that she can contribute something more than good looks and milliners' bills to the stock and trade. . . . So, by her foresight and wisdom, her calm insight and tact, her thrift and frugality, her fertility of resources and largeness of hope and faith, the colored woman can prove that a prudent marriage is the very best investment that a working man can make."[23]

Such a statement may grate on enlightened twenty-first-century feminist sensibilities. Marriage in some constructions represents capitulation to the status quo and the oppression of women. But it is also possible to imagine that for many post-Emancipation blacks, exercising the civil right to marry was as important as exercising the right to vote. In the same vein, although black women, along with other women, were denied the right to vote during this period, they considered the votes cast by black men as theirs as well and exerted pressure to see that those votes were cast in accordance with communal consensus.[24] For postwar black women, marriage and family life were not the final, ultimate accomplishment of a woman's life but a new beginning. This sense of agency, of controlling one's own future, as much as any economic benefits, informs Cooper's elevation of the institution of marriage.

Views of Cooper's Contemporaries on Work

Clearly, Cooper was not the first to argue specifically for black women's labor rights. She followed a tradition perhaps first established in the speeches of Maria W. Stewart in 1832 and 1833. Stewart articulated employment concerns in her Franklin Hall address when she described the difficulty that black

Boston women had in gaining employment, even from other women: "I have asked several individuals of my sex, who transact business for themselves, if providing our girls were to give them the most satisfactory references, they would not be willing to grant them an equal opportunity with others? Their reply has been—for their own part, they had no objection; but as it was not the custom, were they to take them into their employ, they would be in danger of losing the public patronage."[25]

In her address to the World's Congress of Representative Women, some sixty years later, Fannie Barrier Williams echoes this same concern regarding the failure of white women to help black women find work: "It is almost literally true that, except teaching in colored schools and menial work, colored women can find no employment in this free America. They are the only women in the country for whom real ability, virtue, and special talents count for nothing when they become applicants for respectable employment. Taught everywhere in ethics and social economy that merit always wins, colored women carefully prepare themselves for all kinds of occupation only to meet with stern refusal, rebuff, and disappointment."[26] Williams fires off one of her strongest criticisms of the apathy of white women in a November 1894 column for the *Woman's Era*: "We should never forget that the exclusion of colored women and girls from nearly all places of respectable employment is due mostly to the meanness of American women."[27] Several years later in an autobiographical essay, Williams reiterated the sentiment that even progressive white women found it difficult to support the employment efforts of black women as a group, although they could be friendly to one black woman, like Williams herself.[28]

After Mary Ann Shadd Cary argued in her speech at the Colored National Labor Union Convention in 1860 that black women experienced as much employment discrimination as black men did, the delegates passed a resolution that black women be included in future efforts to organize.[29] In a speech to the Women's Congress, published in the January 1878 issue of *Englishwoman's Review*, Frances Harper recalled the many independent black working women she had met during her travels throughout the Reconstruction South. She described women who raised poultry and hogs, farmed, sold baked goods, manufactured sugar, and engaged in bookkeeping, pointing out that many used "their income to buy their own homes without the assistance of men."[30] In her 1886 speech to American National Baptist Convention, Lucy Smith proposed the same kinds of self-employment projects—raising chickens and small fruit, dairying, lecturing, photography, and medicine. With the growth of a market economy after the Civil War, much of the traditional work that wives performed in the home yielded substantial cash crops in many areas. Victoria

Matthews's 1898 speech at the Second Summer Hampton Negro Conference painted a bleak picture of the sexual exploitation of young southern black women lured North to find work. Matthews spoke of the appeal of the high wages and of these victims of unethical recruitment tactics, who found themselves trapped by incurred debts into prostitution; she advocated that they be warned of the dangers that awaited them and taught how to search for jobs intelligently.[31] But most, she pleaded, should stay at home.

While these summarized comments on black women and work do not begin to represent everything black women said about black women and work in the nineteenth century, they do come from some of its most prominent women intellectuals, who themselves were at the same time working women. Most had experienced the bleak working conditions they describe, firsthand. Even so, few mention the wage-earning aspect of the work women performed in their own homes, focusing instead on official women's labor in the public arena.

Cooper and Nineteenth-Century Black Working Women

Discounting the article "Colored Woman as Wage-Earners," even Cooper's discourse on labor issues, especially in *A Voice from the South*, does not address specifically the wage-earning rights of women in the home. This is not particularly surprising when one considers, as Cooper noted in the opening sentences of her essay, that for most black women wage-earning was a necessity, not an option. While faced with many domestic issues, these workers may have been less concerned with how homework was defined than with the possibility of acquiring and maintaining respectable and fairly compensated outside work. Further, as historian Sharon Harley points out, late-nineteenth-century black women, faced with racial and gender discrimination in various workplaces, "more readily embraced their status as mothers, wives, aunts, and sisters than their more embattled status as wage-earners."[32] For example, an 1890 Philadelphia survey revealed that most black women in that city worked in personal service occupations, with only a few employed as clerical workers, hairdressers, and dressmakers. Only 17 percent worked solely in their own homes. Those who worked as domestics were often required to perform a wide variety of chores, including "scrubbing the stoop and tending the furnace," and faced considerable sexual harassment. They earned about $150 a year.[33] The irony here is that the very work that post-Reconstruction middle-class white women had decided was menial and more appropriate for immigrants and emancipated blacks was the work that many black women had come to value when it was performed in their own homes. Consequently, those who wrote and spoke about black women's labor issues focused on inequalities in hiring practices and working conditions and argued for independent sources of employment that would free black women from on-the-job abuse and from financial dependence upon men. Black women paid much less attention to their rights to wages for the work they did at home.

Many have commented on Cooper's apparent lack of identification with the women for whom she claims to be a "voice." It is true that no particulars of Cooper's life appear to inform this essay directly. Cooper herself spent only two years in a traditional domestic relationship and continued to work during that period. The pronoun "I" throughout the essay is not the I of personal experience, frequently found in *A Voice from the South*, but the I of authority.[34] Cooper's use of "I" in "Wage-Earners" asserts her authority to write on women's labor issues. Such metadiscursive phrases as "No one deplores more than I do," "what I mean by social wealth," "Now I hold that," and "as I conceive the matter" convey self-confidence in her right to express her opinions. Nonetheless, autobiographical impulses resonate in her frequent use of the unifying first person plural "we" and "our." First, she employs the "we" uniting writer and reader in a general sense, as in "When we pass from the home and enter the dusty arena of the world." Then there is the "we" and "our" that appeal to group identity, allowing Cooper to declare her community with African American people: "As colored wage-earners, we are today under a double disadvantage" and "We somehow feel that our child ought to appear as fine as the rest." While these pronoun shifts locate Cooper squarely within an African American consciousness, it may be significant that Cooper's "we's" in this essay never refer to "we black women." Her one use of "we" to mean "we women" comes in the section where Cooper has not yet shifted her attention specifically to black women and is writing of all women: "If men will not or cannot help the conditions which force women into the struggle for bread, we have a right to claim at least that she shall have fair play and all the rights of wage-earners in general."[35] This exception may provide additional support for literary critic Mary Helen Washington's claim that Cooper "does not imagine ordinary black women as the basis of her feminist politics," but it does not weaken Cooper's labor arguments in this piece.[36] Cooper and most of the "race women" of this era were caught in their own gender and class binds of DuBoisian double-consciousness. Washington's analysis of this dilemma is worth quoting in full:

> As a middle-class black woman, Cooper, like all of her contemporaries . . . had a great stake in the prestige, the respectability, and the gentility guaranteed by the politics of true womanhood. To identify with the issues and interests of poor and uneducated black women entailed a great risk.

Cooper and her intellectual contemporaries would have to deal with their own class privilege and would undoubtedly alienate the very white women they felt they needed as allies. Burdened by the race's morality, black women could not be as free as white women or black men to think outside of these boundaries of "uplift"; every choice they made had tremendous repercussions for an entire race of women already under the stigma of inferiority and immorality.[37]

They needed to demonstrate kinship with the white women to whom they wrote and spoke by a show of cult culture and refinement, even as they argued for fair employment practices toward black women who had been denied the opportunity and leisure to develop these attributes.

Conclusion

This essay reveals a number of tensions resulting from Cooper's attempt to defend the rights of working women in the context of the gendered division of family labor. Cooper argues for recognition of the wage-earning aspect of the work women do in the home, but seems ultimately more concerned with defining that work as a critical aspect of black women's racial uplift work. Although she encourages women to advocate aggressively for their rights as workers in the public domain, she registers a distinct dislike for "women with elbows" and implies an ideal that they should not have to work. While arguing for the dignity of the work women do within the home, Cooper appears not to question the assumption that these domestic and maternal duties do, in fact, belong to women. While Cooper's arguments resonate with the discourse of domesticity and labor movement rhetoric, she dissociates her interests from those of both groups in previous writings. Although she elevates the domestic work of black women, her own life was not a traditional domestic one nor was her work typical of that of most working black women. This multiple and apparently contradictory positioning brings to mind Mae Henderson's comments on the heteroglossic nature of black women's discourse, one that enables them to speak in multiple public languages. Henderson draws on Mikhail Bakhtin's concept of dialogism, wherein language in its various forms can be properly understood only as dialogue or communication that takes place within specific social situations and which to some extent helps to create those situations. Henderson observes that black women "enter into a competitive discourse with black men as women, with white women as blacks, and with white men as black women."[38] In "Colored Women as Wage-Earners," Cooper's ability to speak in many tongues makes it possible for her to counter black men's claims, such as the one articulated by Kelly Miller, that the presence of "surplus" black women in large cities lead to moral decline. It also enables her to express resistance to a close alliance with white privilege, as in her opening announcement that she is not concerned with "ideal situations." But Cooper's is mainly the intra-racial discourse of a black woman speaking to black men and women, enlarging and redefining their understanding of work. She collapses the separate-sphere distinction between home work and official work for black women. Cooper believed that black women, whether working in their own homes or in the homes and public spaces of others, were working for the race.

NOTES

1. Frances Harper, "The Two Offers" [1859], in *A Brighter Coming Day: A Frances Ellen Watkins Harper Reader* (New York: Feminist Press, 1990), 106.

2. Anna Julia Cooper, *A Voice from the South* (1892; reprint, New York: Oxford University Press, 1988), 42, in reprint.

3. Ibid., 50.

4. Cooper, *A Voice from the South*, 31, 138; and Anna Julia Cooper, "Colored Women as Wage-Earners," in *We Are Coming: The Persuasive Discourse of Nineteenth-Century Black Women*, ed. Shirley Wilson Logan (Carbondale: Southern Illinois University Press, 1999), 205.

5. Ruthe Winegarten, *Black Texas Women: A Sourcebook* (Austin, Tex.: University of Austin Press, 1996).

6. In 1878, Hampton Institute had assumed the education of Native Americans captured and held prisoners of war by the United States following an 1875 uprising; thus the "red" race was incorporated into the school's general uplift project.

7. Anna Julia Cooper, "Colored Women as Wage-Earners," in Logan, *We Are Coming*, 200. Cooper's figures correspond to those found in *Social and Physical Condition of Negroes in Cities*, by Atlantic University Publications (Atlanta, Ga.: Atlanta University Press, 1897), appendix A, 6.

8. Cooper, "Colored Women as Wage-Earners," 200.

9. See Chaim Perelman and Lucie Olbrechts-Tyteca, *The New Rhetoric: A Treatise on Argumentation* (Notre Dame, Ind.: University of Notre Dame Press, 1969), 213, for a discussion of definition as argument.

10. Cooper, "Colored Women as Wage-Earners," 201.

11. Ibid., 202.

12. Ibid., 206.

13. See Barbara Welter's frequently cited essay, "The Cult of True Womanhood, 1820–1860," in her *Dimity Convictions: The American Woman in the Nineteenth Century* (Athens: Ohio University Press, 1976), 21–41, in which she identifies the cult's four cardinal virtues of piety, purity, submissiveness, and domesticity; Spencer quoted in Cooper, "Colored Women as Wage-Earners," 200.

14. Reva B. Siegel, "Home as Work: The First Woman's Rights Claims Concerning Wives' Household Labor, 1850–1880," *Yale Law Journal* 103 (March 1994): 1206; Charlotte Perkins Gilman, *Women and Economics* (Boston: Small, Maynard and Company, 1899).

15. Siegel, "Home as Work," 1216.

16. Cooper, *A Voice from the South*, 58.

17. For a full discussion of these concerns, see Cooper, *A Voice from the South*, 80–145, 228–285.

18. Cooper, "Colored Women as Wage-Earners," 296.

19. Ibid., 203.

20. Ibid.

21. Kelly Miller (1863–1939) served as professor of mathematics and sociology at Howard University and filled various academic roles from 1895 to 1935. Miller was a founder of the American Negro Academy, of which, according to some sources, Cooper was the only female member. The academy published Miller's "A Review of Hoffman's *Race Traits and Tendencies of the American Negro*" as an occasional paper in 1897 (Washington, D.C.). In the review, Miller critiqued Frederick Hoffman's treatise (New York: Macmillan, 1896), purporting to demonstrate the genetic inferiority of blacks. In response to Hoffman's claim that urban blacks were by nature immoral, Miller countered that "a greater than any cause yet assigned as leading to the social degradation of Negroes in cities is the excess of the female over the male element of the population" (32). Miller further develops this notion in his 1908 essay "Surplus Negro Women," in his *Race Adjustment: Essays on the Negro in America* (New York: Neale, 1908), 168–178.

22. Cooper, "Colored Women as Wage-Earners," 205.

23. Ibid.

24. See Elsa Barkley Brown's article on the political activism of Richmond women who, especially during the 1870s, participated in public deliberations and went to the polls with their husbands, although they could not vote, to gain "collective protection" and to affirm the sense of a "collective enfranchisement." Elsa Barkley Brown, "Negotiating and Transforming the Public Sphere: African American Political Life in the Transition from Slavery to Freedom," in *The Black Public Sphere: A Public Culture Book*, ed. The Black Public Sphere Collective (Chicago: University of Chicago Press, 1995), 127.

25. Maria Stewart, "Lecture Delivered at the Franklin Hall," in *With Pen and Voice: A Critical Anthology of Nineteenth-Century African-American Women,* ed. Shirley Wilson Logan (Carbondale: Southern Illinois University Press, 1995), 6.

26. Fannie Barrier Williams, "The Intellectual Progress of the Colored Women of the United States since the Emancipation Proclamation," in Logan, *With Pen and Voice,* 114.

27. Fannie Barrier Williams, "Women in Politics," *Woman's Era* (November 1894): 12.

28. Fannie Barrier Williams, "A Northern Negro's Autobiography" [1904], in *Bearing Witness: Selections from African-American Autobiography in the Twentieth Century,* ed. Henry Louis Gates Jr. (New York: Pantheon, 1991), 14–15.

29. Philip S. Foner and Ronald L. Lewis, eds., *The Black Worker: A Documentary History from Colonial Times to the Present,* vol. 2, *The Black Worker during the Era of the National Labor Union* (Philadelphia: Temple Univerity Press, 1978), 55.

30. Frances Harper, "Coloured Women of America," *A Brighter Coming Day: A Frances Ellen Watkins Harper Reader,* ed. Frances Smith Foster (1878; reprint, New York: Feminist Press, 1990), 271–275.

31. Lucy Wilmot Smith, "The Future Colored Girl," in Logan, *We Are Coming,* 221–228; Victoria Earle Matthews, "Some of the Dangers Confronting Southern Girls in the North," in Logan, *We Are Coming,* 215–220.

32. Sharon Harley, "Race: Gender, Work, and Domestic Roles in the Black Community," in *Black Women in America: Social Science Perspectives,* ed. Micheline R. Malson, Elisabeth Mudimbe-Boyi, Jean F. O'Barr, and Mary Wyer (Chicago: University of Chicago Press, 1990), 160.

33. Gilbert Anthony Williams, *The Christian Recorder: A.M.E. Church, 1854–1902* (Jefferson, N.C.: McFarland, 1996), 8, based on survey in *The Philadelphia Negro: A Social Study*, by W.E.B. Du Bois (1899; reprint, Millwood, N.Y.: Kraus-Thompson, 1973), 102–103, in reprint.

34. See Elizabeth Alexander's analysis of Cooper's skillful use of "I" to perform a range of rhetorical moves in *A Voice from the South*, from expressing conventional formality to "posit[ing] an African-American woman's lived experience as evidentiary." Elizabeth Alexander, "We Must Be about Our Father's Business: Anna Julia Cooper and the In-Corporation of the Nineteenth-Century African-American Woman Intellectual," in *In Her Own Voice: Nineteenth-Century American Women Essayists*, ed. Sherry Lee Linkon (New York: Garland, 1997), 68.

35. Cooper, "Colored Women as Wage-Earners," 203, 204, 200.

36. Mary Helen Washington, introduction to *A Voice from the South*, by Cooper, xliv.

37. Ibid., xlvii.

38. Mae Gwendolyn Henderson, "Speaking in Tongues: Dialogics, Dialectics, and the Black Woman Writer's Literary Tradition," in *Changing Our Own Words: Essays on Criticism, Theory, and Writing by Black Women*, ed. Cheryl A. Wall (New Brunswick, N. J.: Rutgers University Press, 1989), 20. See Mikhail Bakhtin, "Discourse in the Novel," in *The Dialogic Imagination: Four Essays by M. M. Bakhtin*, ed. Michael Holquist (Austin: University of Texas Press, 1981), 259–422.

"All of the Glory . . . Faded . . . Quickly"

Sadie T. M. Alexander and Black Professional Women, 1920–1950

Francille Rusan Wilson

PERSONAL STATEMENT

This is how I came to be a labor and intellectual historian: In my junior and senior years of college, I had a small room with a large window high above the rest of the campus, overlooking a vast expanse of green hills and a road I hoped would lead to tomorrow. Outside that room I appeared to be a self-confident campus militant. Inside it I paced, eyes focused on the far horizon, meditating on the messy and seemingly uncharted transition I was making from colored girl and Negro student to black woman and what else I did not know. One day there was a long line of women standing directly and so close behind me at that window that there was no denying that we were kin. A quick backward glimpse of what could only be seen in my mind's eye did little to get them out of the room. Only by looking forward could I begin to sense them separately: each was a different size and shape, all fully clothed, some wore aprons and head ties properly fastened, others wore big Sunday hats. Dark hands held hoes, baskets, books, or Bibles. Their faces were in shadow, so I couldn't see just how they had lined themselves up. Was my Mama Rusan at the front or the end of the line, and did the formidable Aunt Georgias of both parents stand together? Why so many? Their presence was humbling, mocking, inspiring, and puzzling. What did they want? "We're here. We've always been here," was their silent witness—a gift, softer than a sigh, more palpable than a pulse. I write both to make them visible and to take my place in our line.

This is how I came to write about Sadie T. M. Alexander: This chapter grows out of a series of explorations of the lives of the first generations of black social scientists, my scholarly ancestors. The larger work, *The Segregated Scholars: Black Social Scientists and the Creation of Black Labor Studies, 1890–1950*, looks at ten men and five women who made black workers a legitimate field of study. Sexism and racism prevented black women such as Alexander from earning a consistent income as social scientists, but, much like me at that window, their education gave them professional careers and allowed them to study workers rather than work in kitchens, factories, or farms. Alexander's 1921 dissertation on household budgets of one hundred migrant families in Philadelphia was the first by a black person in economics, but she simply could not get a job. While examining her aborted career as an economist, I realized that the story of Sadie Alexander's reinvention of herself as a lawyer in the 1920s was equally if not more important in gaining a better understanding of the lives of professional black women in the 1920s. Alexander was neither a victim nor a saint. She was a lively actor who rewrote her life's script as she went along.

Sadie Tanner Mossell Alexander on 15 June 1921, the day she received a Ph.D. in economics from the University of Pennsylvania.

PHOTO COURTESY
OF THE UNIVERSITY OF
PENNSYLVANIA ARCHIVES.

Could Black Women Climb in the Professions before the Civil Rights Era?

"Can you beat it? . . . Can you imagine such publicity being attached to a little thing like me?"[1] Twenty-three-year-old Sadie Tanner Mossell was thrilled with the buzz of attention and national press coverage accorded to her march down Broad Street to the Academy of Music with the other graduates of the University of Pennsylvania on 15 June 1921. The route was familiar, for she had donned a cap and gown twice before and stood among the graduating classes, but now cameras were aimed at the first black woman in the United States to earn a Ph.D. and the first black American to be awarded a doctorate in economics. Mossell had apparently achieved two major racial milestones and had her very own firsts to add to the noteworthy accomplishments of her grandfather, father, uncles, and aunts. Her triumph was short-lived. She could not find a full-time job as an economist.

Mossell's attempts to find work in her field were rejected by white corporations because of her race and by the research departments of black social service agencies and black colleges because of her sex. She finally took a position as an assistant actuary with a black insurance firm in North Carolina, a position well beneath her educational achievements but her only permanent offer. Her dissertation had been a study of southern migrant families in Philadelphia, and the irony of her own reverse migration from the North to the South for a job was not lost upon the proud three-generation Pennsylvanian. The close juxtaposition of her joyous graduation day and her keen disappointment at being unable to work as an economist still rankled her fifty-five years later despite her accomplishments as a lawyer, her successful marriage, and two children. Sadie T. M. Alexander vividly recalled her predicament: "All of the glory of that occasion faded, however, quickly, when I tried to get a position."[2] As her rueful comment signaled, race and gender were powerful constraints that limited her and other black women's ability to establish themselves in the professions in the 1920s.

An examination of how Sadie T. M. Alexander tried to establish two careers will help us to better interpret what work meant to educated black women before the Civil Rights era. A number of previous studies have examined early twentieth-century black women's club work, their campaigns against Jim Crow and lynching, and their progressive social service programs. These collective efforts constituted black educated women's self-conscious "lifting," as reflected in the motto of the National Association of Colored Women: "Lifting as we climb." An unwritten assumption by historians has been that an individual's career advancement, or climbing, was self-evident. However, when black women's attempts to enter and advance in professions which were dominated by men and white women are closely examined, we observe major obstacles in their paths.

Although educated black women were able to enter the feminized and largely segregated professions of primary school teaching, social work, and nursing, the two professions of Sadie Tanner Mossell Alexander in the

1920s—economics and the law—amply demonstrate the extent to which their race and sex limited their access to other professions. Mossell Alexander's Ivy League credentials placed her among the most educated women in the United States, while her ancestry and light color made her one of the most advantaged colored persons of her era. Yet she could not find work as an economist in white or black America and had restrictions on the types of cases she received in her first years as a lawyer in her own husband's firm. As we shall see, the two other black women who received doctorates in June 1921 also had significant obstacles in their educational and career paths.[3]

In the early 1900s black male and white female social scientists used segregated and gendered job opportunities to build careers in which they were able to assert authoritative knowledge of the condition of their race or gender. White female social scientists forged what Robin Muncy has asserted was a "women's dominion" of jobs in selected universities and governmental programs. Black men with bachelor's degrees found good salaries and highly respected jobs as social scientists at Negro colleges and as executives at the National Urban League and the YMCA (Young Men's Christian Association). In July 1921, while Sadie Mossell looked in vain for a job as a social scientist, Charles S. Johnson was appointed research director of the National Urban League at a salary three times greater than the average social worker's. Johnson did not even have a master's degree and it was his first full-time job.[4]

Young Sadie Mossell was not alone in her failure to make a living as a black female social scientist. At least four older social science pioneers designed and published excellent studies of black women workers during the labor crisis of World War I, but Elizabeth Ross Haynes, Helen Brooks Irvin, Emma Shields Penn, and Gertrude McDougald Ayer were forced to find other ways to make a living afterwards.[5] Black female social scientists' inability to gain access to either black or women's jobs in the 1920s not only stunted individual careers but also meant that their social science work took place in locations that lacked the authority and stature of their counterparts'. The first black woman to have a career as an economist was Mabel Smythe, who began working in the early 1940s, a generation later.

Black Women's Education in the Early Twentieth Century

At the time of Sadie Tanner Mossell's birth in 1898 there were 25,000 black women teachers but only 252 black female college graduates. There were nine times more black men—2,272—who had graduated from college than women, a fact which inevitably slowed black women's entrance into certain professions. The numbers of black people whose education went beyond primary school was so small during Sadie Mossell's childhood that *The Crisis* magazine carried an annual tabulation of high school and college graduates with the names and photographs of college and high school graduates from the most elite schools. Between 1901 and 1920 the black population grew from 9.9 to 12.3 million but only 4,763 black men and women graduated from college. This number amounted to 0.038 percent of the black American population. W.E.B. Du Bois's educated, talented tenth was in fact not even one-tenth of 1 percent of the black population, but Sadie Mossell was determined to count herself among them.[6]

Most educated black women in the nineteenth century had either attended normal schools or, like Ida Wells-Barnett, had augmented their education with lyceum courses and self-study. Normal schools specialized in teacher training and offered certificates, but their curricula did not offer the required courses in ancient languages, science, and mathematics, courses that were offered the last two years of good college preparatory programs. Financial pressures, family obligations, and the need to earn a living limited black women's entry to college. Wells-Barnett and her fellow late-nineteenth-century journalists Victoria Earle Matthews, Delilah Beasley, and Gertrude Bustill Mossell worked hard to enlarge their sketchy or truncated educations, becoming skillful professionals who used modern historical and social science methods in their newspaper columns, studies, and books.[7] Wells-Barnett may have been expressing many other black women's longing for a bachelor's degree when she wrote to the Fisk University student newspaper that she had "a craving that at times amounts to positive heart-ache to go there and finish [her] education."[8]

Had she been one of the few black women who were enrolled in bachelor's degree programs between Reconstruction and World War I, Wells-Barnett would have found that Negro colleges substituted domestic science courses for the upper-level math and science requirements of their male students. These subjects had to be taken or passed in a special examination before the students gained acceptance in a master's or doctoral program. Sadie Mossell avoided the obstacle of inadequate secondary and college education by attending an exceptionally good high school, which enabled her to matriculate at an Ivy League university, but Negro college graduates were often required to earn a second bachelors before being admitted to a doctoral program. For example, although Eva Dykes—the third black woman to get a Ph.D.—had graduated from Howard University summa cum laude in 1914, she had to enter Radcliffe College as a junior and complete their undergraduate program before she was allowed to begin graduate studies in English.

The first black woman to earn a doctorate, Georgiana Simpson, had an 1885 Normal school certificate and the seminary courses that were typical of the best-trained black teachers in the nineteenth century. She was born in 1866, just four years after slavery was abolished, in the District of Columbia, and began teaching at age nineteen. After teaching for twenty years she began a determined campaign for a university education. She first studied in Germany, then took correspondence courses, and next attended six straight years of summer terms at the University of Chicago from 1906 to 1911 to complete a B.A. Simpson was not married, and it seems safe to infer that she took summer classes because she could not afford to be without her income as a high school teacher. After five more years of summer classes Simpson moved to Chicago for two years, 1919–1921, to meet the university residency requirements for both a master's and a Ph.D. in German.[9]

Sadie Mossell, like the eight other black women who earned doctorates in the 1920s, avoided most of the pitfalls of preparation, financial resources, and gendered curricula, pitfalls that hampered the forward educational progress of most black women. They were the leading edge of an expansion of black women with undergraduate and graduate degrees, but in 1921 there were still three black male college students for every female student. The total number of black Americans with Ph.D.'s increased from twenty-five in 1920 to eighty-five in 1933, while the number of black women with doctorates grew from zero to ten. Mossell was the only black woman with a doctorate in the social sciences for more than a dozen years.[10]

Not one of the first four black women who earned Ph.D.'s got offers to teach at the college level until the end of the 1920s. Although nearby Howard University did not have a single faculty member with a doctorate in English or German, Dykes and Simpson both stayed in their old jobs as teachers at Paul Lawrence Dunbar High School, the newly renamed and relocated M Street High School. It was no coincidence that Mossell, Simpson, and Dykes were all graduates of M Street, which was known for its academic rigor and brilliant faculty members. The fourth black woman to earn a doctorate, Anna Julia Cooper, was also a Dunbar teacher and former principal. Cooper completed her Ph.D. in French at the Sorbonne in 1925.[11] All four women experienced sexism and racism throughout their careers, making Mossell Alexander's experiences emblematic rather than unique.

"A Determination That Nobody Would Beat Us": The Education of Sadie Mossell

Sadie Mossell's family was unusual in that it had professional women on both sides from the 1880s. Her maternal grandfather, African Methodist Episcopal bishop and editor Benjamin Tucker Tanner, encouraged two of her aunts to establish professional careers. When he was editor of the *Christian Recorder*, one of the largest circulating weeklies of the nineteenth century, Tanner was the first to publish journalist Gertrude Bustill. Bustill later married Sadie's father's brother, physician Nathan Mossell, the first black graduate of the University of Pennsylvania. Tanner employed his older daughter, Halle T. Dillon, as his editorial assistant for the *A.M.E. Church Review* and sent her to the Women's Medical College of Pennsylvania when she became a young widowed mother. In 1891 Halle Tanner Dillon Johnson became the resident physician at Tuskegee Institute and was the first woman of any race licensed to practice medicine in Alabama.[12]

The public accomplishments and private tragedies of the Tanner family shaped Sadie Mossell's early education and were central to her sense of herself as a highly competent person who must be self-supporting. Although she was born in Philadelphia in the Tanner family home, she grew up on the campus of Howard University in Washington, D.C. Bishop Tanner was on Howard's Board of Trustees, and his son-in-law, Lewis Baxter Moore, was the dean of the Teachers College at Howard University. Dean Moore was responsible for institutionalizing the social sciences at Howard University and was a model for Mossell's aspirations and political views. He was the first black person to earn a Ph.D. from the University of Pennsylvania and was also a founding member with W.E.B. Du Bois of the Niagara Movement. As Mossell moved between the Moore and Tanner households, she met Du Bois, Booker T. Washington, and most of the black intellectual and political leaders of the early twentieth century. This early exposure to the black intelligentsia made her want to become an educated person and a leader in her own right.

There were three early, private tragedies that made Mossell different from other privileged colored girls in the tiny black mid-Atlantic upper class. Desertion and two sudden deaths left her mother without adequate financial or psychological resources. Aaron Mossell was the first black to complete the University of Pennsylvania Law School, but he left his wife, Mary, and their three children when Sadie, the youngest, was barely one year old. The desertion caused great embarrassment and no little economic distress for her mother, who never offered Sadie an explanation for her father's absence. For many years the child believed her father was dead, but he was in self-imposed exile in Europe. Bishop Tanner and Dean Moore provided material and emotional support for Mary and her children. Tanner bought them a house in Washington, D.C., where Mary moved in hopes of getting a job at Howard University and to be nearer to her sister, Sadie Tanner Moore.[13]

Two other tragedies struck the Tanner family in 1901, shortly after Mary Mossell moved her young family to Washington. Sadie T. Moore and Halle

T. D. Johnson both died, leaving six motherless children. Rocked by the loss of her sisters on the heels of her own abandonment, Mary Mossell left her two older children in the Moore household, and for the next decade she shuttled young Sadie between her home in Washington and her parents' home in Philadelphia. When it was time for Sadie to enter high school, she was relieved to be allowed to live with the Moores for four straight years, 1911 to 1915, so she could attend the M Street High School with her friends rather than the nearly all white Girls High School in Philadelphia.[14]

In the Moore household and at M Street High School, Mossell became supremely confident of her intellectual skills and was encouraged to be academically competitive. She was an editor of the school newspaper and had accomplished teachers who, as she said, "put in us a determination that nobody would beat us." She claimed that she even stopped praying to be able to do her best: "[A]fter a while I began to realize that I didn't need to ask the Lord for that . . . because I only knew how to do it the best."[15] Every ounce of that audacious self-confidence would be called upon when she attended college at the University of Pennsylvania. While Sadie Mossell was, on the eve of World War I, among a minority of black girls for whom high school attendance was unquestioned, she was only able to attend college because of the financial support of her grandparents. Her mother's plight seems to have sharpened Sadie Mossell's determination to have her own career and income. Her later views toward women's employment and careers were shaped by her mother's experiences, her grandfather's material support, and, eventually, her husband's concurrence that she was an intellectual who could and should have a career outside of those traditionally reserved for women.

Mossell had won a scholarship and fully expected to enter Howard University in 1915, although her older sister Elizabeth had only gone as far as normal school. The Tanners seem to have focused their efforts upon Sadie's education, perhaps because she was a very good student and the youngest child of their youngest daughter. Mary Mossell had a different plan, however—she enrolled her daughter in the School of Education at the University of Pennsylvania and refused to budge. Sadie T. Mossell greeted her mother's decision to enroll her at the University of Pennsylvania with a tantrum and tears, but did not dare to disobey. This decision most firmly set her on a path to two nontraditional occupations. She entered the university, which was the site of academic "firsts" by her father and uncles, with great reluctance but with a quiet determination to excel.

In the fall of 1915 Mossell began her studies at the University of Pennsylvania's School of Education and was for the first time segregated largely by gender and racially ostracized: "Let us imagine you came from Outer Space and entered the University of Pennsylvania. . . . You spoke perfect English but no one spoke to you."[16] Unlike the coeducational expansion just under way at Howard University and other black colleges, all but a handful of Penn's female undergraduates were enrolled in either education or the College of Women until the 1960s.[17] Seventeen-year-old gregarious Sadie Mossell was given the silent treatment by her classmates. Coming to campus the first day of classes, she sought directions from students, but her queries were met with stony silence. After making her way to the building unaided, Mossell was stunned to discover that the persons she had appealed to were in the same classroom. "Can you imagine looking for classrooms and asking persons the way, only to find the same unresponsive persons you asked for directions seated in the classroom, which you entered late because you could not find your way? Just suppose that after finding your way to a seat in the classroom, not one person spoke to you."[18]

From that first day on campus until she graduated three years later in 1918, she recalled, "Not one woman . . . spoke to me in class or when I passed . . . on the walks to College Hall or the Library." Since she was the only black woman in her class, she "had no one with whom to discuss assignments."[19] There were perhaps a dozen other black students among Penn's undergraduate and professional schools, and Mossell turned to them for her friendships and solidarity. One classmate, Virginia M. Alexander, alerted her to the arrival on campus in 1917 of her brother, Raymond Pace Alexander. Mossell and Virginia Alexander started a chapter of a new Howard University sorority, Delta Sigma Theta, and they drew on Mossell's ties to the black intelligentsia to invite W.E.B. Du Bois, Carter G. Woodson, and other intellectuals to give lectures to Penn's black students.

Sadie Mossell's shunning was not unusual, and this isolation and hostility knew no geographical boundaries and showed clear signs of worsening over time. While some black students attending elite white colleges suffered overt harassment from white students, most experienced what Arthur Huff Fauset called a "rather determined ambivalence."[20] In 1907, Georgiana Simpson, en route to a B.A., was removed from the woman's dormitory at the University of Chicago by the express order of the president of the university, overruling the assistant dean of women, social reformer Sophisonia Breckinridge, who felt that Simpson was a "very able and learned 'woman of color.'" Forty-one-year-old Simpson was old enough to be the mother of the white southern students who forced her out. That same summer Carter G. Woodson lived in Divinity Hall without incident, but black men would be excluded from Chicago's dormitories by 1911.[21]

New England offered no respite from discrimination against black female college students. When she entered Radcliffe College in 1915, Eva Dykes had to live in a private, segregated boardinghouse. Black men at Harvard could live in its freshman dormitories until they were banned from the otherwise mandatory housing in Harvard Yard in 1921; the prohibition was rescinded a few years later, after a furious public protest by alumni. Eating on or near their campus was very problematic for most black students on white campuses. No restaurants or cafeterias at or near Penn would serve its black students. Mossell's appeal to the provost to place these facilities off limits to all students was briskly rebuffed. Even on campuses where black students were allowed to eat with whites, they were subjected to racist behavior. As a Wellesley College student in 1924, Jane Bolin watched southern students "ostentatiously walk out and stand outside" the freshman dining room to avoid sitting with her. Bolin was also forced to live off campus with the only other black student in her class, and she recalled that her roommate was asked by a faculty member to "play the role of an Aunt Jemima figure (bandanna too!)" in a skit in front of the Wellesley Chapel. That request was withdrawn only after Bolin "remonstrated vociferously."[22]

While the question begs for more detailed research, anecdotal evidence suggests that black women at white elite colleges were more often given the silent treatment and barred from campus activities than were black men who also experienced segregation in housing and restaurants. White women's assertion of racial privilege and prerogatives in college parallels the suffrage movement's attempts at racial exclusivity. Black male students participated in athletics—at Penn most of the male students were enrolled in the professional schools and were on the track team and the debating teams. Black men were also welcomed by most campus YMCAs while black women were not.[23] Black male and female students who were campus leaders were often deliberately left out of the yearbook in a blatant attempt to erase their presence from the official class record.[24] For both male and female black students, segregation and discrimination on white private campuses worsened rather than improved over time.

Whether segregation of and discrimination against black students was less overt in the large public universities of the Midwest and West requires further exploration. But when Ida L. Jackson was an eighteen-year-old freshman at the University of California, Berkeley, in 1920, she was subjected to the same silent treatment that was given Mossell from white students: "One of the most difficult problems . . . was entering classes day after day, sitting beside students who acted as if my seat were unoccupied, showing no sign or recognition, never giving a smile or nod."[25] Jackson's parents were uneducated southern freedmen who had moved to Oakland from Vicksburg, Mississippi—origins quite unlike Mossell's upper-class, educated, northern free black background and more like the working-class background of Virginia Alexander. But like the other women students during this era, Jackson drew upon her family's unconditional support and financial sacrifices in order to graduate, despite her extreme isolation and loneliness. She turned to the handful of other black students on her campus much as Mossell had. They formed a Braithwaite literary club, and she helped to establish a chapter of Alpha Kappa Alpha sorority.

/ / /

The isolation and ostracism that black women faced on campuses of white schools caused a significant number to leave before graduation but provoked those who stayed to demonstrate their worthiness in academic achievements. Jane Bolin had mostly "sad and lonely personal memories" of her four years at Wellesley College. Her "sharpest and ugliest memory" was of an encounter with a guidance counselor who "exhibited obvious physical shock" after Bolin said she planned to apply to law school. She was advised to teach because there was no place for colored women in the law. Upset and in tears, Bolin called her father, who promised her the financial and moral support she needed to complete Yale Law School.[26] Despite her silent treatment, Sadie Mossell's grades quickly climbed from good to distinguished, and she earned her undergraduate degree in three years. The Tanner-Mossell household reorganized itself to excuse her from all domestic responsibilities while she was in undergraduate and graduate school, provoking protests of favoritism from her aunts and firmly establishing Sadie's lifelong rejection of housework. Her mother cared for the bishop and the house and prepared her daughter's lunch, so she would not have to leave the campus until evening. Unlike Virginia and Raymond Alexander, who worked all year long, Mossell never worked in college or graduate school and so was free to study without interruptions. In the sweltering heat of Philadelphia summers, Mossell had a desk and lamp set up for her in the cool Tanner basement on Diamond Street.[27]

Mossell's excellent undergraduate record had attracted the attention of the faculty in history, and she was encouraged to apply for admission to the Ph.D. program. The cordial relationships she had with faculty members seemed to offer an oasis of civility in a hostile environment, and despite a rocky start, her experience as a graduate student at the University of Pennsylvania was a much more positive one than her undergraduate years. It was imperative that she win a graduate scholarship or fellowship because the family breadwinner, Bishop Tanner, was nearing ninety and had only a half-pension from the A.M.E. Church. There were only three types of awards available to women graduate students, but Mossell wanted to win the largest and most prestigious, the Frances Sergeant Pepper Foundation Fellowship. When she graduated with honors in 1918, the history department voted to award her the fellowship, but a university librarian strongly opposed the award, accusing Mossell of disturbing a Ph.D. student's desk. Although Mossell was eventually exonerated, the Pepper Fellowship was awarded to another student. She did, however, receive a university scholarship, which covered her tuition, ending her family's largest financial burden.[28]

Mossell's professors were both supportive and protective throughout her graduate years. History professor A. C. Howland was enthusiastic about her before she had completed a single graduate term. In his reply to a letter W.E.B. Du Bois sent to a number of major universities, seeking qualified black students to assist him in a projected history of World War I, he said, "She is one of the most able students we have had in history for some time and has made a brilliant record for herself in the courses at the university."[29] After a year in history Mossell decided to switch to economics, which seemed to her to be more fitted to the modern era. Mossell received "her heart's desire," the Pepper Foundation Fellowship, in her third and last year of graduate study.

Sadie Mossell's doctoral thesis, "The Standard of Living among One Hundred Negro Migrant Families in Philadelphia," was detailed and analytical. Over her lifetime the widely dispersed black population of Philadelphia had become increasingly concentrated in three wards, which now had or approached black majorities. Her patrician's view was that the newly arriving migrants from the rural South were worsening the racial climate for the old free families. She meticulously investigated housing, employment, and social institutions of a sample of the newcomers, following the tradition established in earlier studies of the black Philadelphians by W.E.B. Du Bois and R. R. Wright Jr. The economics faculty had her study published by the American Academy of Political and Social Sciences, which was "glad indeed" to make an exception to its policy against publishing dissertations, stating that her work was "so replete with interesting information . . . and . . . so suggestive not only as to methods but as conclusions," that others would do well to follow her example. "The Academy sends out this monograph with the hope that it may stimulate other students, particularly of the colored race, to devote their scientific attainments to a study of living and industrial conditions among the Negroes in this country."[30] Now, after having become an economist, all that remained for Mossell was to get a job.[31]

When Mossell switched from history to economics, which was located in the Wharton School, she minored in insurance. Her major professors, Ernest Minor Patterson and Raymond Bye, contacted the major insurance companies in the Northeast in an apparently sincere effort to get Mossell a position, but to no avail. They even considered not recommending any Penn student for insurance jobs that year in protest, but the faculty's indignation did not change the fact that Sadie Mossell, with a Ph.D. in economics, could not get a job. She got an assignment to do a comprehensive study of tuberculosis among black Philadelphians, but her successful completion of this research led nowhere.[32] Even teaching public school was a limited option in Philadelphia because black people were not permitted to teach in the high schools. She had not earned a doctorate to teach elementary school. In the late fall of 1921 C. C. Spaulding, a black insurance company owner in Durham, North Carolina, came to her rescue and hired her as an assistant actuary.[33] Her move to Durham was trumpeted in the black press as a sign of black women's professional progress, but Mossell, who was overqualified for her job, hated the Jim Crow South and was not given the warm welcome into the Durham elite she believed she deserved.

Mossell needed to support herself and was expected to start helping her siblings assist their mother, so she stuck it out at North Carolina Mutual Life Insurance Company for two years. While in the South, her college sweetheart, Raymond Pace Alexander, completed Harvard Law School and returned to Philadelphia to set up a practice in the summer of 1923. Mossell and Alexander married in the fall of 1923, a month after he passed the bar. Although Mossell left Durham without a backward glance, she had made it clear to her husband that she intended to work and did not want to have children immediately. Raymond Pace Alexander supported his wife's determined non-domesticity throughout their fifty-one years of marriage. Newlywed Mossell Alexander wanted a professional career but was still determined not to teach young children. After one miserable year as a housewife and NAACP (National Association for the Advancement of Colored People) volunteer, she gave up the idea having a career as an economist and entered the University of Pennsylvania's Law School with her husband's blessing and financial support. Alexander hoped that her second career choice would prove to be more successful.[34]

Despite years of slights from her fellow students, Sadie T. M. Alexander was not prepared for the hostile reaction of the Law School faculty to her enrollment. She came to feel that her undergraduate honors had helped the graduate school faculty to treat her as a kind of a pet, and she learned belatedly that they had quietly warned incoming white female graduate students not to harass her. There was no such treatment at the Law School. The dean forbade her admission into the women's legal society. Once again she was without study partners, but this time she could review with her husband. The dean refused to either speak to her or call on her in class, and in 1925, he canceled her election to the *Law Review*. When she was elected to the *Law Review* once again in her third year, she was able to serve only because the editor, who was the son of a Law School faculty member, threatened to resign.[35] At her fourth University of Pennsylvania graduation, in 1927, Alexander was surprised to hear her accumulation of degrees mocked by male law classmates, who suggested that she next add "mamma" to the growing list. "The boys looked at the program and they saw my degrees; bachelor's, master's, Ph.D. and they began laughing, . . . what degree is Sadie going to get next? And then somebody yelled, . . . 'Mamma, Mamma!' Mamma didn't come that fast. I passed the bar. . . . My husband opened his office to me and I enjoyed working there."[36]

Obstacles and Opportunities for Black Women Professionals in the 1930s and 1940s

Mossell Alexander's ability to shift careers demonstrated an occupational flexibility that the two other black women who earned doctorates in 1921 did not share. Both Georgiana Simpson and Eva Dykes were single and could have moved to another city, but sexism meant that they were forced to wait for some years until university positions came their way. At Negro colleges, married women were rarely given full faculty appointments and single women's pay was often lower than men's pay. Dykes was personally recruited in 1929 by Mordecai Johnson, the first black president of Howard University, who began to recruit women faculty. When Simpson joined Howard University's German department in 1931, she was sixty-five and taught six years before retiring in 1937.[37] Dykes left Howard in 1944 to teach at tiny Oakwood College in Alabama, where she was the only employee with a Ph.D. Overhearing a male faculty member thanking the president for a raise, she asked the president directly why she was not included and was told the reason was "because you are a woman." Dykes replied, "When I go to the store to buy food or books do they charge me less because I am a woman?" The president was not persuaded by her argument.[38]

Black women did not begin to be hired in permanent positions as social scientists until the late 1930s, when a few pioneers, including Inabel Burns Lindsay, Mabel Smythe, and Merze Tate, gained teaching positions at black colleges. Inabel Burns Lindsay, founder of Howard University's School of Social Work, successfully made the transition from social worker to college professor, albeit as the dean of an increasingly feminized professional school. Before Lindsay arrived, Howard University hired the wives of influential faculty members to teach social work courses as part-time instructors. At least one of these

women, Myra Colson Callis, more than met the qualifications for assistant professor, with a master's degree in sociology from the University of Chicago and
publications.[39]

The social sciences became more welcoming to black women in the 1940s.
Mabel Smythe earned a Ph.D. in economics from the University of Wisconsin
in 1944 and began her teaching career at Lincoln University in Missouri. Merze
Tate, a political scientist with a Litt.D. from Oxford and a Ph.D. in international
relations from Radcliffe, was hired by the history department of Howard University in 1942. A new professional group, the Association of Social Science
Teachers in Negro Colleges, provided publishing opportunities and support
that was not available to Alexander and other black women social scientists in
the 1920s and 1930s.[40]

Although Sadie Mossell Alexander's legal career was still affected by racism
and sexism, over the next fifty years she was able to craft both a private career
as a lawyer and a public life as a womanist intellectual. Economist Julienne
Malveaux suggests that Alexander's failure to make a career in economics was
a "missed opportunity" to make a significant contribution to the literature and
the profession.[41] In fact, Alexander did not completely curtail her research or
writing about black workers in general and black women workers in particular. Her location outside of academia, government, or social welfare organizations hindered her economic writings from being fully incorporated into the
literature of black workers because most of it consisted of public addresses or
was published in nonacademic journals. Alexander did not abandon her training as an economist and put it to use in speeches to numerous uplift and civil
rights organizations. Her continuing familiarity with basic economic data and
trends helped when she was appointed to President Truman's Civil Rights
Commission. She drew on both her aborted career as an economist and her
ongoing work in the law to make forceful arguments for the commission to
examine economic, social, and legal discrimination.[42]

Working as an economist proved to be impossible for Alexander and other
black women in the 1920s and 1930s, but it was possible, although by no means
easy, for black women to establish legal careers in the 1920s. Sadie T. M.
Alexander was one of a small number of black women who successfully practiced law in the 1920s and 1930s.[43]

Black and white women lawyers found it easier to practice when they
worked within a family firm, and most had practices which emphasized
domestic law: divorce, wills, small property cases. When Sadie Alexander
joined her husband's firm, one of his black male partners objected quite
strongly and eventually left the firm. Despite her husband's unequivocal stance
against overtly sexist behavior, Alexander was assigned the domestic court

cases the male attorneys did not want. However, Sadie Alexander did not do housework and she delayed having children until her legal practice was established. Later she employed full-time child-care workers and sent both her daughters to boarding school when they were teenagers. Alexander was free to build her own practice within the firm and used her organizational memberships to become legal counsel for the A.M.E. Church and Delta Sigma Theta sorority. Her marriage and legal partnership gave her more freedom to do uplift work than most women lawyers had, and she was an active board member of the National Urban League, the National Council of Churches, and dozens of other organizations. In the 1950s, after her husband became a municipal judge, Alexander established a successful solo career.[44]

Alexander also was appointed an assistant city solicitor in the 1930s, a part-time position designed to placate or reassure black voters. She was a Republican well into the New Deal, but other black women lawyers who joined the Democratic party in the early 1930s also received patronage appointments at both the city and state level. Just after World War II, Alexander undertook a history of black female lawyers for the National Bar Association and the Haitian Bar. She identified just 57 black women out of a total of 1,400 black lawyers who were practicing in the late 1940s. There were 2.5 million black women workers. The law was still a field that was largely closed to black women, twenty years after Alexander began her practice.[45]

Conclusion

Sadie T. M. Alexander's life spanned the Jim Crow era. The racism and sexism she faced to get an education and begin a career were the norm for black women of her era who chose nontraditional careers. That she and others succeeded to the extent they did is a testimony to their own courage and commitment to racial progress and to the supportive networks of family and friends that each developed. With the exception of Mary McLeod Bethune's New Deal post in the National Youth Agency, black professional women did not have access to the top "race jobs" either. Most executive positions in the National Urban League, the NAACP, the New Deal agencies, and Negro colleges were reserved for black men. Nor were they able to apply for any of the jobs that white female social scientists reserved for themselves in women's colleges, the government, or social service agencies.

The law provided an independent career for Sadie Alexander and a hardy group of pioneers. Unfortunately, the respect they earned from their peers for their legal skills and the widening opportunities for a select few women in state and local court systems did little to change the climate for the women who succeeded them. Sexism made Pauli Murray as lonely and isolated at Howard Law School in the late 1940s as Alexander had been at Penn in the mid-1920s. Years later, in 1965, when Murray failed to get a law school appointment after earning a doctorate from Yale Law School, her description of the stark contrast of emotions between the joy of her graduation day and the somber recognition of her poor prospects on the job market eerily echoed Sadie Alexander's words forty-four years earlier: "Once this day of triumph was over, I faced the somber reality that . . . I still lacked the indispensable contacts I had to have to gain admission into an almost exclusively male preserve."[46] Black women's climb into male professions, such as the social sciences and the law, remained contested and conditional. Pauli Murray's experiences in 1965, the year after the passage of the Civil Rights Act, suggest that the individual and independent successes of women like Sadie T. M. Alexander were not able to fully eliminate the barriers created by racist institutions or sexist practices.

NOTES

1. Letter from Sadie T. Mossell to Raymond Pace Alexander 16 June 1921, Sadie Tanner Mossell Alexander Papers, in the Alexander Family Papers, University of Pennsylvania Archives, Philadelphia, Penn. (hereafter STMA Papers). See also *The Crisis* 22, no. 3 (July 1921).

2. Quote from 10 December 1977 oral history interview of Sadie T. M. Alexander by Walter M. Phillips (WMP), original in the Urban History Archives, Temple University, Philadelphia, Penn., copy in STMA Papers. Harry Washington Greene's *Holders of Doctorates among American Negroes* (Philadelphia: Meador, 1946), 47, describes Mossell as "first in economics as a single field." I have determined that at least one and possibly both of Greene's two earlier economics degree holders were not African American.

3. Stephanie J. Shaw, *What a Woman Ought to Be and to Do: Black Professional Workers during the Jim Crow Era* (Chicago: University of Chicago Press, 1996). Eva Bowles, "Opportunities for the Educated Colored Woman," *Opportunity* 1 (March 1923): 8–10. Georgiana Simpson defended her dissertation on 4 June 1921 and was awarded the Ph.D. in German cum laude at the University of Chicago on 14 June 1921, one day earlier than Mossell, so she was in fact the first black woman to have earned a doctorate. Letter from Andrew Hannah, associate registrar, University of Chicago, to Francille Wilson, 9 March 1998, in the possession of the author. Eva Dykes was the third to receive her degree in English literature at Radcliffe College, 22 June 1921. Since Eva Dykes had successfully defended her thesis in the spring of 1921, it was also asserted that Dykes was the first black woman to have earned a doctorate. Interview of Eva B. Dykes by Merze Tate, 30 November 1977, in *The Black Women Oral History Project: From the Arthur and Elizabeth Schlesinger Library on the History of Women at Radcliffe College,* vol. 3, ed. Ruth Edmonds Hill (Westport, Conn.: Meckler, 1991), 187–227.

4. Robyn Muncy, *Creating a Female Dominion in American Reform, 1890–1935* (New York: Oxford University Press, 1991); George Edmund Haynes, "Negroes," in *Social Work Year Book,* vol. 3, ed. Fred S. Hall (New York: Russell Sage, 1935), 291–297; Nancy J. Weiss, *The National Urban League, 1910–1940* (New York: Oxford University Press, 1974), 216–217.

5. Helen Brooks Irvin, "Conditions in Industry as They Affect Negro Women," *National Conference of Social Work Proceedings* (1919): 521–524; [Gertrude McDougald], *A New Day*

for the Colored Woman Worker (New York: Consumers League for the City of New York, 1919); Emma L. Shields, "Negro Women and the Tobacco Industry," *Life and Labor* (May 1921): 142–144; Elizabeth Ross Haynes, "Negroes in Domestic Service in the United States," *Journal of Negro History* 8, no. 4 (October 1923): 384–442; Francille Rusan Wilson, introduction to *Unsung Heroes*, by Elizabeth Ross Haynes; Elizabeth Ross Haynes, "Negroes in Domestic Service in the United States," in her *The Black Boy of Atlanta* (1921; reprint, New York: G. K. Hall, 1997), xv–xxxvii, in reprint. A discussion of these four women's lives and work is found in Francille Rusan Wilson, *The Segregated Scholars: Black Social Scientists and the Creation of Black Labor Studies, 1890–1950* (Charlottesville: University Press of Virginia, forthcoming).

6. W.E.B. Du Bois, *The College Bred Negro* (Atlanta, Ga.: Atlanta University Studies, 1900), 55–56; Charles S. Johnson, *The Negro College Graduate* (Chapel Hill: University of North Carolina Press, 1938), 8–9, 66–67; [W.E.B. Du Bois], "The Higher Training of Negroes," *The Crisis* 22 (July 1921): 105–113; Bureau of the Census, *The Social and Economic Status of the Black Population in the United States: An Historical View, 1790–1978*, Current Population Reports Special Studies, Series P-23 #80 (Washington, D.C., n.d.), tables 1 and 2.

7. Ida B. Wells, *A Red Record: Tabulated Statistics and Alleged Causes of Lynching in the United States, 1892–1893–1894* (Chicago: Donohue and Henneberry, 1895); Ida B. Wells, "Lynch Law in All Its Phases," *Our Day*, May 1893; Rosalyn Terborg-Penn, "Gertrude Bustill Mossell," in *Black Women in America: An Historical Encyclopedia*, ed. Darlene Clark Hine, Rosalyn Terborg-Penn, and Elsa Barkley Brown (New York: Carlson, 1993); Claudette Brown, "Gertrude E. H. Bustill Mossell," in *Dictionary of American Negro Biography*, ed. Rayford Logan and Michael Winston (New York: Norton, 1982); Elsa Barkley Brown, introduction to *Negro Trailblazers of California*, by Deliah Beasley (New York: G. K. Hall, 1997); Anne Ruggles Gere and Sarah R. Robbins, "Gendered Literacy in Black and White: Turn of the Century African American and European American Club Women's Printed Texts," *Signs* 21, no. 3 (1996): 658–660; Floris Barnett Cash, "Victoria Earle Matthews," in *Black Women in America*, ed. Hine, Terborg-Penn, and Brown; Wanda Hendricks, "Ida Belle Wells-Barnett," in *Black Women in America*, ed. Hine, Terborg-Penn, and Brown.

8. Ida B. Wells, an extract from a personal letter, 6 December 1885, in *The Fisk Herald* 3, no. 5 (January 1886): 5.

9. Andrew Hannah to Francille Wilson, 9 March 1998, letter in author's possession; Catherine Johnson, "Georgiana Simpson," in *Black Women in America*, ed. Hine, Terborg-Penn, and Brown.

10. Johnson, *The Negro College Graduate*, 8–11; Greene, *Holders of Doctorates among American Negroes*; Eva Bowles, "Opportunities for the Educated Colored Woman," *Opportunity* 1 (March 1923): 8–10. There are no breakdowns by gender of black people who earned master's degrees before 1940.

11. "Achievement," *The Crisis* 22 (September 1921): 223, featured a photograph of Georgiana Simpson in her doctoral robes. Simpson's dissertation was titled "Herder's Conception of 'Das Volk.'" Andrew Hannah to Francille Wilson, letter, 9 March 1998. Dyke's dissertation was titled "Alexander Pope's Influence on America, 1710–1850." Interview of Eva B. Dykes by Merze Tate. See also DeWitt S. Williams, *She Fulfilled the Impossible Dream: The Story of Eva B. Dykes* (Washington, D.C.: Banner Books, 1985), 15; Anne Englehart, Staff Assistant, Radcliffe College, letter to Sadie Alexander, 9 May 1979, STMA Papers; Louise Daniel Hutchinson, "Anna Julia Haywood Cooper," in *Black Women in America*, ed. Hine, Terborg-Penn, and Brown.

12. Rosalyn Terborg-Penn, "Gertrude Bustill Mossell," in *Black Women in America*, ed. Hine, Terborg-Penn, and Brown; Jessie Carney Smith, "Halle Tanner Dillon Johnson," in *Black Women in America*, ed. Hine, Terborg-Penn, and Brown.

13. My account of Sadie T. M. Alexander's childhood is derived in part from V. P. Franklin, "Sadie T. M. Alexander," in *Black Women in America*, ed. Hine, Terborg-Penn, and Brown;

and two oral history interviews which contain errors and contradictions: interview of Sadie T. M. Alexander by Walter M. Phillips, October 1977, Temple University Urban Archives; and interview of Sadie T. M. Alexander by Marcia McAdoo Greenlee, 26 January 1977, in *The Black Women Oral History Project*, ed. Hill, 72–85.

14. Jessie Carney Smith, "Halle Tanner Dillon Johnson"; Walter Dyson, *Howard University, The Capstone of Negro Education: A History, 1867–1940*, (Washington, D.C.: The Graduate School, Howard University, 1941), 374–375. Moore married Sarah Tanner in 1895 and married Lavinia Waring about 1903. Alexander never mentions her aunt's death or Moore's second wife in her extensive interviews or her writings.

15. Quote from oral history interview of Sadie T. M. Alexander by Walter M. Phillips, 10.

16. Sadie T. M. Alexander, "A Clean Sweep," *Pennsylvania Gazette* 70, no. 5 (March 1972): 27–28, 30–32. Also quoted in Marvin P. Lyon Jr., "Blacks at Penn, Then and Now," in *A Pennsylvania Album: Undergraduate Essays on the 250th Anniversary of the University*, ed. Richard Slater Dunn and Mark Frazier Lloyd (Philadelphia: University of Pennsylvania, 1990), 43–48.

17. Lisa M. Silverman, "Women at Penn in the 1950s," in *A Pennsylvania Album*, ed. Dunn and Lloyd, 49–52.

18. Lyon, "Blacks at Penn, Then and Now," 43–44.

19. Ibid., 43.

20. Ibid. Arthur Huff Fauset (1899–1983) earned three degrees, including a 1942 Ph.D. from the University of Pennsylvania.

21. Ellen Fitzpatrick, *Endless Crusade: Women Social Scientists and Progressive Reform* (New York: Oxford University Press, 1990), 182. Chapter 2 of Wilson's *The Segregated Scholars* discusses segregation at the University of Chicago. R. R. Wright Jr.'s *Eighty-Seven Years behind the Black Curtain* (Philadelphia: Rare Book Co., 1965) describes his living in the men's dormitories between 1898 and 1906.

22. Jane Bolin Offutt, "Wellesley in My Life," excerpt from *Wellesley After-Images: Reflections on Their College Years by Forty-Five Alumnae*, ed. Wellesley College Club of Los Angeles (Los Angeles: Wellesley College Club of Los Angeles, 1974), 91–92, in *Black Women in Higher Education*, ed. Elizabeth Ihle (New York: Garland, 1992), 147–150.

23. Wilson, *The Segregated Scholars*, chapters 2 and 4 passim; Marcia Synnott, *The Half-Opened Door: Discrimination and Admission at Harvard, Yale, and Princeton, 1900–1970* (Westport, Conn: Greenwood Press, 1979); correspondence from John Hope to Frank J. Miller, Examiner for Secondary Schools, University of Chicago, 24 May 1911 and reply 2 June 1911, John and Lugenia Burns Hope Papers, Atlanta University Center Archives, Atlanta, Ga.; Lyon, "Blacks at Penn, Then and Now," 43–48.

24. Ida L. Jackson has an account of paying for a photo of the AKA sorority in the yearbook and it being omitted. See *There Was Light: Autobiography of a University: Berkley, 1868–1968*, ed. Irving Stone (Garden City, N.Y.: Doubleday, 1970), 249–256. Lyon's "Blacks at Penn, Then and Now," 43–48, discusses the omission of a photo of the track team the year its captain was a black man.

25. Quoted in Stone, *There Was Light*, 253–254.

26. Offutt, "Wellesley in My Life," 150. In 1931 Jane Bolin [Offutt] became the first black woman to graduate from Yale Law School, and in 1939 she became the first black female judge in the United States when she was appointed as a domestic relations court judge in New York.

27. All of Sadie T. M. Alexander's academic records are in the STMA Papers.

28. The University of Pennsylvania, *Catalogue, 1918–1919* (Philadelphia: University of Pennsylvania, 1918), 691.

29. A. C. Howland to W.E.B. Du Bois, letter, 22 November 1918, STMA Papers.

30. Clyde L. King, Editor, foreword to Sadie Tanner Mossell's "The Standard of Living among One Hundred Negro Migrant Families in Philadelphia," *Annals of the American Academy of Political and Social Sciences* 98, no. 187 (November 1921): 169–218.

31. Robert Gregg, *Sparks from the Anvil of Oppression: Philadelphia's African Methodists and Southern Migrants, 1890–1940* (Philadelphia: Temple University Press, 1993), 25–27.

32. Sadie T. Mossell, *A Study of the Negro Tuberculosis Problem in Philadelphia* (Philadelphia: Henry Phipps Institute, 1923).

33. The oral history interview of Sadie T. M. Alexander by Walter M. Phillips suggests that an appeal was made to Spaulding to hire her so that the white students could be placed.

34. Franklin, "Sadie T. M. Alexander"; oral history interview of Sadie T. M. Alexander by Walter M. Phillips; and interview of Sadie T. M. Alexander by Marcia McAdoo Greenlee.

35. Oral history interview of Sadie T. M. Alexander by Walter M. Phillips; law school grades for second and third year and law review letter, STMA Papers.

36. Oral history interview of Sadie T. M. Alexander by Walter M. Phillips, 6.

37. Dyson, *Howard University*, 176; Johnson, "Georgiana Simpson" in *Black Women in America*, ed. Hine, Terborg-Penn, and Brown; DeWitt Williams, *She Fulfilled the Impossible Dream: The Story of Eva B. Dykes* (Washington, D.C.: Banner Books, 1985).

38. Williams, *She Fulfilled the Impossible Dream*, 99–100.

39. Rayford Logan, *Howard University: The First Hundred Years, 1867–1967* (New York: New York University Press, 1969), 367–370, 491; Myra Hill Colson, "Negro Home Workers in Chicago," *Social Service Review* 2, no. 3 (September 1923): 385–413; Lorenzo J. Greene and Myra Colson Callis, *Negro Employment in the District of Colombia* (Washington, D.C., Associated Publishers, 1932).

40. Mabel Smythe, "Tipping Occupations as a Problem in the Administration of Protective Labor Legislation" (Ph.D. diss., University of Wisconsin, 1944); Mabel Smythe, "The Economics Teacher in the Post War Period," *Quarterly Review of Higher Education among Negroes* 12 (April 1944): 173–176; Rosalyn Terborg-Penn, "Merze Tate," in *Black Women in America*, ed. Hine, Terborg-Penn, and Brown.

41. Julianne Malveaux, "Missed Opportunity: Sadie Tanner Mossell Alexander and the Economics Profession," *American Economic Review* 81, no. 2 (May 1991): 307–310.

42. Sadie T. M. Alexander, "Negro Women in Our Economic Life," *Opportunity* 8 (July 1930): 201–203. Among the numerous economic addresses in STMA Papers are "The Role of the Negro Women in the Economic Life of the Postwar South" and "Sugar without Social Security" (about Puerto Rico).

43. The black women lawyers who attended law school at elite white Northeastern schools or at Midwestern state universities had bachelor's degrees, while others attended schools such as Portia School of Law or Howard University, which did not require a B.A. in the 1920s. See J. Clay Smith, *Emancipation: The Making of the Black Lawyer* (Philadelphia: University of Pennsylvania Press, 1993); Ralph Chester, *Unequal Access: Women Lawyers in a Changing America* (South Hadley, Mass.: Bergin and Garvey, 1985); oral history interview of Sadie T. M. Alexander by Walter M. Phillips.

44. The financial records of the Alexander law firm remain to be analyzed by scholars.

45. Sadie T. M. Alexander, "Women as Practitioners of Law in the United States," typescript in box 71, folder 68, STMA Papers; J. Clay Smith, *Emancipation*; Chester, *Unequal Access*; oral history interview of Sadie T. M. Alexander by Walter M. Phillips.

46. Pauli Murray, *Song in a Weary Throat: An American Pilgrimage* (New York: Harper and Row, 1987), 360. Murray was also experiencing discrimination because of her age and her radical politics.

A Sister in the Brotherhood

Rosina Corrothers Tucker and the Sleeping Car Porters, 1930–1950

MELINDA CHATEAUVERT

PERSONAL STATEMENT "Well, with a focus like that, you'll be totally employable, or totally unemployable," a friend commented when, during the middle of the culture wars, I proposed a dissertation on the women of the Brotherhood of Sleeping Car Porters. In most ways, including the teaching job I took upon graduating, my topic was absolutely perfect for me. As a women's studies major at the University of Massachusetts, Amherst, I did "isms cubed": simultaneously learning radical economics and Afro-American studies while casting a critical eye on the racist tendencies of feminism. As an activist and a public policy researcher in Washington, D.C., I examined race- and sex-based discrimination in the workplace for a law office that represented unionized workers. As Ph.D. student in U.S. history, I saw all of these interests come together in my dissertation on twentieth-century black trade union women in a civil rights organization—at least theoretically.

Some view my writing as a white woman about African American women as misguided at best and, at worst, patronizing. Moreover, in contradiction to the historiography of black trade unionism, I chose to analyze my subject using gender as a category of analysis rather than race discrimination or nationalism. But by looking at gender issues within the Brotherhood, I explored the racialization of gender and, particularly, the importance of black manhood rhetoric in African American political thought. Now I found that I might be doubly suspect: I was criticizing black men for their sexist behavior, which, in the days of Anita Hill and Clarence Thomas, was certainly not a new complaint. But again, that was a topic claimed by black women, not white women like me. (And given the racist exploitation of sexual harassment by white feminists in the aftermath of those hearings, I wanted to distance myself from their self-aggrandizing behavior.)

About this time, I organized a dinner at a restaurant for my partner's visiting relatives. We were both appalled when my brother-in-law declared he would drive from his downtown workplace to the southeastern suburbs to pick up his wife before meeting up with us in the restaurant in a northern suburb, a trip that would take more than an hour and a half in rush hour traffic. It wasn't right for "the wife" to drive the Beltway alone, and she was the one with the Lincoln. My partner's family consciously adheres to their religious beliefs and class aspirations to determine proper gender behaviors. This observation forced me to reexamine the apparent sexism of Brotherhood men. And what I discovered was the complicity of women in the Ladies' Auxiliary in enforcing traditional gender roles.

Why would these women undermine their power by insisting on such sexist behavior? Because "ladyhood" and femininity are routinely denied to African American women. By identifying as housewives with interests in trade unionism and domestic politics, the Ladies' Auxiliary asserted a culturally and politically defiant stance. That was how I, as a historian, came to understand how people looked at the world at that particular time and in that particular place. In the mid-twentieth century, when people aspired to suburbs and nuclear families, Brotherhood men and women wanted to have the same benefits as whites. Many African Americans still do, as my brother-in-law's neat, brick suburban home in Prince George's County attests.

Participating in the Black Women and Work seminar over these past several years provided me with the necessary credentials to write about African American women.

---

*R*osina Tucker had a dream job. She worked as the international secretary-treasurer of the Ladies' Auxiliary to the Brotherhood of Sleeping Car Porters, of the American Federation of Labor. She worked with more than one thousand black women in sixty-one locals of a black trade union on economic, political, and social policy issues in Washington, D.C., and she got paid for it.

Rosina Tucker earned her dream job in 1938.[1] Before then, she put in thirteen years as an unpaid organizer for the Brotherhood. She was also the wife of a rank-and-file union porter. Tucker was born in Washington, D.C., in 1881, the daughter of freed slaves. Her father, she wrote, never wanted "any of [his] girls working in white people's kitchens." From her family she learned music. While still in her teens, she published a concert waltz she titled "The Rio Grande Waltz." Her sister Marietta gave Duke Ellington piano lessons.[2]

Throughout her life, Tucker studied the dictionary to learn new words. Though she never finished high school, she took efforts to educate herself: "I learned to study a subject, analyze it, and come to my own conclusion. I developed the art of thinking for myself. I came in contact with people who had an aptness to analyze and discuss momentous events of our times and who were ever striving for self-improvement."[3]

In her autobiography, *My Life as I Have Lived It*, Tucker described herself as a young woman: "I never thought of myself as an attractive girl. I always thought of my two sisters as better-looking than I. . . . I was straight-up-and-down. At fourteen, I stood 5'7", taller even than my brothers—and weighed 145 pounds. My hair was very fine and soft and would break off before attaining any length. Throughout my childhood, I was called 'nappy-headed Rose Harvey' when some of the girls became mad at me. My sisters . . . tended to look to Papa for advice about every detail of their lives, I was surprisingly independent."[4] At seventeen, this independent, nappy-headed girl found herself being courted by the poet and A.M.E. minister James D. Corrothers (1869–1917).[5] Widowed at thirty-five, she had no intention to remarry. But in 1918 a girlfriend pestered her into marrying again. B. J. Tucker, a Pullman porter, became her second husband.

B. J. Tucker "was a man who firmly believed that a woman's place is in the home." He insisted his wife quit her civil service job as a file clerk and take over the housework to free his mother, who lived with the couple, from further work. Although the newlywed Mrs. Tucker chafed at the enforced domesticity and her new husband's assertion of patriarchal authority, she did not disagree with her husband's opinion. But she always added that the man should be the head of the household "only if he has the ability to do so." She later admitted, "I had problems with Berthea . . . right from the start."[6] During their forty-year marriage, the proper role of wives—and of husbands—would be a contentious point between the couple. One can surmise that Tucker's domestic experiences led her to advocate an expanded role for women in the Brotherhood of Sleeping Car Porters and in the community generally.

Tucker was not a housewife who stayed home. She was a community activist and a member of the prestigious Fifteenth Street Presbyterian Church, founded before the Civil War. After serving as a church mother and an adult Bible-study teacher, she became the first woman elected to the trustee board. She drew her strength from her religion. Despite many personal misfortunes, she never questioned the ways of God, although she quarreled with his servants' methods. In 1923, she started her own women's club, "to do something constructive" for children in Northeast Washington, D.C. Working in these organizations gave her the skills, experience, and contacts she needed to organize Pullman workers and their families.[7]

In late 1925, Tucker met A. Philip Randolph, president of the Brotherhood of Sleeping Car Porters (BSCP). The Brotherhood was organized in New York City in August 1925. With Tucker's assistance, Randolph organized the Washington BSCP local right in Tucker's home two months later. For twelve years, the union fought for recognition. In 1937, the BSCP became the first trade union controlled by African Americans to win a labor contract from a major U.S. corporation.

The BSCP achieved firsts in other areas too: It was the first black union granted an international charter by the American Federal of Labor. More importantly, the BSCP was the first union to represent African American women in the railroad industry, a bastion of native white male labor power. The Brotherhood's International Ladies' Auxiliary was the first international African American women's labor organization.[8]

To African Americans in the mid-twentieth century, these firsts made the BSCP more than a just bread-and-butter labor union for Pullman porters. The Brotherhood taught black workers in other trades and industries the power of organization and encouraged them to join the labor movement. The BSCP was a race organization that advocated trade unionism as the solution to the problems faced by African Americans. The union challenged the National Association for the Advancement of Colored People, the Urban League, and Marcus Garvey's Universal Negro Improvement Association, forcing these groups to pay attention to economic issues.

The BSCP argued that good wages earned under decent working conditions would give the black community the power it needed to win political rights and social justice. The Brotherhood led the Civil Rights movement during the 1940s and 1950s. Randolph organized the first March on Washington in 1941, forcing President Franklin D. Roosevelt to issue the first federal executive order prohibiting job discrimination on the basis of race, color, creed, or national origin. And it was local BSCP president E. D. Nixon who bailed Rosa Parks out of the Montgomery city jail in December 1955.

The Ladies' Auxiliary was not only the women's section of the BSCP, but also an organization of African American women working on economic, political, and social justice issues in the name of trade unionism. As BSCP vice president Milton P. Webster described it, "The Brotherhood Ladies' Auxiliary is not a social Auxiliary. . . . There is opportunity for a woman to exercise her ability and intellectual talent. They have a wide opportunity to develop themselves."[9] Most of its members were the wives of Pullman porters. Many worked, particularly if they had good jobs as teachers, sales clerks, and government employees. A few auxiliary members formally belonged to the BSCP. These African American women worked as sleeping-car maids, as porterettes and train maids, and as car cleaners in the Pullman yards.

Rosina Tucker and other auxiliary women worked with the BSCP political campaigns, such as the 1941 March on Washington and the 1958 Prayer Pilgrimage for Integrated Schools. Yet most of the auxiliary's political work was conducted independent of the BSCP. Tucker agreed with the advice given by Lillian Herstein, of the Chicago American Federation of Teachers, who told the founding convention of the Ladies' Auxiliary, "You are going to be an auxiliary of trade union women, and you are going to share the work and responsibilities of the Brotherhood. . . . Don't let them fool you with the decorative jobs. When they can't get rid of the women, they always give them little decorative jobs."[10] Rosina Tucker had no intention of decorating the union hall.

Ideas about what a black woman should and should not do limited the scope of the auxiliary's political protest activities. Tucker's vision for the Ladies' Auxiliary challenged her union sisters' more traditional ideas. She believed in the "union woman." Another model of African American labor women was the "union wife," the picture held by Halena Wilson, the international president of the Ladies' Auxiliary. Tucker and Wilson differed over the appropriateness of wage work for women. Tucker saw that everyone worked, men, women, and children, whether they earned a wage or not. Wilson did not think women should work for wages.

The issue of women's paid work carried over to the volunteer work of the auxiliary. Many in the auxiliary believed that "it isn't lady-like to be a union woman." Tucker agreed with Herstein, "I think it is very lady-like to belong to a union. And the next best thing to it is to belong to a union man."[11] Tucker saw herself as a union woman. Others, perhaps a majority of auxiliary members, preferred to be that "next best thing," the union wife. Halena Wilson, the international president of the Ladies' Auxiliary, saw herself as a union wife.

Tucker was a union woman who wanted the auxiliary to be the big sister of black working women everywhere. In her view, the organizational power of trade unions gave women the means to advance themselves economically and to give themselves a political voice. She was eager to organize unions for domestics, laundry workers, and schoolteachers, the three major occupations in which black women worked. For her, work could be paid or unpaid, but she did not think wage earning should be reserved for men.

Nor did she think politics and organizing should be reserved for men. She said what she thought. She didn't mind challenging people she believed were wrong, especially when she knew they were acting like hardheaded fools. Her minister, the Reverend Francis Grimké, did not think that trade unions could help African Americans, even all-black unions like the Brotherhood of Sleeping Car Porters.[12] Tucker told Grimké he was wrong and spent two years arguing with him until he agreed to support the BSCP. She was just as argumentative with her union brothers and sisters.

Tucker's forthrightness was a quality President Randolph admired, "She is distinguished for an impressive personality and a brilliant mind."[13] When organizing the women, Randolph advised, "Success in organizing [the Ladies'

Auxiliary] will depend largely upon the character and personality of the individual secured as head or President. . . . The aim should be to get as strong and popular a woman as possible."[14] Tucker's intellect, strength, and personality made her essential in the campaign to organize the Washington local of the Brotherhood of Sleeping Car Porters.

When the BSCP was founded in 1925, no one recognized the right of workers to organize. The Pullman Company spied on, harassed, blacklisted, and fired porters and maids whom management suspected of disloyalty. Despite the poor working conditions and the low wages, working for Pullman was considered a good job in those days. And, of course, no one ever wants to lose a good job. President Randolph and Tucker recognized that women's support for the BSCP would be crucial to winning recognition. Union organizers had to work secretly. Tucker writes: "So it devolved upon the wives of the porters to do most of the organizational work . . . I was asked to act as liaison between Mr. Randolph and the Washington division. Material was sent to me and I personally disseminated it to the men. I kept them in touch with what was going on, because it was dangerous for them [union members] to let it be known even to each other that they were members or had expressed any interest in the Brotherhood." Because she was a housewife, spies for the Pullman Company did not suspect her of union organizing. The wives of Pullman porters traditionally called on each other at home, a social nicety Tucker used as a guise to organize. In her handbag, Tucker brought BSCP literature for the family to read. And she left the house with union dues she had collected. Some wives "put their husbands' names on the rolls and paid their dues for years," while others opposed the union, fearing a husband could lose his job. Tucker believed "it was absolutely necessary . . . that Pullman porters' wives be cognizant of their husbands' working conditions. The porter's home had to be a union home. Without a union home, the porter could not be a good union man."[15]

The Washington Ladies' Auxiliary recognized Rosina Tucker's eleven years of work as president in 1935, presenting "her [with] a beautiful brief case."[16] It replaced the handbag in which she carried BSCP literature in the early years of organizing. Upending middle-class notions of women's charity work, they chose a gift symbolic of professional male office workers. This gift, intended for workplace use (or, more accurately, for taking paperwork home from the office) is a sign that the women saw their activities as work, not voluntary service.[17]

The symbolism of this gift is not a single, isolated detail. Tucker believed strongly in the right of women to work. Her husband strongly disagreed. He thought she spent too much time working on auxiliary and Brotherhood affairs and too little time at home. Whether they paid her or not didn't seem to matter. At the time she was not earning money from the BSCP, although upon her election as international secretary-treasurer in 1938, the union paid her a small salary.[18] For her official photo, she chose to be seated at her desk, using the symbols of her office: a membership registry, the official seal, the charter of the Ladies' Auxiliary, and sheet music of the auxiliary's official anthem, "Marching Together."

Tucker was happiest when her Pullman porter husband "was away on his runs." When she felt his demands on her were too great, she took "vacations."[19] During these separations (one of which lasted almost two years) she lived with female friends or her sister and continued to do her work for the Brotherhood. Even at sixty, she remained as independent as she was as a teenager. Union work was more important for her than marriage.

As an auxiliary leader, Tucker kept the wives and female relatives of BSCP men committed to the union. She arranged educational and social programs for each monthly meeting. She joined with African American and white women labor activists in the District of Columbia to develop a wide network of labor organizers. Tucker met Mary Anderson, head of the U.S. Women's Bureau from 1920 to 1944, while organizing the Brotherhood. Anderson spoke several times at mass meetings organized by the Washington auxiliary.[20] During the New Deal years, the Ladies' Auxiliary supported the secondary boycotts called by the Washington Women's Trade Union League (WTUL) and the National Negro Alliance to protest the lack of job opportunities given to African Americans at the Sanitary Grocery Company (now Safeway). They also assisted the WTUL in organizing unions for laundry workers, domestic workers, and hotel and restaurant workers, all largely African American women's occupations. "Word went out that colored maids wouldn't organize but they did," Tucker wrote in the BSCP newspaper.[21] Continuing their focus on the work of African American women, the auxiliary joined with Mary Mason Jones, the African American president of Local No. 27 of the American Federation of Teachers, to sponsor several events.[22] Concluding her report of union activities for 1938, Tucker summarized: "I am proud to make this report . . . because it shows that Washington is labor conscious and that the forces of labor are united to a very great extent and too you should observe . . . that labor in Washington is definitely breaking down race prejudice."[23]

Her organizing work among women stretched across race lines. She did not, however, confine her organizing to women. She also did men's work for the Brotherhood. According to the *Black Worker*, the union paper, "She went up and down the streets of Washington and into the offices of the Washington Pullman supervisor and courageously spoke her piece about the right of porters to join the Brotherhood."[24] President Randolph and some Brotherhood men valued her courage to speak against injustice.

Her husband may not have appreciated his wife's assertiveness, but when he was unjustly laid off, she spoke for him, too. The Pullman Company supervisor took Berthea Tucker off his run to punish him (and his wife) for supporting the union. She did not let the company get away with its union busting: "I decided that I'm not going to take that, I'm going to the office and see the superintendent. . . . I went to the phone and rang up the superintendent. . . . I identified myself as Mrs. B. J. Tucker. There was a silence. 'Wait a minute.' Somebody else came to the phone. I said I wanted to speak to the superintendent, calling him by name. This second man told me that the superintendent was 'in conference.' Now I knew that it was the superintendent to whom I had first spoken and that, when he learned who it was to whom he was speaking, he skipped."[25]

The superintendent stayed "in conference" over the next two days, until Brother B. C. Massey advised Tucker to "see the man *over* the superintendent." Finally she called upon the Pullman manager in his office, walking in past the secretary's unattended desk.

> "I came to see about my husband, Mr. B. J. Tucker."
>
> "What about him?" the official asked.
>
> "He was taken off his run and the man at the sign-out office told him 'Nothing in hell could take him off that run except your wife's activities in the Brotherhood of Sleeping Car Porters!'"
>
> "So?"
>
> Pounding on his desk, I declared, "I want to tell you that nobody has anything to do with what *I* do!"
>
> "Why are you taking the matter up? Why not Tucker?"
>
> "Because they brought me into it. Now! You take care of this matter and put my husband back on his run, or else I'll be back."[26]

Her threat worked. "Well, for a black woman to speak up to a white man like that in those days was considered extraordinary." Naturally, he thought that there was somebody very powerful supporting her. However, Berthea Tucker got his run back immediately.[27]

This confrontation empowered Tucker in her future dealings with Brotherhood men. She believed she earned the right to question the men's decisions, and she acted accordingly. President Randolph supported her, using her speaking talents in other unionization drives and political campaigns. He called on her to help organize the Provisional Committee of the Colored Locomotive Firemen in 1940. She went on to help organize Pullman yard workers and car cleaners in the Washington yards during World War II. For the 1941 March on Washington, she spoke on street corners and in movie theaters to raise public awareness of the movement.[28]

Rosina Tucker was a union woman. The lyrics of "Marching Together," the anthem she composed in 1939 for the BSCP Ladies' Auxiliary, define what she meant by a union woman. She portrayed women as equals, encouraging them to work with their husbands in the "great campaign" "to bring truth and justice nigh." She praised women for the "manly hardships" they bore. Women of the Brotherhood fought "injustice of all kinds," "our bondage to relieve."[29]

The union woman was a worker. She did not necessarily receive a wage for her labors; she could be a housewife dependent upon her husband's income. Tucker's many disagreements with her husband show that she did not believe wage earning or union protection should be reserved for men. She recognized that women did not always earn wages for their labor and that the wages African American women earned were rarely comparable. Nor did she think that women should have to rely on men for financial support. Thus all women could benefit from trade unions, because all women needed economic power.

Economic power meant political power. Rosina Tucker was a citizen, too. In addition to her union work, she fought for equal rights for disenfranchised residents of the District of Columbia, black and white. Her political activism during the 1941 March on Washington took her into local Washington politics. She was elected president of the newly reorganized Public Interest Civic Association in 1942 and became a delegate to the citywide Federation of Civic Associations. That group fought vigorously against the District commissioners' order to racially segregate public parks and recreational facilities (even though the District's federally supervised parks had just been integrated by Secretary of the Interior Harold Ickes). That segregation order started the Civil Rights movement in Washington.[30]

In her work as chair of the Social Service Committee, Tucker surveyed racially segregated public welfare institutions and schools in the city, issuing a report that bitterly indicted the District's facilities for African American children. She lobbied for funds to equalize facilities, forcing Congress to appropriate millions of dollars to correct the problems, although it refused to desegregate the facilities.

Tucker wanted to create a "suitable living environment" for children and testified in Congress on behalf of the "Working Mothers of the District of Columbia" to extend federal funding of day-care centers "that are so much needed by the Negro Working Mother."[31] In 1950, she became the only African American woman on a committee to investigate children's services in the District. The conditions at both institutions, publicized in a series of newspaper articles, created such outrage that Congress raised the District's appropriation so that new facilities were constructed within five years. She worked to combat juvenile delinquency that she thought was made worse by segregation in the local boys' clubs and the public parks.

Here again, Tucker's belief that trade unionism could solve the race problem is evident. Juvenile delinquency, she wrote, was the result of too few job

opportunities and a lack of education and training programs for both teenagers and their parents. It was not, as Daniel Patrick Moynihan would later
claim, the result of broken homes, poor parental supervision, and working
mothers. To combat what was called "the boy gang" problem, Tucker worked to
develop new recreational programs for youth. In 1955, when she was seventy-
four, the Washington chapter of the NAACP presented her with its Silver Cup
Award for distinguished civic work.[32]

Despite the recognition and honors Rosina Tucker received for her work,
many in the auxiliary thought her too forward in her approach. They had a
different image of African American trade union women. Halena Wilson, the
international president of the Ladies' Auxiliary, believed in the union wife.
Wilson's union wife enjoyed the domestic security of her husband's union
wages and used her power as a consumer to buy union-made goods. Labor
unions protected men's jobs and, by extension, protected a man's nonworking
wife and family. Women protected their husbands' jobs through their understanding and support for the labor movement. According to Wilson, "The
porter's wife's primary interest is in the security of her husband's job. She
wants to know that the paycheck will be continuous and naturally she wants
it to be as large as possible. . . . Hundred of mothers and wives have learned
from experience that the fate of organized labor determined very largely the
fate of their homes. . . . In many instances wives have been known to reinstate
and keep a husband's dues paid up without his knowledge of it, so that he
may be in a position to receive the desired protection in case any trouble
arises on the job."[33]

This image of the union wife reserved wage earning for men. Like most
people in her time, Wilson thought of work as a set of duties and responsibilities, often requiring physical labor, for which a person earned a wage. Yet she
used the word "work" to describe the activities of the Ladies' Auxiliary. For
example, while planning to organize "a legislative program, a political education program, a consumers' education program, etc.," she thought to appoint
"women to do the research work and to keep abreast of current events [that]
may develop a sense of importance [and] would prove beneficial to the Auxiliary as a whole."[34] Wilson always described auxiliary members as "nonworking women," even though the Chicago chapter, of which she was local
president, held its meetings at night, "for the convenience of members who
work during the day."[35]

The union housewife needed to support the labor movement, according to
the auxiliary president. This was the "very important" work of the auxiliary
because "the labor movement has done a poor job of educating the wife and
mother of its real or potential members. There is evidence also, that this neglect has been largely responsible for women's general indifference, and poor

understanding of a movement that has such a vital bearing upon the well-being of themselves and their families."[36]

For the well-being of Brotherhood families, Wilson encouraged wives to shop the union label, honor product boycotts called by trade unions, organize cooperative buying clubs, and teach children the value of labor. Wilson's own auxiliary drew on Chicago's extensive resources to set an example for other locals. Consumer education was popular, and a series of lectures on this topic led eventually to the formation of a food cooperative located in the Chicago union headquarters in 1943. For almost five years, the co-op offered members basic grocery items and an alternative to the small, overpriced corner markets common on the city's South Side.[37]

Both Wilson and Tucker viewed children as the next generation of labor activists. For Wilson, this meant a war of words against the Junior Achievement programs recently introduced in many public schools after World War II. She believed these programs sought to instill a "Hitlerian pattern of working with the minds of the youth of the country." Children were being taught how to raise capital through the sale of stocks, how to sell their products, to "circumvent existing labor laws and how to oppose organized labor."[38] Working with the International Executive Board of the Brotherhood, Wilson drew up an elaborate plan to organize Junior Auxiliaries across the country. The plan was never realized because of the recession and retrenchments after the war.[39]

The work of the Ladies' Auxiliary sought to complement rather than compete with that of the Brotherhood of Sleeping Car Porters. Rosina Tucker agreed with Wilson that women should understand the labor movement but, unlike the auxiliary president, thought that women could and should participate in concerns beyond household domesticity. From her home in Washington, Tucker sought to improve the lives of all women through the labor movement.

NOTES

1. Rosina Corrothers Tucker, "My Life as I Have Lived It," manuscript in the Rosina Corrothers Tucker Papers (hereafter RCTP), Leadership Conference on Civil Rights, Washington, D.C.

2. Tucker, "My Life."

3. Ibid.

4. Ibid.

5. Richard Yarborough, "James David Corrothers," in *Dictionary of American Biography,* vol. 50, *Afro-America Writers before the Harlem Renaissance,* ed. Trudier Harris (Detroit: Hale Research, 1986), 52–62. Their son, Henry, became a well-known collegiate and professional athlete.

6. Tucker, "My Life."

7. Ibid.

8. Among U.S. trade unions, the BSCP Ladies' Auxiliary was the largest one composed of African American women almost exclusively. While the other African American railway brotherhoods had auxiliaries, none had chapters outside the United States; the BSCP Auxiliary had five Canadian divisions.

9. "Report of the Proceedings of the Southwestern Zone Conference Brotherhood of Sleeping Car Porters, Houston, Texas, April 24–29, 1949," mimeograph, Brotherhood of Sleeping Car Porters Papers, Chicago Historical Society (hereafter BSCP-CHS), box 5, 20.

10. "Midwestern Regional Conference of the Ladies' Auxiliary," *Black Worker* 3 (October 1937): 4; Lillian Herstein's speech is transcribed in "Report of the Proceedings of the First National Convention of the Ladies' Auviliary to the Brotherhood of Sleeping Car Porters," mimeograph, BSCP-CHS, 41–43.

11. Herstein's speech, BSCP-CHS, 43.

12. In 1927, from his retirement, Reverend Grimké endorsed the BSCP. Manuscript notes for Tucker's "My Life," RCTP.

13. A. Philip Randolph to Rev. Bernard Ruffin, letter, 24 June 1974, RCTP.

14. "Cooperation Plan of the Women's Economic Council," n.d., Brotherhood of Sleeping Car Porters Papers, Schomburg Center for Black Culture, New York Public Library, New York.

15. Tucker, "My Life."

16. "Women's Economic Council," *Black Worker* 2 (February–March 1936): 2.

17. In 1940, at a testimonial dinner sponsored by the BSCP to honor Tucker, "The Auxiliary presented Sister Tucker with a handsome black leather pocketbook with her initials in gold. There are so many compartments that she will have to partly fill it with tissue paper." Lottie Moore to Dorothy Williams, 2 March 1939 [1940], C. L. Dellums Paper, Bancroft Library, University of California, Berkley (hereafter CLD-UCB), box 39.

18. Tucker's and Wilson's salaries were hardly more than a stipend, since the union leadership believed they were working for pin money. Wilson earned $60 per month, Tucker earned $40 in 1938, and this increased only slightly during World War II. When the national office stopped subsidizing the auxiliary, forcing the two officers to finance the organization based on the five-cents-per-month dues collected from each member, their salaries dropped to less than $100 per month. In 1949, when her husband forced her to support herself financially, a very embarrassed Tucker wrote to President Randolph: "Since I am assuming all of by obligations financially, and since it is impossible for me to carry on with the salary I am now receiving. I am asking you to find it in your heart to increase my salary, I am not asking for charity, but an increase because I feel that after serving thru the years for such a small amount an increase is deserved." Tucker to Randolph, 4 November 1949, Brotherhood of Sleeping Car Porters Papers, Library of Congress, Washington, D.C. (hereafter BSCP-LC), box 75, folder 8. Randolph claimed it was impossible to pay her any more because of the recession. Randolph to Tucker, 15 December 1949, BSCP-LC, box 75, folder 8.

19. Tucker, "My Life." In 1951, Tucker appealed to the BSCP International Executive Board for a raise: "I am not asking you to give me an increase simply for the sake of giving, but I know that with the amount of work I have done, . . . I have earned an increase and since this is a labor organization, which all of us have fought together to establish for better working conditions, shorter hours and more pay, certainly those who are actually doing the work should receive a living wage. With this in mind, I think the least respectable amount offered me should be no less than $150/month." The board refused, however, to supplement her pay, in part because they did not endorse her decision to separate from her husband. Tucker to Milton P. Webster, 5 September 1951, BSCP International Executive Board Minutes, 1951–1953, A. Philip Randolph Papers, Library of Congress, Washington, D.C. (hereafter APR-LC), box 11.

20. Melinda Chateauvert, *Marching Together: Women of the Brotherhood of the Sleeping Car Porters* (Urbana: University of Illinois Press, 1998), 44, 79.

21. Rosina Tucker, *Black Worker* 4 (May 1938): 2, a report on Washington auxiliary activities.

22. Ibid. See also Mary Mason Jones's speech, "The Negro Woman as a Factor in the Economic Life of America," *Black Worker* 4 (August 1938): 2.

23. Ibid.

24. A. Philip Randolph on Rosina Tucker, *Black Worker*, January 1957, clipping in RCTP.

25. Tucker, "My Life."

26. Ibid.

27. Ibid.

28. Chateauvert, *Marching Together*, 165; Tucker, "My Life."

29. Rosina Corrothers Tucker, "Marching Together," words and music copyright 1939, RCTP.

30. Tucker, "My Life"; Rosina Corrothers Tucker, radio broadcast, "The Public Interest Civic Association," 10 April 1955; Rosina Corrothers Tucker, "To the Board of Commissioners of the District of Columbia," 17 October 1946, RCTP; Rosina Corrothers Tucker to Alice C. Hunter, D.C. Recreation Board, 21 June 1949, RCTP; Rosina Corrothers Tucker, "To the Members of the Board of Education," 29 June 1929 [1949], RCTP; Social Service and Welfare Committee Report, 26 April 1946, RCTP; "Brother Anderson Protests against New Jim Crow Ruling," *Black Worker* 11 (September 1945): 2; Constance McLaughlin Green, *The Secret City: A History of Race Relations in the Nation's Capital* (Princeton, N. J.: Princeton University Press, 1967), 263–264, 269–273, 286–290, 291–295, 310–311.

31. Eileen Brooks to Rosina Corrothers Tucker, 11 March 1946, RCTP; [F.C.A., Social Services Committee], "Summary of Findings" (ca. 1951), RCTP; Minutes, United Community Services, Subcommittee on Institutions, Committee on Public Welfare Services, 9 February 1951, RCTP; Recommendations, Industrial Home for Colored Children and Industrial Home School for Colored Girls, formerly National Training School for Girls, Subcommittee on Institutions, 25 April 1952, RCTP; Program, "Junior Village, D.C. Department of Public Welfare . . . Dedicated by Commissioners of the District of Columbia," 9 September 1956, RCTP; "District Challenge to Lift 450,000 out of Their Heritage of Poverty," "This Is Life in Junior Village: Lonely, Crowded, Hopeless," "Junior Village Report Proposals," "3 Agencies Fill Junior Village," *Washington Post*, 29 November 1959, clippings in RCTP; Report of the Research Committee, Area P, 21 October 1954, RCTP.

32. Mrs. Elizabeth Craig, draft article for the *Black Worker*, 7 February 1955, copy in RCTP; program for the Washington, D.C., National Association for the Advancement of Colored People Annual Dinner, 1955, copy in RCTP.

33. [Halena Wilson], 'Program of the Sixth Biennial Convention and Twenty-Third Anniversary of the Ladies' Auxiliary," draft, n.d., BSCP-CHS, box 10, file 5; see also "Report of the Proceedings of the Sixth Biennial Convention of the International Ladies Auxiliary: Detroit, September 13 to 15, 1948," mimeograph, BSCP-CHS.

34. Wilson to A. Philip Randolph, 1 July 1956, BSCP-LC, box 74, file 3.

35. "1949 Annual Report of the Chicago Ladies' Auxiliary," BSCP-CHS, box 32, file 2.

36. Ibid.

37. Agnes Thornton, "Brief History of the Brotherhood Consumer Cooperative Store," n.d. [1948], BSCP-CHS, box 34.

38. Halena Wilson, "NAM Changes Its Tactics," *Black Worker* 8 (March 1946): 7.

39. Chateauvert, *Marching Together*, 151–152.

PART 3 / *Women's Work through the Artist's Eyes*

Declaring (Ambiguous) Liberty

Paule Marshall's Middle-Class Women

MARY HELEN WASHINGTON

> The life they had made by separating themselves
> from mothers and fathers, from home ground.
> It was precisely this separation that had made each
> of them possible. And now the distance was too great.
> And it was the distance that irked and prodded the
> family to blame and accuse. Even when they didn't really
> want to, they would still say, "It is that life that you made that
> is killing you." Even if they named sin in their complaints, it
> was not sin they blamed, it was straying from their watchful eyes.
> Not retribution for acts, but for separation, for declaring liberty.
>
> —Thulani Davis, *Maker of Saints*

PERSONAL STATEMENT   My mother, Mary Catherine Dalton, and her five sisters (Helen, Sarah, Elsie, Cora, and Bessie) migrated to Cleveland, Ohio, in the early 1920s from Indianapolis, Indiana, and, in spite of their many talents, found every door, except the back ones, closed to them. My youngest aunt, Helen, was trained as a bookkeeper and was so good at her work that the white manager of Guardian Savings Bank of Indiana hired her to work at the branch in the black section of Indianapolis. The Cleveland Trust Company was not so liberal, and Cleveland, being integrated, had no official black branch, so she learned to run the elevator at the bank. My aunt Bessie (who called herself Bessie Beaven Riffe), the entrepreneurial sister, started at the Cleveland Trust as a cook but quickly moved up to managing the lunchroom at the downtown branch of Cleveland Trust on Euclid and Ninth Streets. Aunt Bessie ordered the food, created the recipes, designed the menu, hired and fired, and left the bank at 2:00 (like the other executives) to shop at the fashionable places in downtown Cleveland. Aunt Bessie's supervisor at the bank was a white woman who, knowing my aunt was a smart, competent manager, saw to it that she never got the title.

199

One by one, Aunt Bessie hired all of her sisters, including my mother, to work in the bank's cafeteria. My mother was the salad girl, working during the Great Depression for eleven dollars a week, a depressing job in a depressing age. She went to John Hay night school to get her high school diploma, one of the few blacks in a classroom of immigrants. At age thirty-three, having met my father, who was also employed at Cleveland Trust, she wrote to her best friend, Evelyn, "Your old maid sister is to be married September, 18, 1939 unless I change my mind. Smiles and more smiles." In typical 1940s fashion, she gave the bank two weeks' notice as soon as the wedding date was set. What is striking to me is how clear was the expectation that a woman should exchange her life in the world for marriage and motherhood, how unquestioned the assumption that, for a woman, this was a vertical move.

The work I saw my mother engaged in seemed like drudgery to me. She did laundry in an old wringer washing machine and hung it on the lines in the basement or in the backyard. There was no dryer. She washed and starched curtains and nailed them to a stretcher. She and my grandmother canned food and filled the cellar pantry. I see her work now through different eyes. She cooked wonderful meals even when there was little money. She organized our play, so that we always had coloring books, cutout dolls, jacks, books, games, double-dutch ropes, skates, at least one bike. She taught me and my two older sisters to embroider as we sat by the upright radio at night and listened to "The Shadow," "Doctor Christian," and "The Great Gildersleeve." Though she was a trained pianist, a student in Indianapolis under Lily Lamond and in Cleveland at the prestigious Music Settlement, my mother never played the piano again after all eight of her children arrived. Instead, she gave us lessons. Her entire life was devoted to giving us a better life.

In the 1950s I entered high school at Notre Dame Academy, and it was there I discovered the women who showed me that an intellectual life was possible for women: Sister Owen, Sister St. Louis, Sister Mailee, and Sister Kathryn Ann. In freshman English, Kathryn Ann made us bring empty oatmeal boxes to class to use as drums to accompany the poetry we girls read aloud. We read difficult books like Saint-Exupéry's *Wind, Sand, and Stars* and *Moby-Dick,* and the poetry of e. e. cummings, and she showed us how to be creative, idiosyncratic, probing thinkers. In the 1960s, when the nuns in the Catholic Church started to stir things up, she left the convent. Much later I learned that Kathryn Ann was (and still is) a poet and writer, that when she began to get public notice for her poetry (some of it apparently not sufficiently conservative for the nuns in her order), her superiors quashed her poetry writing.

If I add Paule Marshall to this galaxy of female influences in my work life, I begin to see a pattern. I turned to Marshall because her women characters are all in the act of struggling to free their creative spirits. The work of my mother and her sisters was never fully recognized or respected, so it was natural that my first scholarly work was to rescue the stories of neglected black women writers, and I loved the work I did for my first two anthologies—finding lost black women writers. More than I ever realized, my mother, the nurturer and organizer of other people's lives, and Kathryn Ann, the teacher and developer of other people's growth, are deeply embedded in my psyche. But so are Mary Catherine, the pianist, and Kathryn Ann, the poet.

---

*M*iddle-class black women have so often been represented in contemporary popular culture as vain, materialistic, selfish, and often betrayers of the black community that this image has almost become a naturalized trope. As long as a woman is working class, she can be portrayed as loyal and admirable; but a black woman who achieves success in the professional world is, in current popular culture, dangerous, disloyal, and destructive. One of the reasons for this conflict is that black people are often uneasy about middle-class status. As Valerie Smith points out in her essay on black men and work, middle-class black men in film texts almost always have to perform some act of solidarity with working-class black men, something that shows that they are "down with the brothers."[1]

For black women this breach is much harder to repair. Black women, more often than black men and more often than women of other ethnic groups, are expected to expiate for their deviance in choosing careers and becoming successful. Several films featuring a successful but self-centered career woman estranged from family and community come immediately to mind. In the 1975 film *Mahogany*, directed by Berry Gordy, the ambitious fashion designer Tracy (Diana Ross) betrays both her home community and her devoted, community-activist boyfriend, Brian (Billy Dee Williams), by becoming highly successful in the European world of high fashion and by sleeping with white men. To atone for her transgressive behavior, Tracy is asked at the end of the film to make an act of public confession, agreeing to marry Brian, and to give up her ambitions as a designer. In a more recent film, *Soul Food*, produced in 1997, this trend of dissing the professional woman continues. Teri, the lawyer, played by Vanessa Williams, is the one sister out of three unable to hold on to her husband or to produce children. Since the family is a surrogate for community, this husband-less, childless woman, distrusted by her sisters and unwilling to carry on family traditions, represents a profound alienation from communal values. An earlier film, *The Spook Who Sat by the Door* (1973), about black men working together to form a revolutionary guerrilla movement, is perhaps the classic example of portraying the black career woman as destructive to her community. The only two women in the film, a prostitute and a social worker, are pitted against each other. The prostitute, dressed like an African queen, infiltrates the government to aid the revolutionaries. The social worker, dressed in fashionable Western clothes, betrays them to the police.[2]

The film *Waiting to Exhale* (1996), based on the novel by Terry McMillan, is particularly instructive because it is one of the most popular in the genre of films about successful black women afflicted with disastrous personal lives. Of the four highly successful women in this film (Bernadine, Savannah, Gloria, and Robin), none is shown at the workplace for more than three or four minutes, so that if there is any meaning in their work or any reward besides money for conspicuous consumption, that meaning is excluded from our knowledge about them and from their knowledge about themselves. Without any attention to their work (or to their relationships with family, community, church, etc.), the film is then free to focus on their inability to succeed at their main goal of finding a man and getting into a traditional marriage. It has almost become axiomatic that films will find a way to sabotage a black woman character who has independence, autonomy, brains, and a good job.

Even young women barely on their way to middle-class status can be viewed as undermining the good of the black community. A recent report from the NAACP on the state of black America concludes that as black women "outpace" black men in both graduate and undergraduate schools, the most troubling gap for black America is not the one that divides black and white but "the gulf between black men and women in educational attainment."[3] The result of these attitudes toward black women's achievement is that black women are almost never shown in film or written texts (or musical texts for that matter) as skilled, confident, engaged workers.

This denigration of black middle-class women is a relatively recent phenomenon. Well into the twentieth century, when black women's professional choices were limited to teaching, nursing, some form of social service, and occasionally writing, literally all professional work done by women could be enlisted on behalf of the race. In the early 1900s, writer Pauline Hopkins said that she wrote stories in order to "advance the race." Another early writer, Frances Harper, said that she was using her literary gift to overcome "mountains of prejudice." Even dancing could be turned into race uplift. The young dancer Florence Mills, starring in the hit musical *Shuffle Along* in 1922, saw her work as a crusade on behalf of racial justice and literally believed that every white person pleased by her performance was a friend won for the race.[4] One of the main purposes given for a girl being educated at Spelman College was to produce "a redeemed and elevated womanhood for the Negro race." In 1902,

The National Association of Colored Women's Clubs adopted the motto "Lifting as We Climb" to express the utopian but problematic notion that privileged black women could not and would not rise in the world without lifting up the others below them.

The demands of racial uplift and racial loyalty have meant that writing about the lives of middle-class women who do not uphold these ideals would always produce endings for fictional women of conformity or death—even in the fiction of black women writers.[5] Women in the 1920s fiction of Jessie Fauset and Nella Larsen dramatize perfectly the limited options open to women who desire careers. Fauset's characters most often choose conformity, giving up their transgressive desires for conventional marriages. Larsen's nonconforming women die. In the 1930s, Zora Neale Hurston wrote about women who were safely a part of the working class. Ann Petry's Lutie Johnson, striving for a career as a singer in *The Street* (1946) ends up alone and defeated, losing her only son because of her career ambitions. Petry's nonconventional female pharmacist is a pathetic spinster. The main character in Gwendolyn Brooks's *Maud Martha* (1953) desires a life of art, but that desire is suspended as the novel ends with her discovery that she is expecting her second child, keeping her within a traditional, domestic life.[6] Even in the fiction of contemporary U.S. black women writers, black women of privilege are rarely depicted as intelligent, resourceful, dynamic, and/or fulfilled human beings.

Given this limited survey of middle-class black women characters (and my survey is admittedly brief and cursory), I am sure that somewhere there is a middle-class black woman, in a literary text, who is represented as successful and satisfied and therefore unsettles my categorizations. In this essay, however, I turn to Paule Marshall precisely because she is interested in probing the lives of women whose ambitions create tension and conflict in their lives. From her short stories "The Valley Between" (1954) and "Reena" (1962) to her 1991 novel, *Daughters,* and her autobiographical statements, which I put in dialogue with her fiction, Marshall reenacts this black female drama over class status, professional ambition, and material success. Because Marshall is a politically committed writer, she often attempts to resolve these tensions in the lives of her upwardly mobile characters by making them community workers and political activists. Much is hidden behind those overt political strategies, and I am interested in looking beneath the masks and devices Marshall uses to camouflage the more troubling and threatening aspects of women's desires for achievement and status. In the first part of this essay, I focus on the story "Reena" because desire and anxiety about work, professional status, and privilege emerge here in overt ways as well as in subtexts and disguises, almost as if Marshall's subconscious was working to both suppress and expose them.

"Reena" has had a curiously neglected history, appearing first in *Harper's* magazine as part of a special supplement for the October 1962 issue, called "The American Female," then, as Marshall reports, "languishing" until it was reprinted in 1970 in Toni Cade's landmark anthology of black feminism, *The Black Woman*, and in my anthology, *Black-Eyed Susans: Classic Stories by Black Women*, in 1975.[7] Marshall told the editors at *Harper's* that she would attempt a "kind of story-essay" about the women she knew best: "the comparatively small group of young black women: those from an urban, working-class and lower middle-class, West Indian–American background who, like [her]self, had attended the free New York City colleges during the late forties and fifties." Writing in this hybrid form of a "story-essay," part autobiography, part fiction, allows Marshall to engage in a sleight of hand as she both allows and restricts our access to her autobiographical story. The three characters—the narrator, Paulie; her friend Reena; and Reena's ex-husband, Dave—could easily be read as aspects of Marshall herself. *Paulie* is obviously a play on Marshall's first name, *Paule*, which is pronounced *Paul*, "like a man," but looks as though it might be pronounced *Paul-ee*.[8] Like Marshall, Paulie is a writer (from Brooklyn) with two published books. Marshall's first book, *Brown Girl, Brownstones*, was published in 1959; her second book, *Soul Clap Hands and Sing* (short stories), was published in 1961, a few months before she published "Reena." Like Marshall, whose family is from Barbados, Paulie and Reena are West Indian (Reena's mother is West Indian, her father is from Georgia), and both graduated from one of the free city colleges in New York in the late 1950s, as did Marshall. The third character, Dave, Reena's ex-husband, struggles with issues in his career as a photographer, issues that are similar to the ones Marshall, at age thirty-three, was facing in her own writing career.

When the story opens, Reena and Paulie meet again, after twenty years, at the wake of a woman they both call Aunt Vi. They spend the entire night catching up on the past years, with Paulie, as always, mostly listening as the garrulous Reena recounts the past twenty years of her life. Though both women resisted taking "safe" jobs as "tidy little schoolteachers, social workers, and lab technicians," it is Reena who has been the radical.[9] In the 1950s when she is in college, Reena is rebellious and unconventional, cutting her hair in an Afro, wearing African dresses to accentuate her dark skin, becoming involved in an interracial affair, leaving home to live on her own. In her most political period, she is suspended from school for demonstrating in left-wing groups against lynching in the South and against McCarthyism. After working as a welfare investigator, which she despises for the system's treatment of the poor, she lands a job with a small progressive newsmagazine.

Though Reena is atypical, both Paulie and Reena are meant to represent black middle-class women of the 1950s and 1960s. Despite their talent and preparation, their lives as adults are marked by race and gender boundaries. Armed with her college degree and looking for a job as a journalist in Manhattan, Reena is turned down over and over because of her color. At one point, even her mother succumbs to the notion of the black ceiling and accuses her of stepping out of her place: "'Journalism! Journalism! Whoever heard of colored people taking up journalism. You must feel you's white or something so.'"[10] While class and education cannot overcome racial barriers they face in the job market, these very qualities diminish their chances in the black marriage market: "All those years they spent accumulating their degrees and finding the well-paying jobs in the hope that this could raise their stock have, instead, put them at a disadvantage. For the few eligible men around—those who are their intellectual and professional peers, whom they can respect (and there are very few of them)—don't necessarily marry them, but younger women without the degrees and the fat jobs, who are no threat, or they don't marry at all because they are either queer or mother-ridden. Or they marry white women."[11] Then, in one of the most powerful moments in the narrative, Paulie and Reena, both voices merging, recite together a litany of the reasons black men give for rejecting women of their backgrounds: "'too middle-class-oriented . . . Conservative . . . Too threatening . . . Castrating . . . Too independent and impatient with them for not being more ambitious . . . contemptuous . . . Sexually inhibited and unimaginative . . . Not supportive, unwilling to submerge our interest for theirs.'"[12]

The anger in this passage is so palpable that we might reasonably expect the plot of female anger and assertion to continue. Instead, a male figure intervenes. The narrative unexpectedly shifts away from Reena and Paulie to Reena's then husband, Dave, and his struggles to be a successful black photographer in New York. In Reena's version of the marriage, the couple refuses the bourgeois lifestyle but continues to live close to Harlem so that they can work on social and political issues. While this social and political involvement seems easy and untroubled, the career conflicts in Dave's life emerge, representing some of the most difficult psychological issues for any artist, especially a black one. Because of his fear of taking risks, Dave leaves freelance work and takes a "secure" job with a black magazine, where his work consists of (in Reena's words) photographing the "unrealities" of "the high-society world of the black bourgeoisie." Reena pushes him to open his own studio, to put his experimental work in prestige camera magazines; and gradually the awards and the money begin to come in. But Dave is still dissatisfied with these lesser rewards because, according to Reena, what he really wants and is unable to admit, is "the big, gaudy commercial success that would dazzle and confound that white world down-town and force it to see him."[13] Finally, unwilling to submerge herself in Dave's problems any longer, Reena returns to her old job, and the marriage falls apart under Dave's accusations that she is only working to point up his deficiencies and failures.

The similarities between Dave and Paule Marshall are striking. Dave's struggles closely resemble Marshall's own dilemma as a writer, but, perhaps because in 1962 it was unacceptable for a woman (especially a black woman) to be so absorbed in her own career, it was easier for Marshall to allow those ambitions in a male character. Like Dave, Marshall took a job after college working for a small black magazine, *Our World*, where, for a time, she was the food and fashion editor and eventually a feature writer. In the early 1950s *Our World* was *Ebony*'s closest competition, and like *Ebony* the magazine did pro-files of show business figures, prominently displaying "the hundreds of pairs of shoes, the swimming pools." As part of her fashion editing, Marshall was invited to select the models for the feature stories, but the ones she selected, who looked more like her—with dark skin and African features—were often the ones the editor found "not suitable": "I was terrified that if I didn't get out of there, I'd end up being a hack writer for a second-rate magazine. I went home and started *Brown Girl* [*Brown Girl, Brownstones*, Marshall's first novel, published in 1959] as a kind of antidote to sustain me and make it possible for me to go in there and knock that stuff out."[14]

Another striking similarity between Marshall's life and Dave's is that work creates conflict in their marriages. Reena and Dave divorce because he is too diffident to pursue his dreams; the conflict in Paule Marshall's marriage is over her determination to pursue hers. When she began writing *Brown Girl, Brown-stones*, Marshall was a young married woman, about twenty-six years old, liv-ing in St. Albans, working during the day for *Our World* and at night on her first novel, *Brown Girl, Brownstones*. Turning to that novel after an exhausting day at the magazine, Marshall says, "I never had a more exhilarating writing experience."[15] When she was writing her second book, *Soul Clap Hands and Sing*, however, she had just had her first (and only) child, and things became much more difficult as the conflict between her writing and her husband's idea of her role as wife and mother began to surface:

> It was an easy book to write. But it was also difficult in the sense that I'd just had a baby. And even though my first husband liked the fact that I was a writer, he couldn't quite reconcile himself to the hard work involved. He objected to the fact that I was away from the house working on the book. With the money I got from *Brown Girl*, I went and got help to stay here with my son. I went off to a friend's apartment and worked every day on *Soul*

Clap Hands, and there was strong objection to that. Yet I went ahead and did it. There were, he sensed it, I knew it, my need and determination to be my own woman. To do my own thing. I think this is something women have to acknowledge about themselves—their right to fulfill themselves.[16]

In contrast to this portrait of herself as a transgressive woman, writing in spite of her husband's objections, imperiling her marriage, leaving her child while she goes off to write, Marshall makes Reena, at the end of her story, maternal and giving, her desires turned toward community and family. The psychological probing present in Dave's story now disappears. Reena's exciting job is summed up neatly in the narrative in two simple sentences: "Then her job. She was working now as a researcher for a small progressive magazine with the promise that once she completed her master's in journalism (she was work-ing on the thesis now) she might get a chance to do some minor reporting."[17] In comparison to Dave's story, this passage is smooth and untroubled as if all the turbulence and disorder of desire has been skillfully and safely projected onto the absent male character. In contrast to the powerful undercurrents and tensions of Marshall's own work life, Reena's life is described as a seamless inte-gration of family, work, and community. At the end of the story, she is com-mitted to a number of social action groups. She is heading a delegation of mothers to City Hall to protest conditions in the schools in Harlem, and she starts a neighborhood organization to fight slumlords. She has plans to take her daughters on a pilgrimage to Washington to fight for more rapid school desegregation, and she is saving to take her children to live in Africa so that they will understand black people's true place in history: "'They must have their identifications straight from the beginning. No white dolls for them.'"[18] Reena has now been reconstructed as an acceptable woman worker, her desires turned toward family and community. Is work for middle-class black women still, in 1962, such an anxiety-producing category that even a woman's anxiety about it must be credited to a man? I maintain that Dave is a disguise for those issues that Marshall found too threatening to reveal openly: the tensions between career and marriage, risk versus security, and, perhaps the most un-acceptable for a politically committed writer like Marshall, the desire for acceptance and approval in the white world.

Marshall seems to resolve these tensions over work by making her middle-class women characters community workers and social activists. In her second novel, *The Chosen Place, The Timeless People* (1971), the main character, Merle Kinbona, is never shown in her professional work. Having failed to take her degree in England or to succeed as a teacher in her small West Indian town, she works as an innkeeper and unofficial but powerful community leader. In *Daughters* (1991), Marshall's more recent novel, the main character, Ursa,

abruptly resigns from her job as a successful corporate executive to become
a community worker and political activist.[19] I want to openly confess the
dilemma these choices create for me. On the one hand, I read these choices
for women to become active in social and political and community life as
Marshall's critique of capitalism, her insistence that her women characters be
committed to the work of social and political change and not defined by or
absorbed in wage work. On the other hand, I ask myself if this is just another
form of racial uplift that black women must undertake in order to be acceptable women. Is the concern that black women must show for their communities a way of assuaging the guilt of having moved beyond their communities?
Is the work women do for the community Marshall's way of critiquing the
bourgeois values of a consumerist, capitalist culture? Are my own biases creating these binaries between professional achievement and communal good, or
are these binaries written into Marshall's narratives?[20]

I must confess here that my dissatisfaction with the way Reena is reconsti-
tuted as a community and social activist is very personal. Black women have
always been encouraged to do uplift work and have been given respect for
doing that kind of work. Our ambivalence and anxiety are over working in our
careers. Witness the growing numbers of young career women who feel that
their good jobs are the cause of their unmarried status or their unsatisfying
personal lives. As a university professor, I was for years unable to work well
because of the absence of models in my life who would encourage and sustain
my work. I know how working-class women work. I saw my mother and
grandmother and aunts work, and I have great respect for that work. I belong
to Paulie and Reena's generation, the first generation in my family to do professional work, and I long for descriptions of women at work in their professions. I want to see this work described in detail because that is one way of
showing respect for women's work. I want to know what these woman do all
day, the various stages of their work, their interactions with colleagues, the
resources and skills they need for their work, the problems they solve, the decisions they make, their triumphs and failures. I want an ultrasound picture of
such women at work, so that I—we—can experience black women characters
immersed in, happy in, disturbed by, good at, proud of, even dissatisfied with
their work. I want to experience a woman's face lit up with energy and excitement about her work, like that woman scientist I read about who, whenever she
made a particularly important discovery, skateboarded down the halls of her
lab. I am sitting here in front of my computer at a writers' colony where I have
secluded myself in order to do this writing, where I am the only black person
present, and I know that what enables my own work is my ability, however limited, to imagine such a woman.

I also know that the harried, career-driven, overachieving workaholic is a status symbol in the current cultural mythology of middle- and upper-class America, and I am certainly not trying to elevate or promote that kind of career obsession. I am talking about love of one's chosen work, the psychic freedom to derive pleasure from the work one has been trained to do, a kind of abandonment, a relishing of a job well done, of spending one's energy on a task without holding back, a complete absorption in the work.

But shouldn't we be very careful about buying into the class-based notion that work is liberatory for women? In her essay on black women and work, Helene Christol argues that we must question liberal notions that women's access to the world of work is a form of emancipation. It is, she insists, often another form of control in a modern, industrialized society, masquerading as the key to psychological or economic freedom for women.[21] We could very easily end up valorizing that mass market image of the successful corporate executive as a black woman, a media ideal of self-aggrandizement and consumerism that is being packaged and sold in slick magazines and even slicker movies. "Middle-class black woman" is not a fixed, stable category. It is always being constructed—and marketed. We are, to paraphrase Marx, always being reshaped to serve the needs of capital.

Marshall has always been skeptical about narratives of black middle-class progress. In her first novel, *Brown Girl, Brownstones,* she critiques her own Barbadian-American community in Brooklyn for its relentless and destructive pursuit of money, status, and property: "The novel was an attempt to articulate feelings long held about the acquisitive nature of the society and what I feel to be its devastating impact on human relationships."[22] As a writer committed to goals of radical social justice and black solidarity, Marshall has often been accused (once by a *New York Times* reviewer) of being too political. In the 1950s and 1960s, she belonged to the left-wing American Youth for Democracy and to the Association of Artists for Freedom.[23] She was in marches and demonstrations in those decades and became a strong supporter of a militant black cultural and political nationalism. When the Artists for Freedom sponsored a symposium in 1964, "The Black Revolution and the White Backlash," Marshall gave a speech calling for "independent black organizations and 'the closing of the gap' between black intellectuals and the masses."[24] She was a close personal friend and admirer of Malcolm X and was considering becoming active on a full-time basis in the newly formed Organization for African Unity, founded by Malcolm X after he left the Nation of Islam.[25] All of her texts bear the imprint of her belief in resistance to all forms of oppression, and I think we must read Marshall's texts through this political lens, but we must do so cautiously, recognizing that Marshall's stated intentions are not always the most reliable guides to her fiction.

Without question, the characters Marshall most admires are those who maintain close ties to black communities, work for the poor, and reject consumer-driven lives. She is, in fact, almost singular among black American writers in her determination to construct privileged women characters who retain vital and enabling links to their communities. Both Reena and Ursa fit this profile. Reena's plans for her future have multiple strands, linking her to home, family, and community. Note the ways Marshall writes these images of connection into "Reena." First she creates a diaspora subject by making Reena's mother West Indian and her father African American and during the entire story collapsing any distinction between West Indians and other blacks by alternately using the terms "Negro" and "black." The images that pervade this story (and all of Marshall's fiction) are images of connection: "lines of allegiance," "interrelated landscapes," Reena's hands reflecting "the whole of black humanity.[26] Reena's plan to return to Africa so that her children will "see black people who have truly a place and history of their own," an image of a reverse Middle Passage, is another sign of reconnection.[27] It is important to remember that "Reena" is staged as an extended act of reconnection. Reena and Paulie reunite, after twenty years, in a nightlong encounter in the bedroom of Aunt Vi (with Reena actually sitting on Aunt Vi's Victorian bed of roses), a domestic who spent much of her life living in white homes, with only "Thursdays and every other Sunday off." In recognition of how Aunt Vi's life paved the way for theirs, Reena offers a toast to Aunt Vi and says to Paulie, "'Our lives have got to make more sense, if only for her.'"[28] I see Marshall constantly creating these connections in order to undercut that archetypal insider-outsider split in which the middle-class character is "educated" to identify with the dominant culture and to become dissociated "from kin and kind."[29]

In her 1991 novel, *Daughters*, Marshall puts her main character, Ursa, at the pinnacle of corporate success, but, because Marshall wants to expose the exploitative nature of corporate structures, the novel refuses to portray this work. Ursa Mackenzie is the associate director of a Fortune 500 company, so successful that her father, the prime minister of a fictional West Indian country called Triunion, expects her to become president of a top company. With all of the signs of success in place—the expensive car, apartment, clothes—Ursa abruptly resigns her position with the company, goes to work for a foundation that supports minority causes, and divests herself of the status symbols of that former life:

> She gave up the apartment in Park West Village she could no longer
> afford, sold her furniture, her car—a new Toyota Corolla she had bought

only the year before—even sold the better part of her clothes, all those NCRC suits, as she called them. She didn't even bother to renew her membership at the health club on West End Avenue, where she had gone to swim at least twice a week. And as if reverting to the sixties even as the eighties were getting under way, she got up one morning, washed and washed her hair—all the TCB relaxer down the drain!—Then, once it was dry and standing in a bush all over her head, she parted it down the middle, divided the hair on either side of the part into two thicknesses and carefully plaited it to form a single wreath of a braid that started at her forehead, trailed down behind her ears, and was joined at the back. Her hair was just thick and long enough to manage it.[30]

In *City of Quartz*, his study of Los Angeles, Mike Davis says these entitlements of "designer Downtown living" directly affect the lives of the poor and working classes. In other words, the terms "work" and "class privilege" are inseparable. Luxury lifestyles for the middle class, Davis writes, are constructed so that work, recreation, and consumption for the privileged can be free from "unwonted exposure" to the working class and the poor, lives made possible by new repressions of the space and movement of those undesirable classes.[31] In remaking Ursa, the corporate executive, into a worker-activist, Marshall is asking this charged political question: Without a concern for distributive justice for the majority of black people, what good is personal professional advancement?[32]

Marshall answers this question in *Daughters* by showing the other, shadow side of contemporary labor politics—the massive joblessness and permanent unemployment among the poor and working classes. Ursa's first assignment in her new job is to do a study of political change in Midland City, a small, mostly black city (probably modeled on Newark), where her old friend Mae Ryland, a grassroots organizer, still lives and works with the poor. When she visits Mae, two teenaged girls, one in maternity clothes, the other holding a newborn, come into Mae's office; the baby's twitching limbs betray his mother's drug addiction: "Some of 'em come in here you can hardly tell which one's the mother, which one's the baby." In all of Marshall's writing, it is the work of characters like Mae Ryland that most interests Marshall. We see that interest in the way she shows Mae in action—at work—counseling young women, fighting the mayor and city hall, studying the plans that will affect her clients. Mae Ryland reminds Ursa to remember her true "vocation," not just what she does to make a living: "'I know you out here trying to do a little somethin' that's about somethin' till we can get to the real work. And that's what I mean to do: give you some *real* work!'"[33] After this visit to Mae Ryland, Ursa, now moved to political action, undertakes the campaign that Marshall considers Ursa's real work: she engineers her corrupt father's defeat as prime minister of Triunion.[34]

That haunting phrase in Ursa's mind as she listens to Mae Ryland talk about her work with the poor, "there was no separating the landscapes that filled her mind," indicates Marshall's intention to make the relationship between wage work and working for political and social change an essential one. These interconnected landscapes converge in Ursa's mind because the work one does to make a living is never for Marshall a discrete enterprise; it intersects, overlaps, crisscrosses, is interwoven with all the other aspects of her characters' living. In his essays on the spirituality of work, theologian Matthew Fox reminds us that the origin of work was in what was needed to be done in order for a community to survive. But in an industrialized and postindustrialized world, the question of the community's needs has been subordinated to what needs to be done in order to increase the gross national product. Ursa's choices—to resign her corporate job, to fight her father's political corruption, to support her friend Mae's dreams of transforming the inner city—like Selina's decision (in *Brown Girl, Brownstones*) to renounce her mother's materialism or Reena's fight to make her children aware of poverty and racism, are perhaps, for Marshall, the real work, the work that matters.[35]

But I must return to my contention that behind these sanctioned political scripts are the suppressed and threatening stories of female ambition. At least once before "Reena," Marshall wrote a story which she later admitted was deliberately constructed to disguise her own desire to write. In her very first short story, "The Valley Between," published in 1954, the main character, Cassie, defies her husband and returns to college in an effort to escape the numbing boredom of her life as housewife and mother. Marshall wrote in a later introduction that she made all of the characters in this story "white" in order to, as she says, "camouflage my own predicament because by the time I wrote 'Valley' I was married also—an early, unwise first marriage."[36] The young wife in "Valley" eventually gives in to her domineering husband and leaves school out of the fear she will be a bad mother and because she is unable to assert herself against her husband's male power. Marshall clearly felt this same pressure in the 1950s to be a wife and mother in a conventional marriage and to regard female ambition as transgression. In her justly famous essay "From the Poet's in the Kitchen" she speaks of her desire to become a writer as "the dangerous thought of someday trying to write myself."[37] Marshall herself summoned a very powerful male to give her the permission to write. In the 1960s, when she was troubled over her feelings that her life as a writer—when students in the South were risking their lives in the struggle—might be merely self-indulgent, Marshall says she called her friend Malcolm X to consider becoming a full-time activist. Malcolm encouraged her to pursue her own way of being political: "He cautioned me that struggle takes place in many arenas and on many levels. He said it was very important that the word be a part of the struggle and that writing could be a very beneficial way of being political."[38]

What rarely gets acknowledged about Marshall's writing is that the critique of gender inequality *is* a political story and another way of being "beneficial" to the community.[39] I would argue that the story in *Daughters* of Astral Forde's date rape and subsequent back-alley abortion is the most compelling "political" story in that novel. And the unconventional relationship between Ursa, her friend Viney, and Viney's son Robeson—a kind of homosexual marriage—suggests a conscious revision of earlier plots that force women into heterosexual romance. I want to call special attention to the fact that Reena's divorce is a first in African American literature, the first divorce chosen by a woman, not because of abuse, but out of her need for psychological freedom and self-fulfillment. That Marshall's fiction disrupts those patterns that lock women into conventional female stories, that she is deliberately challenging those plots, allowing her female characters to rebel against sexual and gender domination, is evidence enough of her politicalness.

The more troubling and vexing questions in Marshall's fiction surface with characters that are unable or unwilling to carry out Marshall's political missions. I think of Dave, who cannot tame the demons of professional ambition or his desire for commercial success in the white world. Is it so abhorrent that a talented artist should desire such success, and must that desire be denied? And, more critically for the purpose of this essay, can women have these desires without being considered race traitors? I turn for an answer to that question to the shadowy, silenced character Paulie, who drifts mysteriously in and out of the narrative, representing the uncertainty and risk attached to such desires. Despite Marshall's stated goal of keeping her characters connected to their (racialized) communities, she makes Paulie's story one of disconnection and distance. Paulie opens the story by admitting that the funeral for Aunt Vi stirs up memories of her unpleasant Brooklyn childhood. She deliberately comes late to the wake and downs three drinks to prepare for this encounter with the past. She has not held onto the people from her past, including her old friend Reena, whom she has not seen in twenty years. Reena stays on for Aunt Vi's burial, but Paulie leaves her hometown immediately after the wake, taking the subway into Manhattan, where we can assume she now lives. Several months after the encounter with Reena, Paulie leaves the country, noting in the last two lines of the story that although she invited her old friend to her going-away party, Reena did not come. In this casual, almost offhand image of the writer leaving to take an international journey, Paulie, the storyteller, the figural representative of Marshall herself, a figure of contradiction and ambivalence, is freed into ambiguous liberty. Marshall puts Paulie in a long tradition of writers who are free to critique and to redefine community, free to retain the most stable or the most tenuous ties to it, and free even, from time to time, to leave it—a story that has yet to be written, it remains unnarrated and, even at this late date in history, perhaps unnarratable.

NOTES

1. Valerie Smith, *Not Just Race, Not Just Gender: Black Feminist Readings* (New York and London: Routledge, 1998), 67–68.

2. Obviously, economic issues are at the heart of these portrayals, and we must ask who profits from films which sell consumerist, romantic, unattainable fantasies to predominantly young, black, working-class spectators. This essay is part of a larger project examining representations of work in the film and fiction of black women. I will be looking at films by black women filmmakers to see how they are revising and critiquing these mainstream, commercially driven portrayals. The works of black women filmmakers, such as Cheryl Dunye, Euzhan Palcy, Julie Dash, to name a few, show work as central to women's lives.

3. "Report on Black America Finds a College Gender Gap," *New York Times*, 26 July 2000, A-16.

4. See Darlene Clark Hine, *Hine Sight: Black Women and the Re-construction of American History* (New York: Carlson Publishing, 1994), 13. Hine agrees with historian Linda Perkins, who maintains that racial uplift was a central thread in the organizational as well as the individual pursuits of black women throughout the nineteenth century.

5. See critical work on nineteenth- and early-twentieth-century black women writers by critics Hazel Carby, Deborah McDowell, Frances Foster, Carla Peterson, Claudia Tate, Barbara Christian, Gloria Hull, Thadious Davis, Marilyn Richardson, Jean Humez, Elizabeth Ammons, Jean Fagan Yellin, Dorothy Sterling—to name just a few of the writers who have commented on this theme in the literature. See also Mary Helen Washington, *Invented Lives: Narratives of Black Women, 1860–1960* (New York: Doubleday, 1987); Mary Helen Washington, "Anna Julia Cooper: The Black Feminist Voice of the 1890s," in *Legacy: A Journal of Nineteenth-Century American Women Writers* (fall 1987): 3-15, which also appears as the introduction to Anna Julia Cooper's *A Voice from the South by a Black Woman of the South*, ed. Henry-Louis Gates, Schomburg Series (New York and London: Oxford University Press, 1988) and is reprinted in *Presenting Women Philosophers*, ed. Sara Ebenreck and Cecile T. Tougas (Philadelphia: Temple University Press, 1999).

6. See my essay on *Maud Martha*: "Taming All That Anger Down: Rage and Silence in Gwendolyn Brooks' *Maud Martha*," in *Black Literature and Literary Theory*, ed. Henry-Louis Gates (New York: Methuen, 1984), 249–262.

7. Paule Marshall, "Reena," *Harper's* 225 (October 1962): 155–163. Marshall was commissioned to do this story by *Harper's* magazine as part of a special supplement for the October 1962 issue, called "The American Female"; *Harper's*, a white, male-dominated magazine—a clearly inhospitable forum—opened its pages for the first time in its history to consider women. Except for one essay about working-class women and Marshall's story, the entire *Harper's* supplement was about white, middle- or upper-class, heterosexual, nonfeminist women caught in the dilemma of having too much time on their hands and not enough to occupy their intelligence and energy. With the exception of the pictures of black women which accompany Marshall's essay-story, all of the illustrations feature white women, including the black-and-white drawing on the cover page. On the cover, beneath the heading "A Special Supplement of *Harper's*," the words "The American Female" are cut out in black and

white letters shaped as the curvaceous, reclining body of a young white woman, smiling contentedly, a large bow atop her head, her hair cut in a pixie style. Within this symposium, "Reena" stands as a one-woman refutation of the race, gender, and class politics of the *Harper's* supplement. See also Toni Cade, *The Black Woman* (New York: New America Library, 1970); and Mary Helen Washington, *Black-Eyed Susans: Classic Stories by and about Black Women* (New York: Doubleday, 1975).

8. Paule Marshall, *Reena and Other Stories* (Old Westbury, N.Y.: Feminist Press, 1983), 71. This is the way Marshall told me to pronounce her name when I met her in the 1970s.

9. Marshall, *Reena and Other Stories*, 78.

10. Ibid., 86.

11. Ibid., 85.

12. Ibid., 85–86.

13. Ibid., 88.

14. Paule Marshall, interview with author, New York City, August 1998.

15. Alexis DeVeaux, "Paule Marshall: In Celebration of Our Triumph," *Essence* 10 (May 1981): 98.

16. Ibid., 123.

17. Marshall, *Reena and Other Stories*, 89.

18. Ibid.

19. Paule Marshall's newest novel is *The Fisher King* (New York: Scribner, 2000).

20. One of the most excellent sources for stories about black middle-class women, their relationship to work, and their ambivalent relationship to community is Sara Lawrence-Lightfoot's book, *I've Known Rivers: Lives of Loss and Liberation* (New York: Addison-Wesley, 1994). Lawrence-Lightfoot interviews six black professionals, allowing them to tell their stories firsthand, in depth, searching for the meanings and complexities in the choices they have made as African Americans of privilege. I call attention to the first interviewee, Dr. Katie Cannon, an ordained Presbyterian minister, with a Ph.D. from Union Theological Seminary, and an associate professor at the Episcopal Divinity School in Cambridge, Massachusetts. Cannon talks openly about the psychological distance between her life as a professor and a minister and the world of her childhood in Kannapolis, North Carolina, where she grew up in poverty. After years of struggling to get out of the "inhibiting" and "stifling" world of tiny Kannapolis and into college and the seminary, Katie is now an "exotic stranger" to the folks at home, an unmarried woman minister. Cannon articulates eloquently the difficult compromises of leaving a black world and living in a white one. For moving beyond boundaries, for "declaring liberty," Cannon faces the disapproval and disappointment of her family and a loss of a sense of belonging; but she values what Lawrence-Lightfoot calls the "abundance" of a world where she has space, time, and resources.

21. Helene Christol, "Paule Marshall's Bajan Women in *Brown Girl, Brownstones*," in *Women and War: The Changing Status of American Women from the 1930s to the 1950s*, ed. Maria Diedrich and Dorothea Fischer-Horning (New York: Berg, 1990), 141–154.

22. Paule Marshall, "Shaping the World of My Art," *New Letters* 40, no. 1 (autumn 1973): 108. In this essay Marshall begins to write openly about the link between her aesthetic and political aims in *Brown Girl, Brownstones*: "I wanted to express through the study of this black family how over-emphasis on the material which is the national ethic often destroys the ability to care and feel for each other." Ibid., 108.

23. The Association of Artists for Freedom included, among others, Ruby Dee, Lorraine Hansberry, John Killens, LeRoi Jones, James Baldwin, Louis Lomax, and Ossie Davis.

24. "The Black Revolution and the White Backlash," reprinted in *A Verbatim Transcript of a Forum* (New York: Martin C. Johnson, 1964).

25. One memorable story Marshall tells about Malcolm X demonstrates the trust and affection between them. He spent the last New Year's Eve of his life at her apartment at 407 Central Park West in New York. "I was having a New Year's Eve party, and I called Betty [Shabazz] to invite them. She told me that they had not been doing anything social for so long that they'd like to come. Since it was traditional among blacks to have black-eyed peas and some form of pig on New Year's, I had pig feet and pig snout, and I guess the smell got to him because he even ate some of the pig that night. Malcolm was the center of attention, but he spent the entire evening with his back against a wall, guarding his back as though knowing what awaited him. He would be dead that February [1965]. We were definitely friends, and he was a great mentor." Phone conversation with author, College Park, Maryland, September 2000.

26. Darlene Clark Hine, *Twentieth-Century Caribbean and Black African Writers* (Detroit: Gale Research, 1996), 192. Hine notes that Edward Brathwaite calls Marshall's work "literature of reconnection" to underscore the diasporic intent in her fiction.

27. Marshall, *Reena and Other Stories*, 90.

28. Ibid.

29. In her critical study of silences in Asian American women writers, *Articulate Silences: Hisaye Yamamoto, Maxine Hong Kingston, Joy Kogawa* (Ithaca: Cornell University Press, 1993), King-Kok Cheung notes how often those who are cast as the "Other" in American society are pressured to identify with the dominant culture and "to dissociate [themselves] from kin and kind," as in Maxine Hong Kingston's *Woman Warrior*. This dissociation is more complicated for African Americans who continue to be racialized in certain ways regardless of class or gender. There is also more pressure from within the group for blacks to remain aligned with the group, and I maintain that that pressure is exerted more forcefully on black women.

30. Paule Marshall, *Daughters* (New York: Atheneum, 1991), 48.

31. Mike Davis, *City of Quartz* (London and New York: Verso, 1990).

32. My own informal definition of "distributive justice" is based on a conversation with Reverend Bruce Bavinger, S.J., pastor of my church, St. Aloysius Church in Washington, D.C. Distributive justice demands an equitable distribution of the world's goods, a balancing so that each member of a group receives his/her proper share. We all share a moral obligation to work toward this balancing, to think in terms of our role within a collective, our role in providing proper material sustenance to the whole community.

33. Marshall, *Daughters*, 297, 300.

34. In contrast to the portrayal of black women as betrayers of community, the characters in Marshall's fiction who are the most likely to become corrupt and addicted to materialism or power are men. This is true of every novel from *Brown Girl, Brownstones* to *Daughters*. In *Brown Girl*, the father, Deighton, dreams of owning a big white, colonial-styled house back home in Barbados so that he can show off to the folks there that he has made it. However much the Bajan women speak and plan in *Brown Girl, Brownstones*, men dominate at the Barbadian Homeowners Association, and their plans are to empower the West Indian community and to exclude other African Americans. Avey's husband, Jay, in *Praisesong for the Widow*, is seduced by money and prestige. In *The Chosen Place, The Timeless People*, it is the barrister, Lyle Hutson, and his bourgeois friends and colleagues who are willing to exploit the poor, and it is Merle Kinbona, the main woman character, who tries to keep middle-class blacks from capitalistic greed. In *Daughters*, the two characters who are willing to sell out their communities are men—Sandy Lawson, the mayor of Midland, and Ursa's father, the prime minister of Triunion—while the women, Ursa and Mae Ryland, work to expose this corruption.

35. Matthew Fox, *The Reinvention of Work: A New Vision of Livelihood for Our Time* (New York: HarperCollins, 1994), 3–4.

36. Marshall, *Reena and Other Stories,* 15.

37. Paule Marshall, "From the Poet's in the Kitchen," in *Reena and Other Stories,* 11.

38. Author's phone conversation with Paule Marshall, College Park, Maryland, 6 September 2000.

39. John Cook, in an article entitled "Whose Child? The Fiction of Paule Marshall," *CLA Journal* 24 (September 1980): 1–15, comes to this same conclusion, that Marshall's "major private subject" is "sexual conflict." Shirley Parry also examines these issues in "Ambivalence toward Community in Paule Marshall's Fiction" (Ph.D. diss., University of Maryland, College Park, 1993). Parry, who has a forthcoming book on issues of gender, sexuality, and community in Marshall's fiction, was the first person to call my attention to issues of homosexuality in *Daughters.*

Searching for Memories / Visualizing My Art and Our Work

Deborah Willis

> They struggle to instill in their children some sense of dignity, which will help the child to survive. This means of course, that they must struggle, solidly, incessantly to keep this sense alive in themselves.
>
> —James Baldwin, *Nobody Knows My Name*

PERSONAL STATEMENT James Baldwin's observation in his memoir about Harlem residents created a sense that in teaching children photography one can teach and explore the value of self, family, and memory in documenting everyday life. Photographing friends, family members, and objects is a transformative act and, one may hope, instills a sense of joy and dignity. Since the beginning of photographic history, family photographs have had a special connection to the viewer. They can be viewed as evidence of a special event and used to illustrate a story.

The photograph has long been used as an instrument of memory. As a photographer, educator, and curator, I have used photography to tell stories about family life and in the past have asked students and artists to use the photograph in a narrative form to explore personal memories. When I became aware of the photograph as an important storytelling device, I was a young girl growing up in North Philadelphia. My father was the family photographer and his cousin owned a studio near our house. We were often photographed by both of them, and later I spent many hours placing photographs in the family album. This was in the 1950s and early 1960s, and the small number of television shows of the black family did not portray what I experienced in my own family. I spent hours watching television and looking at books and magazine as a young girl, as many as I was allowed between chores and homework, and found myself imagining how different our lives were from the published and televised images. Our family had black toys and images of black life hanging on our walls and on the mantel. The images that I found did not, except for one book, Roy DeCarava's *The Sweet-*

paper of Life. As I grew up, I often read visually the picture books and picture magazines in our home.

In 1968, while a student at Temple University, I began working for the Center for Community Studies and traveled often to West Virginia with the staff to assist in helping to set up employment training for families living in Appalachia. I thought about my own family life and wanted to take photographs on my trips to Huntington, West Virginia, and document the work of the VISTA volunteers and the families they assisted. I wondered how I could document this experience without "looking down" on the families. I believe that was the beginning of my desire to fulfill my childhood dream of becoming a photographer.

I began teaching photography in my late teens in North Philadelphia. I later moved to Brooklyn and worked for the Neighborhood Youth Corps Photography program in Ocean Hill–Brownsville. It was the summer of 1969 and my first year in New York City as a budding photographer. I entered Brooklyn as a young black woman sporting an Afro, ready to photograph and teach in the neighborhood. Wide-eyed on a mission and naïve about the politics of the community leaders, I found myself in the midst of the decentralization of the public school system, political uprisings, and the aftermath of the 1968 riots. I was excited about the possibilities of photography. But attempting to devise a lesson plan was not an easy task while political issues were in the forefront of the neighborhood town meetings and weekly staff meetings. But what I remember most about that experience is the frequent request from young people in the program and on the streets: "Hey Miss, take my picture." I often complied with my 35-mm Minolta, with a quick click of the shutter, and then tried to get them to focus on the assignment.

As I attempted to enter their lives through photography and my daily lesson plans, I found it difficult to reach the parents, who often resisted my "college student" gaze into their community. I had daily confrontations with one woman, but that's another story! I wanted the students to photograph in their homes, playgrounds, neighborhood stores, and churches and on the "famous" brownstone stoops. They wanted to photograph each other posing or mugging for the camera! Their parents wanted them to only photograph the "positive" images in the community. The struggle was an ongoing daily process for the first four weeks. After a month of teaching darkroom techniques, I found it important for them to learn how to talk about what they experienced while photographing, and I asked them to keep a diary and to write about the photographs they printed as well as the pleasures and difficulties in making the photographs. What I learned from this experience was that these young people had a voice and understood how to deconstruct their home life in provocative ways. They knew joy, sorrow, and loss. They talked about large families, grandmothers and fathers, big brothers and sisters, and the babies of their families. By looking at their photographs and talking about making them, they began to realize that their lives had importance and that their photographs illustrated that their community was broader than what was depicted in daily presses, which was often crime, welfare, and the struggle for equal education.

Over the past ten years, I thought about this experience and my own life as an artist and wondered how and why I maintained my interest in the "visual." Was it because of my mother's beauty shop and how she transformed the women in our community? Was it because of my father's advocation, or was it the experience of discovering the works of Roy DeCarava and Langston Hughes? I am amused when I think about my own son, who was ten years old when I published my first book on black photographers. At the time, he was unaware of the work I was doing, but he later began to study photography in the university; and I recall that he used the family album the same way I did as a child, arranging and rearranging photographs in my parents' albums to the dismay of my mother, who often felt that she had to hide them from him.

My personal experience with photography has many dimensions, and in my artwork I attempt to relive family memories by incorporating old photographs with contemporary images I made while exploring the nuances of those memories. In photographing my family, I found a way of entering the past and commenting on societal issues that I believe helped to shape my interest in visual culture.

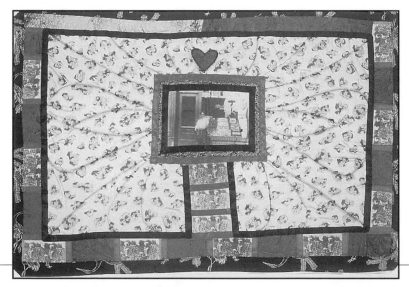

No Man of Her Own, *1992, fabric, photo linen, by Deborah Willis*

Washboard series:
With Curling Iron,
2000, by Deborah Willis

Daddy's Ties, *1992, by Deborah Willis*

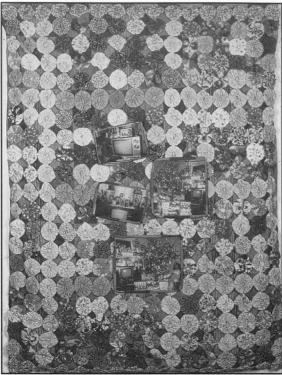

Date Unknown,
*1994, fabric,
photo linen quilt,
by Deborah Willis*

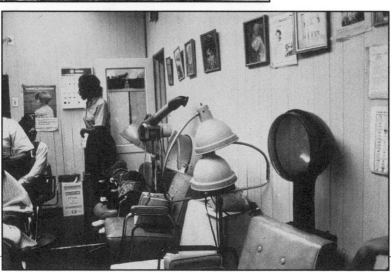

Beauty Shop, Philadelphia, 1999, gelatin silver print, by Deborah Willis.
COURTESY OF THE BERNICE STEINBAUM GALLERY, MIAMI, FLORIDA.

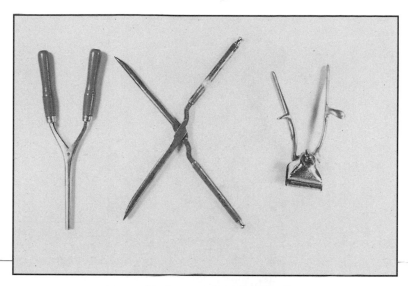

Beauty Tools, *2000, by Deborah Willis.*
COURTESY OF THE BERNICE STEINBAUM GALLERY, MIAMI, FLORIDA.

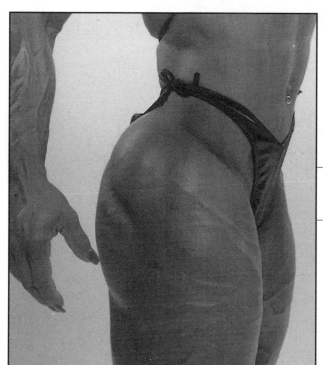

Bodybuilder #16,
*1997,
by Deborah Willis*

Bodybuilder #19,
1997,
by Deborah Willis

*I*n her provocative 1974 essay, "In Search of Our Grandmothers' Gardens," Alice Walker challenges us to imagine the experiences of our creative female ancestors and calls upon black women to define their own identity as black women artists throughout history: "What did it mean for a black woman to be an artist in our grandmothers' time? In our great-grandmothers' day?.... How was the creativity of the black woman kept alive, year after year and century after century, when, for most of the years black people have been it was a punishable crime for a black person to read or write? And the freedom to paint, to sculpt, to expand the mind with action did not exist."[1] When I first read these words, I wanted to explore the possibilities of these experiences and reinvest in the work of other black female artists as a way of locating my own identity as an artist. Ever since I was a child art has played a part in my life. I am fascinated by the work of nineteenth-century women artists and am equally intrigued with the photographic images in my family album of the women in my own family. I began my artistic career in the late 1960s; I reference my family's artistry and creativity in my own artwork. Author and poet Michelle Cliff writes candidly about the responsibility of black women artists in reevaluating the image of black woman as object. In her 1992 essay "Object into Subject," she writes, "[B]lack women have been doubly objectified as black, as women; under white supremacy, under patriarchy. It has been the task of black women artists to transform this objectification: to become the subject commenting on the meaning of the object or to become the subject rejecting the object and revealing the real experience of being."[2]

I share this story as an introduction to how I use photographs from family albums and my own photographs to make constructed and fabricated histories about black women and women in my family. I recall my own childhood in North Philadelphia in the mid-1950s with great detail. For the past twelve years, my artwork has been shaped by autobiography. I especially remember when I was required to finish the ironing before I was allowed to go a Saturday matinee. The women in my extended family shared weekly chores, gossiping the time away in my mother's beauty shop, sometimes talking about my aunts and cousins, who were washerwomen (as were the majority of urban female day workers in the 1880s). Thinking about what these women mean to me today, I reimagine their lives in autobiographical quilts, combining family photographs, fabric, mementos, and text. Through my art, I have been able to express my emotions visually. One of my quilts focusing on the domestic work of women in my family is descriptively titled "Thursday and Every Other Friday Off" and is subtitled "No Man of Her Own" (1996). It is a tribute to my maternal great-aunt, Annie Chappelle. She was a striking woman with a smile that would light up a room; she was also a domestic live-in worker whom I often photographed when I was young. Prompted by one of those photographs, I searched my family album for other photographs that would support the story of the quilt. The central photograph of my aunt in this quilt is one that I snapped when I was twelve. She is standing on Ridge Avenue, a once busy business district in North Philadelphia, outside a shoe repair shop, wearing a white starched blouse. She posed for me in front of a movie poster titled "No Man of Her Own." When I initially made the snapshot, I did not notice the poster, but looking at that image today, I am intrigued with that moment and the evocative title of the movie.

I see and use photographs as evidence of a particular experience. My photographs are part of an ongoing documentation of black women workers in America. The visuals in my family album evoked so many memories that I began to design quilts, in my sketchbook and later on my computer, of some of the experiences. The memory of my aunt and her work experience, evoked by the one photograph, generated another kind of search. I started to expand my story quilts about my family to cover the archival photographs of black women who worked in the home and the fields. I looked for historical moments in photographs to link her personal story to that of other black women, women working in the cotton fields during slavery. One day in the mid-1990s, while researching the Washer Women's Strike of 1881 in Atlanta, I looked at one photograph closely and thought about my aunt's experience as I recalled an incident that revealed her inner strength. At church she tried to organize other maids, encouraging them to ask for higher wages as she had with her own employer. I do not recall if she was successful or not, but I remember the pride I felt in watching her. I wondered about the 1881 strike and thought of my aunt's attempts at consciousness-raising. I also thought about the strike and wondered, if it had been widely publicized, what its impact could have been on domestic workers today. Those strong washerwomen struck back at their oppressors, and their stories could provide insight to modern women. In my work, I link the historical past with my own personal history. In doing this, I become the storyteller, the spectator, and the artist. I was trained as an artist, studying photography at both the undergraduate and graduate levels. Artistic training allows me to frame with cultural history and to examine the role memory plays in creating art. My quilting process, which includes photographs printed on photo linen, a pre-sensitized photographic product, enables me to explore historical memory through text and used fabrics, such as silk, cotton, and satin.

In 1990, I began to incorporate the quilting tradition to create my artwork, in part because members of my family have always been quilters and storytellers. My maternal grandmother, Lillian Holman, had thirteen children and recycled clothing, blankets, and other hand-me-downs until they were no longer recognizable in their original form. Then she would make quilts of the salvageable items. My grandmother gave quilts to all of her children and some of her older grandchildren throughout her eighty-eight years. Gram, my name for her, died in 1990. My paternal great-aunt, Cora Glover, was also a quilter as well as a ceramist and canner. Visiting her as a child in the early 1950s, I marveled at the fact that she called herself an artist. Aunt Cora lived in Philadelphia from 1941 until the mid-1970s, when she moved back to her birthplace in

Orange County, Virginia, and became known as the lady canner and quilter. She died in 1986.

Three important female relatives and my parents influenced my work. As a young man, my father, Thomas Meredith Willis, had dreamed of being a tailor. He attended the Berean Institute, a trade and business school for blacks, and after graduating in the later 1940s, he opened the Willis Tailor Shop in West Philadelphia. His interests in tailoring and stitching fascinated me because he pieced together seemingly difficult pieces to create wonderful fashions for men and women. He was also a no-nonsense police officer with huge, veined hands. After my father's death in 1990, I worked with my mother and sisters to make a quilt about his "image" from ties that we gave him as presents for Father's Day, Christmas, and birthdays throughout the years. It was an interesting way to hold on to our individual ties to him. I began to see his quilt as Egungun, a Yoruba deity that represents the ancestral community. The lively quilt, with colors and photographs, was a testament to our love and respect for him. The grieving process had just begun and would last for some eight years as I looked to his photographs to make autobiographical art.

My mother, Ruth Ellen Willis, was a hairdresser. I spent many hours sitting around listening to the stories of the women who were live-ins and day workers and who came on Fridays and Saturdays to get their hair straightened, curled, and dyed for Sunday church services. They often spoke freely about the women they worked for and shared stories of both humorous and humiliating encounters with their employers. The photographs I made of the women in our family wearing colorful and stylish hats are also used within my story quilts. Family photographs are my reference, in which to construct a family story; the narrative shifts with each memory from other family members.

My photographs preserve these collective memories. Creating visual diaries through photo quilts and black-and-white photographs allows me to tell stories visually in the tradition of African American story quilts. Quilts remind us of who we are and how our ancestors have influenced us and the larger society. Many of my own personal memories affected my early artwork, in which I attempted to recapture childhood memories, quiet moments, and inspiring stories.

I often think about my own experiences as a black woman artist and imagine those of other black women artists who are considering and reconsidering their own images. In doing so, it forces me to question what we have imagined about black women and what has been represented about them through art. By reinterpreting this visual history, I merge gender, race, family, and public history in an effort to become more aware of the visual by decoding past and present images of black women.

I continue to photograph and use my own family photographs and archival references to incorporate stories and social politics into my art, inviting a larger public to imagine these experiences—both collective and individual—of African Americans in the nineteenth and twentieth centuries. In constructing a photo story through memory, I situate my own family and the lives of other African American families. By telling my story, I make it possible for others to visually consider the shared experiences of many black women workers, many who had or have their own cottage industries as laundresses, hair-care specialists/beauticians, day-care providers, and personal trainers. Autobiography is essential to my work. Biography is useful in exploring the cultural values, traditions, and perceptions in the black community. Collective and individual memories are the foundation for my work. I am concerned with the present and its linkage to the past: identity through its connection to community and ideas that are fully imagined through spirituality and the art-making process.

My most recent work focuses on the black female body. In the series entitled *Nancy Lewis: Bodybuilder*, I am attempting to focus on the female body, contextualized and situated in the present, pointing to how work is manifested physically in the black female body, shorn of covering and developed and amplified in muscles and tendons, shoulders and calves. The depiction of physical work and its impact on the development of the body has oftentimes been relegated to men, and thus the world of physical work is constructed as one that is gender specific. This series attempts to speak to that notion and to how the black female body, if viewed under the lens of actual work, deconstructs and reconfigures the image of women, pointing to literal strength and not to figurative, emotionally specific moments.

NOTES

1. Alice Walker, "In Search of Our Grandmothers' Gardens," in *The Norton Anthology: African American Literature* (New York: W. W. Norton, 1997), 2380.

2. Michelle Cliff, "Object into Subject," in *Imagining Women: Cultural Representation and Gender*, ed. Frances Bonner et al. (Oxford, U. K. and Cambridge, Mass.: Blackwell Publishing Milton Keynes, Polity Press in association with Open University, 1992), 142.

PART 4 / *Detours*
on the Road to Work:
Blessings in Disguise

Labor above and beyond the Call / *A Black Woman Scholar in the Academy*

MARILYN MOBLEY MCKENZIE

Even in those institutions in which they are treated well, black women professors in white colleges and universities are always aware that their presence represents a disruptive incursion into spaces never intended for them.

—Nellie Y. McKay, "Troubled Peace"

As tenured faculty of color we cannot let ourselves be used to illustrate that the system is working and that other strategic changes are no longer necessary.   —Elizabeth Higginbotham

Often, we must be able to affirm that the work we do is valuable even if it has not been deemed worthy within socially legitimized structures. Affirming in isolation that the work we do can have a meaningful impact in a collective framework, we must often take the initiative in calling attention to our work in ways that reinforce and strengthen our sense of audience.

—bell hooks, *Breaking Bread*

PERSONAL STATEMENT / I am a product of a mixed marriage. Not in terms of race, but of class. I say this because although both of my parents came from working-class backgrounds, the class division in their marriage came when my mother stopped doing domestic work to become a homemaker and my father was able to leave his job as a factory worker to take advantage of the two degrees he earned by going to school at night. He became an educator—first a teacher, then a principal, and later a school board administrator. But my parents' divorce and my desire to remain with my mother meant a shift in class status from upper middle class back to working class. My mother had to return to work, but this time she chose work in retail sales, moving over time from sales clerk to department manager.

In retrospect, I never discussed how the shift in socioeconomic status affected me. I was in the same circle of the best and brightest at school, but I didn't socialize with them as much, partly because I was rarely invited and partly because I declined even when I was. My father's work had given my family status. My mother's work did not. My mother and I grew closer, dependent on each other in new ways, once my father was gone. She began to tell me stories of her early work life as an adult. I learned how angry she felt about doing domestic work in the homes of prominent white families in Fairlawn, Ohio, when members of those families, especially their adult children, were reluctant to acknowledge her when they would see her out in public.

Over the years, her anger became my anger. I couldn't always name what I was angry about. I suppose it was a combination of things: that the woman I loved and knew as my mother had had to do work some black people look down on, that each of her pregnancies had managed to worsen her problem with varicose veins, that my father's desire that my mother not work outside the home meant she was caught off guard when their marriage ended, that their divorce changed my social status, and that I had once been ashamed of this part of my mother's past as a working woman.

I'm sure it's this complicated personal past regarding black women and work that has shaped my attitudes toward work in the academy. On top of this anger and complicated family history came my college education in the 1970s at Barnard College. Attending Barnard during the 1970s meant new exposure to socioeconomic class distinctions in the black community. Some of the women were from mixed families like mine. Some were from upper-middle-class black families. And some were from working-class families. What brought us all together was activism in campus politics, black studies courses, and community work in Harlem and Morningside Heights. No one tolerated anybody feeling better or lesser than anyone else because of where they had come from or who their parents were. My self-consciousness began to drop away. I began to thrive on the ethic of giving back to the community as a measure of self-worth. Later, as a high school English teacher in Shaker Heights, Ohio, I accepted the invitation from a dear sister friend to consider becoming a Delta, only after she identified it as a public service sorority. (Barnard had no black sororities and no one had ever identified Delta Sigma Theta as a public service sorority before she did.) The desire to distance myself from my earlier class status and to build on the ethic of service I had learned and partly lived made me eager to become a Delta.

Once I became an English professor, my complicated relationship between class and status, service and work emerged again. This essay documents one of the complicated manifestations of my desire to balance my professional identity as a scholar with my personal commitment to service as an extension of my commitment to social change. This essay, in a sense, is a meditation on my recognition of how my attitudes toward service—something I once even referred to as "domestic labor"—almost sabotaged my research agenda.

$\mathscr{A}$t the 1989 Modern Language Association convention, Nellie McKay, one of the nation's foremost scholars of African American literature and culture, presented the paper "A Troubled Peace: Black Women, Race, and Class in the Halls of Privilege."[1] She spoke with refreshing candor, to one of the best-attended forums, about the complex challenges black women face in establishing careers at predominantly white institutions. The public sharing of personal and professional concerns made its most visible presence, however, at the now famous conference "Black Women in the Academy: Defending Our Name, 1894–1994," held at the Massachusetts Institute of Technology in 1994. Although I was unable to attend this historic gathering of black women scholars, the reports I heard from one woman after another were that it brought the community of scholars together in a way that had a profound impact on their lives. More than anything, this conference enabled black women who had struggled in silence to exchange their isolation for a communal experience of sharing and to learn how to cope with the nuanced forms of racism and sexism so familiar to us all. Partly influenced by the historic Massachusetts Institute of Technology conference, Lois Benjamin's recently published volume of essays, *Black Women in the Academy: Promises and Perils*, explores the status of black women from all the various positions we occupy, from professor to administrator.[2] What we have, then, is a continuum of dialogue in which black women have moved beyond our personal experiences in the academy to raise our collective voices about our work and our identity. McKay aptly describes some of the themes that shape this dialogue:

> The black women I know complain constantly of overwork: more is expected of them than of others by students, other faculty, administrators, and the professional organizations to which they belong. And that work is infinitely varied, including the expectation that they will assume responsibility for working out the problems that black and Third World students encounter in the academy. Students (even white ones) in need of counseling on academic issues as well as psychological ones continually appear on the doorstep of the black mother, the great bosom of the world. The black women feel sure, too (or is this paranoia?), that their performances are more carefully scrutinized than those of others.[3]

I believe it is the unique forms of service we render, more than anything else, that create the physical and mental exhaustion that so many black women scholars experience to a greater degree than others. The exhaustion that McKay describes is multiplied several times over when a black woman is the only one in her department, or when she is one of a precious few on her campus and is, therefore, constantly expected "to present and represent the race," to use an apt phrase coined by literary critic Claudia Tate.[4] My recent decision to shift my focus from administrative work back to my scholarship not only was an occasion to reflect on the nature of the intellectual work and service I had done, but was also an occasion to reflect on the ongoing dialogue that connected my experience to the larger context of the collective experience of other black women scholars in the academy. In this essay, I discuss the process by which I came to terms with the ambivalence that comes from reconciling the competing demands of our institutions and others with our own personal and professional goals, dealt with the nature of the ambivalence itself, and found some strategies we might use individually and collectively to assist those scholars who come after us.

In 1989, only two years after receiving my Ph.D. in English, at the same Modern Language Association (MLA) convention where McKay had served as a keynote speaker, in one of the follow-up forums, I presented a paper entitled "Stepping on Toes: Responding to Diverse Interpretive Communities as an African American Womanist Scholar." What that paper represented for me was an early attempt to articulate the ambivalence I was already feeling and observing among black women scholars as we attempted to negotiate our way through our own professional needs and desires and the expectations that the academy placed upon us. Conflicted feelings of fulfillment and frustration emerge from our attempts to contribute to the well-being of our students and our institutions at the same time that we try to devote the necessary attention that our research and scholarship agendas demand. Even at that early point in my career, I was aware that the very work that I loved and was being called on to do—that is, the work of extending myself to students over and above my classroom duties and engaging in various forms of service—was the very work that dangerously threatened to sabotage my visibility as a serious scholar. My presentation at that session was itself a departure from my more familiar conference papers on Toni Morrison, black literature and culture, and the study of narrative, where I was accustomed to speaking in strict academic discourse with few, if any, personal references to myself. Though I was somewhat timid at first, I recall a real need to discuss the connection between my scholarship and my perceptions about the context in which I was attempting to produce it.[5] In one sense, my paper was not so much a departure as it was a new application of analytical and critical skills from reading literary texts to reading the narrative I was constructing of my own life in the academy. Moreover, I was applying these skills to a reading of the academy itself. Given that the context for my paper was a workshop sponsored by the Commission on the Status of Women in the Professions, I regarded the setting as a safe space to share serious issues for women in general and for black women in particular.[6]

The dawn of a new century seems an apt moment to revisit my earlier attempt to read and reflect on our lives and work in the academy and the tensions that emerge from the contradictions between our own goals and those of our institutions. The ambivalence that I took for granted at an earlier stage of my career is much more complex than it once was. By mapping the shift in my ambivalence from a negative site of alienation, disillusionment, and resentment to a more positive site of authority that integrates my identity with the various modes of work that needs to be done, I discovered a need to move beyond descriptions of our plight to an exploration of the consequences we experience. In other words, I no longer see our conflicted attitudes as a bad thing, but as a logical consequence of the unique roles that black women perform in the academy. Even though I have come to terms with my own professional identity crisis that grew out of trying to do justice to these multiple roles, reflecting on this crisis has merit. Most of all it reveals that we cannot underestimate the need to reflect on the academy as a workplace. As we engage in our intellectual work and attempt to transform the academy into a better place for ourselves and our students, we also need to gain a greater understanding of what I call the politics of labor—that is, the power relations, the conflicting demands, and the implications of both on our productivity and professional well-being. Thus, this essay will explore three components of the politics of labor: the "service trap," the politics of hypervisibility, and the conflicting definitions of success.[7] My goal is not to claim a neat and tidy response to these issues and concerns, but to share a cautionary tale based on my responses to them and to suggest how we might come to terms with the challenges we face as black women scholars in the academy. The seriousness of these issues requires a level of frank discussion that enables us to break polite silences and to challenge the practices that created them.

That I recently felt a greater sense of urgency about these issues than I did ten years ago when I presented the paper at the MLA convention is actually not so surprising. For one, I am situated differently in the academy now than I was then. No longer an assistant professor concerned about the tenure process, I am now an associate professor with tenure. Though I now have senior status, I seek to be a full professor, well aware that I cannot achieve full professor status at my university until I publish my next book. This awareness prompted me to examine the consequences of the trajectory my career had taken. Like many, I came into the academy under the presupposition that I would be evaluated on the basis of my teaching, scholarship, and service (and in that order). Over time, however, the call of service overshadowed the expectation that I would remain an active scholar in my field. But the pressure to write and publish was no longer coming primarily from outside sources, such as my chair, my department, or my dean, but from within. Moreover, I had to confront the personal and professional consequences of two decisions. The first was shifting my institutional identity from a full-time faculty position to an administrative-faculty position, and the second was shifting back to my identity as an associate professor. As a consequence of founding and directing the African American studies program at my university in 1992, just five years into my tenure-track position as an assistant professor of English, I discovered I had created a predicament for myself that I had not anticipated. Namely, I had seriously slowed down my once more rapid progression toward full professor to combine my full-time duties as an associate professor with part-time duties as an administrator of a fairly visible interdisciplinary program.

Indeed, over time, the work of institution building can take a toll. It can make the level of "saturation" in one's scholarship (to use Stephen Henderson's term), the level to which we are accustomed, impossible; and, as a result, we can become alienated from larger book projects while we remain productive in terms of smaller projects such as articles and book reviews.[8] It is this alienation from my larger research projects that prompted me to take action. I decided, in response to what was a virtual professional identity crisis, to resign from the administrative position. Of course, in the case of both decisions I had to weigh what economists call the "opportunity costs" that accompany any decision to choose one option over another equally viable one.[9] In other words, while few would argue with the value of establishing an African American studies program, given what many know about the very political nature of such work, many would question whether the year a scholar receives tenure is the best time to take on so tremendous a task.[10] Many might also argue whether release time from one of five courses is sufficient support for the director of a new academic program, but this point raises labor issues that are beyond the scope of this essay.[11] It was my reflections on these decisions, especially the latter one, coupled with my reading of the larger political context in which I made them, that prompted me to revisit my early life in the academy and to examine the current status that my colleagues and I face today. The identity crises many of us face can be attributed to the politics of labor in academe. In other words, I could not reflect on my personal situation in academe without examining the structural realities and institutional practices of the larger context in which I worked. What I seek to do here is discuss how the politics of labor operate, how I responded to them, and how we might redefine our work in relationship to them.

The "Service Trap," or the Personal Is Political

The feminist mantra that the personal is political is one many of us have taken seriously since the early days of the women's movement. We have been filling the space freed up from years of containment with narratives and analyses, about the personal dimensions of our lives, that male-dominated institutions had not permitted. But as black women, we have had to negotiate carefully when and where we speak. And as we have joined in coalition with white women, we have done so in the hopes that race would not be so over-determined that we would always have to speak out against racism or discuss the intersection of racism and sexism by ourselves. In other words, when it came to race matters, we wanted it to matter to all of us, not only in our scholarship, but also in various spheres of influence in our personal and professional lives. We appreciate the ways in which scholars are integrating racialized readings of gender in their analyses of literary and cultural texts, but, as Ann duCille and others have eloquently explained, we worry about the ways in which "race and gender alterity has become a hot commodity" while the realities of our lived lives are still misunderstood or ignored.[12] When our fellow women scholars can analyze race in texts but shy away from doing so in everyday life interactions outside of the texts they study, we have a tangible manifestation of the politics of labor. The consequences of not sharing the work of addressing race matters in personal public spaces often fall on the shoulders of black women. To call attention to the psychic and emotional consequences of others' expectations that we shoulder this work is one way to address the politics of labor.

One of the best illustrations of the politics of labor is one I observed at a conference I attended in 1996. The Nineteenth-Century American Women Writers in the Twenty-First Century conference, which was held at Trinity College, included a banquet and a choral performance by a local Connecticut community group on the last night. The performance of nineteenth-century songs, which included some based on Harriet Beecher Stowe's *Uncle Tom's Cabin*, became increasingly more offensive with subtle and not so subtle references to black people's apparent but surprising contentment with enslavement, even when the going was rough. The black women scholars who sat at my table were particularly offended, and our facial expressions registered our displeasure. It was clear, however, that many of our white women colleagues, though they also sensed that the lyrics were problematic, expected one of the black women to rise to the microphone to protest and offer a critique. They even encouraged one black woman to do so. This black woman then in turn informed me that she had been asked to say something to the audience (made up primarily of scholars and a few community people) about the offensive part of the evening's entertainment. When she expressed her reluctance to do so, and asked me what I felt she should do, I responded that she need not say anything if she did not feel led to do so. When it was clear that neither this woman, the only black woman of the conference organizers, nor any of the other black women scholars at my table felt responsible for addressing what was an embarrassing moment, one of the white women in the audience rose to the microphone and expressed her regret over the intrusion of such offensive lyrics into an otherwise wonderful program and conference. She encouraged all those who felt so inclined to remain afterwards to "process" their feelings. As an audience, we were encouraged to thank our guest performers, nonetheless, for their beautiful singing. The program ended with applause and the murmur of hushed tones as the audience dispersed throughout the auditorium and into the hallways.

As one of the guest speakers invited to do endnotes at the closing session of this conference the next morning, I selected this incident as one of the central points for my reading of the conference. I explained that the offensive lyrics should not be viewed as an intrusion into the conference as much as another example of the nineteenth-century discourse we had been addressing in the sessions leading up to the banquet. The issue really was one of interrogating how a racist form of popular culture from the previous century could show up at our conference in the place designated for entertainment. Even more interesting to me were the ways in which white women anticipated and actually expected the black women present to address this embarrassing moment so that they would not have to. What the black women achieved the night before by choosing not to speak was a symbolic, if not real, reprieve from the very type of service many of us do on our campuses. That is, we chose to give ourselves a break from the familiar pattern of white women assuming that to speak in such a situation would be to speak for us. What we hoped instead, was that the same analysis we had heard throughout the papers delivered could come from them in this social situation. We needed them to speak, not for us, but for themselves. Instead of accepting the burden as though it was only ours to address, we chose to give them an opportunity to engage in the work of addressing the racist comments for themselves. Their reluctance to respond raises questions about whether anything would have been said at all if black women had not been present.

It could be argued that I indeed engaged in the very intellectual work my colleagues and I had collectively refused to do the night before. But as one of the designated endnote speakers, I was situated differently from my colleagues at that point. The night before, we all felt a great deal of ambivalence as we experienced the moment from a dual perspective: as black women and as black scholars. As members of the audience, we resisted the pressure to show up as the only qualified intellectuals to address the racial issue in question and exercised our sense of agency to redefine our identity as a strategic response to the moment. By so doing, we created a space for our white colleagues in the audience to interrogate the moment and their response to it.

The shift from the personal response to the collective political one is a strategy very familiar to black women. It is one thing to offer the intellectual labor of racial analysis because it is called for under the circumstances and because many black women have historically provided some of the best forms of this analysis. It is quite another thing to choose when and where we will provide this hard intellectual labor. Moreover, at a conference where white women scholars had been perfectly willing to engage in racial analyses of literary texts, it was particularly disturbing for those same women to suddenly seem unable to extend their analyses to the real-life text in front of us. If the nation of the United States is indeed the "house that race built," as Wahneema Lubiano's collection of essays by that name argues, then we need to interrogate who is expected to do the hard labor of addressing these issues when they show up in public spaces, on our campuses, and the like.[13] More often than not, as the black presence on campus, black women, and to a lesser extent black men as well, are expected to help maintain domestic tranquillity, especially regarding black students and often regarding racial matters and diversity issues. Toni Morrison's discussion of the nation as a "racial house," shaped by race and racism, eloquently suggests why the intellectual service I am describing is so politically charged, when she explains:

> [S]o much of what seems to lie about in discourses on race concerns legitimacy, authenticity, community, belonging. In no small way, these discourses are about home: an intellectual home; a spiritual home; family and community as home; forced and displaced labor in the destruction of home; dislocation of and alienation within the ancestral home; creative responses to exile, the devastations, pleasures, and imperatives of homelessness as it is manifested in discussions of feminism, globalism, the diaspora, migrations, hybridity, contingency, interventions, assimilations, exclusions. . . . In virtually all of these formations, whatever the terrain, race magnifies the matter that matters.[14]

What happens when our white colleagues share responsibility for the work of interrogating how racism affects everything from the curriculum to campus climate rather than assuming that the black folk on campus are the only ones able to do it? The politics of labor involved in our decision to resist or accept these roles contributes to the ambivalence we feel, but how we respond to this ambivalence determines whether the work we do reinforces the service trap or transforms it into a site of authority. An abbreviated narrative of my life in the academy follows and suggests how I made this shift in understanding the politics of my own labor.

From the very beginning of our work in the academy, many of us combined an activist sensibility with our training in literary criticism. Like scholar-activists before us, such as Anna Julia Cooper and Francis Harper, we had both our intellectual projects and the desire to transform the context in which we did our work. This is especially true for many of us who were student activists during the 1960s and 1970s. Thus, many of us view our work in terms that are over and above reductive notions about teaching and regard our intellectual project as one of engaging minds in and outside of the classroom in critical analysis of both the aesthetic and political dimensions of human experience represented in texts, literary and otherwise. To take on this mindset is to view our scholarship and teaching as sites of intervention in ongoing dialogues about American literature, women's literature, black women writers, black studies, and cultural studies. Like many professors who value the intellectual and political revolutions that challenged us to enter our professional lives to make a difference, I brought a complex notion of pedagogy to the classroom, one informed with a sense of history and a responsibility to teach American literature and black literature, in particular, to diverse communities of students and to advocate that they be open to new knowledge about oppression, race, gender, and class and that they be willing to engage in dialogue about many of the very issues with which the nation had not yet come to terms.

What I brought and continue to bring to my teaching of African American literature is a near obsession with the value of what Gerald Graff calls "teaching the conflicts."[15] Thus, in the tradition of an African American studies methodology that considers both the text and the contexts which produced it, I teach my students to understand the conflicted terrain of cultural, social, and political contexts, a terrain that would prompt Frances Harper's black female protagonist in *Iola Leroy* (1892) to utter the words, "I would like to do something of lasting service for the race."[16] Likewise, when I teach Toni Morrison's *Beloved* (1987), it is critical that my students understand the historical conflicts that would enable Baby Suggs, on one hand, to minister to the spiritual and emotional needs of the enslaved community yet, on the other hand, to struggle with "the sadness . . . at her center, the desolated center where the self that was no self made its home . . . having never had the map to discover what she was like."[17] Unlike that of those who view responsible teaching and advocacy with suspicion and see them as mutually exclusive binary opposites, my goal has consistently been to enable students to interrogate and understand their ideological positions and "the assumptions in which we are drenched," to quote Adrienne Rich, even if they choose to hold onto them.[18] Thus, the very nature of the subject matter I teach has meant that I routinely and self-consciously go over and above the call of my job description to teach literature. I am well aware that many white women scholars and progressive male professors of both races regard their teaching in much the same way as I do.

But what happens when black women transfer the rigorous intellectual labor involved in this teaching to other work on campus? What happens when we take our informed positions on race, gender, and class and the intersection of the three categories to committee work, task forces, and administrative positions, either voluntarily or upon request from students, department chairs, deans, provosts, and even presidents? When we consider the issue of positionality for black women scholars, our presence in and out of the classroom creates a unique arena of expectations that have an impact on the scholarship we produce and the service we contribute. For me and for many black women, our positions create an expectation, on the part of our institutions, that we will be more visible, more active, and more available than our white and male counterparts. When a black woman has a predisposition to serve, an activist sensibility to make a difference, and a heightened sense of responsibility to marginalized communities of which she is a part, she is particularly vulnerable to expectations that she will contribute over and above what is expected of others and that she will do the service that others have elected not to do. It is only in reflecting on my own three positions—before, during, and after my work as director of African American studies—that I was able to understand more fully how our work as black women scholars in the academy is both enabled and complicated by the demands placed on us by others and by those demands we place on ourselves.

When the very subject matter of our scholarship is connected to the issues that put us in demand, we have a good problem, but a vexing one nonetheless. We enjoy identities as experts in our field but feel overburdened by the demand that we be resident scholars for all racial matters, as I indicate in "Campus Expectations of the Minority Professoriat," published in *Black Issues in Higher Education* during the fall of 1992.[19] When we are the only black professor, or one of a precious few, the status of resident scholar brings both personal satisfaction and feelings of alienation. At the same time that we try to make our campuses more hospitable intellectually and culturally, not only for black students, but for all students, we help stave off our own alienation. Our work becomes a way to galvanize other scholars doing work in African and African

American studies around a common cause in a way that can make a visible difference on our campuses. As Nellie McKay notes, "The exception to . . . individual racial isolation in the workplace of white academia occurred when a black faculty member was a part of a black studies program."[20]

Though I have felt welcome on my campus, for the most part, I nevertheless felt isolated in terms of my research interests until I began the work of establishing the academic minor in African American studies. From 1992 to 1998, with the exception of the one semester of faculty research leave that I took, only after colleagues reminded me that I was eligible for one (since, by then, I had become so engrossed in administrative duties that I had forgotten to apply), I was engaged in the serious work of establishing, developing, and running the program. What began as limited service to my department, college, and university was multiplied far more than I ever expected. From meetings to memos, from phone calls to conferences, from welcome addresses to keynote speeches, my identity had changed. One striking example of this change was when the president of the university announced my name in 1994 at a ceremony where I was to receive a five-year service award and he jokingly said, "Are you sure this is right? It seems like you've been here longer than that!" In retrospect his question is very telling of just how visible I had become. I was still teaching, holding conferences with my students, grading papers, producing an article here and there, and even attending a professional meeting once in a while, but my life in the academy had changed, and I was forced to alter my relationship with my own research and scholarship. Meanwhile, I was serving on diversity committees, meeting with students who were angry over racial and/or sexual incidents, and working with colleagues to enhance the status of our program with the limited resources available. What few knew was how many community speaking invitations I received and accepted. I was constantly weighing when to "just say no," as so many of my colleagues encouraged me to do.

My research leave during the spring of 1997 was the first substantial opportunity I had to focus on my second book on Toni Morrison. Unfortunately, a semester leaves hardly any time to give one's research the attention a project such as mine demanded. As a consequence, I returned in the fall of 1997 with my book still incomplete. When my dean asked whether I wanted to be reappointed to the position of director of African American studies, I answered yes without even thinking, I had become so accustomed to that familiar identity. Yet, as the new semester got under way, my conscience compelled me to acknowledge that I needed to change my mind. Feelings of alienation from my scholarship and disillusionment with administrative duties created a restlessness for change. As Ruth Farmer argues, black women administrators often have positions with high visibility but are often not given the power to make many of the substantive changes that would really transform the academy.[21] My research leave had made it clear that I was ready to shift my priorities, even if others were not expecting me to do so. Thus, despite a glowing evaluation from the reappointment committee, I announced in the spring of 1998 that I would resign from the director's position, effective 1 July 1998. Though I was certain I had made the right decision (I actually made it in the fall of 1997 but was encouraged by the faculty to wait until the spring to announce it), I struggled for weeks with feelings that I was abandoning the program, abandoning the students, and reneging on my own expressed commitment to the work of institution building. The relief from this struggle came only from analyzing the politics of labor that created the ambivalence toward the very work that had shaped my life in the academy up until my leave. Interestingly enough, like James Baldwin, who said he did not write about being black because he expected that to be his only subject but because "it was the gate [he] had to unlock before [he] could . . . write about anything else," I discovered that analyzing the politics of labor was actually work I had to do before I could turn my full attention back to my other research projects.[22] In a word, I had to analyze how the service work I had done and was doing had changed me and my perspectives on the academy and on my scholarship. Moreover, I sought to know how my work in the academy was similar to and different from that of other black women. I discovered that although Yolanda Moses is right "that there is very little research specifically concerning black women in academe, how [we] are faring and what issues are of concern to [us]," there is ample evidence, nevertheless, that more black women scholars are beginning to discuss the issues we confront, the strategies we might employ, and the meanings and representations of our work in the academy.[23]

The Politics of Labor and Hypervisibility

Given that black women often have a cultural orientation to service, based for some on our knowledge of a tradition of racial uplift and social activism and based for others on our own involvement as students, activists, and community leaders, many of us are at risk, as I was, of being trapped by our commitment to our students and by our desire to bring about institutional change. Many of us take seriously the words "Lifting as We Climb," the famous motto of the National Association of Colored Women, as a kind of personal mantra.[24] While I am aware that some black women scholars, many of whom are at senior levels in the profession, feel less conflicted and vulnerable to the service trap and have already comfortably negotiated their way through the ambivalence of which I speak, I am concerned about those who have not. My focus is on those who have not yet come to terms with the struggle of negotiating the competing demands of self and other, personal and professional, academy and community. In fact, we need to find ways even to admit that these competing demands exist, that despite our good intentions we can often inadvertently sabotage ourselves, giving so much that we have little time to attend to those parts of our identity that matter. It is often only after we are caught in the cycle of giving to the detriment of our attention to our research and, as some could testify, to the detriment of our personal lives that we recognize the underside of our commitment to serve.

The service we contribute often has invisible, unspoken dimensions to it. Many of us take pride, as I did, in the fact that students seek us out as more available, more compassionate, and more receptive, but we also know that the work we do outside the classroom is often emotionally and mentally draining. Above and beyond my teaching, I was and am often called upon to meet with sororities, fraternities, black student groups, and campus organizations. Sometimes these are occasions for students to meet me informally, to get acquainted, but, at other times, they are difficult sessions in which students seek guidance in coping with racial slights, overt racism, and their perceptions about campus climate. Over the years I have also had increasing instances of my own students requesting conferences ostensibly to discuss a paper topic or class assignment, only to learn that what they really needed was to discuss some very personal matter. Even though I have customarily had to send some students on to another office or trained professional who could better assist them, that does not negate my presence as the first point of contact for many students in crisis. Thus, I am certain I have other colleagues in the profession who can bear witness to the sense of gravity we feel when students come to us with problems from bigotry in the classroom to sexual assault, alcoholism and drug abuse (their own, a friend's, or some family member's), pregnancy, abortion, homophobia, and the spiritual discomfort some feel when exposure to new ideas, knowledge, and values challenges those they brought from home.

To a certain extent, we respond to these matters out of our disciplines, out of our intellectual work in African American, feminist, and cultural studies, and in this sense, these conferences are a form of intellectual work themselves, representing the intersection of theory and praxis, especially when we can encourage students to do research into the very issues they are confronting. The reality is that we are often not trained to handle many of these issues, even when we are good listeners. Moreover, many of us become ambivalent about our identity in these roles, for often, like nurturing mothers, we discover the serious need to establish boundaries between ourselves and our students, and we worry when such lines become blurred.[25] As Susan Apel indicates, the disproportionate amount of such work falling on women's shoulders "is not surprising given that women are viewed as primary caretakers in the culture as a whole."[26] Yet as Darlene Clark Hine reminds us, any discussion of black women's labor must be historicized to account for the unique roles we have played since slavery as caretakers, over and above that of any other group.[27] In other words, though all women scholars experience the politics of gender in our work, black women scholars experience it to a greater degree. What many black women scholars and I have discovered is that the time we take to advise and mentor students in these very personal ways cannot be measured because we are often the difference between whether a student remains in school or not. Thus, though we may feel overwhelmed by such work, we often continue to make ourselves available, not wishing to let our students down, not willing to be perceived as disinterested, and definitely not willing to be perceived as abandoning our historic role to give back or to lift as we climb. We experience our work not just as nurturing, but as liberating for our students and for ourselves. Yet when we go out of our way to create a safe place both in our classrooms and in our offices for these kinds of conversations, then we can expect to experience the attendant weight of such labor-intensive and emotionally intensive work. That black and female professors, in general, and black women professors, more specifically, often do the majority of such work is probably not surprising. The toll that such work takes on our personal and professional lives is what needs to be examined. Moreover, we probably need to examine the self-imposed burden many of us feel from the intraracial ethic of commitment to service, an ethic that has historically been intricately woven into African American life and culture.

The question is, what are black women who find themselves in these predicaments to do, and what are the implications of redefining and/or renegotiating their relationship to their institutions? Unfortunately, except for these recent examples of collective sharing, many black women are reluctant to give voice to these concerns in public, fearful that their grievances will be viewed as whining, as symptoms of their need to claim victim status or to see themselves as self-sacrificing martyrs, or as an abdication of their historic role. In *Slaying the Mermaid: Women and the Culture of Sacrifice*, Stephanie Golden's study of the differences between black and white women's responses to service and community, she points out that during the 1960s and early 1970s, while white women were focusing on their own individual development, "African-American women . . . felt a duty to subordinate their desire for individual development to the needs of black people as a whole, putting their energy into holding families together and supporting men under assault."[28] Though this generalization is somewhat reductive and simplistic in its suggestion that service and self-development are mutually exclusive, it does point to the gender politics embedded in black nationalist agendas that still sometimes account for the negative labels that black women receive within the black community for calling the expectation that they will do certain work into question.[29] I believe we must resist these labels as forms of silencing, as just one more manifestation of the service trap. In place of this silencing, we need to create more safe places for black women to discover new coping strategies, not only to survive, but also to thrive as we do our work. We also need to negotiate a space between giving too much and being available, between being used up and giving of ourselves in ways that are mutually fulfilling for us and those we serve. For those of us who value our identity as scholars, we seek to be available to our students and not neglect or sabotage our scholarship.

I have been focusing on the politics of labor for black women scholars as opposed to other professionals in the academy for a reason. While I am aware that many who now identify themselves as administrators were once scholars, I am interested in those black women who see themselves as teacher-scholars first and foremost and who maintain an active commitment to teaching, research, writing, and publishing. When women in this category combine their scholarship with the service work I have described, it is their scholarship that often suffers. At the same time that they value their contribution to their students and their institutions, they pay a price in unpublished manuscripts and invisibility in the larger community of scholars. If we are not publishing our work, we are not actively engaged in producing new knowledge or new perspectives on old knowledge. Thus, we cannot get cited, and the academy is diminished by the absence of our contribution. I am aware, however, even as I argue this, that the significance of the spoken word and the oral tradition make some question the privileging of the written word, a privileging that is inherent in my position. The reality is that our calling as scholars demands that we engage in the work of producing and preserving knowledge, not just in disseminating it as professors. The so-called culture wars not only have sometimes put us in frontline positions in the campus politics that precipitated these wars, but also have curtailed the degree to which those of us engrossed in service could participate in the debates through the publication of our scholarship in response to them.[30] Thus, while many of us may be very visible in the sense of our service work on our campuses, and even in our communities, the very form of labor that has cultural capital in the academy in terms of promotion and tenure, not to mention authority, legitimacy, and credibility, is the work that many of us do not get to do.

Black feminist critic duCille brilliantly describes the situation of black women scholars on white campuses as one in which we "experience both hypervisibility and a superisolation by virtue of [our] racial and gender difference," on one hand, even as we find ourselves "drawn as exemplars and used up as icons [and] . . . find [ourselves] chewed up and spit out because we did not publish."[31] As mentioned earlier, Claudie Tate refers to this "hypervisibility" of black women scholars as the pressure to "present and represent the race." Fortunately, as this discussion suggests, a growing number of black women scholars and writers have been producing an impressive body of scholarship in their respective disciplines. As duCille and others have argued, our presence as scholars, critics, and theorists can no longer be denied. Our intellectual labor has challenged received knowledge, contributed new knowledge, and altered private and public discourse on any number of subjects. As Jane Gallop argues in *Around 1981: Academic Feminist Literary Theory:* "[T]he centralization of race and black women's writing to academic literary feminism . . . already has to its credit two major accomplishments: the inclusion of questions of race in critical considerations of gender and the inclusion of writing of African-American women in academic practice—critical and pedagogical, feminist and mainstream—in particular, the works of Hurston, Walker, and Morrison."[32] But when black women are engaged in service to the detriment of their productivity as scholars, we need to admit that we are then vulnerable to being dismissed and to not being regarded as serious scholars in our field. Hypervisibility in one arena can make us less visible in another. Moreover, our intellectual labor is often categorized in ways that marginalize when and where our scholarship is even cited or acknowledged. In fact, the original title of this essay was "Who's Quoting My Sisters? The Politics of Labor and the Work of Black Feminist Criticism in the Academy."[33] But the complex terrain of the politics of citation is beyond the scope of this essay.

New Definitions of Success

It has been personally and professionally difficult to articulate some of the concerns raised in this essay. In discussing the issue of service, I have attempted to suggest that the politics of labor have often rendered black women scholars invisible in ways that matter to us and that count in academe at the same time that we have engaged in institution building that has made us very visible in other ways. The reality that some of the work we value the most—in terms of being available for our students, making our campuses more hospitable for them, ourselves, and the courses we teach—is work that often does not count in the larger scheme of things is something many of us want to change. We

especially do not like feeling that this work of institution building has put us at
a disadvantage in terms of promotion, tenure, and the prestige we desire and
deserve as scholars. The politics of labor I have described are already complex,
but they are also complicated by a national climate of major paradigm shifts in
the academy. On some campuses, the whole notion of tenure is being challenged. On several campuses there have been challenges to affirmative action
guidelines to such an extent that the black presence is dwindling even as more
doctoral students claim to be African Americanists. Then there is the catch-22
that black women seemingly want it both ways—that is, we want to engage in
the work of institution building, but we want that work to count. Nevertheless,
we want the service work of institution building to be shared by our male colleagues, our white colleagues, and all those who see the value of making the
curriculum more inclusive and our campuses more hospitable. In other words,
it is time for our colleagues to be more invested in sharing the work. We must
individually and collectively encourage our institutions to acknowledge our
contributions, and we must diligently and carefully make the case for them
when they are reluctant to do so. Our chairs, deans, provosts, and presidents
need to know that our intellectual labor informs the service we contribute and
that, because of the racial and gendered realities of our nation, the service we
contribute will continue to be needed. The irony of making the case for
redefining perceptions of our work is that no one will make the case for us.
Consequently, we will have to make the effort ourselves and enlist the support
of allies. What we seek is what Linda Singer calls a "recognition of reciprocal
indebtedness" so that the politics of labor shift in a more equitable direction
for black women in the academy.[34]

But the process of shifting my identity from that of an administrator and
institution builder back to my former identity as a professor and scholar has
changed my perspective on my work as well. Though the ambivalence
remains as a given, I have come to see my scholarship as an extension of the
service work I have described and as a site of authority from which I can now
make a new contribution. While I no longer wish to use my intellectual energies to the same degree in certain forms of service, I cannot diminish the
value of that work, not only to my institution, but also to my own intellectual
growth and development. Moreover, it could be argued that this article and
the research projects I have returned to are the forms of service that demand
my attention at this point in my life. Even our students need to be encouraged
to understand the significance of our scholarship to our teaching, to our identities, and even to the production of knowledge. By sharing this information
with them, we not only take better care of ourselves, but we prepare them to
have appropriate boundaries even as we contribute to their intellectual and

emotional development. If the work we do has any meaning at all, then we must actively encourage and recruit new students for doctoral programs. We must mentor one another about timing decisions about administrative work versus teaching. And given the renewed and earlier emphasis on publishing, we must encourage our graduate students to present papers at conferences, become active in professional meetings, and seek mentoring early in their academic careers, if they are to avoid some of the pitfalls that have challenged us. Rather than dwelling on ambivalence as a negative dimension of the profession, I have come to view my journey in the academy thus far as a rich and complex one that has a narrative that is both my own and one that I share with so many other black women. In the midst of my professional identity crisis, I reread Wahneema Lubiano's "Constructing and Reconstructing Afro-American Texts: The Critic as Ambassador and Referee" and Mary Catharine Bateson's *Composing a Life*.[35] Lubiano's work was a reminder not only that the black woman's presence in academe has been commodified, but also that our scholarship is contested terrain that often amplifies the ambivalence we bring to the academy at the same time that it requires that we play multiple roles at once. Bateson's work resonates with my ability to see the various fragments of my life story as part of a larger narrative that I am still composing. I have come to view my reconnection with my scholarship as the phase that my professional life cycle calls for at this moment. The work I do as a scholar perhaps should not be weighed as better while the work of institution building gets weighed as lesser. Instead, even though institutional practices for measuring our work continually need to be challenged and critiqued, we must find ways to make peace with the fact that we desire to contribute differently at different times, not so much because we will or will not be rewarded or compensated adequately, but because the work matters. Thus, I am ultimately calling for a different measure of success, one that recognizes our need to do different work at different times. And we must develop networks of support around those who choose to do institution building so that the losses to their scholarship can be minimized. We must also educate our department chairs, deans, and provosts to the complex nature of the service we contribute. To educate them means we must wisely use what Karla Holloway calls the "storytelling space" of our "intellectual and personal histories" to enlist their support in changing the academy.[36] When and if they are reluctant to hear such stories, we have an obligation to enlist support among our own ranks, to engage in collaborative work, and to network with our colleagues elsewhere so that the burden does not unduly rest on any one individual. Rather than being penalized for the service that has compromised our research agendas, we should instead be compensated both in time and money to transition back into our professorial roles. Or, when it is clear that we are gifted administrators, we should be compensated, not with fancy titles that carry little visibility or power, but with responsibilities that give us a voice in changing policy and in making decisions.

In retrospect, I am able to look back at lives transformed, boundaries crossed, and ideas shared, things that would not have occurred had I not chosen to accept a position as a faculty leader. While the academy needs to devise new ways to integrate our service into new measurements of our labor, we must not underestimate the value of our labor in other terms. I have come, therefore, to look at my administrative experience as the intersection of theory and praxis, as a site of authority, and as the intellectual reservoir that now informs my research and scholarship. I am reminded that often when I have been called upon to speak before student groups, women's groups, or community organizations, I have shared what I refer to as the three most important existential questions we all need to ask ourselves. These questions are, Who am I? What is my work? And how will I contribute? Ultimately, these are questions about identity, calling, and service, respectively, and they are questions that we answer differently at different phases of our personal and professional lives. Having come to terms with the politics of labor, I have been able to celebrate the work that I have done, return to my scholarship with new insights, and contribute in yet another way to the larger work of transforming the academy into the kind of intellectual home that our students deserve and that we envision.

NOTES

1. Nellie Y. McKay was one of four speakers at the forum "Access to the Academy: Crossing Boundaries." Her forum paper, "A Troubled Peace: Black Women, Race, and Class in the Halls of Privilege," has since been published in *Black Women in the Academy: Promises and Perils,* ed. Lois Benjamin (Gainsville: University of Florida, 1997), 11–22.

2. See Benjamin, *Black Women in the Academy.*

3. McKay, "Troubled Peace," 21.

4. Claudia Tate used this phrase in one of my informal discussions with her. The phrase resonates with many black women at predominantly white institutions.

5. For an eloquent statement about the challenge of using our personal voices in our scholarship when our training in graduate school has not prepared or encouraged us to do so, see Sharon Harley's "Reclaiming Public Voice and the Study of Black Women's Work," in *Gender, Families, and Close Relationships,* ed. Leigh Leslie et al. (Thousand Oaks, Calif.: Sage Publications, 1994), 189–209. I thank Bonnie Thornton Dill and the Black Women and Work editorial board for sharing this essay with me.

6. The 1989 MLA convention in Washington, D.C., featured a forum titled "Access to the Academy: Crossing Boundaries," which was sponsored by the Commission on the Status of Women in the Profession and the Gay and Lesbian Caucus for Modern Languages. The forum was then followed by workshops featuring four different communities—African

American, lesbian, working class, and postcolonial—which were encouraged to continue the dialogue begun in the open forum. My workshop session, which was organized by Valerie Smith, was titled "Black Feminist Perspectives in/on the Academy."

7. I am indebted to Bonnie Thornton Dill for the term "service trap" to describe the complex set of issues I am examining as they relate to work we are called upon to do.

8. Black literary critic Stephen Henderson, whose work on the Black Arts Movement of the 1960s offered some of the first theoretical perspectives on what some call the Second Black Renaissance, used the term "saturation" to signify the depth of immersion into and evaluation of a poem, from the perspective of the poem itself and the wider context of the black experience from which it comes. See Stephen Henderson, *Understanding the New Black Poetry: Black Speech and Black Music as Poetic References* (New York: Morrow Quill, 1973), 62–69. One of the larger projects that I am eager to return to and complete is "Spaces for the Reader: Toni Morrison, Black Studies, and the Praxis of Cultural Studies," a manuscript on Toni Morrison's narrative poetics and cultural politics. Other projects include a study of the intersection of narratives of multiculturalism and pedagogy and a novel about a black woman's journey from exile to sanctuary to rebirth in the wake of her divorce.

9. The term "opportunity costs" does not so much refer to monetary compensation as it does to the general idea of tradeoffs involved in making decisions. Choices always mean we get to receive one set of experiences or rewards versus another. I refer to my progression toward full professor as rapid because the publication of my first book in 1991 meant that I could apply for tenure a year early. Almost simultaneous with receiving tenure, I began the work of establishing the African American studies program at George Mason. What I am discussing in this essay are the pros and cons of deciding to do that particular kind of work at that particular time in my academic career.

10. In fact, as I recall, two of my colleagues, Barbara Christian and Margaret Wilkerson, both of whom had encouraged me to take an offer to come to Berkeley, advised me to think carefully about the encouragement I was receiving to start an African American studies program. Based on their work as pioneers in black studies at Berkeley, they understood both the attraction and the consequences of such work.

11. The internal affairs of my own university are not really the subject of this paper, but I do believe there is a larger institutional issue that is common to many campuses regarding the work of African American studies, black studies, and other ethnic studies programs. Faculty who are named to such administrative positions are rarely afforded the same kind of support that department chairs receive. Moreover, very few such programs even receive department status, and this becomes an institutionalized form of control over their growth and visibility. I recall that the former president of my university, who was in office when the program was approved, made it very clear that he would approve a minor and not a major, an interdisciplinary program and not a department. The claim that this structure would best support the college and university commitment to diversity is problematic and contestable. When coupled with the scarcity of resources allocated to such programs, this claim is absurd.

12. See Ann duCille, "The Occult of True Black Womanhood: Critical Demeanor and Black Feminist Studies," *Signs* 19 (1994): 591.

13. Wahneema Lubiano, ed., *The House That Race Built: Original Essays by Toni Morrison, Angela Y. Davis, Cornel West, and Others on Black Americans and the Politics in America Today* (New York: Vintage, 1998).

14. Toni Morrison, "Home," in *The House That Race Built*, ed. Lubiano, 5.

15. See Gerald Graff, *Beyond the Culture Wars: How Teaching the Conflicts Can Revitalize American Education* (New York: Norton, 1992).

16. Frances E. W. Harper, *Iola Leroy, or Shadows Uplifted* (1892; reprinted, New York: Oxford University Press, 1988), 262.

17. Toni Morrison, *Beloved* (New York: Knopf, 1987), 140.

18. Adrienne Rich, "When We Dead Awaken: Writing as Re-vision," *College English* 24 (October 1972): 18. For an excellent discussion of the history, practice, and debates around advocacy, see Patricia Meyer Spacks, ed., *Advocacy in the Classroom: Problems and Possibilities* (New York: St. Martin's Press, 1996).

19. Marilyn Mobley McKenzie, "Campus Expectations of the Minority Professoriat," *Black Issues in Higher Education* 9 (17 December 1992): 10–13.

20. McKay, "Troubled Peace," 11.

21. Ruth Farmer, "Place but Not Importance: The Race for Inclusion in Academe," in *Spirit, Space, and Survival: African American Women in (White) Academe*, ed. Joy James and Ruth Farmer (New York: Routledge, 1993), 196–217.

22. James Baldwin, *Notes of a Native Son* (Boston: Beacon Press, 1955), 5. In some ways my participation in the Black Women and Work Project gave me an opportunity to discuss the politics of labor and to discover the connection between this analysis and my more familiar research and scholarship. The Black Women and Work Project has thus been a crucial factor in this turning point of my career.

23. See Yolanda T. Moses, "Black Women in Academe: Issues and Strategies," in *Black Women in the Academy*, ed. Benjamin, 23.

24. See Paula Giddings, *When and Where I Enter: The Impact of Black Women on Race and Sex in America* (New York: Bantam, 1984), 97–98.

25. I thank my Black Women and Work colleague Adrienne Davis for pointing out that this work raises issues of boundaries.

26. Susan B. Apel, "Gender and Invisible Work: Musings of a Woman Law Professor," *University of San Francisco Law Review* 31 (1997): 1016. I thank Taunya Banks from the Black Women and Work Project for sharing this article about how gender and labor issues affect law professors.

27. See Darlene Clark Hine, "'In the Kingdom of Culture': Black Women and the Intersection of Race, Gender, and Class," in *Lure and Loathing: Essays on Race, Identity, and the Ambivalence of Assimilation,* ed. Gerald Early (New York: Penguin Books, 1993), 337–351.

28. Stephanie Golden, *Slaying the Mermaid: Women and the Culture of Sacrifice* (New York: Harmony Books, 1998), 119.

29. Wahneema Lubiano analyzes these black nationalist agendas and the gender politics embedded in them in "Black Nationalism and Black Common Sense: Policing Ourselves and Others," in *The House That Race Built*, ed. Lubiano, 232–251.

30. See Graff, *Beyond the Culture Wars;* and Henry Louis Gates Jr., *Loose Canon: Notes on the Culture Wars* (New York: Oxford University Press, 1992) for discussions about how curriculum changes from ethnic studies to women studies and from feminism to multiculturalism have changed public discourse about the academy and higher education.

31. See duCille, "The Occult of True Black Womanhood," 605.

32. See Jane Gallop, *Around 1981: Academic Feminist Literary Theory* (New York: Routledge, 1992), 241.

33. This title is the original one I submitted upon being invited to join the Black Women and Work Project. I appreciate the valuable critiques I received from my colleagues in the group—especially Mary Helen Washington, Saundra Nettles, Taunya Banks, Bonnie Thornton Dill, Sharon Harley, Caleen Jennings, and Shirley Logan, among others—as my thoughts on these issues evolved. Valuable conversations with Rev. June Gatlin, Marita Golden, Gloria Murray, and Linda Nelson helped me revise the essay into its present form.

34. Linda Singer, "Feminism and Postmodernism," in *Feminists Theorize the Political,* ed. Judith Butler and Joan W. Scott (New York: Routledge, 1992), 465.

35. See Wahneema Lubiano, "Constructing and Reconstructing Afro-American Texts: The Critic as Ambassador and Referee," *American Literary History* 1, no. 2 (summer 1989): 432–437, for the complex set of ambivalences that have shaped recent critical debates. Also see Mary Catherine Bateson, *Composing a Life* (New York: Plume, 1989), for her discussion about how she and five other extraordinary women integrated change and discontinuity into their very busy professional lives.

36. Karla F. C. Holloway, *Codes of Conduct: Race, Ethics, and the Color of Our Character* (New Brunswick, N.J.: Rutgers University Press, 1995), 10.

When the Spirit Takes Hold, What the Work Becomes!

JUDI MOORE LATTA

I am what historian-theologian Vincent Harding called a "working witness," one who comes to the spiritual work of African American women as a participant-observer in search of the sacred. My Christian evangelist West Indian grandmother Druscilla, watching me play with my friends and listening to my four-year-old child-talk, predicted that I would be a missionary working on behalf of others. My parents concurred that I would eventually "do something for other folks" and always knew that that something would build upon the lessons I learned from observing those around me.

My ideas about what constitutes work were shaped while I grew up in the segregated South on the campus of the historically black Florida A & M University (FAMU) as the only child of two college professors. As an educator from the 1940s through the 1960s, my father, Oscar Moore, earned a reputation as a "gentleman and a scholar" among his many students and colleagues, who described him, even at his funeral in 1996, as a "moral man with principles." On his road to his doctorate at Boston University—a road that took him from Cambridge, Massachusetts, to Charleston, West Virginia, to Lawrenceville, Virginia, and then to Tallahassee, Florida—he had shined shoes, literally shoveled horse manure, hustled baggage, been an athlete and a coach. My mother, LaVerne Moore—his partner for fifty-three years—was an educated woman who, in the late 1930s, hated every moment of being "the only one" in her classes during four years at the predominantly white University of Cincinnati. She married and then earned a master's degree and academic hours beyond the degree at Boston University. When her advisor offered her a fellowship toward a Ph.D., she declined, opting to leave her studies and come back to Tallahassee to take care of Dad and me. During her professional career, she was a teacher's teacher, responsible for launching students in FAMU's School of Education. I watched her for years do an incredible balancing act—teaching four classes a semester as one of two professors in the university's area of Fundamentals of Education, mentoring students who would be among the strongest secondary school teachers of color in the state of Florida, working as an active member of St.

Michael and All Angels Episcopal Church in Tallahassee, organizing our household with unparalleled passion and skill, and finding "bargains" to keep our home running on the budget of a "colored teacher's salary." Mother never called what she did work, but rather "what I need to do." But it is clear that work with head and hands for both of my parents was no stranger. Work for them meant having self-control, extending oneself beyond the moment, and answering a call to service.

I always knew that in the work I did I wanted to tell stories, so it was no surprise to those who knew me that I majored in English when I went to Hampton Institute as an undergraduate, then went to Boston University for my master's in English Language and Literature, and later received a Ph.D. in American Studies at the University of Maryland. I wanted to find the voice to tell audiences the stories that put the people I knew and met at the center. And I wanted my stories to validate people's experiences. Storytelling, I always believed, was sacred territory, and participating in it and teaching it to others was my calling. So becoming a university professor, a documentary radio producer and reporter working for National Public Radio, and a television producer of lifestyle features meant answering my call.

Along the way I met women whose work connected them in spiritual ways to something larger than themselves: Barbara Boardley, my nursery school teacher and Girl Scout leader, who taught me how to work for an extended family of people who are not blood relatives; Nancy McGhee, my high school English teacher, who nudged me to put lives into poems; Jessie Lemmon Brown, my professor at Hampton, who urged me to keep writing until it meant something; Bernice Johnson Reagon, my Smithsonian collaborator at National Public Radio, who reminded me how precious and fine the work of telling stories can be. And there were more.

The women in the essay that follows are two of the many I have met over the years. Telling stories about their spiritual work not only helps me understand my own work, but also helps me fulfill my grandmother's prophecy.

---

*T*his essay is about women who are not legitimized by patriarchy and whose principal work is considered outside of the orthodox labor force. Their authority to be bold in what they do comes from God, and, as a result, they see themselves as in the employ of the Eternal. At issue here is the spiritual work of two contemporary African American women who may not call themselves missionaries but who clearly work as evangelists, ambassadors, teacher-counselors, disseminators of the Word of God. Sister Leona Davis and Donna Sams Heart, who come from different sacred music communities, do the work of ministry, witnessing for the Spirit through the substance and character of their actions.[1] They say that this work sustains them, allows them to face the everyday challenges of living, helps them to help others. Their words are those of Christian women, and while language is not a transparent vehicle for making meaning, it does provide a window through which we can examine the attitudes and beliefs they put into practice.

What happens to a woman when the Spirit takes hold of her? What difference does it make in her life? The women explored in this essay suggest that they are inspired, moved, and directed to be what sociologist Cheryl Townsend Gilkes has called "women God raised up," or women set apart for sacred purposes.[2] Yet their spiritual work does not fragment and separate them from the world and from the people they have been called to serve. One works within the context of a congregational hymn-singing tradition and the other within a rehearsed gospel choir tradition. Both women see themselves on a mission, in partnership with a Higher Force, answering a calling.

There are three overlapping vantage points from which I view these women's stories, three circles of understanding connected to my own work: the first is from my perspective as a lifetime member-worker within black Christian church congregations; the second is from my perspective as a documentary radio producer on a production team; and the third is from my viewpoint as a teacher and student within a university setting. All of my life I have seen and known women in ministry who believe in the spiritual dimensions of life and do the work of comforting and advising, protecting and informing; but in the early 1990s, when I served as senior producer for the public radio series *Wade in the Water: African American Sacred Music Traditions,* the phrase "spiritual work" gained new meaning.[3] I came to understand spiritual work as that which is most important in one's life, makes a difference in someone else's life, is believed to be ordained by God, and for some is performed through music in answer to what the Biblical scriptures identify as a high calling.

Bernice Johnson Reagon, conceptual producer and primary scholar of the *Wade in the Water* series, introduced those of us on the radio production team to African American composers, arrangers, directors, and singers from a variety of historical and contemporary sacred music communities that had been, for most Americans, invisible. I felt a kinship with these communities and took seriously my responsibility to translate aspects of their experiences into a production plan for twenty-six one-hour documentaries. This, for me, was spiritual work because I was serving as a vehicle for the transformation of long-silent communities into stories. I felt I had been given a sacred responsibility to make this information accessible to a listening public.

When the radio series ended, I felt compelled to continue my work, and, as a result, I began graduate study in the academy, investigating these sacred music communities in greater depth. At the university my work became ethnography—which enables a researcher to enter a culture, participate in it, observe it, and then describe it—and in the process I met Donna Sams Heart and Sister Leona Davis, women whose spiritual work extends from and is motivated by their music. On several occasions between October 1995 and January 1998, I interviewed and observed them, taking written notes, making audio recordings, and feeling connected with their stories. In their commitments they are not lukewarm. In fact, their work—which they would call "God's work"—described below, might best be characterized by a quote from the Biblical prophet Jeremiah: "His word is in my heart like a fire, a fire shut up in my bones" (Jeremiah 20:9).

"Fire Shut up in My Bones": A Calling to Spiritual Work

What form does fire take when put to work? Sister Leona Davis calls herself an "ambassador for the Lord," and passionately declares, "I do sing sometimes; I pray and I also testify" to the end of "bringing some souls to Christ." An ambassador is one sent or appointed on a special mission to represent a sovereign. In the Christian church this role frequently is performed by those who preach. Yet Sister Leona is not called a preacher and has never delivered a formal sermon, nor has she been ordained in any church. However, she sees her singing and personal testimonies as a sacred assignment: "When I was young, . . . we used to be on the porch and I would be the preacher. I would try to sing like some of the . . . Deacons . . . old sisters, mothers in the church. Seem like God gave me a gift of preaching at the time, but I would never accept it. [Now] it seem like something becomes a part of me."

A similar preaching fire compels Donna Sams Heart to perform ambassadorial tasks "to help somebody else." She comes from a tradition of missionaries, a family of singing women evangelists, and, like them, she has used her music to do the work of a spiritual counselor, determined to serve/console/reassure others. She puts it this way: "And I have this drive that I must be about my Father's business, come what may. Whatever door He chooses to open, if He opens it, I'm going through."

Both women consider themselves led by the Spirit—the sovereign they acknowledge—to do important work that embodies three types of actions: first, the work of telling others about Christ; second, the work of modeling what it means to live a Christlike life; and third, the work of encouraging others who are disillusioned and disappointed. In these ways they share a connection with other African American women, from sacred music communities, who have a cosmological vision that honors the centrality of Jesus and an attitude toward what they do that echoes author Shri Aurobindo's understanding of work as "action done for the Divine and increasingly in union with the Divine."[4]

In one episode of the *Wade in the Water* radio series, concert singer J. Robert Bradley described the early-twentieth-century spiritual work of his mentor, Lucie Campbell, considered the first woman to compose gospel music: "[Campbell] was a preacher, but in those times women were not allowed to preach. If she wanted to keep her job, she couldn't say that she was a preacher, so she put it in music."[5] In this statement, Bradley spoke volumes about some spiritually convinced and convicted black women working within the context of the Christian religious tradition. Lucie Campbell's paid profession, her "job" for thirty-three years, was as a high school English teacher; but she was equally devoted to her volunteer music ministry. As music director of the National Baptist Convention from 1916 through her death in 1963, she created new gospel songs, preserved and updated old ones, and encouraged new talent to perform the music, thus expanding the repertoire. Since the convention represented at the time the largest gathering of African Americans in the world, her work was pivotal. "Miss Lucie," as she was affectionately called by many who knew her, controlled what gospel singers appeared before the convention audiences. She determined what black Baptists sang for more than four decades because, as ethnomusicologist Horace Boyer observed, she "introduced a new song each year," composing original lyrics which reflected her Christian convictions; some of these songs became gospel standards: "He Understands, He'll Say 'Well Done,'" "Jesus Gave Me Water," "Touch Me Lord Jesus," among others.[6] In one verse of her composition "Something Within," she wrote about the fire driving her spiritual work:

Have you that something, that burning desire?
Have you that something that never doth tire?
Oh, if you have it, that Heavenly Fire
Let the world know there is something within.[7]

Campbell was a composer, an arranger, a counselor, a director, and a teacher who used her songs and her work with singers to pronounce her calling, to tell others about Jesus, to encourage Christian living. The portraits I will draw of Sister Leona and Donna Sams Heart reveal Christian women committed to work that is important to them, that is believed to be ordained by God, and that is intertwined with music. It is ambassadorial work that is faith driven and Spirit inspired.

Sister Leona and the Prayer Band

By definition, a prayer band is a community of worshippers who meet for regular prayers, testimonies, and sacred singing and who commit to mutual support of members. During production of the *Wade in the Water* radio series, I was introduced to the United Southern Prayer Band of Baltimore, Washington, and Virginia—made up of members, from a network of Baptist churches, who met in all-night services once a month. A few years later, this group became part of my academic investigation of singing spiritual communities. In this prayer band, the music is unrehearsed and the worshippers use no instruments except for their voices and their bodies to "raise a hymn" or offer "a word for the Lord."[8]

The United Southern Prayer Band was formed in 1944 by a group of African Americans who migrated to the mid-Atlantic region from South Carolina and brought their Baptist worship style with them. At one time, the group boasted more than eight dozen members from throughout the region, but in recent years the numbers have dwindled as the average age of prayer band members continues to climb toward the mid-eighties. On most evenings now, the number of participants is usually fewer than thirty. These participants are members of different local churches and they hold their United Southern Prayer Band meetings alternately between Baltimore and Washington in churches to which their members belong.[9] Their goal, one explained, is "to help people find a better religion."

I met Sister Leona Davis when I went to my first all-night service as an assignment for an ethnography course I was taking. (I later learned that some prayer band members give their women members the title "Sister" as a sign of respect for their Christian bond.) On that night in the fall of 1995, as I entered Central Baptist Church, I came as an observer and took a seat on the back pew, voluntarily on the margins because I thought this might be a good vantage point from which to record the unwritten rules of the ritual. From the beginning, I could feel the passion in worshippers' voices and see the electricity in their whole bodies as they sang and spoke with conviction, clapped their hands with great enthusiasm, and supported each other with verbal responses. First, there was an opening prayer and then one woman who had entered the church leaning on a cane stood straight and, apparently emboldened by the Spirit, with a strong voice raised a song: "Ever happened to me, ever happened to me, O Jesus is the best thing ever happened to me."

Another woman, who looked to me to be in her late fifties, Sister Leona Davis—white hat glittering—gave a testimony and led the congregation in singing "Jesus Will Fix It for You." Then three songs, two testimonies, and one prayer into the service, she turned and waved me forward, inviting me (a stranger) to leave my back pew seat and join her a few rows from the front. Torn between my academic-journalist frame of reference and my African American Christian upbringing, I tried to decide if it was more important to keep up the intensive note-taking in my journal or to become a worshipper. "Guide me O, thou great Jehovah." I closed my notebook and raised my hand in praise.

A few days later I interviewed Sister Leona, who told me she had frequent and casual conversations/prayer with the Lord, in which, she said, "I'm in here talking to Him like I'm talking to you." Painting a picture as though telling a short story, she gave details of her coming to the prayer band meeting on the night we first met, and, in so doing, she revealed much about her attitude toward spiritual work. My own academic work, as that of every ethnographer, involves writing the cultural scene so as to make it recognizable to those who are in it. What follows, then, are my recollections of the picture story Sister Leona painted for me in words and spirit about the evening of the all-night meeting.

Heaven opened up and the rain poured down as she backed her sedan out of the parking lot of her apartment complex in Southeast Washington, D.C. With the sequins of her white hat glittering in the moonlight, she took one last glance out of her rearview mirror to make sure the guard was still circling the complex as he did every weekend night. She was torn—excited to be going to the prayer band meeting on this Saturday night but anxious about staying too much beyond 2:00 A.M. That was the time the guard went off duty. If she could get back before he left, she would feel safe coming home, climbing the two flights of steps to her apartment. As it had so many times before, music comforted her and offered reassurance. "I will trust in the Lord, I will trust in the Lord, I will trust in the Lord till I die," she sang softly the familiar tune and felt better. Somehow, keeping her eyes "stayed on Him" and a song in her mouth strengthened her and assured her that she was not alone.

With all this rain, "thank God," she thought, that she didn't have to go to Baltimore tonight; this evening she only had to drive four blocks to Central Baptist Church at the corner of Pennsylvania and Branch for the gathering of the prayer band. Even if there were only twenty or so members, it was good to find people from different churches wanting to sing and pray. Actually, she was not sure of any other reason why—after six years—she was still going to the once-a-month all-night meetings, and she talked to the Lord just as if He was sitting next to her on the front seat of the car. Speaking as she had so many times before, Sister Leona said, "I'm getting out of it. Lord, you know I can't go up and down the road by myself at night. It's getting too dangerous out here." And just as He had so many times before, the Lord reminded her that she had a testimony that could not wait and a "job that had to be done."

Sister Leona's "job," in this case, meant her spiritual work as missionary—her duty as an ambassador to tell others about her blessings. Several days before—without money, without access to legal assistance in a court case she faced—she had prayed, "Lord, I need a lawyer to speak for me." Her prayers had been answered when a prominent attorney had taken her case pro bono: "And when I got there [in court] they was telling me, 'Oh, you got the best lawyer. He's a good man.' And I wanted to tell them, said to myself, 'I didn't get him, God gave him to me.'" With the court case won, she felt that her spiritual duty was to proclaim publicly, or "witness," at the all-night meeting how God had answered her prayer. Nothing could silence her—not inclement weather, not fatigue, not fear for her personal safety because of her late hours. She was convinced that her testimony would announce her blessing, her life would serve as a model of how to put God first, and her singing "what the Lord laid on her heart" would encourage others in her community who might be encountering comparable life challenges.

Witnessing and encouraging in the context of the church are related, but different, concepts. The one who witnesses, sharing the language of the legal profession, "testifies" or acknowledges publicly a Divine presence in her personal life and in so doing fulfills a part of the promise she has made to tell someone else about how her life has been transformed by God. Sometimes the act of witnessing takes the form of a gesture—raising one's hand in agreement with someone else. However, the one who encourages may witness but may also use other strategies in her spiritual work. For example, in addition to a spoken testimony, she might sing her witness, hum a song, or physically touch someone as a sign of support and compassion.

When Work Is Not a Job

When Sister Leona describes what she does for the Divine, she borrows what she sees as positive from the language of work and leaves what is not. For example, at one time or another in the life of this sixty-year-old woman, "work" and "job" have been synonymous terms. At other times the meanings of these terms have been at odds with each other, one suggesting what she has been spiritually called to do and the other suggesting what she is economically compelled to do.

Being raised as one of six children in a family of poor sharecroppers in rural Alabama, she came to understand manual labor, physical exertion, and low pay in a secular world as the elements of wage-earning work. When Sister Leona moved North in the early 1970s, she found low-paying work that was physically taxing and has resulted in her early retirement. She talks about this work as a job, and the tensions are evident in her language: "I had to *come out*. I had carpal tunnel syndrome. I was working for Giant Food. I been in and out of little pieces of jobs, you know, and never got a foothold of getting back into a good job. I'm trying. When I came out I wasn't old enough to retire or anything, and now they tell me I got to wait till I get sixty-two to even draw my retirement from Giant. The woman say, 'If you draw it now, you'll loose 20 percent.' I was with Giant for twenty-two years. Think about you been on a job so long. They done got the best part of my life." Within this context, a job and the spectrum of activities associated with it have negative connotations, with the illusive opportunity for a "good job" always somewhere beyond her grasp. When she refers to having to "come out," she suggests that she had to leave the job because having such a job is an *insider's* position to which she is not privileged.

At the same time, Sister Leona holds another view of work, a view that grows out of the experiences of a twelve-year-old whose father dies, leaving her mother to care for her children with what could be pieced together from seasonal, exploitative, and underpaid service jobs. In the midst of these difficulties, her mother, led by the Spirit, turned to the church, where she did the work of a witness, including "leading songs and moaning" during prayer services.

Song leading is an important type of spiritual work in African American worship services, since not everyone has been "given the gift" to set the pace, choose the song that fits the need, and "keep the service moving" in a congregational setting. Sister Leona's mother may have been a dependable worker at her paying job, but she saw as her duty the work of song leading (keeping the music going) and witnessing (telling others about her faith-walk with God). When Sister Leona faced her own crisis and had to "come out of the job," the nature of her work shifted to the spiritual realm. On the recommendation of a former coworker in the retail business, she became active with the prayer band and, as she describes it, her "commitment changed."

According to Bernice Johnson Reagon, in the essay "Developing Black American Cultural Programs," one way of demonstrating one's commitment in the prayer band, as in other religious rituals, is where one sits in the church sanctuary during the service.[10] Space has a significant function in ordering the worship. A relationship exists between where individuals sit and the leadership roles those individuals hold. Anecdotal evidence suggests that usually three to four times more women participate in the prayer services than men, but most men—no matter what time they enter—generally occupy the seats facing the congregation as well as the front row of the pews. Sister Leona, who was among the first to arrive at the prayer band meeting on the night of my first observation, sat several rows from the front pew with other women, who, I later learned, consciously left the front seats vacant and available for men. In the tacit rules of the ritual, sitting across the front gives a man automatic authority to make a prayer, give a testimony, or raise a hymn. But it is generally the women who take unacknowledged leadership in certain aspects of the meeting.

On several occasions, for example, as the time to begin the service inched past the nine o'clock traditional starting hour and the congregants sat waiting for the service to begin, I watched Sister Leona nonverbally suggest that the prayer meeting start. She visibly and frequently consulted her watch and began to hum audibly as she rocked back and forth. While she did not make a direct attempt to open the service because she believes "the [male] band leaders are supposed to do that," she did obey what the Spirit told her to do.

In starting the service in such an indirect way, Sister Leona was externally yielding to the tradition while internally remaining loyal to the "fire shut up in [her] bones." She was not disobeying the man-made unspoken rules that assigned gender roles but was obeying the rules of a higher power that assigned work irrespective of gender. Her goal was to get the work of God done in spite of the limitations of tradition placed upon her. Her situation is one example of how some women doing work they consider sacred respond to the call of the Spirit.

Donna Sams Heart and the Choir Rehearsal

Donna Sams Heart's sacred music community was in some ways similar and in other ways quite different from Sister Leona's. Where Sister Leona served in a small congregation singing unrehearsed songs, Heart (with her husband and son) sang in several large gospel choirs. Both the performances and the choirs' rehearsals became sites where Heart practiced her spiritual work. On a Saturday afternoon in October 1996, I visited a choir rehearsal at Ebenezer AME Church, the largest African Methodist Episcopal Church in Prince Georges County, Maryland, in fact, the largest AME Church in the world. During production on *Wade in the Water* we had recorded this choir in performance and in worship, and on this day I was here to observe the choir in rehearsal as part of my academic study.[11]

Donna Sams Heart, in her thirties, greeted as many people as she could while helping other choir members to move chairs and adjust portable walls in the room. The rehearsal had not yet begun and they were busy preparing the space to receive the nearly two hundred choir members expected—ranging from infants to senior citizens—who would soon be seated according to their singing voices: altos on the left, sopranos on the right, basses and tenors in the center. In a few short minutes they would become Kaleidoscope—a mass choir, several community and church choirs joined together. Heart greeted her friend Gloria, chaplain of one of the choirs, who wore a sweatshirt revealing her bias, "Jesus By Popular Demand." Gloria in turn quipped, "I really should be somewhere else" as she planted herself firmly in what would soon become the alto section of the room.[12] This statement was a vocal expression of an internal ambivalence shared by others. Clearly, Gloria had made a conscious decision to be at choir rehearsal rather than "somewhere else," but she questioned whether or not it was a luxury she could afford.

Now they were assembled—two hundred strong. Heart took her place among the more than fifty sopranos and seemed to continue her spiritual work automatically. She squeezed the hand of the woman beside her, who sat quietly and looked as if she needed encouragement. What followed was a devotion period when choir members (mostly women) gave "praise reports," offering a word of testimony to what the "Lord had done" for them this day/week/month. Then came the request for choir members to "touch and agree"—an instruction they understood to mean stand, form a circle, hold hands, bow heads, and pray. Moving to a spiritual high point, they concluded devotion with instant applause and followed it with announcements about choir business. When the singing began, the director motioned to Donna Sams Heart, sitting in the back row of the soprano section. She rose to take the lead on "We Shall Behold Him" and her voice soared, causing hands to be raised in witness to what she sang. The choir rehearsal was transformed into a church service as the Spirit took hold. Throughout the room people were moved to respond by clapping hands or crying. Donna Sams Heart—director of her own choir, member of three others, soloist in this choir, singing evangelist—was using her voice as the center of her ministry to encourage. In an interview later, she explained: "And in a choir we come from all different walks of life. Music will do for you what nothing else will do. People come to choir rehearsal with all kind of trouble and concerns on their mind. But when you come into the choir rehearsal and you see it as a ministry . . . for the sole purpose of lifting of the name of Jesus, then it allows you to focus and say, 'OK, that's personal; let's drop personal and get on one accord.'"

When Music Makes Possible the Work of the Church

It is important to keep in mind that some spiritual workers distinguish between "church work" and "the work of the church" with the former phrase used to refer to the myriad activities and worship rituals which occur under the auspices of the organized church, but not necessarily under Divine inspiration. In that sense, the term "church work" is a euphemism for busywork or uninspired action performed without spiritual direction. The phrase "the work of the church," however, is a reference to those Holy Spirit–filled principles and concepts of religion put into action—not necessarily dependent on affiliation with a single established institution.[13]

Doing "the work of the church" is second nature for Donna Sams Heart, whose work tasks encompass teaching in the broadest sense. I empathize with her because my own work in the academy has made clear for me the sacredness of teaching, the spiritual responsibility of approaching another's mind and helping to move it from where it is to where it could be. The idea of teaching in its broadest sense is also familiar to me, since I grew up in a household where both of my parents were university professors and my father was a baseball coach who drew from his coaching the life skills he taught me. From him I first learned that coaching is more than athletic prowess. Saundra Murray Nettles has suggested that the concept of coaching offers a framework for examining other types of work. Nettles writes about "four elements that are part of what effective coaches do: (a) they teach; (b) they assess performance; (c) they structure the learning environment; and (d) they provide social support."[14]

Being a coach, Nettles suggests, requires having specialized knowledge of a field and of the people who will operate in that field. It involves resolving conflicts, empathizing, and leading. Clearly, in this sense, Donna Sams Heart, who uses in choirs what she calls her "God-given musical talents," is a coach—one who combines the techniques of coaching with an understanding of the transformative possibilities of music as spiritual work. When good coaches teach, they become role models and thought stimulators, conduits of culture; they provide feedback and encourage participation; they extend the lessons of their disciplines to larger life experiences. Heart is a good coach because she transmits culture and teaches choir members music theory, gospel music history, and biblical principles. In addition, she uses stories to pass along commonsense lessons at every opportunity.

Heart's work takes place within the context of the contemporary gospel choir movement that soared in popularity among singers of sacred music during the second half of the twentieth century. Ever since gospel choirs began in the 1930s, these ensembles have been built on a rehearsed tradition in which both repertoire and style have been transmitted orally. At the center of that transmission process is the teacher/coach—called the director—who through formal and informal instruction conveys performance approaches, assesses performances, structures the learning environment, and provides social support. When led by the Spirit, this person is doing the work of ministry.

While the literature on workers in the church has separately linked education to religion and music to religion, it has seldom brought the three—education, music, religion—under one umbrella. Sociologist Cheryl Townsend Gilkes suggests that black women's church work generally encompasses "active membership in local churches, clubs, and religious auxiliaries, as well as teaching Sunday school."[15] Extending this notion and chronicling the nineteenth- and early-twentieth-century work of women in the black Baptist Church, historian Evelyn Brooks Higginbotham explains that the role of missionary and teacher in the church frequently was assumed by those who taught in schools outside of the church and who worked with a fervor.[16]

Throughout this documented history, there are accounts of black women who have accepted the work of teaching—defined to include the meaning of coaching—in tandem with their calls to ministry. In *Daughters of Thunder*, Bettye Collier-Thomas describes the work of "Black preaching women" whose teaching moments came because "they believed that the Holy Spirit empowered them to act, think, speak, and simply be."[17] It is clear that these black women have claimed education and teaching, broadly defined, as part of their spiritual work.

For Donna Sams Heart, spiritual work embraces more than teaching songs. She feels that it is important for her to bring "the right attitude" to the choir rehearsal and to teach others to do the same. She describes this way of being in the choir as she describes the proper attitude necessary to perform what she calls her "nine-to-five job . . . as executive secretary and office manager." Her words reflect a blurred line between sacred and secular as she explains how one should come to spiritual work in choirs: "You come with the attitude to work. Singing is a job within the ministry because you have to come with the right attitude. You come to work."

Having the right attitude, she insists, is important when one is associated with more than one aggregation—each demanding its own schedules, rehearsals, rules, and even uniforms. Before she learned to listen to what the Spirit told her to do, Heart had "crowded her schedule" to the point where she was "no good" to any of the groups or to her husband and teenage son (both gospel musicians)—since she was trying to be everywhere at once. Because she had only evenings and weekends away from her private-sector job, the demands on her time were overwhelming. When we talked, I asked her how she found the time for her music ministry. She replied, "You make it." But then she quickly recalled learning to "juggle schedules" and to "prioritize" her work as she said, "And I remember early on in ministry, years ago, I did not know how to say 'No,' . . . and I was ripping and running and I was worn out." Prioritizing meant learning to do first those things that "truly lift up the name of Jesus."

Beyond Teaching Song

On the night of 18 November 1996, in Prince George's County, Maryland, I recorded the first of several interviews, and Heart took care to distinguish between her work roles within choirs: soloist, soprano, secretary, director. Sometimes they are separate; most frequently they overlap; always they are embraced by her understanding of herself as teacher and, what can be called in the context of this essay, coach. As one who educates, Heart seeks to help choir members grow spiritually. Within the context of the choir rehearsal, her opportunity frequently arises during the devotion period—the time set aside at the beginning of the session. It is then that she sees herself as a catalyst, one who serves as a means to an end: "You go right into your opening prayer, a scripture reading. . . . Right after that you open the floor for people to give, we call it 'victory reports.' . . . If you have something exciting to say, don't sit there and contemplate. Pop, flip, say it. . . . You could overcome for your testimony and you could bless somebody else. If you can't find a reason to be happy right now, you can borrow one of mine until you can come up with one. And [that] allows the director—it's so much easier for any director that has a group of people that's already focused. You can get more work done; you can get better singing."

A second teaching role Heart plays in her work directing a community choir is to help members grow technically as they grow spiritually, teaching them music theory while encouraging them to prepare for leadership. "You always educate your choir. Make them feel like they're always learning something, and not just a new song. They come to grow spiritually. You know, never leave the way you came. Feel better. And then feel like, 'I didn't know that all those five lines was a staff' or 'I didn't know that that was a measuring bar line.' And it makes them feel important. And I always say to them, 'Listen. You may be a director one day. You never know where God's gonna take you from this point on.'"

There is another point of intersection between Heart's role as choir director and her work as educator, a point that is reflected in the language she uses to describe how she encourages choir members to learn new material. As we sit in her living room, talking about her work, she reveals her approach. "You have homework in our rehearsals," she proudly boasts as she borrows the terminology of the secular classroom to describe what she instructs singers to do: "Every singer should have homework. You should always bring a tape recorder to your rehearsals because, you know, you can't commit every single thing, song, or even announcement, concept that the director is giving to you. And you want to take that home, digest it, and live with it. And when you come back to the next rehearsal, you're all these steps ahead. . . . You're growing."

Homework assignments can be as challenging for the worker-director giving the assignments as for the worker–choir member getting them. When she moves from one aggregation to another, she changes roles and positions—and, thereby, her relationship to homework assignments—but she maintains her grounding. She says, "No matter what, you have to know who to satisfy [at] each level. And, of course, you do that with the help of the Holy Spirit."

It is with the help of the Holy Spirit that Heart uses the homework concept as she shifts from being director of one choir into being soloist in another—remaining a spiritual worker in both. Taking her own advice, when she is worker-singer, Heart regularly brings a tape recorder to choir rehearsal so that she can take thorough notes. In this, her unpaid work, she practices what she preaches. Her aim is to connect with the spiritual, since "the Lord can do inside what none of us can do." The tape recorder allows her to hear, after the fact, any extrinsic pointers she may have missed during the rehearsal, and her additional studying of the Bible allows her to hear the inner voice speaking to her—all with the aim of empowering her music ministry: "I'm not just singing, my whole body language—I'm interpreting, my whole body language. I'm including you. I'm pulling you with me into the song. It takes time to do that. Some people can do that naturally, but even with the natural talent, you have to keep practicing. So that's homework. . . . And then you read your Word.[18] And that's part of the homework."

Lives Continuing to Sing: An Update

On that rainy night when I first met Sister Leona, I heard her stand and recite Psalm 27:6 from memory as part of her testimony in the sacred space and time of the all-night meeting of the prayer band. She said, "And now shall mine head be lifted up above mine enemies round about me: therefore will I offer in his tabernacle sacrifices of joy; I will sing, yea, I will sing praises unto the Lord." As she testified that night, she described the obstacles placed in her way and "the Lord who stepped in" to remove them as being "reason enough" for her to sing praises. That same night her praise testimony in song, "Jesus Will Fix It for You," reinforced what she spoke. Three years after our initial interviews she still attended all-night prayer meetings and did God's work as an "ambassador to bring some blind person to the Lord." By 1998, her secular work life had changed. Instead of being unemployed, she performed clerical tasks in a part-time job as a secretary. Ironically, she was not quite satisfied with either sacred or secular work, though the implied differences are clear: "On my paying job I have turned in my resignation twice. In my spiritual work, I don't want to turn in a resignation, but I do want to move around. If I see what I can do better in another place, I want to go."

While Sister Leona separated her paying job from her work for the Lord, Donna Sams Heart saw the two worlds as overlapping. "My resources are different, but I'm serving the public in both places," Heart said, as she celebrated her seventeenth year as executive secretary for a private trade association that supplies information about asbestos. "I see my job as an opportunity the Lord has given me to help. I have helped my neighbors and the Lord has blessed me with a job. . . . It's a destined place for me to be." Similarly, she felt destined to her role in choirs, where her work is her service: "God always puts me in front . . . so that keeps me in prayer. God brings people to me for counseling and I feel I need to be ready at all times. I have to know God's Word. I see myself as a seed planter. I have to keep myself studying, . . . and gospel music is nothing but the Word of God put to notes."

"On One Accord": The Language of Work

There is a shared language among spiritual workers. For Donna Sams Heart, a ministry is in operation whenever and wherever she sings. She says, "I see myself as simply a vessel from heaven going through me, out." Similarly, for Sister Leona Davis, the ministry is in her testimonies and songs, and her words suggest that she views herself as a tool directed by a guiding hand: "I had to go to the Lord for Him to lead me." Calling themselves "a vessel" or "a tool," these women describe their sacred responsibility.

In both their sacred and secular work, the women talk about a compelling force outside of themselves, a force which controls them and drives them to accomplish tasks. What is different in the way they describe work performed primarily as a source of income and the work performed as a spiritual assignment is the relationship between themselves as workers and the force that controls their actions. On the one hand, they contest "being used" and occasionally abused by the powers-that-be on their secular jobs, and, on the other hand, they allow themselves "to be used" as instruments by an omniscient power in the grand scheme of sacred work. The women are not always willing to perform spiritual tasks assigned to them and tell numerous stories about resisting their calling to such tasks because doing the work may take a physical or mental toll on them. It may mean that they must make sacrifices that are difficult. As a result, one question they both ask is, "Lord, why me?" Nevertheless, their

narratives cite Jesus as their example of what it means to be selfless and obedi-
ent to Divine will, and they describe their prayers for His will—not theirs—to
be done in their lives. This is their expression of the "fire shut up in [the]
bones."

The lives profiled here represent pockets of experiences of women whose
work and, subsequently, whose language evolve out of their spiritual way of
seeing the world. These are Christian women whose speech, peppered with
directions from the Lord, reflects a meshing of the secular and sacred worlds of
work. Other African American women have shared similar experiences, but the
accounts have been few. For this reason, telling these stories is important. The
women teach; they witness; they encourage; they spread the Word of God; they
are mentors, counselors, coaches, ambassadors. They may not call themselves
spiritual workers, but clearly their lives and the work most important to them
make them so. This work, done for the Divine and enabled by music, at once
links them to those to whom they feel compelled to minister and gives them a
boldness that empowers their actions.

Notes

1. The names of these women have been changed. The incidents and quotations attributed to them are based on interviews and ethnographic observations conducted from 1995
through 1998 in the Washington Metropolitan area. This fieldwork is part of a larger study
on the effects of the politics of radio production on African American sacred music representations. "Spirit" here is a reference to the Holy Spirit, which Christians believe is part of
the Godhead trinity (Father, Son, Holy Spirit) guiding human actions.

2. Cheryl Townsend Gilkes, "'Together and in Harness': Women's Traditions in the Sanctified Church," *Signs* 10, no. 4 (1985): 683.

3. *Wade in the Water: African American Sacred Music Traditions* was a twenty-six-part
radio series developed by National Public Radio and the Smithsonian Institution (Washington, D.C.) under the direction of conceptual producer Bernice Johnson Reagon and made
available on public radio in 1994.

4. Shri Aurobindo, *The Deeper Truth of Work* (Pondicherry, India: Shri Aurobindo
Archives and Research, 1972), 444.

5. J. Robert Bradley, *Wade in the Water*, episode 14.

6. Horace Boyer, "Lucie E. Campbell: Composer for the National Baptist Convention,
"*We'll Understand It Better By and By: Pioneering African American Gospel Composers*, ed.
Bernice Johnson Reagon (Washington, D.C.: Smithsonian Institution Press, 1992), 82.

7. Luvenia George, "Lucie E. Campbell: Her Nurturing and Expansion of Gospel Music
in the National Baptist Convention, U.S.A., Inc.," *We'll Understand It Better by and By: Pioneering African American Gospel Composers*, ed. Bernice Johnson Reagon (Washington, D.C.:
Smithsonian Institution Press, 1992), 115.

8. In the folk experience of African Americans, "to raise a hymn" is a reference to the ability to begin a song in a key and tempo, using a solo voice under spiritual guidance, in such a
manner that a congregation or group can join in and continue the song.

9. To be a part of this prayer band, individuals must be members in good standing in
their respective churches.

10. Bernice Johnson Reagon, "Developing Black American Cultural Programs: Negotiating the Distances Within and Between," in *Black American Culture and Scholarship: Contemporary Issues* (Washington, D.C.: Smithsonian Institution, 1985), 90–91.

11. This choir was under the direction of Reverend Donald Vails.

12. Gloria explained later in an interview that what she meant by this statement was that she should have been at home studying for an upcoming exam in a night course in which she was enrolled at a local community college rather than singing in the choir rehearsal. The Spirit, she said, had led her to come to the rehearsal.

13. Both terms are what ethnographer James Spradley calls "cover terms" that describe many activities connected with or perceived to be connected with spiritual work. James P. Spradley, *The Ethnographic Interview* (Fort Worth: Harcourt Brace Jovanovich College Publishers, 1979), 103–105.

14. Saundra Murray Nettles, *Coaching in Community Settings* (Baltimore: Johns Hopkins University Center on Families, Communities, Schools, and Children's Learning, 1992), 35.

15. Cheryl Townsend Gilkes, "The Roles of Church and Community Mothers: Ambivalent American Sexism or Fragmented African Familyhood?" *Journal of Feminist Studies in Religions* 2, no. 1 (spring 1986): 43.

16. Evelyn Brooks Higginbotham, *Righteous Discontent: The Women's Movement in the Black Baptist Church, 1880–1920* (Cambridge, Mass.: Harvard University Press, 1993), 14.

17. Bettye Collier-Thomas, *Daughters of Thunder: Black Preachers and Their Sermons, 1850–1979* (San Francisco: Jossey-Bass Publishers, 1998), 12.

18. "The Word" is the term commonly used in Christianity to refer to the spiritually inspired Word of God found written in the Bible. Learning the Word is an important means for living a sanctified life.

About the Contributors

Taunya Lovell Banks is the Jacob A. France Professor of Law at the University of Maryland School of Law. Her scholarship centers on the connections between law and race, gender, and, to a lesser extent, class. Banks was one of the law professors of color at the first Critical Race Theory Workshop in 1989, and critical race theory forms an important part of her scholarly perspectives. In 1993, she was part of the Minority Discourse III residential research group at the Humanities Research Institute (University of California, Irvine). Other research projects include "Gender Bias in the Classroom," a widely cited survey of student perceptions of the classroom environment at five law schools, and "Colorism: A Darker Shade of Pale," in which she argues that courts should recognize colorism claims in employment discrimination cases. A current project examines the status of free black women in mid-seventeenth-century Virginia.

A. Lynn Bolles is a professor of women's studies and affiliate faculty in anthropology, Afro-American studies, and comparative literature at the University of Maryland, College Park. Formerly, she was director of Africana Studies at Bowdoin College; her research focuses on the African diaspora, particularly in the Caribbean. Among her works are *My Mother Who Fathered Me and Others: Gender and Kinship in the English-Speaking Caribbean* (1988); *In the Shadow of the Sun* (coauthored with C. D. Deere et al., 1990); *We Paid Our Dues: Women Trade Union Leaders in the Caribbean* (1996); and *Sister Jamaica: Women, Work, and Households in Kingston, Jamaica* (1996). At present, Bolles is finishing her project on race, class, and women tourist workers in Negril, Jamaica, and a textbook on Pan-Caribbean women's experiences. An active member of numerous professional organizations, Bolles is a former president of the Caribbean Studies Association and current chair of the Association of Feminist Anthropologists for 2001–2001. Bolles is acting director of Afro-American Studies. She is also on the editorial board of *Urban Anthropology.*

MELINDA CHATEAUVERT is an instructor in the Afro-American Studies Program at the University of Maryland, College Park. She holds a B.A. and an M.A. in women's studies from the University of Massachusetts at Amherst and the George Washington University, respectively. She has also worked as the research director of the Pay Discrimination Institute, a nonprofit legal defense fund for race- and sex-based pay equity litigation. She earned a Ph.D. in United States history from the University of Pennsylvania in 1992. She is currently researching sex workers, public sex, and labor activism. Chateauvert's book, *Marching Together: Women of the Brotherhood of Sleeping Car Porters,* was published in 1998.

ADRIENNE DAVIS is a professor at the University of North Carolina–Chapel Hill School of Law. She was previously professor of law and codirector of the Gender, Work, and Family Project at the Washington College of Law at American University. She teaches property, contracts, and a variety of advanced legal theory courses, including courses on law and literature, race and the law, feminist jurisprudence, and reparations. She is the author of several articles, most recently, "The Private Law of Race and Sex: An Antebellum Perspective," published in the *Stanford Law Review.* Davis is active in academic organizations and legal practice. She is a member of the board of the Center for the Study of the American South and the Cultural Studies Program at the University of North Carolina and is on the editorial board of the *Law and History Review.* She is a former editor of the *Journal of Legal Education* and past chair of the law and humanities section of the American Association of Law Schools. She is a consultant with a litigation project seeking reparations for African Americans and is a lecturer with BARBRI-NILE. She is a frequent lecturer on the topic of legal history and legal theory and appears on radio and television talk shows.

BONNIE THORNTON DILL, project coordinator of the Black Women and Work Project, is professor of women's studies, affiliate professor of sociology and Afro-American studies, and director of the Consortium on Race, Gender, and Ethnicity at the University of Maryland, College Park. Before coming to Maryland in 1991, she was professor of sociology at the University of Memphis, where she founded and directed the Center for Research on Women, which, under her leadership, gained national prominence for outstanding work on the intersections of race, class, and gender. Her research focuses on these issues, particularly as they are reflected in the lives and work of African American women and their families. Her published works include *Women of Color in U.S. Society,* coedited with Maxine Baca Zinn (1994), and *Across the Boundaries of Race and Class: Work and Family among Black Female Domestic Servants* (1994). Her journal articles, published in *Signs, Feminist Studies,* and the *Journal of Family History,* among others, have been widely reprinted. Dill has been the recipient of several prestigious awards, including the Distinguished Contributions to Teaching Award and the Jessie Bernard Award, for research in gender studies, both given by the American Sociological Association for the work of the Memphis State Center for Research on Women. Dill is married to Dr. John R. Dill, and they are the proud parents of three children: an aspiring musician and twin college seniors.

SHARON HARLEY, coprincipal investigator of the Ford Foundation–funded Black Women and Work Project and principal investigator of the Ford Foundation–funded Women of Color Project, is an associate professor and former chair of the Afro-American Studies Program at the University of Maryland, College Park, where she teaches courses on Afro-American history, black culture, women's history, and women's work. Harley received her Ph.D. in United States history from the Department of History at Howard University. The recipient of numerous scholarships and fellowships, including the Smithsonian Postdoctoral Fellowship, she has conducted considerable research in the area of black women's history, focusing on the history of black wage-earning women and black women's organizational activities. She served as coeditor of *Afro-American Women: Struggles and Images* (1978, 1998) and of *Women in Africa and the African Diaspora* (1987), in which she contributed scholarly articles. Among her other works are "For the Good of Family and Race: Gender, Work, and Domestic Roles in the Black Community," published in *Signs* (1990); "When Your Work Is Not Who You Are: The Development of a Working-Class Consciousness among Afro-American Women," in *Gender, Class, Race, and Reform in the Progressive Era* (1991); "Reclaiming Public Voice and the Study of Black Women's Work," in *Gender, Families, and Close Relationships: Feminist Research Journeys* (1994); and "Speaking Up: The Politics of Black Women's Labor History," in *Women and Work: Exploring Race, Ethnicity, and Class* (1997). She is currently the principal investigator of the Ford Foundation–funded Center for African American Women's Labor Studies project.

TALLESE JOHNSON received her Ph.D. in sociology from the University of Maryland, College Park, in 2000. Her research interests include welfare reform, poverty, work and family intersection, and race and social stratification. She is currently a postdoctoral fellow at the Carolina Population Center, University of North Carolina, Chapel Hill.

JUDI MOORE LATTA is professor of communications in the Department of Radio, TV, and Film at Howard University. Formerly employed by National Public Radio, she served there as senior producer of the twenty-six-part series "Wade in the Water: African American Sacred Music Traditions," as NPR's first education reporter, and as executive producer of Special Programs. Her work on local television and radio networks has won numerous awards, including the George Foster Peabody Award for excellence in broadcasting, and recognition from American Women in Radio and Television, the Corporation for Public Broadcasting, the National Education Association, the National Federation of Community Broadcasters, the Unity Awards in Media, the National Association of Black Journalists, the CEBA Awards, the National Academy of Television Arts and Sciences, and the Gabriel Awards. She has designed and conducted in-service radio and television training workshops throughout the United States for independent and station-based producers. Latta is a native of Tallahassee, Florida, and a summa cum laude graduate of Hampton Institute. She was a Woodrow Wilson fellow and a Ford Foundation dissertation fellow. She holds an M.A. in English from Boston University and the Ph.D. in American studies from the University of Maryland.

SHIRLEY WILSON LOGAN is an associate professor of English at the University of Maryland, College Park, where she teaches courses in rhetoric, composition, and nineteenth-century African American literature. Her publications include *With Pen and Voice: A Critical Anthology of Nineteenth-Century African-American Women; We Are Coming: The Persuasive Discourse of Nineteenth-Century Black Women;* and essays in *Listening to Their Voices: The Rhetorical Activities of Historical Women; In Other Words: Feminism and Composition;* and *Nineteenth-Century Women Learn to Write.* Her current project is a critical biography of Francis Watkins Harper.

MARILYN MOBLEY MCKENZIE is an associate professor of English and founder of African American studies at George Mason University, where she served as director of African American studies from 1992 to 1998. She is currently serving another term as interim director of African American studies and is on the faculty of women's studies and the doctoral program in cultural studies. Her articles have appeared in the *Southern Review,* the *Women's Review of Books, Colby Library Quarterly, Signs, Sage, Emerge Magazine,* and various collections of published essays. Her first book, *Folk Roots and Mythic Wings in Sarah Orne Jewett and Toni Morrison: The Cultural Function of Narrative,* was published in 1991 and reissued in paperback in 1994. A charter member and former president of the Toni Morrison Society, McKenzie now serves as a member of its advisory board. She is a former editor for *Feminist Studies* and does scholarship on black women writers, African American studies, curriculum change, and women's issues. Her works in progress includes two manuscripts, "Spaces for the Reader: Toni Morrison's Narrative Poetics and Cultural Politics" and "The Strawberry Room," a novel about a woman's passage from personal and family crises to spiritual recovery.

CARLA L. PETERSON is a professor in the department of English at the University of Maryland, College Park, and affiliate faculty of the women's studies and the American studies departments. She has also served as chair of the Committee on Africa and the Americas. She received her Ph.D. in comparative literature from Yale University. Her area of research is nineteenth-century African American literary culture, with a focus on fictional and nonfictional narrative, intersections of race and gender, and minority discourse. Peterson has been the recipient of several fellowships from the American Council of Learned Societies, the American Association of University Women, the New York Public Library Center for Scholars and Writers, and others. She is the author of a book that traces the careers of ten antebellum black female social activists through an analysis of their speeches and writings, *Doers of the Word: African-American Women Speakers and Writers in the North (1830–1880)* (1995). Major recent articles include "Reconstructing the Nation: Frances Harper, Charlotte Forten, and the Racial Politics of Periodical Publication," in *Proceedings of the American Antiquarian Society* (1998) and "The Color of Memory: Interpreting Twentieth-Century U.S. Social Policy from a Nineteenth-Century Perspective," coauthored with Rhonda M. Williams, in *Feminist Studies* (1998). Her current projects include a historical work, *Family History in Public Places: Reconstructing African American Life in Nineteenth-Century New York,* and a literary study, *New Negro Modernity: Reassessing African American Novels of the Nadir.*

MARY HELEN WASHINGTON is professor of English at the University of Maryland, College Park, and coprincipal investigator of the Black Women and Work Project. She has been the recipient of fellowships from the Bunting Institute, the Harvard Divinity School, Wellesley Center for Research on Women, and the Center for African American Studies at UCLA, among others. Washington is author of *Invented Lives: Narratives of Black Women, 1860–1960* (1987) and editor of both *Memory of Kin: Stories about Family by Black Writers* (1991) and *Black-Eyed Susans/Midnight Birds* (1990).

RHONDA M. WILLIAMS was a political economist and acting director of the Afro-American Studies Program at the University of Maryland. She was also an affiliate faculty member in the women's studies and American studies departments. Williams's research interests included the race-gender dimensions of economic restructuring, the nexus of culture and economic policy, race ideology, discrimination theory, and antidiscrimination policy. Her work has appeared in the *Review of Economics and Statistics, American Economic Review, Review of Black Political Economy, Review of Radical Political Economics,* and *Feminist Studies.* She also has been published in numerous edited volumes. Williams graduated cum laude from Harvard-Radcliffe College in 1978 and received her doctorate in economics from Massachusetts Institute of Technology in 1983. She passed away in the fall of 2000.

DEBORAH WILLIS is a professor of photography and imaging at New York University's Tisch School of the Arts and its Africana Studies Program. From 1980 to 1992, she served as exhibition coordinator and curator of photographs and prints at the New York Public Library's Schomburg Center for Research in Black Culture. While there, she lectured and published widely on the contributions of African Americans to contemporary and historical photography. She has curated many exhibitions, identifying important artists now well recognized due to her insight and scholarship. Among her most notable projects are "Imagining Families: Images and Voices" (1994); "Constructed Images: New Photography" (1989); and "Black Photographers Bear Witness: 100 Years of Social Protest" (1989). She is the author of *VanDerZee: The Portraits of James VanDerZee* (1993); *Lorna Simpson* (1992); *J. P. Ball: Daguerrean and Studio Photographer* (1992); *Black Photographers, 1940–1988: An Illustrated Bio-Bibliography* (1988); *Reflections in Black: A History of Black Photographers* (2000); and editor of *Picturing Us: African Americans' Identity in Photography* (1994). She has taught the history of photography and photography at City University of New York, Duke University, and the Brooklyn Museum. Deborah Willis was previously collections coordinator for the Center for African American History and Culture of the Smithsonian Institution.

FRANCILLE RUSAN WILSON is an associate professor of Afro-American studies at the University of Maryland, College Park. She is a labor and intellectual historian whose forthcoming book, *The Segregated Scholars: Black Social Scientists and the Creation of Black Labor Studies, 1890–1950,* is a collective biography of three generations of African American intellectuals. Her other interests include the history of black working women, African American biography, and historiography. Wilson's research interest in black women and work dates from the late 1970s, when she did field research in Nigeria and Zaire on African working women. More recently, she has become interested in recovering early studies by black American female social scientists and social workers. Wilson received a Ph.D. in history from the University of Pennsylvania and has degrees from Harvard University and Wellesley College.

Index

"Access to the Academy: Crossing Bound-
aries" forum, 250n.6
affirmative action, 9, 87, 93, 97–98, 248
African American studies, 240–241,
242–243, 251n.11
African Methodist Episcopal (A.M.E.)
Church, 263
Afro ("natural") hairstyle, 18–19, 20
agricultural workers, 1, 5, 106–107
Aid to Families with Dependent Children
(AFDC), 69, 74, 75–76, 80, 92
"Ain't I a Woman?" speech, 134
Alexander, Raymond Pace, 172, 176
Alexander, Sadie Tanner Mossell, xix;
doctoral studies of, 165–166, 175;
education of, 168, 171–172, 174–175;
family background of, 169–171; job
discrimination against, 166–167,
175–176; in law school, 176–177; legal
career of, 178–180; marriage of, 176
Alexander, Virginia M., 172
A.M.E. Church Review, 170
American Airlines, in hair-grooming code
case, 19–20
American Federation of Labor, 187
American Federation of Teachers, 190
American Negro Academy, 152, 162n.21
Anderson, Mary, 190
Angelou, Maya, x–xi
antebellum period. *See* free black women;
slave women
Anti-Slavery Bugle, 134
Apel, Susan, 245
*Around 1981: Academic Feminist Literary
Theory* (Gallop), 247

art, storytelling in, 218–228
Association of Social Science Teachers in
Negro Colleges, 178
Aurobindo, Shri, 258
Austin, Regina, 52, 59
Ayer, Gertrude McDougald, 167

Baber, Lorenzo Dow, 41
Bakhtin, Mikhail, 160
Baldwin, James, 218, 243
Bambara, Toni Cade, 51, 204
Banks, Taunya Lovell, xviii, 13–28, 62;
about, 273; personal statement,
13–14
Barnard College, 232
Basch, Norma, 130
Bateson, Mary Catharine, 249
Beaches, Bananas, and Bases (Enloe), 43
Beasley, Delilah, 168
Beloved (Morrison), 121, 240
Benjamin, Lois, 233
Bergmann, Barbara, 95–96
Berry, Mary Frances, 48
Berry, Richard, 82
Bethune, Mary McLeod, 8, 179
black colleges, 168, 177–178
"Black Community, The: Its Lawbreakers
and the Politics of Identification"
(Austin), 52
"Black Diamond Express to Hell," 63
*Black-Eyed Susans: Classic Stories by Black
Women* (Washington), 204
Black Issues in Higher Education, 241
Black Panther Party, 51
Black Woman, The (Cade), 204

Black Women and Work Project, xvi, xvii
"Black Women in the Academy: Defending
Our Name, 1894–1994" conference, 233
*Black Women in the Academy: Promises
and Perils* (Benjamin), 233
Black Women in the Labor Force
(Wallace), 88
black working women: in antebellum
period (*see* free black women; slave
women); comparisons to white women's
progress, 89, 94; in criminal enterprises
(*see* underground economy); in Jamaica
(*see* Jamaica, tourism workers in); labor
force participation of, 8, 9, 89–91;
in postbellum period, 4–7; racial
economic inequalities among, 88–98;
Roots, Resistance, and Representation
symposium on, ix, xvi; single mothers
(*see* single mothers in rural South);
studies of, xii, xvi–xvii, 52. *See also*
discrimination; job opportunities; labor
market; labor movement; occupations;
professional black women; wages
Blau, Francine, 95
Blue Cross–Blue Shield, in colorism case,
18–19
blues singers, in underground economy,
57, 60
boarding house proprietors, 4, 6
Boardley, Barbara, 255
Bolin, Jane, 173, 174
Bolles, A. Lynn, xviii, 29–47; about, 273;
personal statement, 29
bootleggers, 50, 51, 52, 58
Boyer, Horace, 258
Boylan, Anne, 138
Bradley, J. Robert, 258
braided hairstyles, 19–22
Breckinridge, Sophisonia, 172
Brooks, Gwendolyn, 203
brothels, 50, 56, 57, 65n.15
Brotherhood of Sleeping Car Porters
(BSCP): in Civil Rights movement, 187;
Ladies' Auxiliary of, xix, 185, 187–194;
organization of, 186–187
Brown, Gwendolyn Hicks, 37–38
Brown, Jessie Lemmon, 255
Brown Girl, Brownstones (Marshall), 204,
206, 209, 212, 216n.34
Burroughs, Nannie Helen, 6, 7, 17, 55

Butterwood Nan, 108, 111, 112
Bye, Raymond, 175–176

Caldwell, Paulette, 13, 20, 24
Callis, Myra Colson, 178
Campbell, Lucie, 258
"Campus Expectations of the Minority
Professoriat" (McKenzie), 241
Capital Spotlight, 56
Carroll, Diahann, 9
Cary, Mary Ann Shadd, 133, 157
cashiers, 73–74
Cecelia's restaurant (Washington, D.C.), 57
Chappelle, Annie, 225, 226
Chateauvert, Melinda, xix, 184–196;
about, 274; personal statement, 184–185
child care, in kinship network, 78–79
Chosen Place, The Timeless People, The
(Marshall), 207, 216n. 34
Christian, Barbara, 251n.10
Christian Recorder, 170
Christol, Helene, 209
church workers, 255–257; calling of,
257–258, 269–270; choir director,
263–264, 265–268; prayer band leader,
259–263; work of the church and,
264–265
City of Quartz (Davis), 211
Civil Rights Act of 1964, Title VII, 17, 20,
24
Civil Rights Commission, 178
Civil Rights movement, 187, 192
class: economic opportunity and, 91;
income inequality and, 85; intrarace
colorism and, 17, 49, 53; among
Jamaican tourism workers, 31–36; shift
in, 231–232. *See also* middle-class black
women
Clayton, Horace R., 17
Cleage, Pearl, 18
clerical workers, 6, 9
Cliff, Michelle, 225
Club Madre (Washington, D.C.), 53–54, 56
Cobb, Thomas, 113
Cody, Cheryl Ann, 110
Cole, Johnnetta, x
college faculty: black women, 150,
177–178, 233–250, 254; black women
students and, 86–87, 174, 175–177;
response to racism and, 237–240

colleges and universities: and affirmative action, 9, 87, 93, 97–98, 248; African American studies, 240–241, 242–243, 251n.11; black colleges, 168, 177–178; discrimination against black students, 172–174, 176–177; doctoral candidates, 165–166, 168–169; economics programs, 85– 87; graduation rate, 167–168; social activism in, 232

"Colored Women as Wage-Earners" (Cooper), 149, 151–156, 160

colorism. *See* skin color

Committee on Fair Employment Practices (FEPC), 7

community welfare activism: of black women's organizations, 138, 232; collectivist ethos and, 6–7; of college students, 232; in labor movement, 8, 186–194; in Paule Marshall's fiction, 207–208, 210; as trap, 243–246

comparable worth principle, 91–92

Composing a Life (Bateson), 249

"Constructing and Reconstructing Afro-American Texts" (Lubiano), 249

Cook, John, 217n.39

Cooper, Anna Julia, xviii–xix, 146, 148; education and career of, 149–151, 169; on fair compensation, 155; on family values, 155–156; on household labor, 149, 151–154, 158, 160–161; kinship with white women, 159–160

Corrothers, James D., 186

courts: on affirmative action, 98; on gender/race discrimination, 24–25; on hair-grooming codes, 18–22; on physical appearance standards, 23–24; on skin-tone discrimination, 15, 16–17; on slave women's labor, 108, 111–112, 113–114, 117

coverture, 136, 140, 141

Craft, Christine, 23–24

criminal activities. *See* underground economy

Crisis, The, 168

Crummell, Alexander, 152

D'Amico-Samuels, Deborah, 43–44

dance halls, 58–59

Darling, Marsha, 138

Daughters (Marshall), 203, 207–208, 210–212, 213, 216n.34, 217n.39

Davis, Adrienne, xviii, 103–127; about, 274; personal statement, 103–105

Davis, Angela Y., 59, 60, 106, 116

Davis, David Brion, 118

Davis, Leona (pseud.), 255–256, 257, 259–263, 269

Davis, Mike, 211

Davis, Thulani, 199

DeCarava, Roy, 218–219, 220

Degraffenreid v. General Motors Assembly Division, 24–25

Delta Sigma Theta, 232

DeParle, Jason, 81

Dill, Bonnie Thornton, xvi, xviii, 67–83; about, 274–275; personal statement, 67–68

discouraged workers, 90–91

discrimination: against black men, 95; against college students, 172–174, 176–177; colorism, 13–18, 55; decline in significance thesis, 94–95; federal executive order against, 187; gender and, 24–25, 96; hair-grooming codes, 18–22; intrarace colorism, 15, 16–18, 53; in job evaluation, 92; job segregation and, 91, 94, 95, 107, 167; in Paule Marshall's fiction, 205; postbellum, 6–7; against professional women, 166–167, 169, 175–176, 179–180, 205; reverse, 98; wage, 9, 89, 91–92, 95; white women's role in, 157

Disney Corporation, grooming codes of, 23

distributive justice, 211, 216n.32

"Doers of the Word" (Peterson), 128

domestic workers: artist's image of, 225; class divisions and, 232; free black women, 3, 4; Jamaican tourism workers, 43; labor movement and, 6–7; postbellum, 158; slave women, 1–2; in underground economy, 57

Domestic Workers Union, 7

Douglass, Minnie ("Memphis Minnie"), 60

Drake, St. Clair, 17

dressmakers, 3

Drylongso: A Self-Portrait of Black America (Gwaltney), 63

Du Bois, W.E.B., 168, 170, 172, 175

duCille, Ann, 237, 247
Dunbar, Paul Laurence, 147
Dykes, Eva, 168, 169, 173, 177

Ebenezer AME Church, Maryland, 263
economists: "declining significance"
    perspective and, 87–88; job
    opportunities for, 88, 167;
    mainstream, 86–87; racial analysis
    of, 87, 88–98
education: attainment of, 167–168, 202;
    and church work, 266; free black
    schools, 3; and M Street High School,
    150, 169, 171; normal schools, 168–169.
    See also colleges and universities
Elders, Joycelyn, 9
Ellison, Ralph, 147
employment discrimination. *See*
    discrimination
employment. *See* job opportunities; labor
    market; occupations
Engel, Karen, 21
Enloe, Cynthia, 43
entertainers: advances of, 9; black public's
    attitude toward, 63; in underground
    economy, 57, 60

factory workers, in war industry, 4, 7–8
Fair Labor Standards Act, 7
family income: black women's
    contribution to, 8, 91–92, 152; in
    kinship network, 77, 79
fancy girl trade, 116–117
Farmer, Ruth, 242–243
Fauset, Arthur Huff, 172
Fauset, Crystal Bird, 8
Fauset, Jessie, 203
female-headed households, 91, 93–94.
    See also single mothers in rural South
feme covert, 131, 139, 140, 143
feme sole, 137, 140
feminist-abolitionists, 131, 139, 141, 143
Flagg, Barbara, 21
Florida A & M University (FAMU), 254
food stamps, 76, 77
Frazier, Hillman, 82
free black women, 1; in kin networks,
    136–137; labor conditions among, 2–3;
    marriage among, 136; occupations, 3–4;
    social activism of, 131–138; women's

rights movement and, 129–130, 142,
    143–144
Freeman, Alan, 20
Frelinghuysen University, 151
"From the Poet's in the Kitchen"
    (Marshall), 212
Fuller, Margaret, 139

Gallop, Jane, 247
Garrison, William Lloyd, 132
Gates, Henry Louis Jr., xii
gender discrimination: in physical
    appearance standards, 23–24; race
    and, 24–25; vs. race-class exploitation,
    95–96; wage, 177
gender roles: in domestic sphere, 137–138,
    148, 153, 200; slave women and, 107,
    119, 134; underground economy and,
    58–61, 62–63
General Motors, gender/race
    discrimination at, 24–25
George v. State, 113–115, 117
Gilkes, Cheryl Townsend, 266
Gilman, Charlotte Perkins, 154
Glover, Cora, 226–227
Glover, Lillie May, 59
Golden, Stephanie, 245
Gordy, Berry, 201
gospel music, 258, 263–269
Graff, Gerald, 240
Gray White, Deborah, 106, 110
Griggs, Sutton, 147
Grimké, Angelina, 130–131, 133, 139
Grimké, Charlotte Forten, 3
Grimké, Francis, 188
Grimké, Sarah, 139
grooming standards: Afro hairstyle and,
    18–19, 20; braided hairstyle and, 19–22;
    gender and, 23–24, 25–26
Guinier, Lani, 9
Guy-Sheftall, Beverly, xii
Gwaltney, John Langston, 63–64

hairdressers, 2, 220, 222
hair-grooming code discrimination, 14,
    18–22
Hakkem, Regina, 39–41
Hamer, Fannie Lou, 8
Hampton Institute, 151
Harding, Vincent, 254

Harley, Sharon, xv, xvi, xviii, 1–10, 48–66, 158; about, 275; personal statement, 48–52
Harper, Chancellor, 115
Harper, Frances E. W., 3, 129–130, 139, 148, 157, 202, 240
Harper's magazine, 204, 214–215n.7
Harris, Abram, 86
Harris, Cheryl, 16
Harris, Patricia Roberts, 9
Harvard University, 173
Haynes, Elizabeth Ross, 167
Heart, Donna Sams (pseud.), 255–256, 257, 263–264, 265–268
Henderson, Mae, 160
Henderson, Stephen, 236, 251n.8
Herman, Alexis, 9
Herring, Cedric, 17
Herstein, Lillian, 188
Higginbotham, Evelyn Brooks, 62, 63, 266
Hine, Darlene Clark, xii, 119, 126n.73, 245
Hoffman, Frederick, 162n.21
Holloway, Karla, 249
Holman, Lillian, 226
Holmes, Violet, 16
hooks, bell, 103, 105, 231
Hopkins, Pauline, 202
Hopwood, Cheryl, 98
Hopwood v. Texas, 98
household labor: property rights and, 153; True Womanhood cult and, 137–138, 148, 153; wages for, 149, 152–154, 160
Houston, Charles Hamilton, 8
Howard University, 168, 169, 170, 172, 177–178, 180
Howland, A. C., 175
Hudgins v. Wright, 108, 109, 111–112, 117
Hunter, Tera W., 52, 62–63
Hurston, Zora Neale, 203, 247

I Know Why the Caged Bird Sings (Angelou), x–xi
Incidents in the Life of a Slave Girl (Jacobs), 2, 132, 134, 135, 136
income inequality, 85, 86
indentured servants, 107, 124n.46
"In Search of Our Grandmothers' Gardens" (Walker), 224

Internal Revenue Service (IRS), colorism suit against, 15, 16–17
Iola Leroy (Harper), 240
Irvin, Helen Brooks, 167
I've Known Rivers (Lawrence-Lightfoot), 215n.20

Jackson, Ida L., 173–174
Jacobs, Harriet, 2, 131, 132, 134, 135, 136–137
Jamaica, tourism workers in: class/color hierarchy among, 31–36, 44; day in the life of, 36–41; invisibility of, 44–46; occupations of, 32, 43–44; social mobility of, 44; tourism development and, 41–42
Jean, Joyce, 56
Jefferson, Thomas, 109–110
Jeffries v. Ham's County Community Action Association, 25
Jenkins, Beverly Jeanne, 18, 21
Jennings, Caleen, xvii
job discrimination. *See* discrimination
job opportunities: for free blacks, 156–157; for middle-class women, 6, 199–200; for professional women, 150, 177–179; in rural South, 73–74; in war industry, 4, 7–8
job training, 74, 78, 95
Johnson, Charles S., 167
Johnson, Halle Tanner Dillon, 170–171
Johnson, Mordecai, 177
Johnson, Tallese, xvii, xviii, 67–83; about, 275; personal statement, 68–69
Jones, Barbara A. P., xviii, 87, 89–91, 94
Jones, Carolyn Pitt, 114
Jones, Jacqueline, 106–107, 119
Jones, Mary Mason, 190
jook joints, 50, 53, 59

Keith, Verna M., 17
Kelley, Robin D. G., 52, 63
King, Nicole, xvii
Kingston, Maxine Hong, 216n.29
kinship networks: free black women in, 136–137; single mothers in, 74–75, 77, 78–79, 82
Kolchin, Peter, 108

labor force participation, 8, 9, 89–91, 97

labor market: decline in working-class
jobs, 90; discouraged workers and,
90–91; gender and, 96; segregated, 91,
94, 95, 107, 167; self-employment, 5,
157–158. *See also* discrimination; job
opportunities; occupations; professional
black women; wages
labor movement: black women in, 8, 185,
186–194; contract law in, 142–143;
domestic workers and, 6–7; failure to
defend black workers, 154; union wife
image, 193–194; wage slavery analogy,
140–142
Latta, Judi Moore, xix, 254–270; about,
275–276; personal statement, 254–255
laundry workers, 2, 4, 6–7
Lawrence-Lightfoot, Sara, 215n.20
lawyers, 178–180
Lee, Jarena, 133
Lee, Robert, 56
Lewis, Penny, 36–37
Lewis, Ruby, 15, 17, 18
Liberator, 132
Lincoln University, 150, 178
Lindsay, Inabel Burns, 177
Logan, Shirley Wilson, xix, 1–10, 146–163;
about, 276; personal statement, 146–148
Lowell mills, 140
Lubiano, Wahneema, 239, 249

Mabley, Moms, 53–54
McBride, Corinne, 22
McGhee, Nancy, 255
McKay, Nellie Y., 231, 233
McKenzie, Marilyn Mobley, xix, 231–253;
about, 276; personal statement, 231–233
MacKinnon, Catharine, 119
McMillan, Terry, 202
MacPherson, C. B., 142
McTell, Kate and Willie, 60
Madre, Odessa Marie, xviii; background
of, 48–49, 53, 54–55; financial success
of, 62, 64; on gender roles, 60; illegal
operations of, 53, 56; nightclub of,
53–54, 56; philanthropy of, 58; target of
intrarace colorism, 49, 53, 55–56
Mahogany (film), 201
Malcolm X, 209, 212–213, 216n.25
Malveaux, Julianne, xviii, 87, 88, 91–93,
178

March on Washington (1941), 187, 192
market vendors, in Jamaica, 35, 36–37
marriage: among free blacks, 136; professional women and, 205, 212; skin
color consciousness in, 17; slavery-of-
sex analogy, 139–140; True Womanhood
cult and, 137–138, 148, 153; union wife
image, 193–194; wage equality in,
152–154
Married Women's Property Act, 142–143
Marshall, Paule, xix, 200; as black
nationalist, 209–210, 212–213; as
magazine writer, 206; marital conflict
of, 206–207, 212; middle-class women
in work of, 203–206, 207–214; white
aesthetic norms in work of, 17
Marx, Karl, 86
Massachusetts Institute of Technology
(MIT), 86–87, 233
Matthaei, Julie A., 59
Matthews, Victoria Earle, 157–158, 168
Maud Martha (Brooks), 203
Merkert, Russell, 15
middle-class black women: in domestic
sphere, 137–138, 148, 153, 200; in
fiction, 203–214; negative image in pop-
ular culture, 201–202; organizations of,
6, 8, 138; racial uplift goal of, 203–204.
See also professional black women
Miller, Kelly, 156, 162n.21
Milloy, Courtland, 54, 55, 160–161
Mills, Florence, 202
Mississippi: economy of Delta region,
72–73, 82; welfare reform in, 81–82.
See also single mothers in rural South
Mitchell, Valerie Welsey, 52
Moore, LaVerne, 254
Moore, Lewis Baxter, 170
Moore, Oscar, 254
Moore, Sadie T., 170–171
Morrison, Toni, 9, 103–104, 105, 120, 121,
239, 240, 242, 247
Moseley-Braun, Carol, 9
Moseley, Walter, 52
Moses, Yolanda, 243
Mossell, Aaron, 170
Mossell, Gertrude Bustill, xii, xvi–xvii, 168
Mossell, Sadie Tanner. *See* Alexander,
Sadie Tanner Mossell
mothers. *See* single mothers in rural South

Mott, Lucretia, 139
Moynihan, Daniel Patrick, 193
M Street High School (Paul Lawrence
    Dunbar High School) (Washington,
    D.C.), 150, 169, 171
Muncy, Robin, 167
Murray, Pauli, 180
music: blues singers, 57, 60; gospel, 258,
    263–269; prayer band, 259–263
My Life as I Have Lived It (Tucker), 186

Nancy Lewis: Bodybuilder (Willis),
    223–224, 228
National Association for the Advancement
    of Colored People (NAACP), 8, 176,
    179, 187, 202
National Association of Colored Women's
    Clubs, 166, 203, 243
National Baptist Convention, 258
National Negro Alliance, 190
National Public Radio, *Wade in the Water*
    series, 256, 258, 259
National Urban League, 8, 167, 179
Neely, Barbara, 52
Neighborhood Youth Corps Photography
    program, 219–220
Nettles, Saundra Murray, xvii, 265
Neverdon-Morton, Cynthia, xvii
Niagara Movement, 170
Nineteenth-Century American Women
    Writers in the Twenty-First Century
    conference, 237–238
Nix, A. W., 63
Nixon, E. D., 187
No Man of Her Own (Willis), 220, 225
normal schools, 168–169
numbers game, 51, 52, 58

Oakwood College, 177
Oberlin College, 150
"Object into Subject" (Cliff), 225
occupations: of free black women, 3–4;
    postbellum, 6; professional, 166, 167,
    202; in rural South, 73; segregated, 91,
    94, 95, 107, 166, 167; of slave women,
    1–2; of tourism workers, 32, 43–44; in
    underground economy, 52. *See also
    specific occupations*
Olmsted, Frederick, 106, 110
Our Nig (Wilson), 132, 134–135

Our World, 206
Owens, Ruby, 57, 61–62

Painter, Nell, 107, 119, 120, 126–127n.74
Palmer, Mary, 38–39
Parks, Rosa, 8, 187
Parry, Shirley, 217n.39
partus sequitur ventrem rule, 108
Patterson, Ernest Minor, 175–176
Penn, Emma Shields, 167
Pepper Foundation Fellowship, 175
Perelman, Chaim, 161n. 9
Personal Responsibility and Work
    Opportunity Reconciliation Act
    (PRWORA), 80
Peterson, Carla L., xviii, 128–145; about,
    277; personal statement, 128–129
Petry, Ann, 203
photography, as storytelling device,
    218–228
physical appearance: gender-neutral
    grooming codes, 23–24; hair-grooming
    codes, 14, 18–22; of Jamaican tourism
    workers, 35; skin tone and, 13–18; white
    aesthetic norms for, 17, 20, 23
Plato, Ann, 3, 148
possessive individualism, 142, 143
Potter, Eliza, 2
poverty, in rural South, 72–73
Powell, Adam Clayton, Sr., 61
Praisesong for the Widow (Marshall),
    216n.34
prayer band, 259–263
Price, Joseph, 152
professional black women: advances of,
    9; in Jamaican class/color hierarchy,
    34–35; job discrimination against,
    166–167, 169, 175–176, 179–180, 205;
    job opportunities for, 150, 177–179;
    marital conflicts of, 206–207; in
    marriage market, 205; negative
    images in popular culture, 201–202;
    in New Deal agencies, 8; occupations,
    166, 167, 202; in Paule Marshall's
    fiction, 203–214; role models for,
    208–209. *See also* colleges and
    universities
prostitution: of slave women, 116–117;
    in underground economy, 50, 56, 57,
    65n.15

Pullman Company, 189, 190–191

quilts, autobiographical, 225, 226–227

race: collective response to racism,
237–240; economic theory and, 86;
labor force participation and, 8, 89–91,
97–98. *See also* discrimination
*Race Rebels: Culture, Politics, and the Black
Working Class* (Kelley), 52, 63
Radcliffe College, 85, 168, 173
Rainey, Gertrude "Ma," 59, 60
Randolph, A. Philip, 186–187, 188–189,
191
rape: prohibitions of, 125n.53; of slave
women, 113–116
Reagan, Ronald, 87, 93
Reagon, Bernice Johnson, 255, 256, 262
"Reena" (Marshall), 17, 203–206, 207, 210,
213–214
reproductive value of slave women,
109–110, 117
reverse discrimination, 98
Rich, Adrienne, 241
Richmond African school, 3
Rivers, LaToya, 22
Rockettes, color discrimination in, 15–16
Rogers, Renee, 19–20, 21
Rogers v. American Airlines, 19–20, 22, 24
Rooks, Ronica, xvii
Roosevelt, Franklin D., 187
Roots, Resistance, and Representation:
Sister Scholars Study Black Women and
Work symposium, ix, xvi
rural South. *See* single mothers in rural
South

St. Augustine's Normal and Collegiate
Institute, 150
Samms, Loretta (case history), 70–78, 80
Sans Souci Hotel, 57
Scott, Cecelia, 57
Segregated Scholars, The (Wilson),
164–165
self-employment, 2, 5, 157–158
Seneca Falls convention, 129, 139
service sector, 9. *See also* Jamaica, tourism
workers in
sexual abuse: of job seekers, 75, 158; of
slave women, 104, 112, 113–121, 134

sexual economy of slavery, 105–106,
117–121
sexuality, silence about, 104, 120, 126n.73
sharecroppers, 5
Sharp Street School (Baltimore), 3
Shaw, Anna, 154
Siegel, Reva, 154
Simms, Margaret, xviii, 87, 88, 92–93
Simpson, Georgiana, 168–169, 172, 177
Singer, Linda, 248
single mothers in rural South: and
economy of region, 72–73; job goals of,
70–71, 77–78, 79–80; kinship support
for, 74–75, 77, 78–79; lack of job
opportunities, 73–74, 81; in low-wage
jobs, 69, 78, 79; personal connections
in job search, 74–75; welfare assistance
for, 71, 75–77, 80; welfare reform and,
80–82
sister, definition of, x–xi
Sister Circles, historical roots of, x
skin color: employment discrimination
and, 13–18; intrarace colorism and,
15, 16–18, 49, 53; in Jamaican class
hierarchy, 32–36; marriage patterns
and, 17
slavery: conspiracy of silence around, 104;
population increase in, 108–109; sexual
economy of, 105–106, 117–121; slavery
of sex analogy, 131, 139–143; wage
slavery analogy, 140–142
slave women: domestic workers, 1–2;
enslaved status of children, 108, 109,
111–113; field workers, 1, 106–107;
gender roles and, 107, 119, 134; prostitution of, 116–117; reproductive value
of, 109–110, 117; sexual abuse of, 104,
112, 113–117, 134; wage labor of, 2
*Slaying the Mermaid: Women and the
Culture of Sacrifice* (Golden), 245
Sleeping Car Porters. *See* Brotherhood of
Sleeping Car Porters
*Slipping through the Cracks: The Status of
Black Women* (Malveaux and Simms),
88
Smith, Bessie, 59
Smith, Jessie Carney, xi–xii
Smith, Lucy, 157
Smith, Miranda, 8
Smith, Valerie, 201

Smith v. Delta Air Lines, 21
Smythe, Mabel, 167, 177, 178
social activism. *See* community welfare
   activism
social wealth, 155–156
socioeconomic status. *See* class
"Something Within" (Campbell), 258
Soul Clap Hands and Sing (Marshall), 204,
   206–207
Soul Food (film), 201
South. *See* single mothers in rural South;
   slavery; slave women
*Southern Workman and Hampton School
   Record*, 151
Southland, 152
Spaulding, C. C., 176
Spelman College, x
Spencer, Herbert, 153
spiritual workers. *See* church workers
Spook Who Sat by the Door, The (film),
   201–202
Stanton, Elizabeth Cady, 139, 143
"Stepping on Toes: Responding to Diverse
   Interpretive Communities as an African
   American Womanist Scholar"
   (McKenzie), 234–235
Sterling, Dorothy, 128
Stevenson, Brenda, 116
Stewart, Maria W., 2, 131, 144, 148; on
   black men, 137; on domestic sphere,
   137–138; on labor conditions, 1–2, 135;
   on labor rights, 156–157; on sexual
   abuse, 133–134; writings of, 132
Stowe, Harriet Beecher, 237–238
Strasser, Susan, xvii
Street, The (Petry), 203
street vendors, 3, 35, 36–37

Tanner, Benjamin Tucker, 169–170, 174
Tate, Claudia, 234, 247
Tate, Merze, 177, 178
Taylor, Donald, 81–82
teachers, 3, 6, 8, 176, 266. *See also* college
   faculty
Temporary Assistance for Needy Families
   (TANF), 80–82
Terborg-Penn, Rosalyn, xvii
Terry, Lucy, 148
Thomas, Alfrenell (case history), 78–79,
   80, 82

tobacco workers, 8
*To 'Joy My Freedom: Southern Black
   Women's Lives and Labors after the Civil
   War* (Hunter), 52
Tomlins, Chris, 107
tourism workers, in Jamaica. *See* Jamaica,
   tourism workers in
transportation, job opportunities and, 79
"Troubled Peace, A: Black Women, Race,
   and Class in the Halls of Privilege"
   (McKay), 233
True Womanhood, cult of, 137–138, 148,
   153
Truly Disadvantaged, The (Wilson), 94
Truman, Harry, 178
Truth, Sojourner, 131–133, 134
Tubman, Harriet, 51, 130
Tucker, B. J., 186, 190–191
Tucker, Rosina Corrothers: background of,
   185–186; political activism of, 187,
   192–193; salary of, 195nn.18, 19; as
   Sleeping Car Porters' Ladies' Auxiliary
   leader, xix, 185, 187–194; as union
   organizer, 186–187, 189, 190, 191
Tuskegee Institute, 170

Uncle Tom's Cabin (Stowe), 237–238
underground economy, black women in:
   arrests of, 62; financial success of,
   61–62; in fringe operations, 56–58;
   gender roles and, 58–61, 62–63;
   invisibility of, 50–51; legitimate
   businesses of, 53–54, 56; motivations
   for criminal activity, 48–49, 52, 53,
   54–56; patterns of involvement, 52–53;
   public denunciation of, 58, 62–64;
   racial stereotyping of, 51–52; types of
   enterprises, 50, 53, 56
unemployment, 8, 9; class and, 91; in rural
   South, 73–78, 79, 82
United Auto Workers, 8
United Southern Prayer Band, 259–262
Universal Negro Improvement
   Association (UNIA), 187
universities. *See* college faculty; colleges
   and universities
University of California, Berkeley,
   173–174, 251n.10
University of Chicago, 172
University of Maryland, xvi

University of Pennsylvania, 166, 171–172, 173, 174–175, 176–177

"Valley Between, The" (Marshall), 203, 212
Voice from the South, A (Cooper), 151, 154, 158, 159

Wade in the Water radio series, 256, 258, 259
wages: comparable worth principle, 91–92; contribution to family income, 8, 91–92, 152; decline in, 89; discrimination, 9, 89, 95; fair compensation, 155; gender gap in, 177; growth in, 8; for household labor, 149, 152–154, 160; low-wage jobs, 69, 78, 79; slavery analogy, 140–142
Waiting to Exhale (film), 202
Walker, Alice, 18, 224, 247
Walker, Madame C. J., 62
Walker, Maggie Lena, 6, 62
Walker, Tracy, 15, 16–18
Wallace, Phyllis, xviii, 87, 88, 93–94
Wal-Mart, 73–74
war industry, 4, 7–8
Washington, Mary Helen, xix, xvi, 15, 159–160, 199–217; about, 277; personal statement, 199–201
Washington, Booker T., 170
Washington Post, 54, 55
We Are Your Sisters (Sterling), 128
welfare: impact of reform, 80–82; insufficient benefits, 75–77, 80; work combined with, 77, 78, 80, 81
Wellesley College, 173, 174
Wells-Barnett, Ida, 51, 147, 168
Wendy's, hair-grooming code at, 22
Wesley, Charles, 86
white women: affirmative action and, 97–98; failure to support black women workers, 157; as indentured servants,

107, 124n.46; job segregation and, 95–96, 107; labor force participation of, 90, 97; progress of, 89, 94; sexual norms of chastity and, 115. *See also* women's rights movement
Wilberforce College, 150
Wilkerson, Margaret, 251n.10
Williams, Fannie Barrier, 157
Williams, Patricia, 16
Williams, Rhonda M., xviii, 84–100; about, 277–278; personal statement, 84–87
Willis, Deborah, xix, 218–228; about, 278; personal statement, 218–220
Willis, Ruth Ellen, 227
Willis, Thomas Meredith, 227
Wilson, Francille Rusan, xix, 1–10, 164–183; about, 278; personal statement, 164–165
Wilson, Halena, 188, 193–194, 195n.18
Wilson, Harriet, 131, 132, 134–135, 148
Wilson, William Julius, 94
Wollstonecraft, Mary, 142
Women and Economics (Gilman), 154
Women's Rights Convention, 129, 143
women's rights movement: black women and, 129–130, 142, 143–144, 154; contract rights and, 142–143; household labor and, 153–154; petition rights and, 142; response to racism, 237–240; slavery-of-sex analogy in, 131, 139–143; wage slavery analogy in, 140–142
Women's Trade Union League (WTUL), 190
Wood, Janet Sims, xvii
Woodson, Carter G., 172
Work of the Afro-American Woman, The (Mossell), xii, xvi–xvii
Wright, Fanny, 142
Wright, Richard, 147
Wright, R. R. Jr., 175